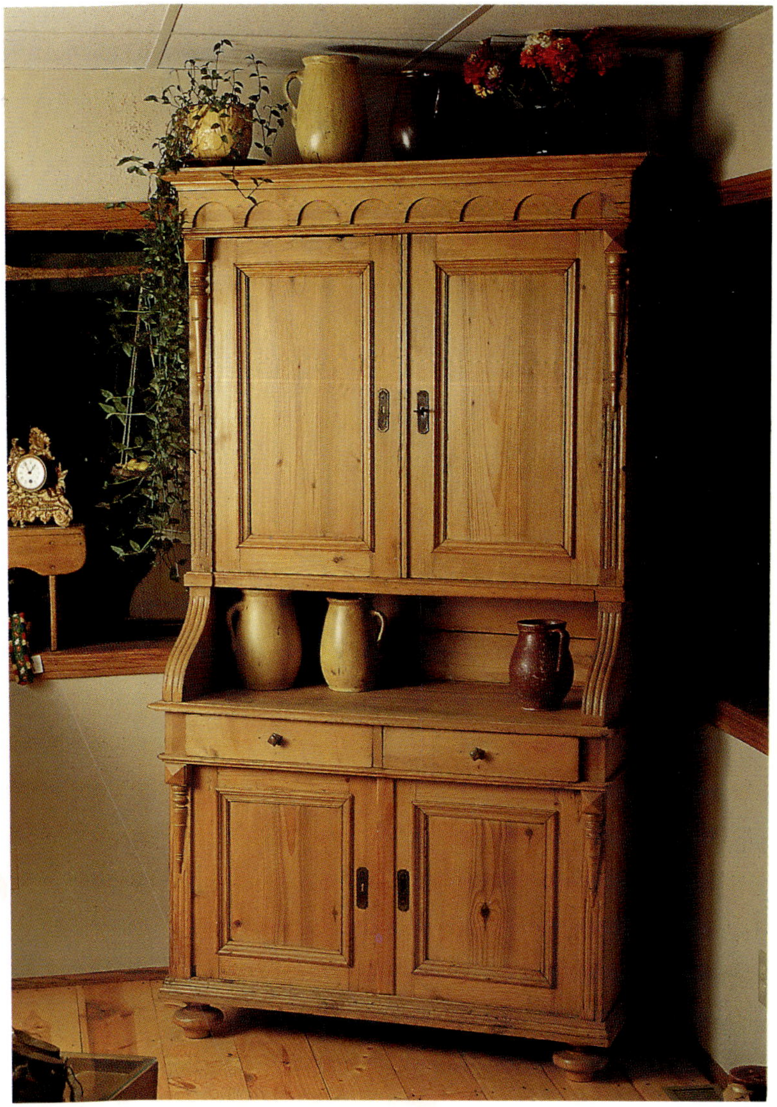

Pine Furniture

THE COUNTRY LOOK

Nancy N. Schiffer

PHOTOGRAPHY BY BRUCE WATERS

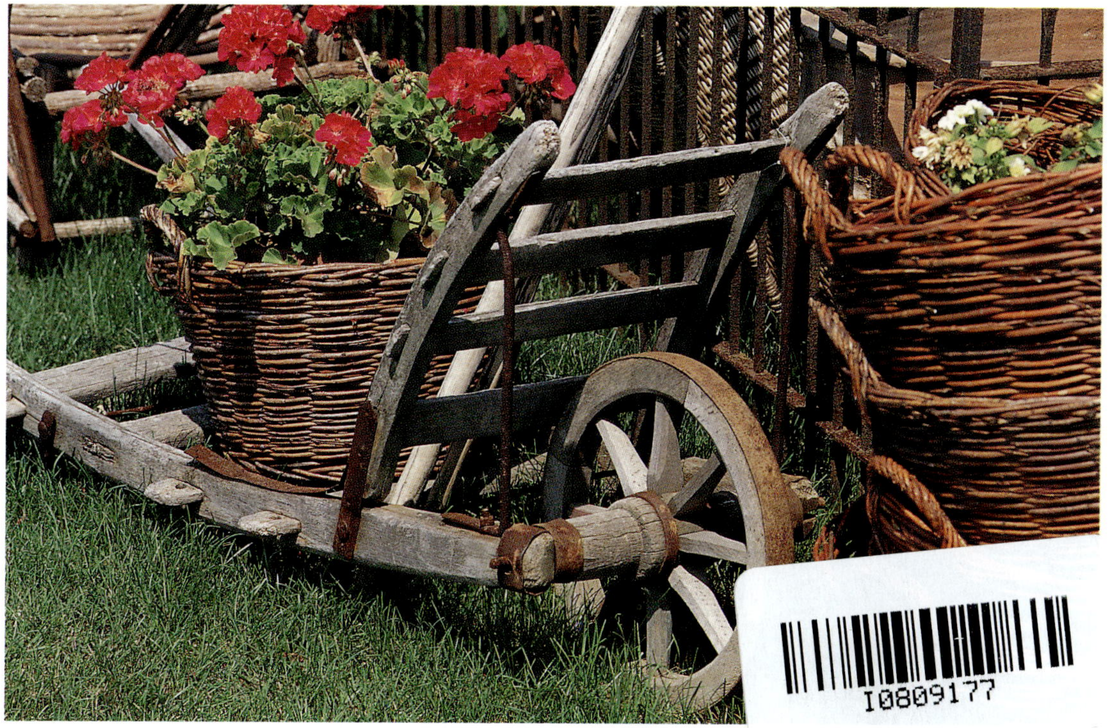

Schiffer Publishing Ltd

4880 Lower Valley Road, Atglen, PA 19310 USA

Published by Schiffer Publishing Ltd.
4880 Lower Valley Road
Atglen, PA 19310
Phone: (610) 593-1777; Fax: (610) 593-2002
E-mail: Schifferbk@aol.com
Please visit our web site catalog at www.schifferbooks.com
or write for a free catalog.
This book may be purchased from the publisher.
Please include $3.95 for shipping.

In Europe, Schiffer books are distributed by
Bushwood Books
6 Marksbury Rd.
Kew Gardens
Surrey TW9 4JF England
Phone: 44 (0)181 392-8585; Fax: 44 (0)181 392-9876
E-mail: Bushwd@aol.com

Please try your bookstore first.

We are interested in hearing from authors
with book ideas on related subjects.

Library of Congress Catalog Card Number: 98-88029

Designed by Bonnie M. Hensley
Type set in CopprplGoth Bd BT/ZapfHumnst BT

ISBN: 0-7643-0742-8
Printed in China
1 2 3 4

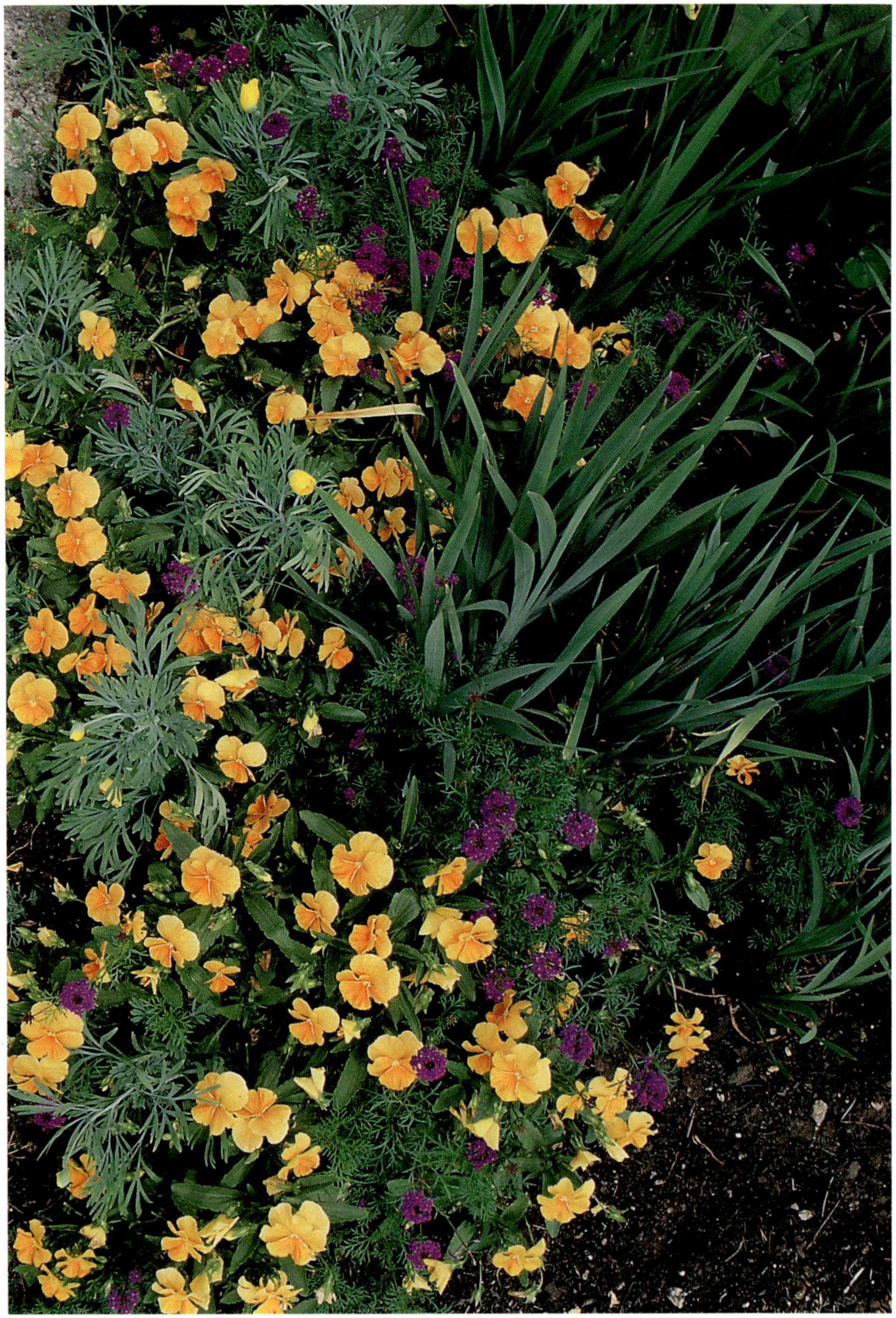

CONTENTS

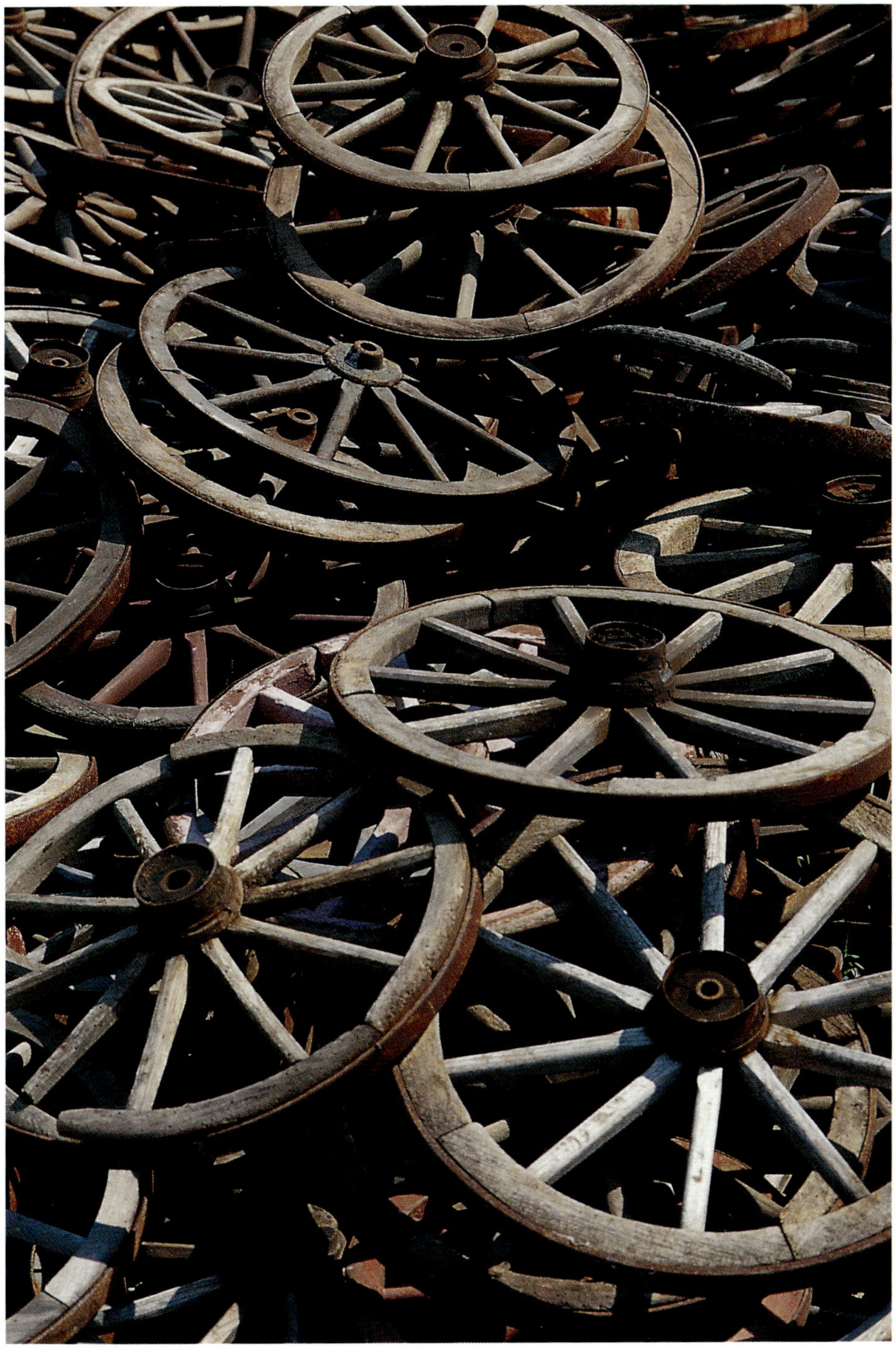

Acknowledgments

Warm gratitude is conveyed to the Franke family of Albertville, Minnesota, who welcomed our cameras into their business, International Country, just northwest of Minneapolis. Here we found the Scandinavian smiles of Tom, Mona, Tim, Todd, and Tommy Franke, and their spouses and staff, among the antique pine and outdoor furnishings they collect and sell. We are grateful for their many contributions.

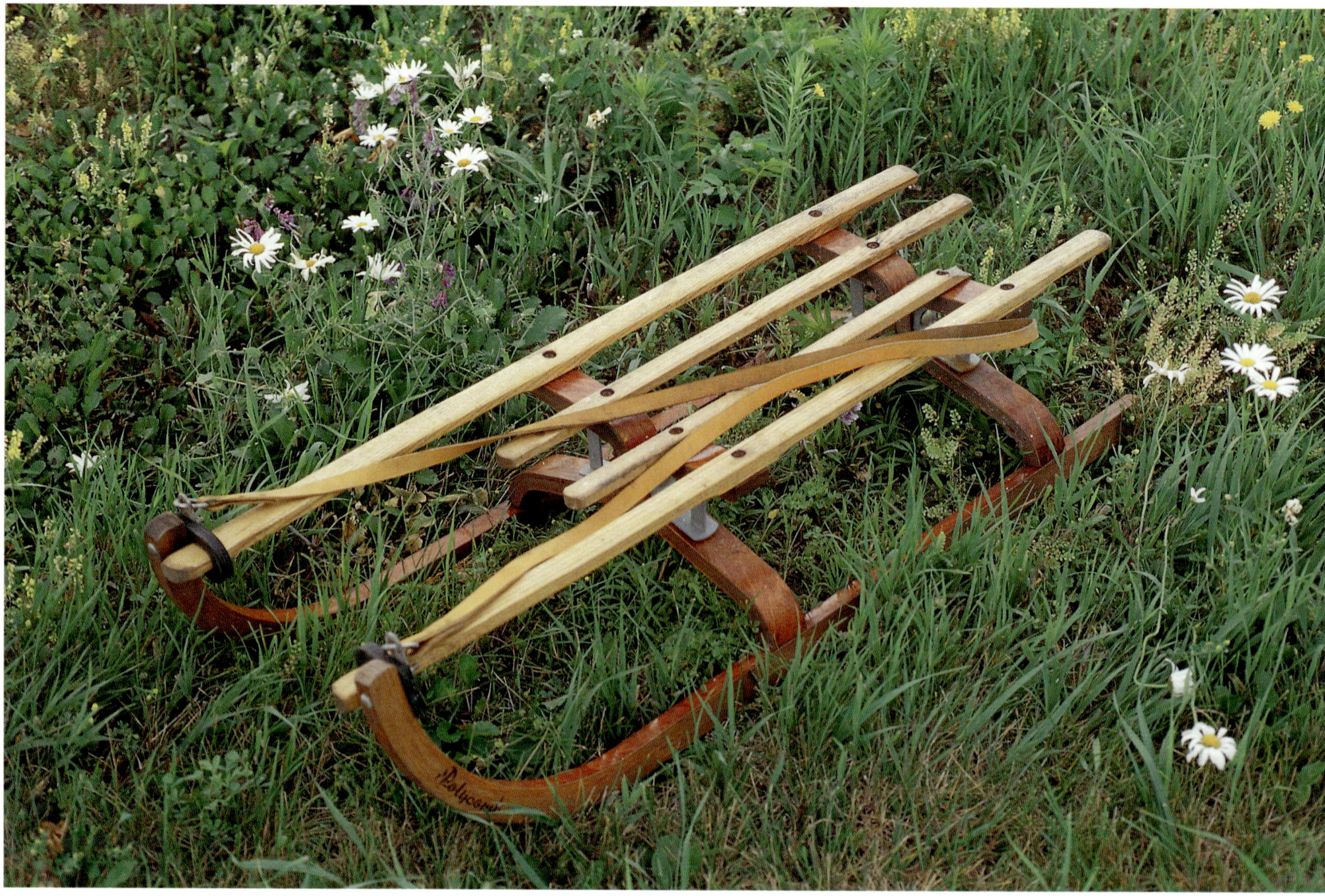

A Welcoming Place

Introduction

The warm tones of old paint on soft pine wood in antique furniture convey stability to a home and security among its inhabitants. They help to create a welcoming place to live. The pine furniture and tools gathered in this book have come from distant places in Europe, the United Kingdom, and Scandinavia. They continue to function perfectly well now as when they were first built. Original painted decoration was of primary importance to the design of this furniture; its construction details were of only secondary importance. If the painted ornamentation remains in good condition, the original character of the piece is relayed. However, when the painted surface is damaged or missing, the construction details become more evident. In fact, today, oxidized pine wood itself is appreciated for its glowing tone and varied surface appearance.

Antique pine furniture possesses various stylistic features of construction. The following construction groupings are noted with simplified style characteristics. Readers are invited to study each country's styles carefully to discover the many features that characterize each period. This list is furnished merely as a starting point.

Baroque, c. 1730-1780.
Deeply canted corners and deep moldings, German influence. Corresponds roughly with English Early Georgian and Chippendale styles.

Louis XVI, c. 1780-1800.
Less canted corners and more shallow moldings, architectural, French influence. Corresponds roughly with English Late Georgian, Sheraton, and Hepplewhite styles.

Empire, c. 1800-1820.
Pediments and applied decoration, French influence. Corresponds roughly with English Regency style.

Biedermeier, c. 1825-1840.
Pediments but no applied decoration, French influence in Austria. Corresponds roughly with English Early Victorian style.

Rococo, c. 1850-1870.
Scrolled feet and crests, strong French influence. Corresponds roughly with German Louis-Philippe and English Mid-Victorian styles.

Renaissance Revival, c. 1880-1900.
Stiles turned, applied decoration, and more restrained design. Corresponds roughly with French Revival style.

Arts & Crafts, c. 1900-1910.
Stiles flat and incised decoration, restrained design. Corresponds roughly with German early Jugendstil style.

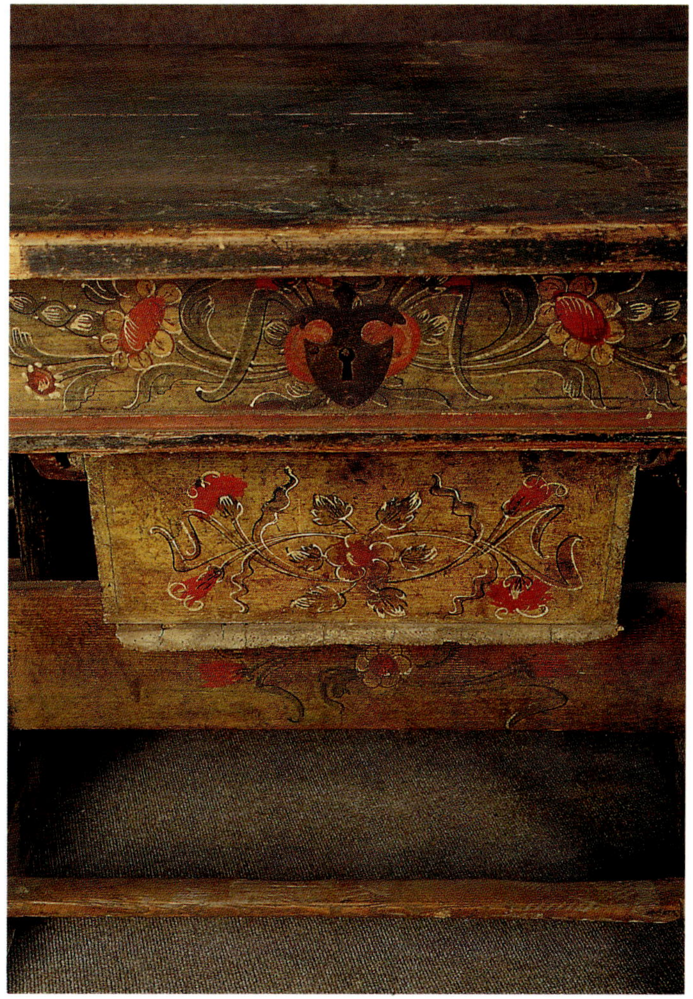

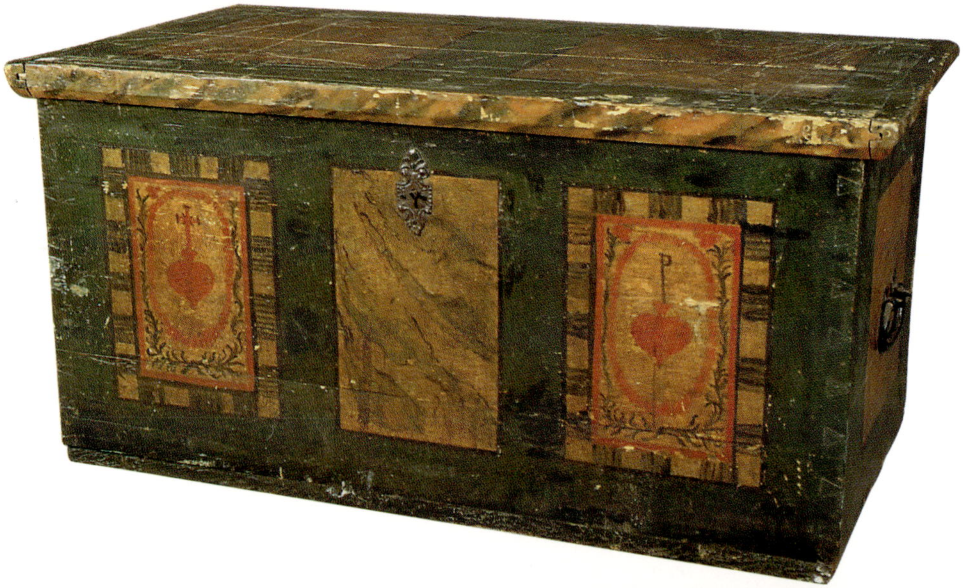

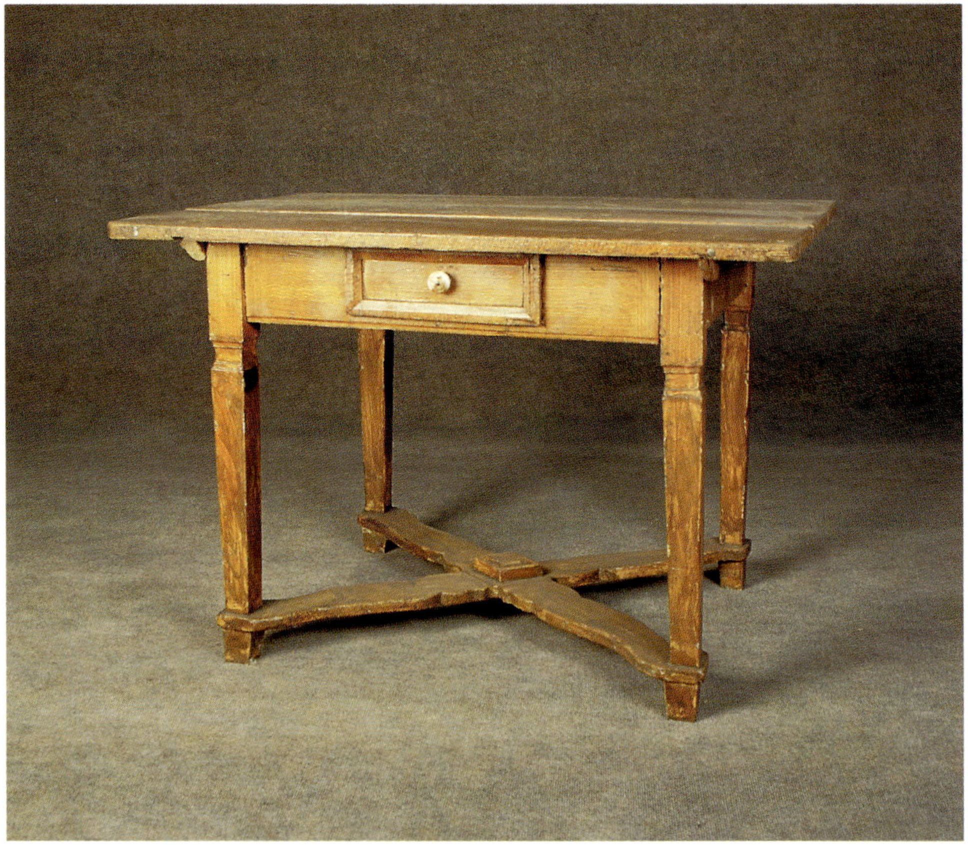

Rectangular table with overhanging top on battens, single drawer, square shaped legs on a flat crossing stretcher. Top inlaid "IHS" with cross and heart. $595.

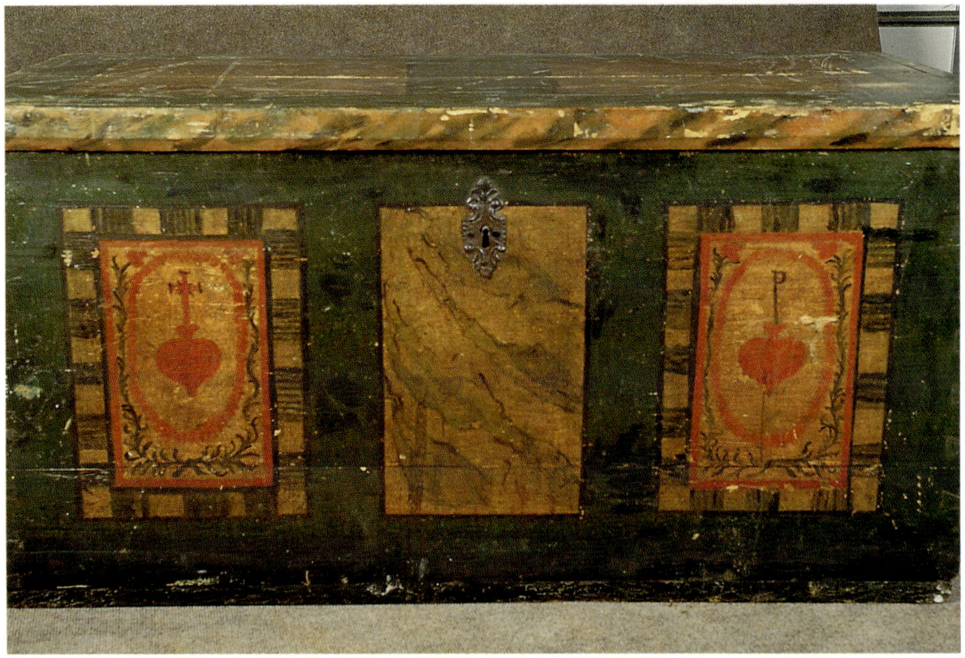

Large painted blanket chest with dark green painted background and rectangular panels with two heart decorations of traditional religious design. $695.

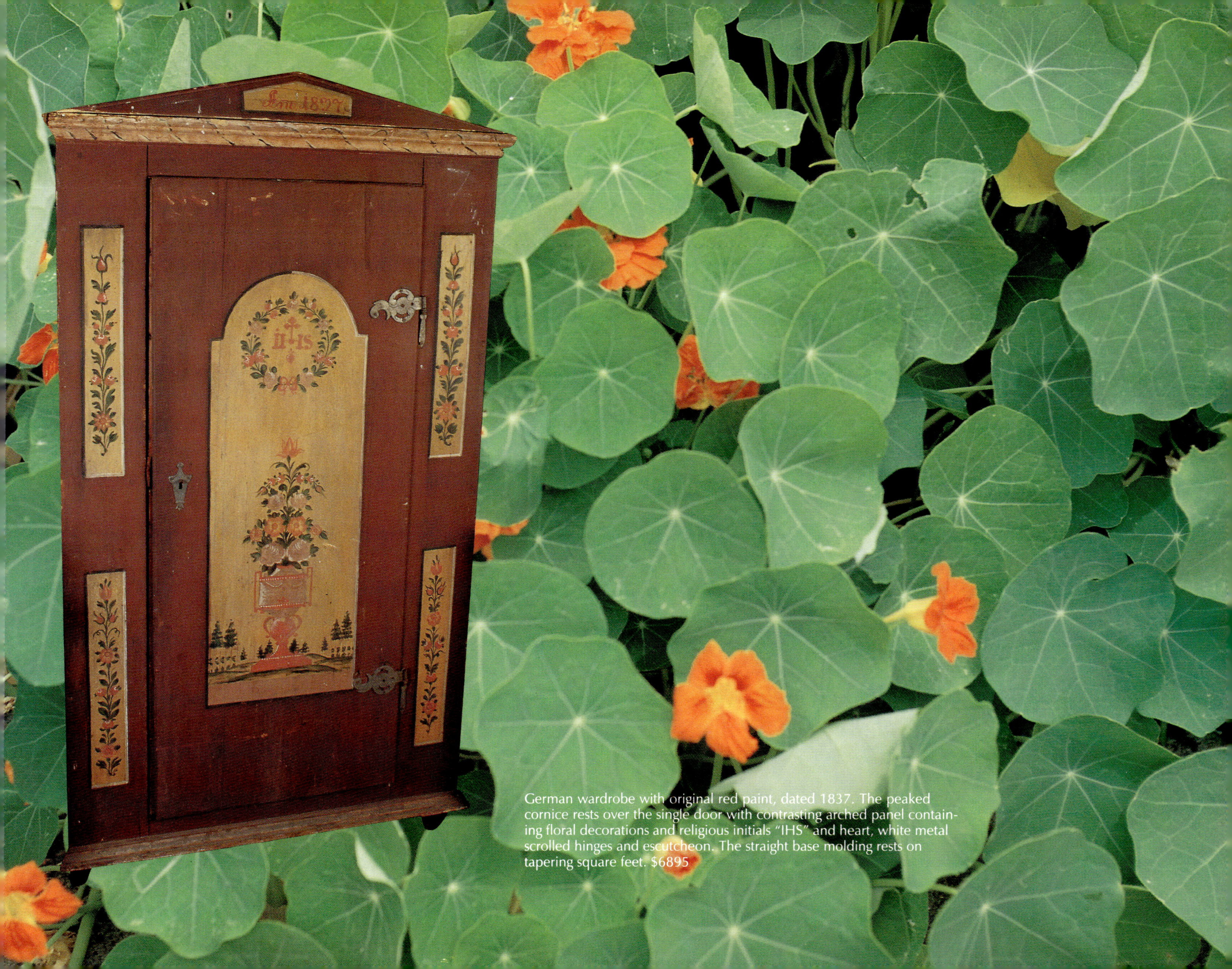

German wardrobe with original red paint, dated 1837. The peaked cornice rests over the single door with contrasting arched panel containing floral decorations and religious initials "IHS" and heart, white metal scrolled hinges and escutcheon. The straight base molding rests on tapering square feet. $6895

Please, Have A Seat

Settees, Chairs, and Benches

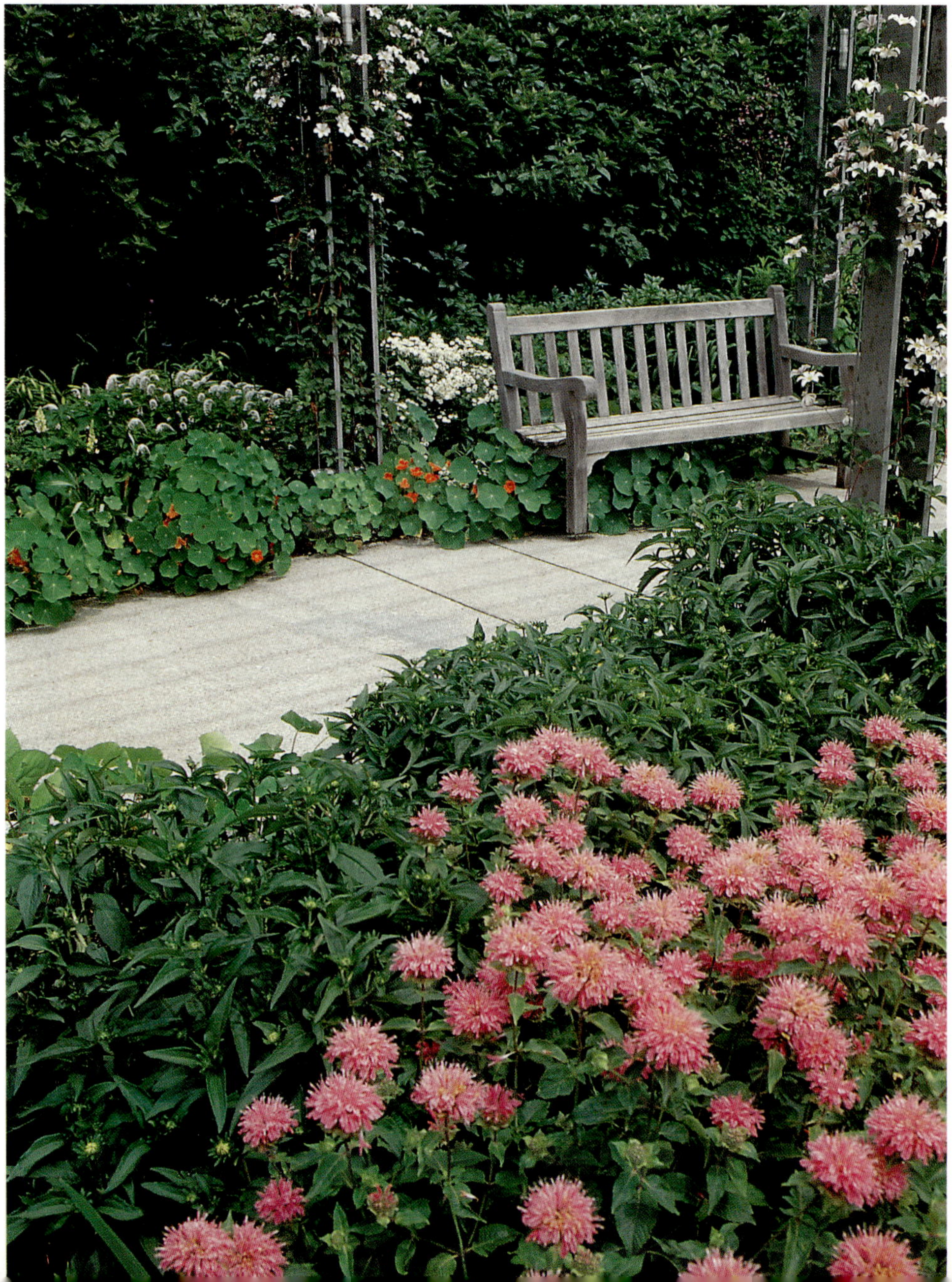

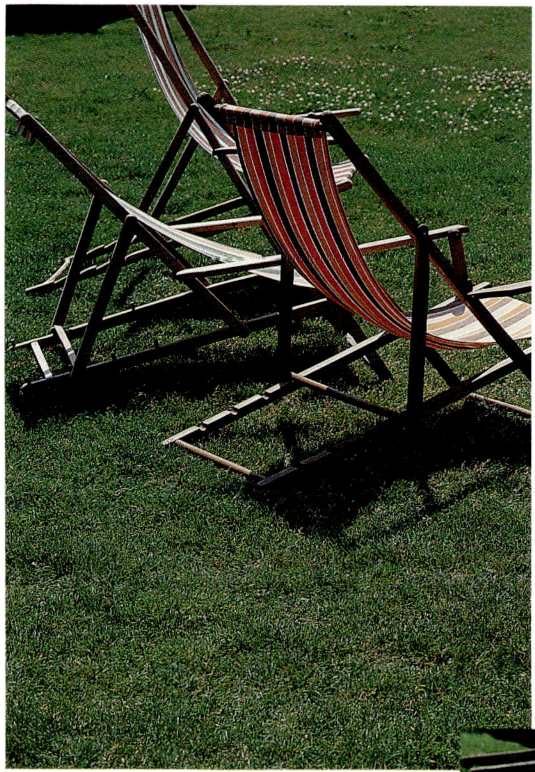

Left, below and opposite page top left: Old French beach chairs of striped canvas and soft wood folding frames. $60.

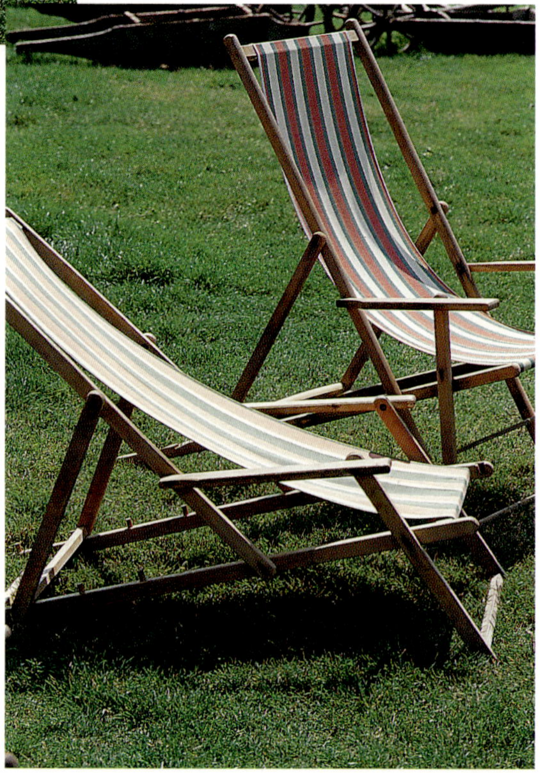

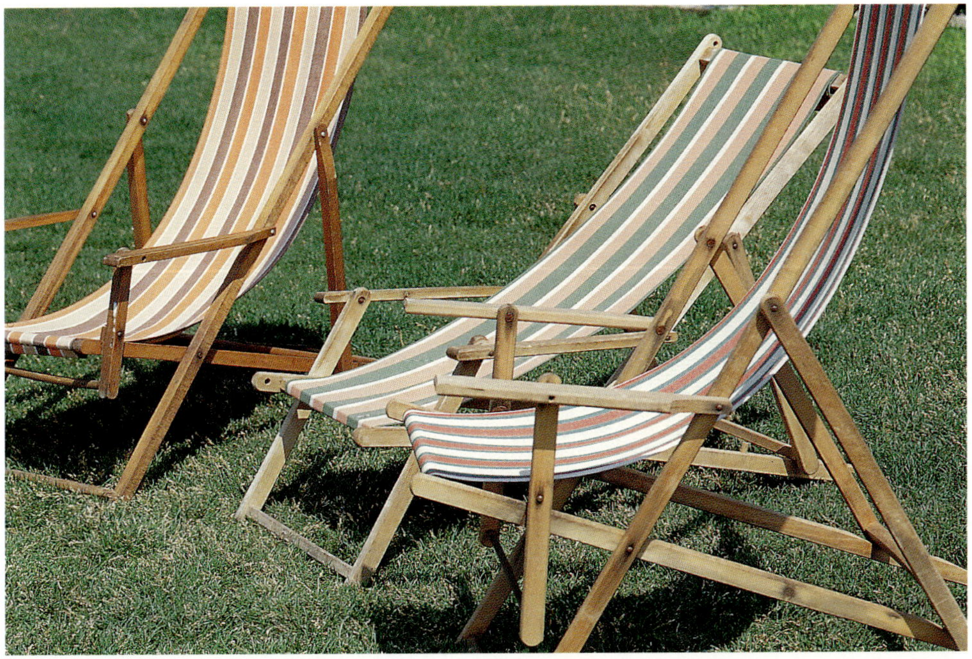

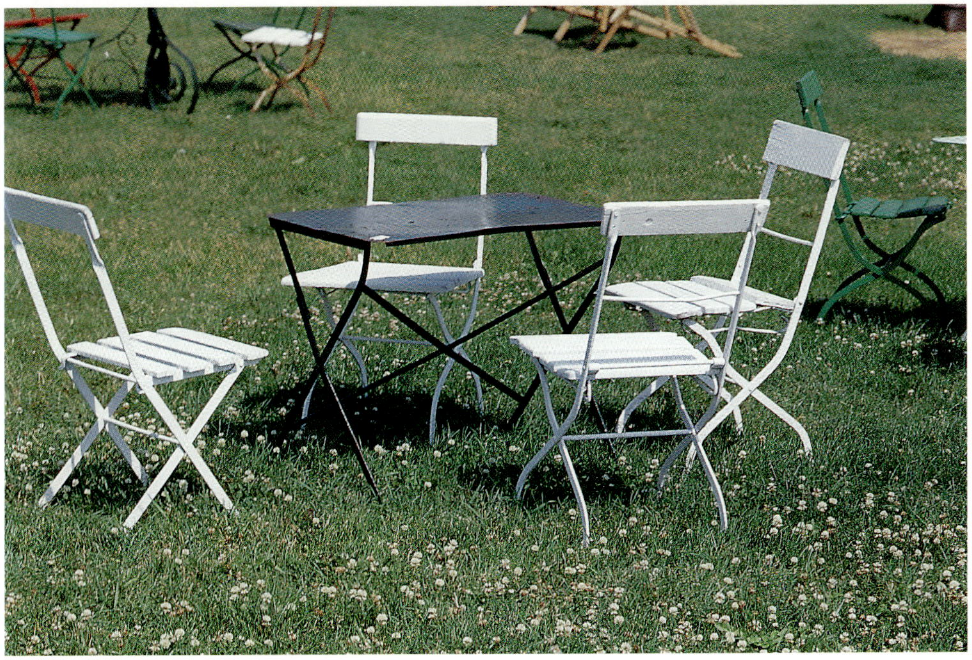

Green folding table and four white folding chairs of iron and painted wood, c.1910.

Right: Rustic bentwood garden chair with honeysuckle vine construction, and a modern birdhouse in use for the summer.

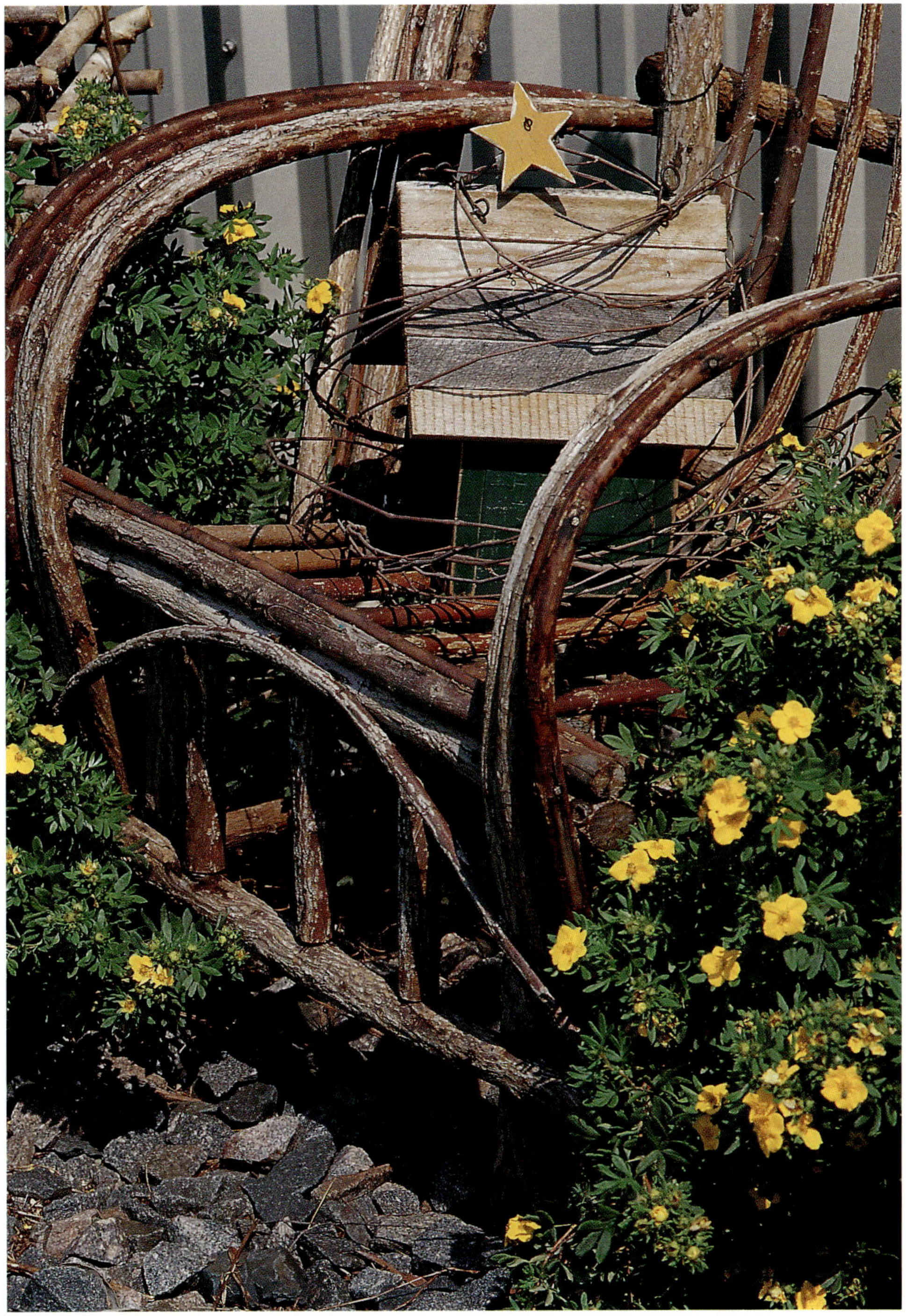

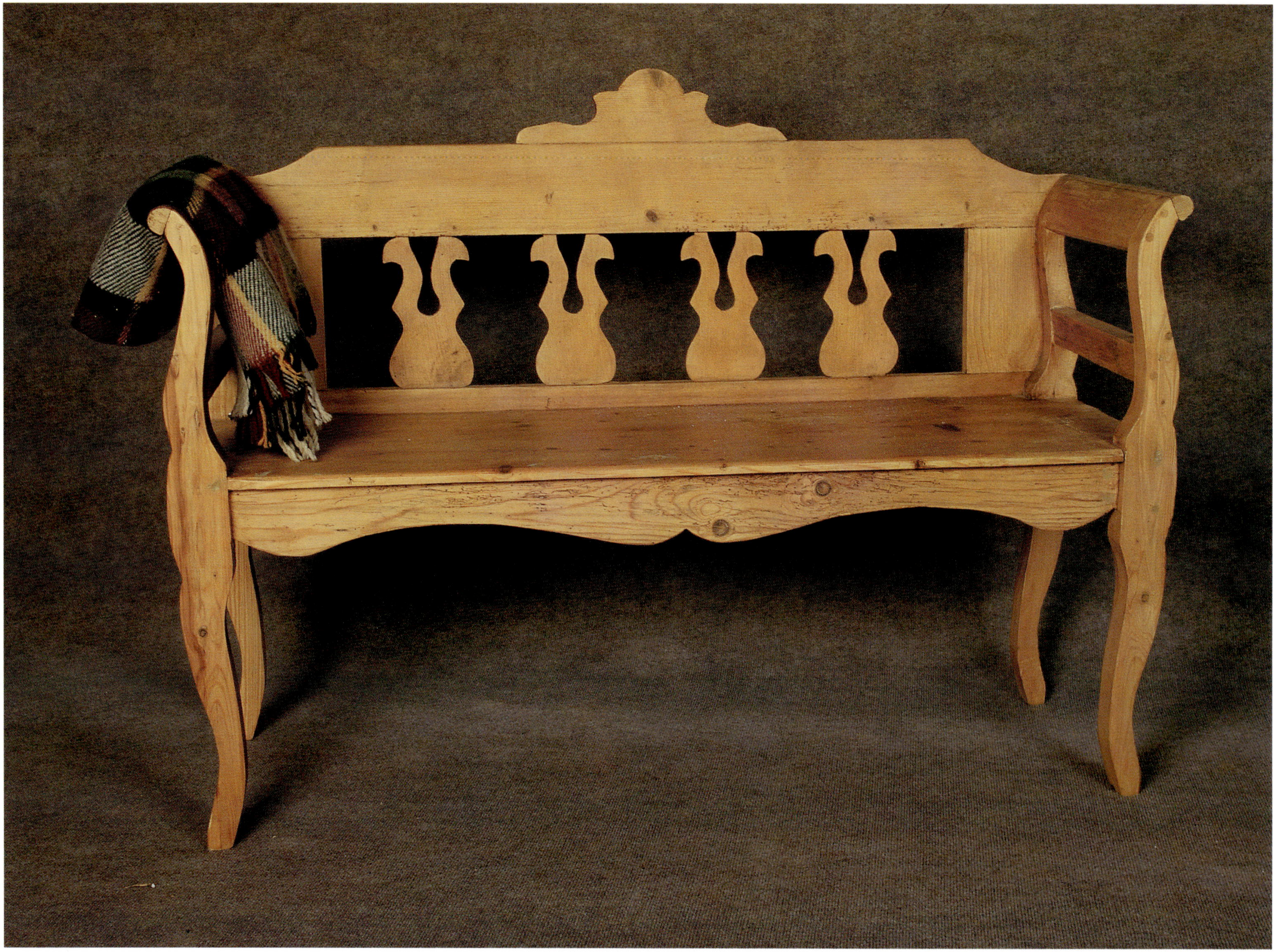

Opposite page: Small pine settee with serpentine legs and fiddle-shaped splats, Rococo style. $625.

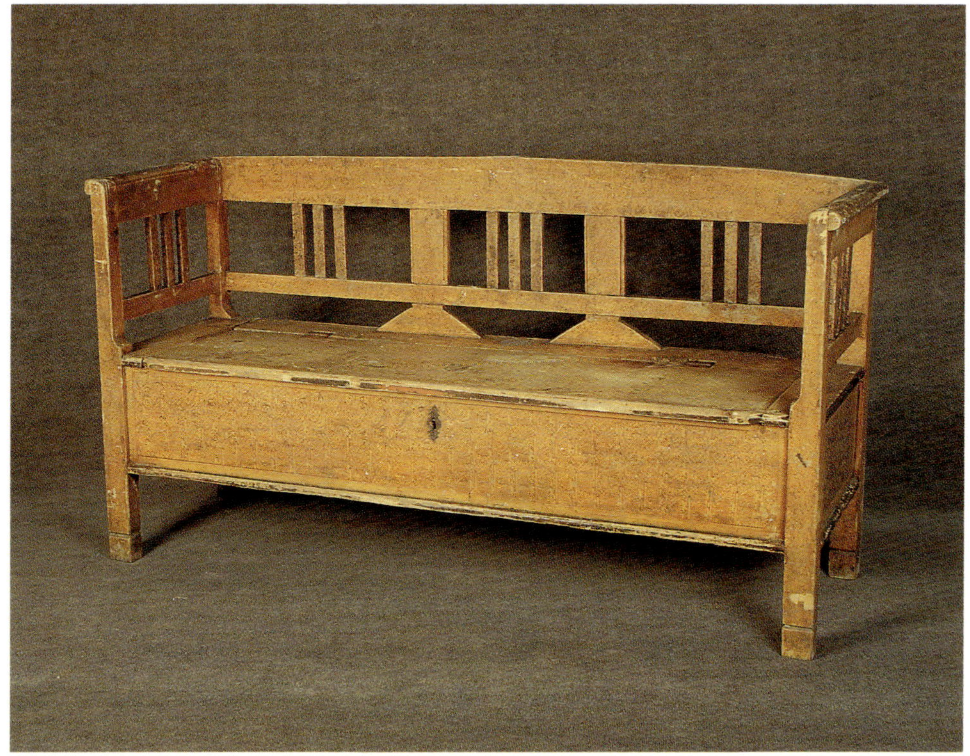

Storage bench/settee with original grain painting and hinged seat, Hungarian, Rococo style, c.1850. $995.

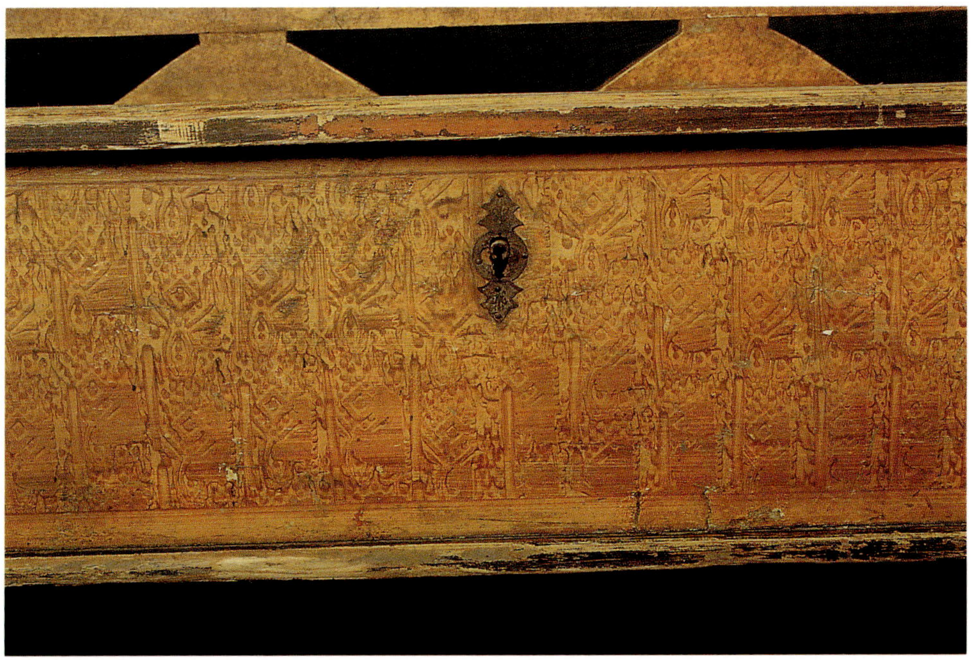

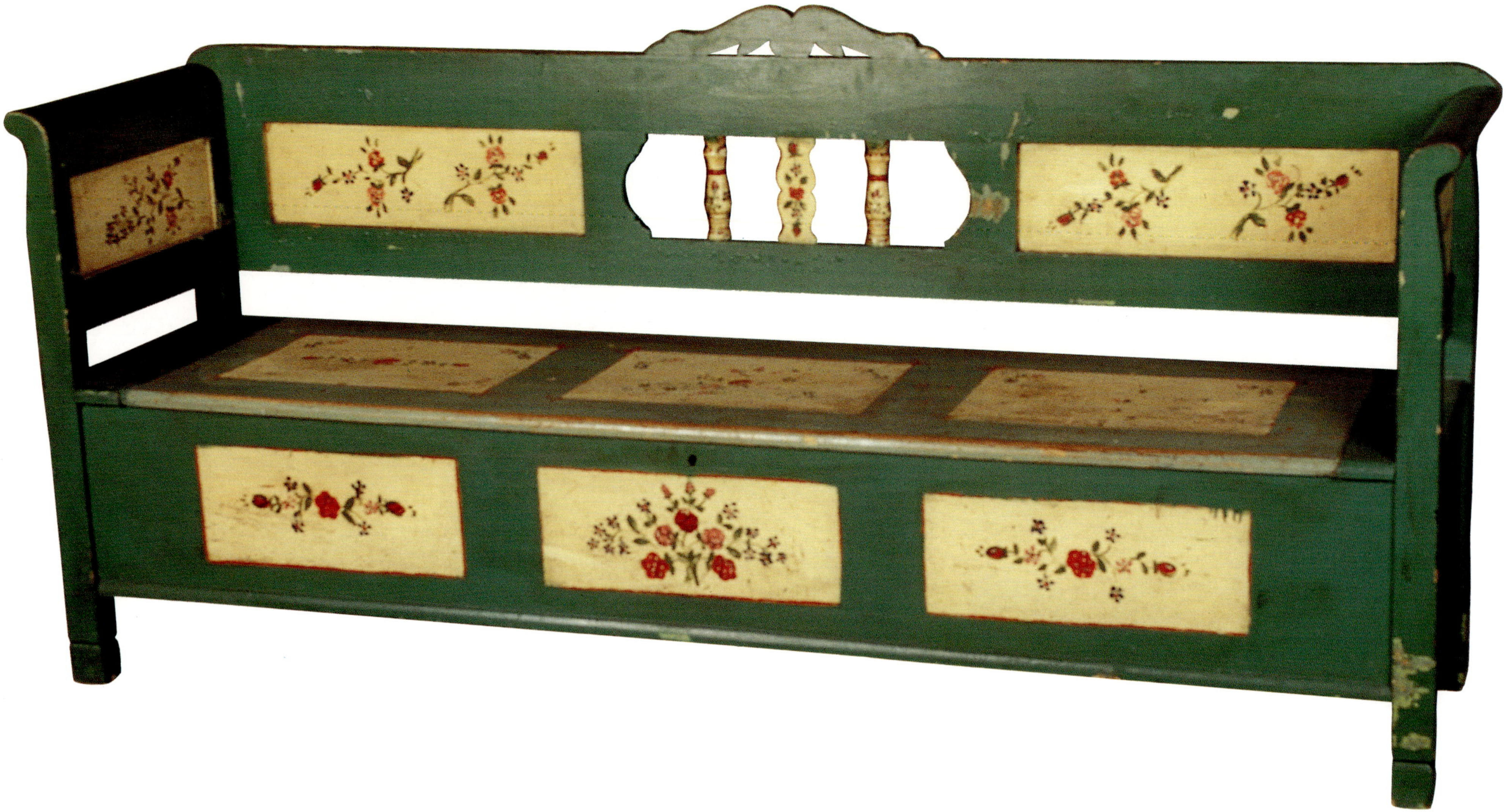

Decorated storage bench/settee painted green with white panels and floral painted details. The seat is hinged to open, Romanian, Rococo style, c.1860. $895.

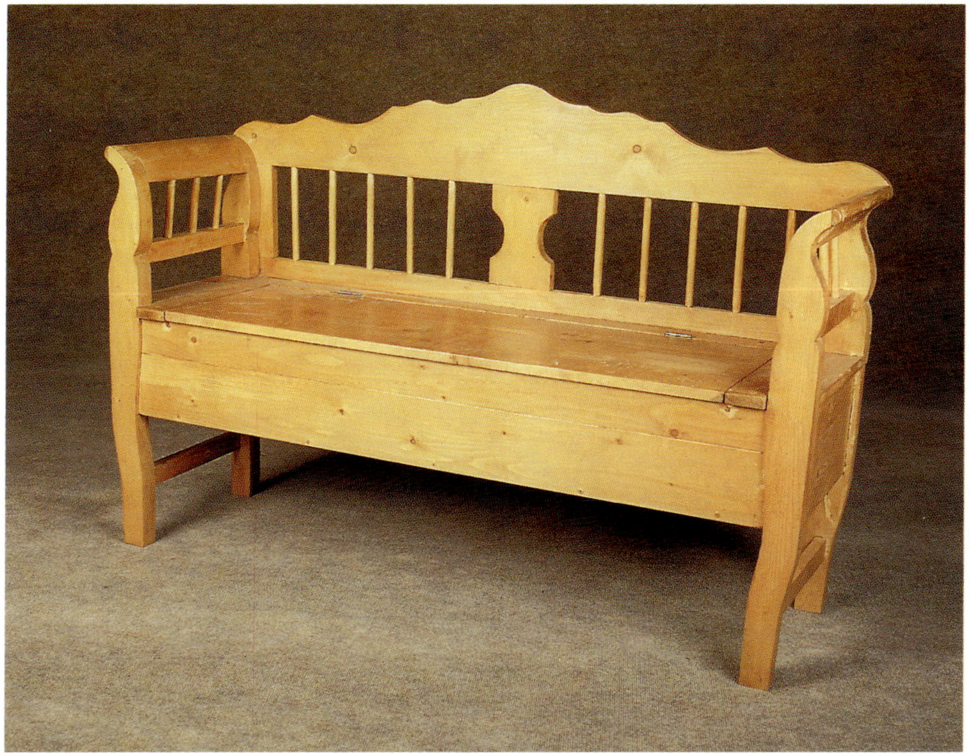

Pine settee with back support, scrolled arms, and a hinged seat on rectangular serpentine legs, Rococo style. $695.

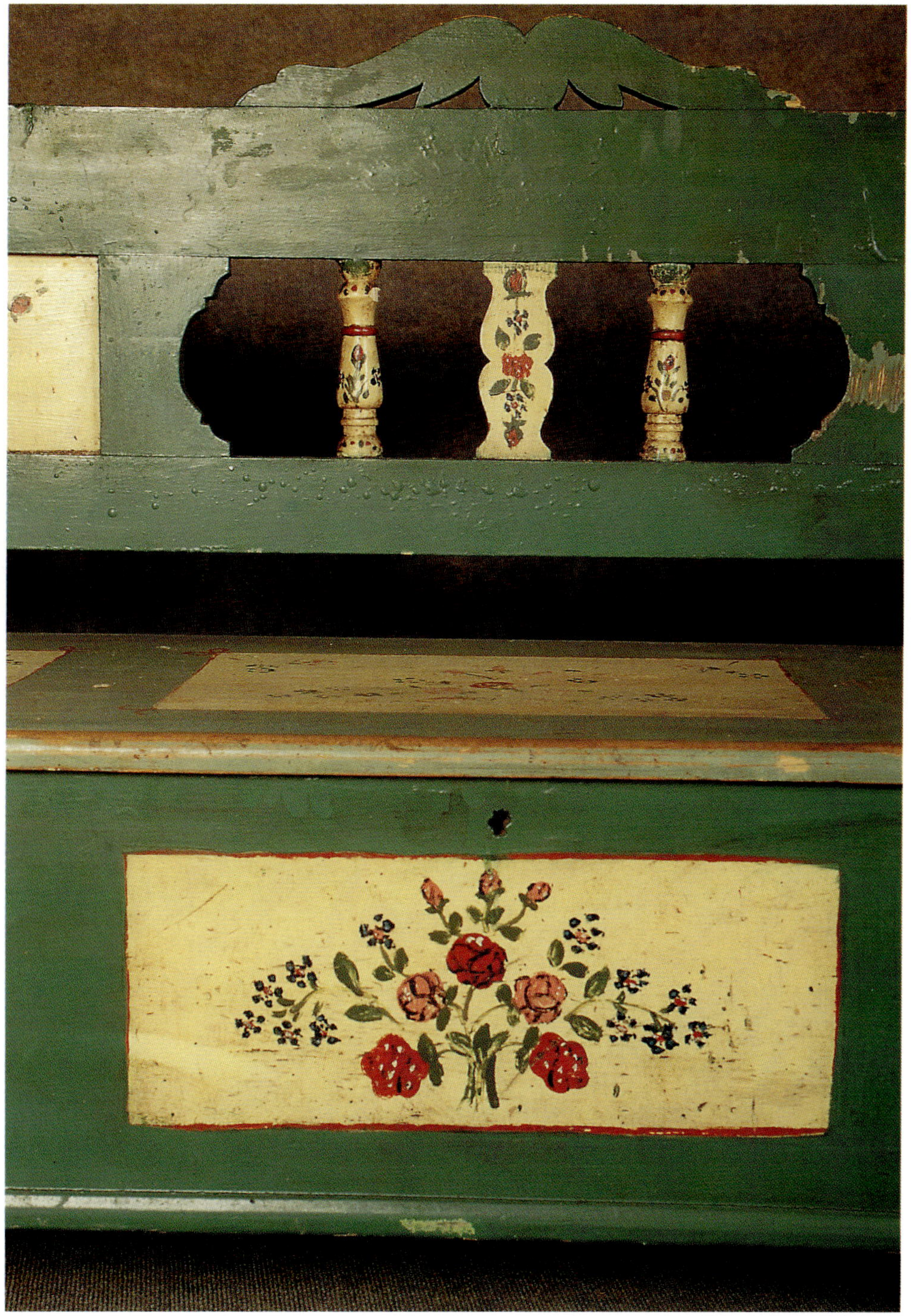

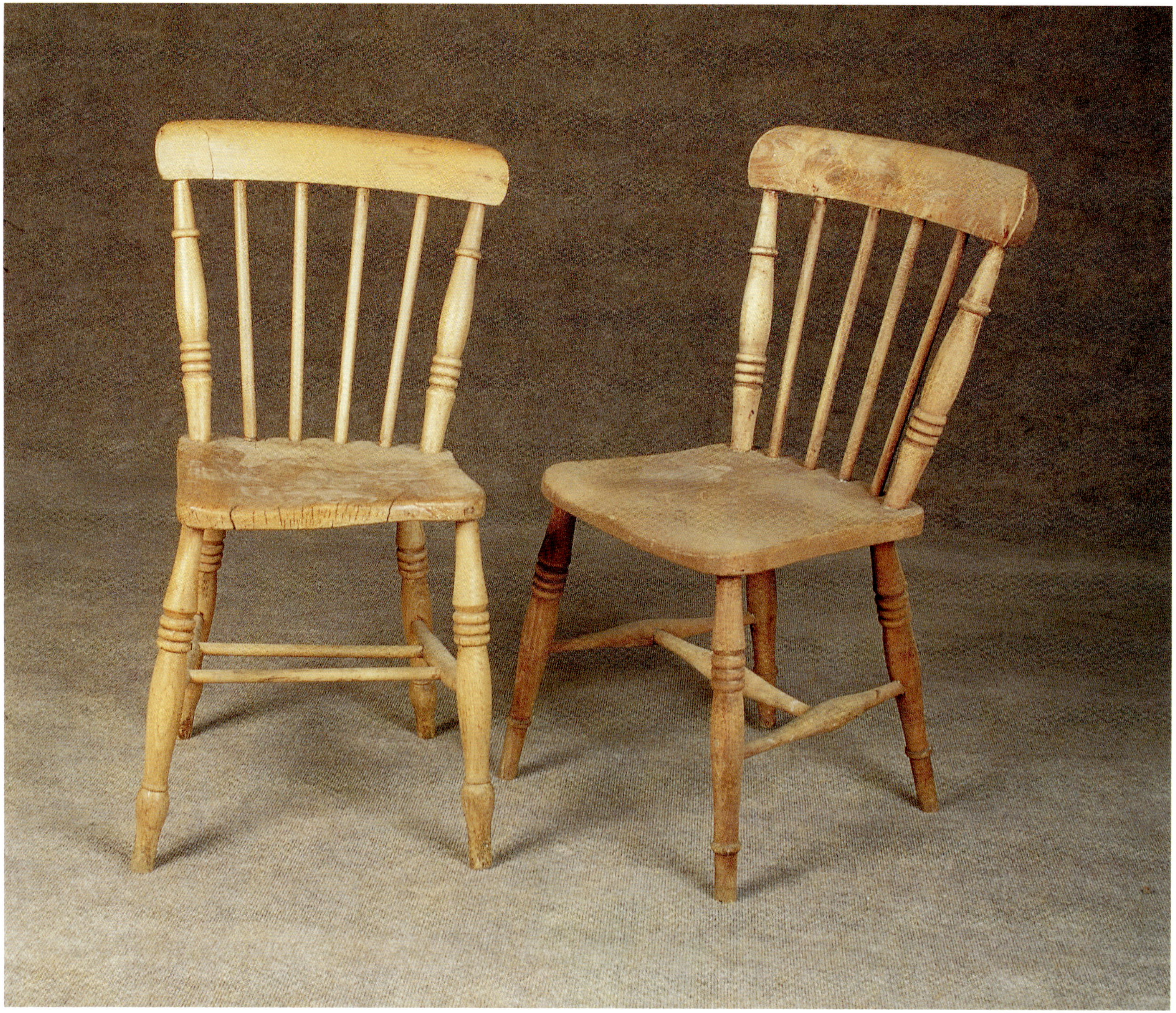

Pair of spindle back side chairs with deep crest, four plain spindles and two turned stiles, plank seat, and four turned legs joined by stretchers. $125.

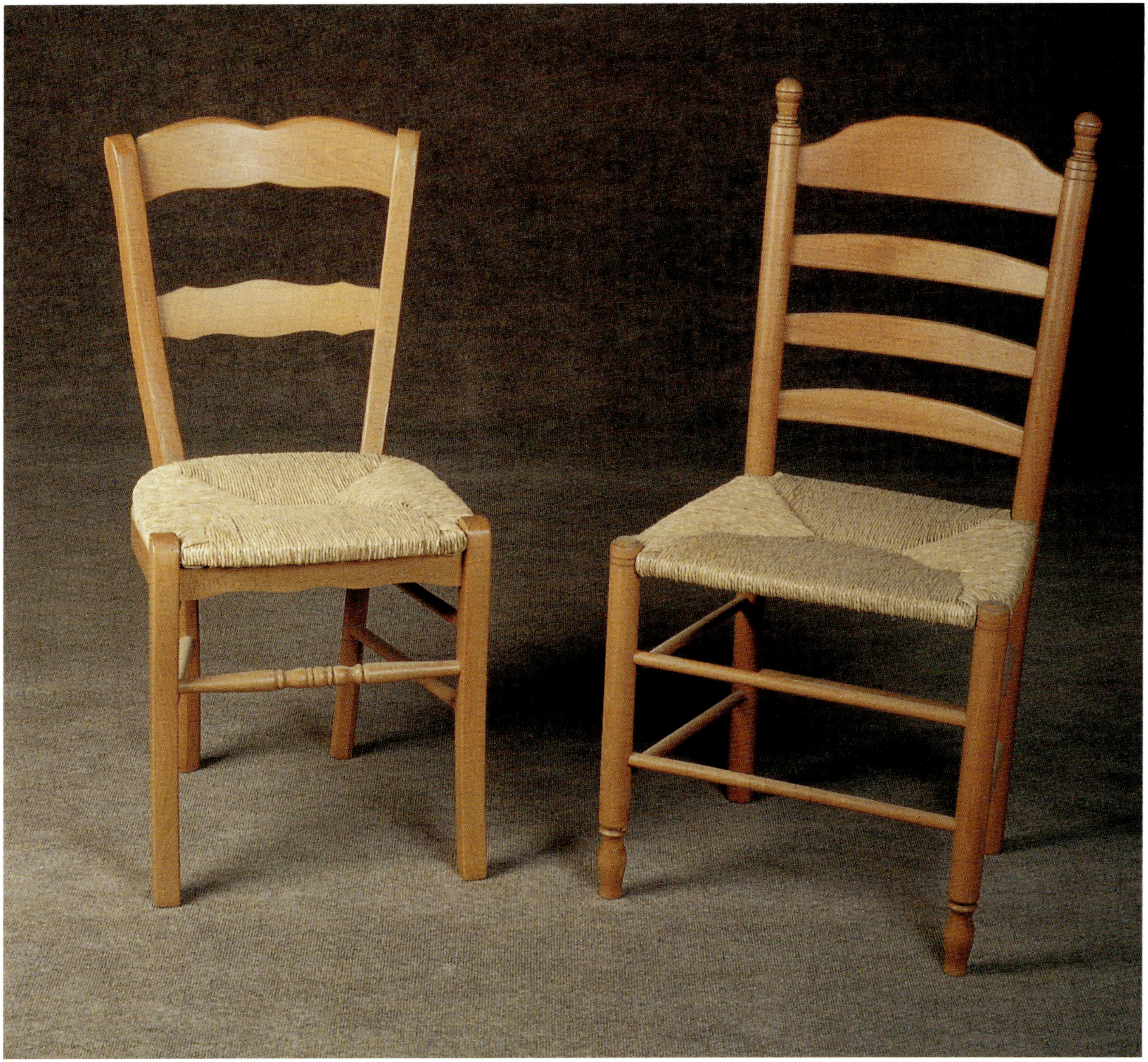

Two rush-seated chairs, one with a shaped crest and back support on square flaring legs, the other with slats and turned legs joined by stretchers.

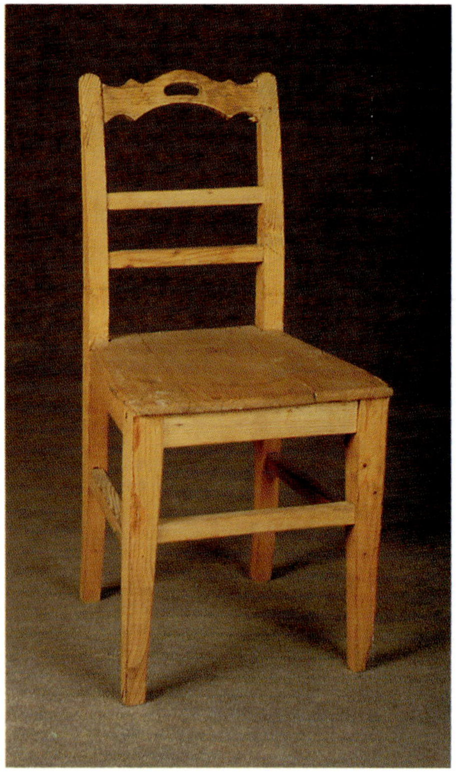

Pine side chair with arched and cut-out crest, two horizontal back supports, rectangular seat on a straight skirt and rectangular legs $125.

Child's painted high chair with raffia seat and plain round legs with stretchers, arm rests missing.

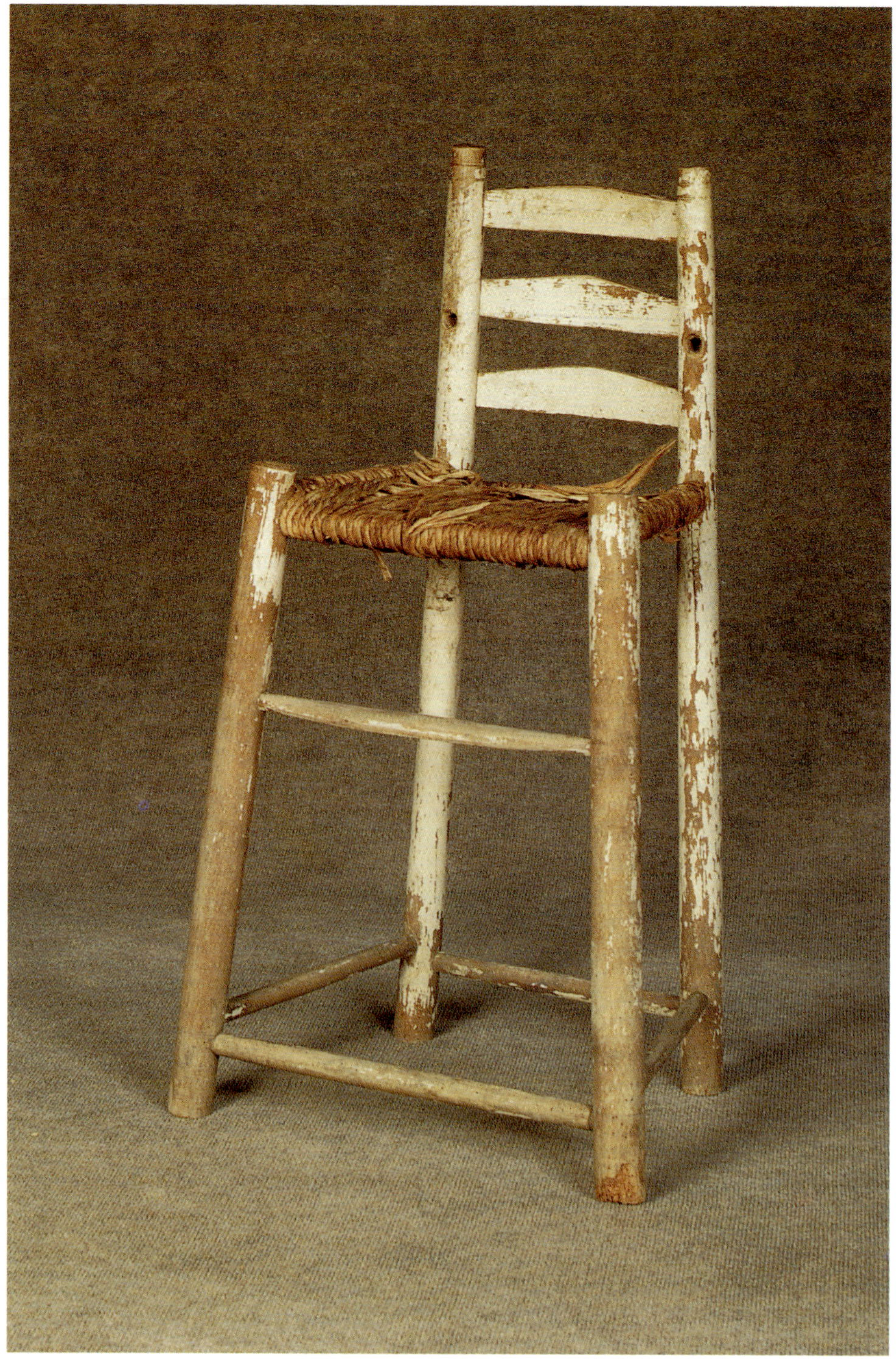

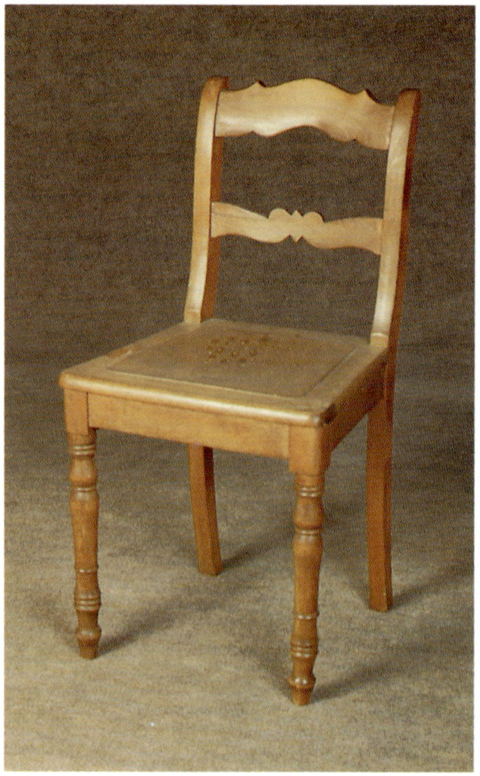

Small chair with two shaped horizontal slats, pierced seat, and turned legs, Renaissance Revival style. $125.

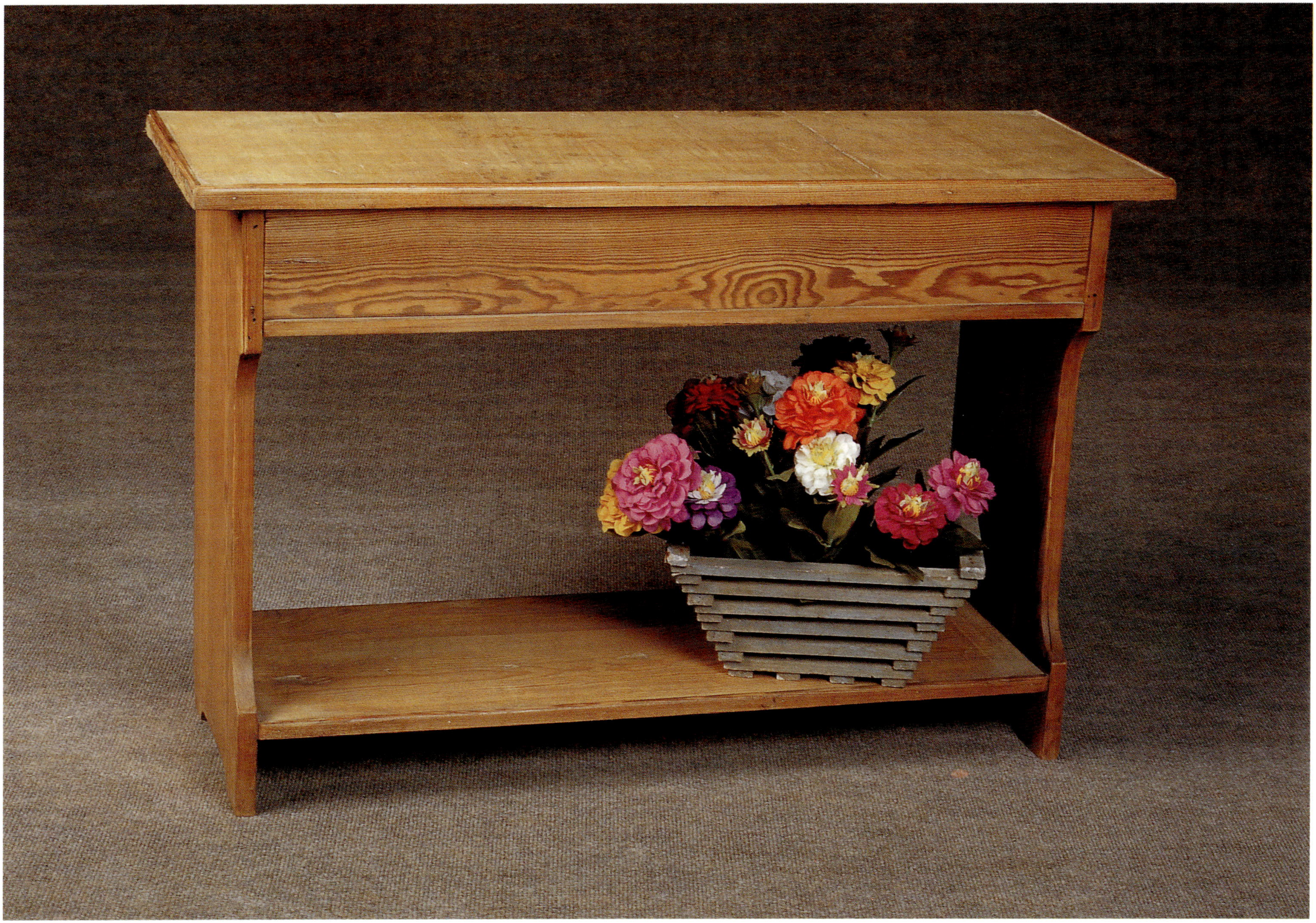

Small bench with hinged top and lower shelf. $265.

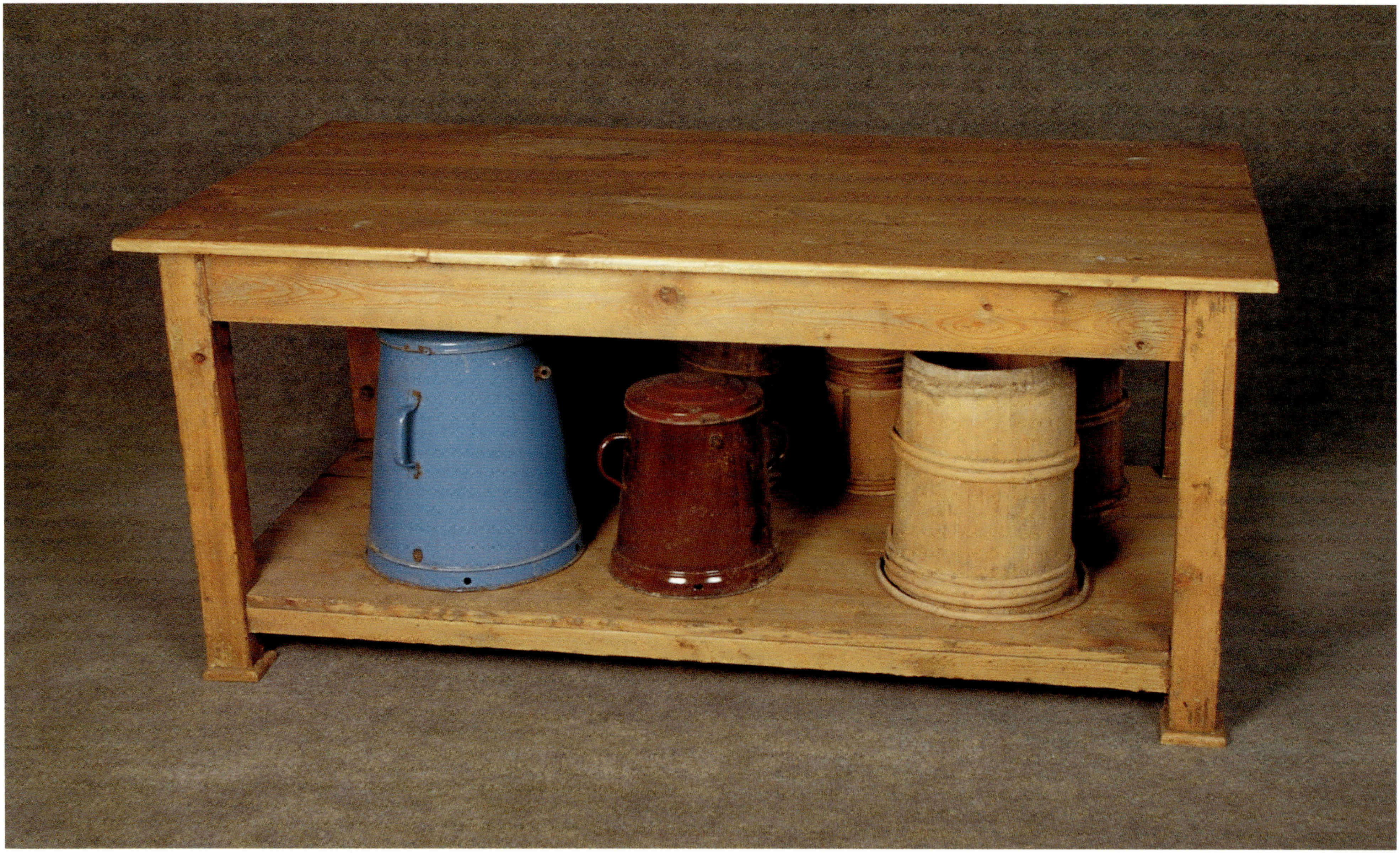

Rectangular bench with a straight skirt and four square legs joined by a shelf and box stretcher, resting on block feet, Arts & Crafts style. $895.

Opposite page:
Top left: German shoemaker's bench on four plain turned legs. $95.

Bottom right: Canted leg stool with scalloped edges to the sides and central stretcher. $65.

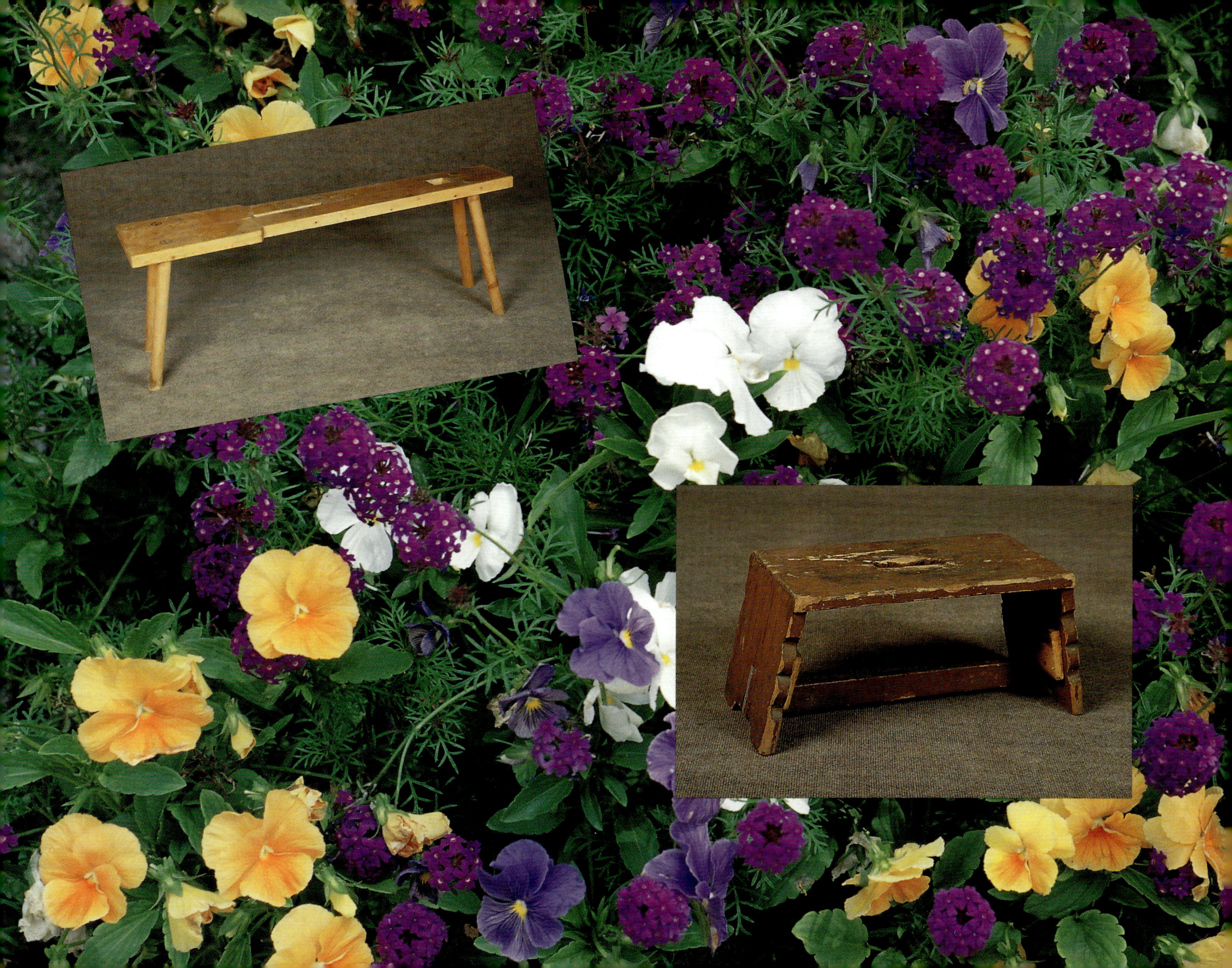

Time For Everything

Clocks

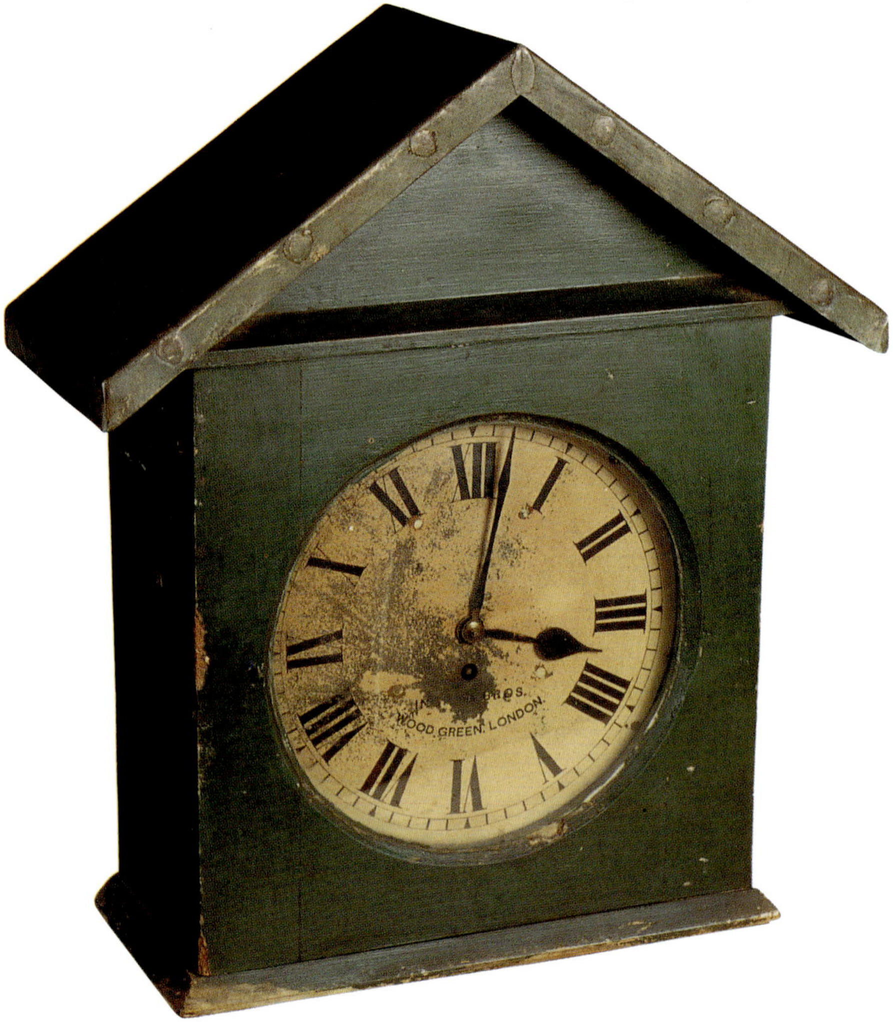

English shop clock with white face marked "Ingraham Bros. Wood Green, London," in peaked case painted green. $895.

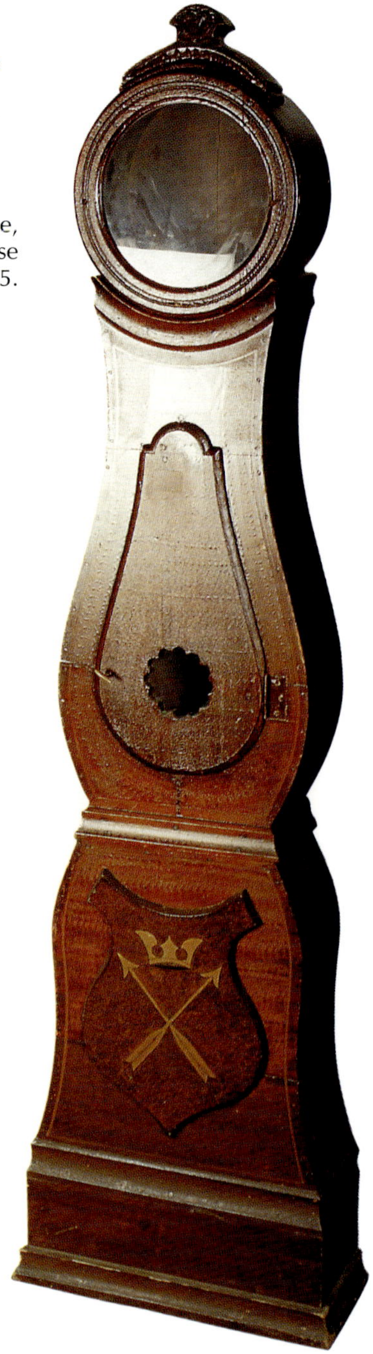

Swedish grandmother clock with round face, painted case, and molded straight base molding, Rococo style, c.1860s. $3295.

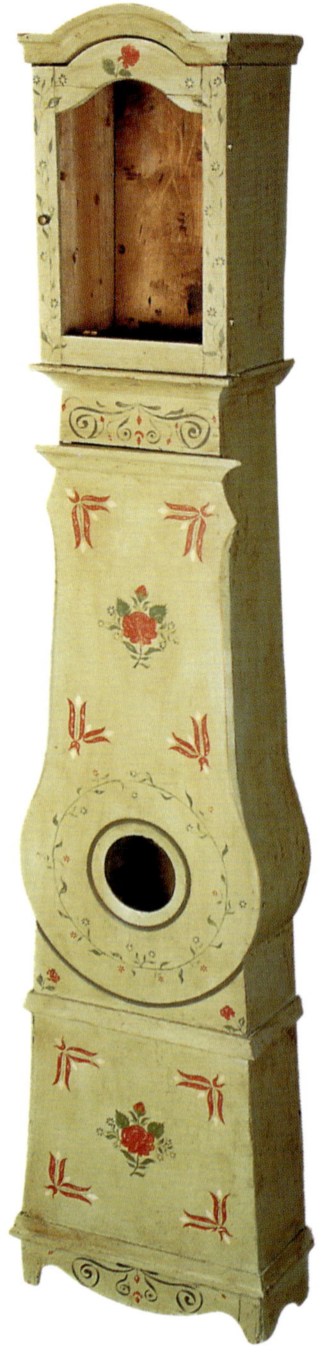

Tall case clock lacking the face and works in a painted case of light green with red floral and garland decoration, 87" high, Rococo style.

UNPACKING

Trunks and Blanket Chests

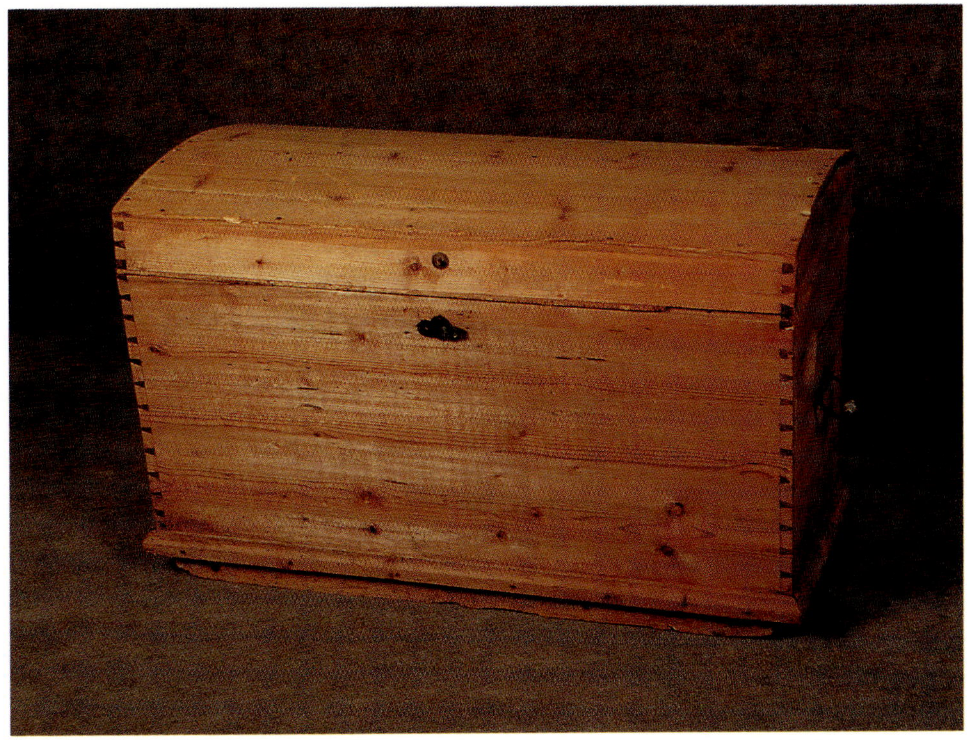

Pine domed-lid trunk with dove-tailed corners, iron bail handles, and molded base on long front and back trestle feet. $295.

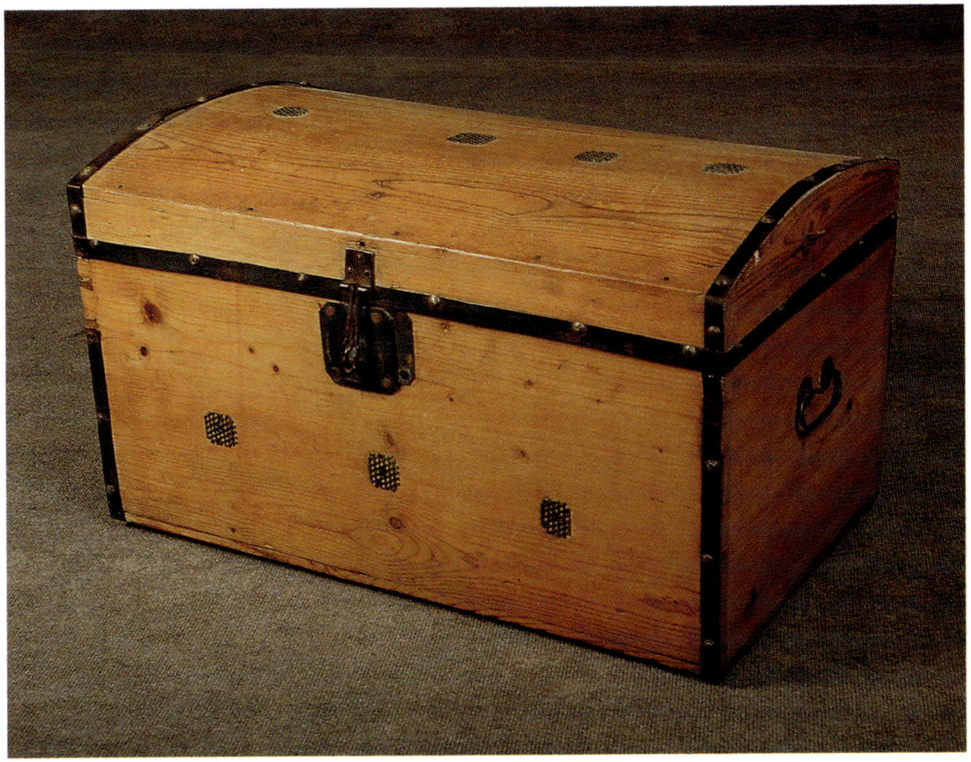

German domed-lid trunk with iron straps and hinges. $350.

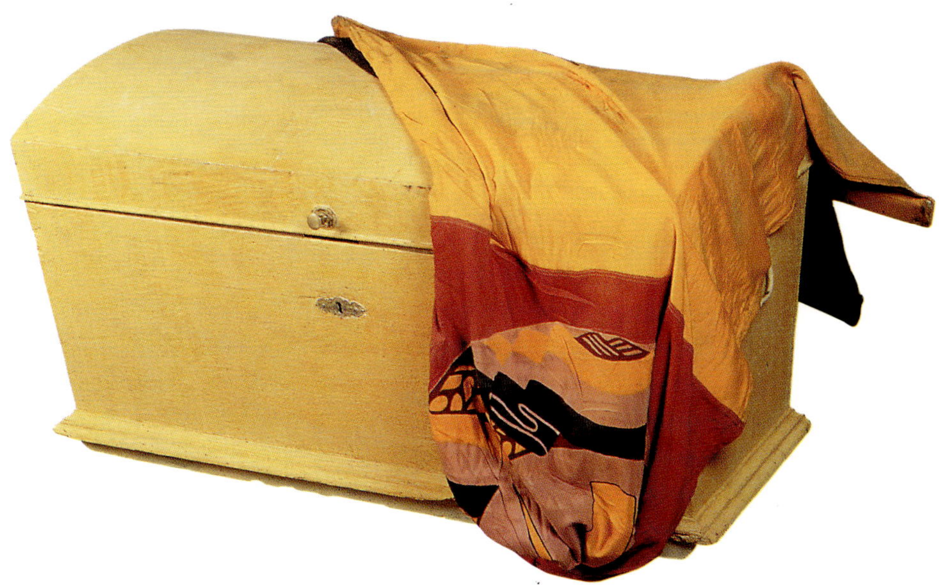

Yellow painted domed-lid trunk with metal pull and escutcheon and a deep base molding. $250.

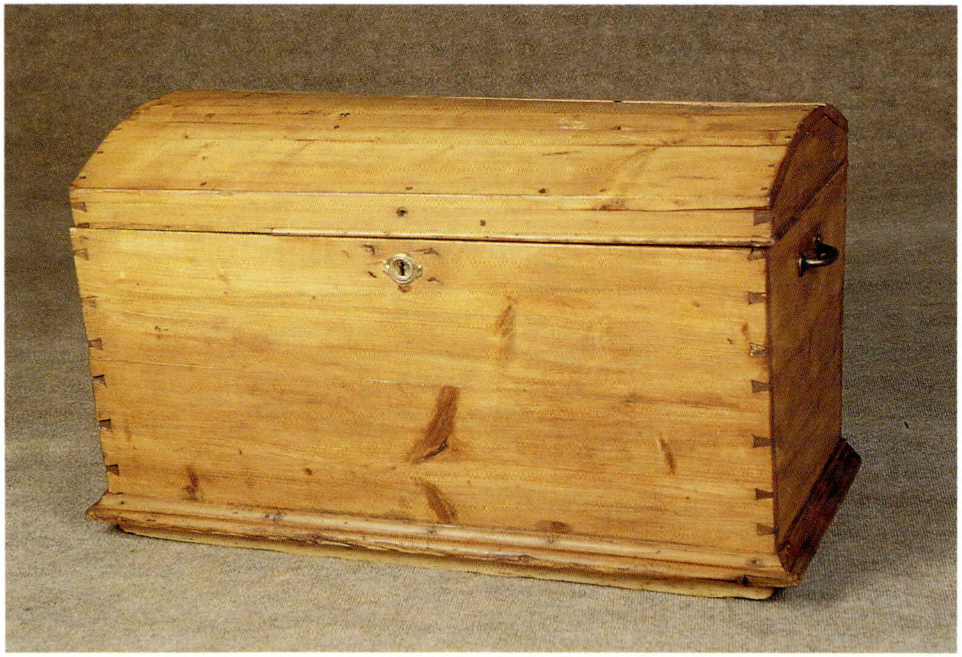

German, pine domed-lid trunk with dove-tailed corners and molded base.

Opposite page:
Top left: Unusual lidded trunk, rectangular with cut corners and tapering sides. The lid rests on the sides and is hinged in the middle. The top and long sides are painted blue with white reserves and floral decoration above a band of red at the base. The short sides have iron bail handles. $850.

Bottom right: Small, blue painted, domed-lid trunk of pine.

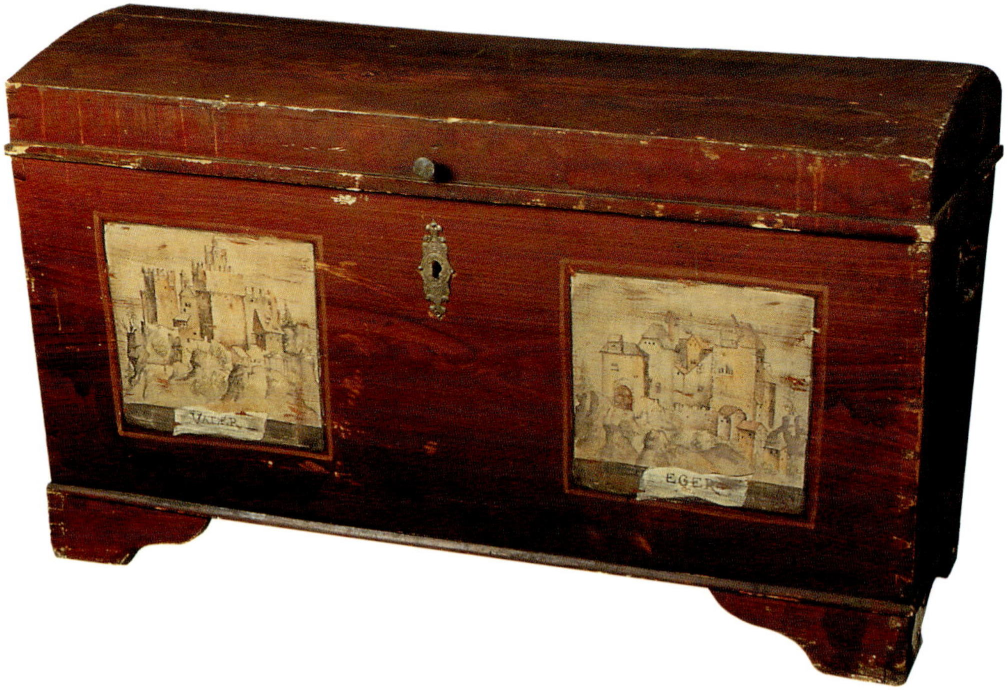

Painted, German domed-lid trunk with architectural scenes painted in the front two panels which are labeled "Valer" and "Eger." $425.

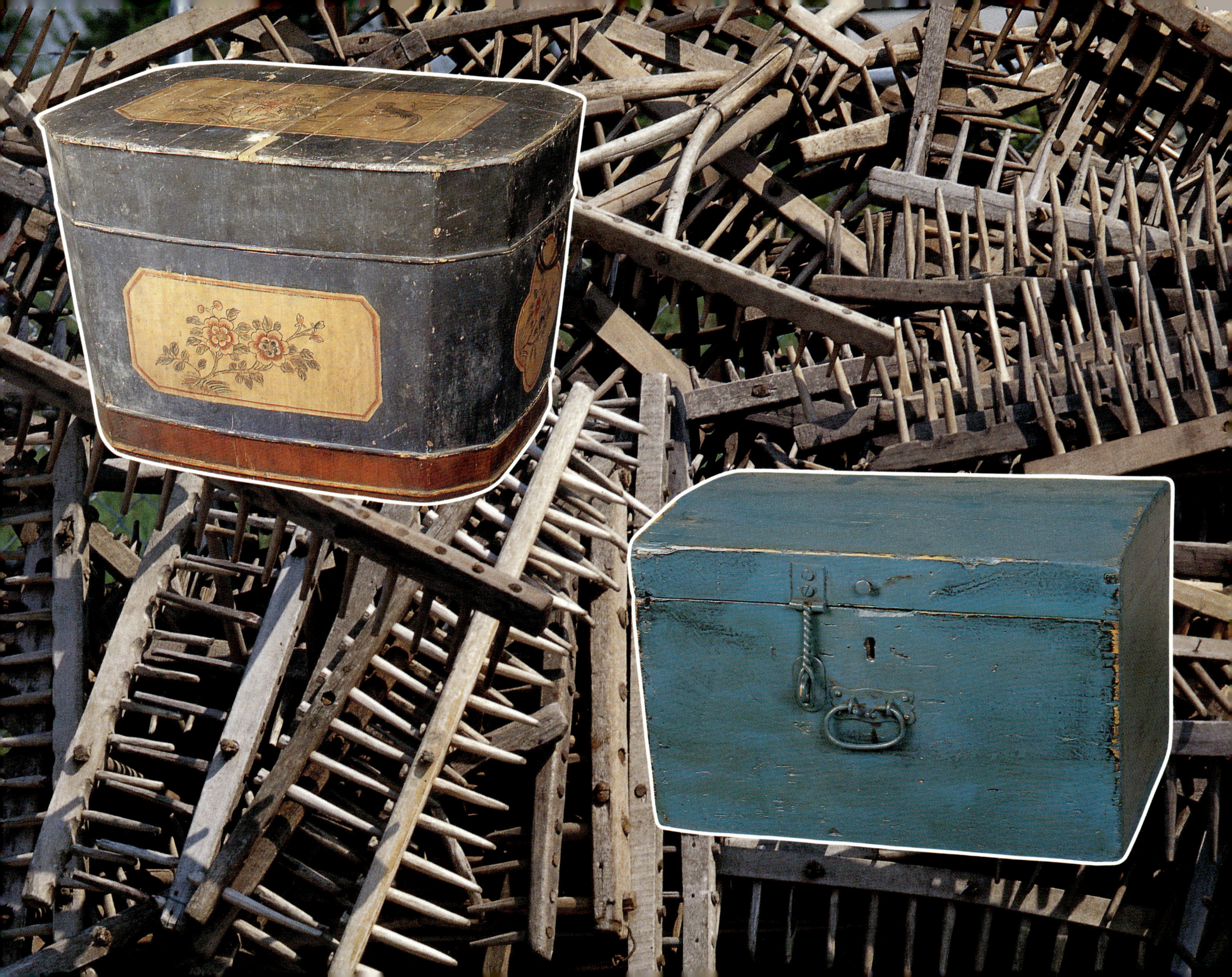

Blanket Chests

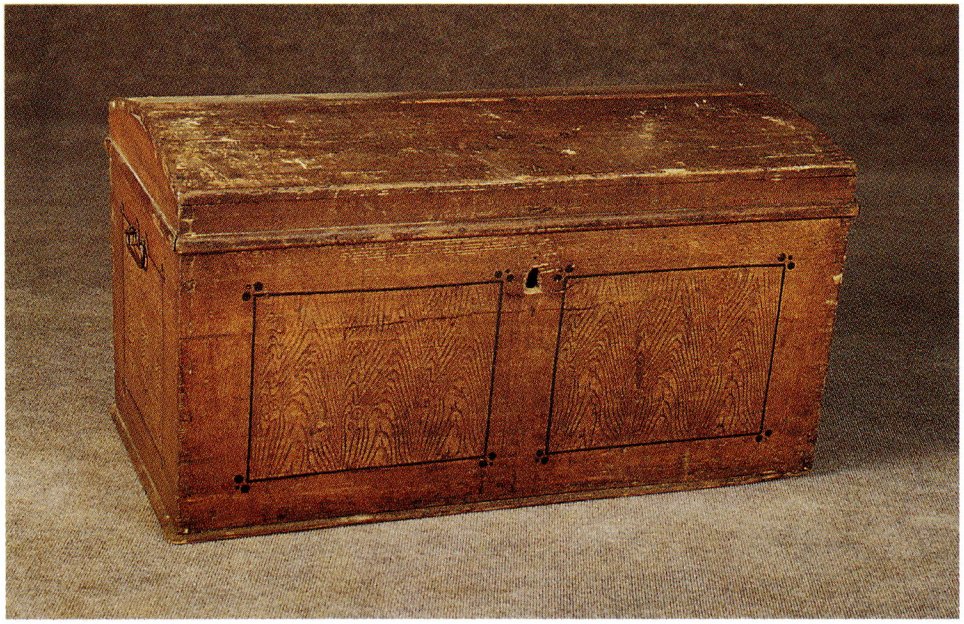

Small, German, painted blanket chest with domed lid and grain painted panels outlined in black. $395.

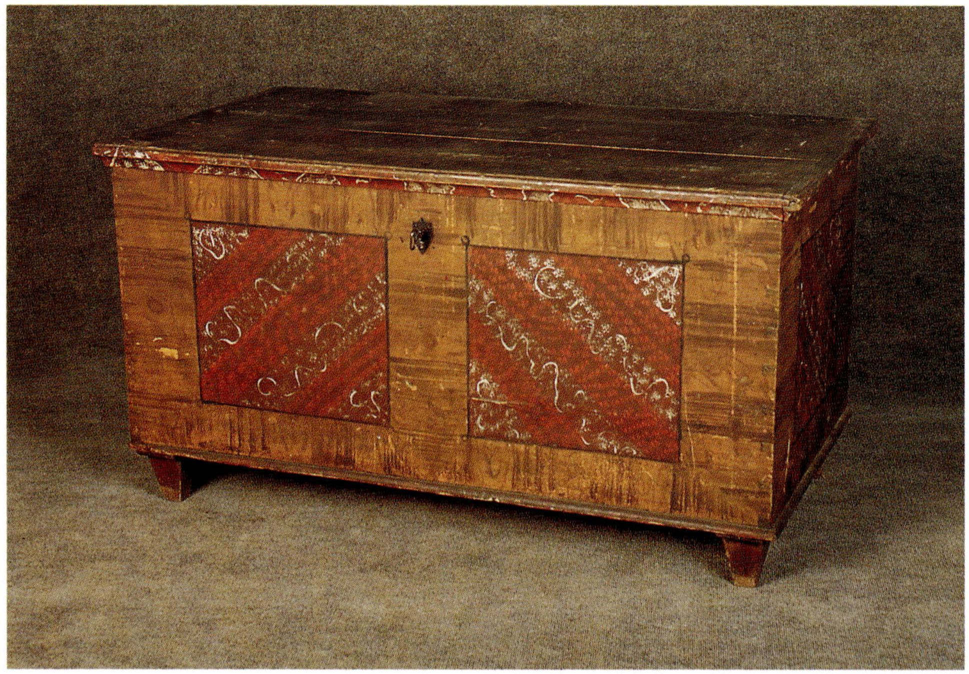

Blanket chest with hinged lid and grain painting, front panels decorated with red and white squiggle lines. The case rests on tapering square feet. $595.

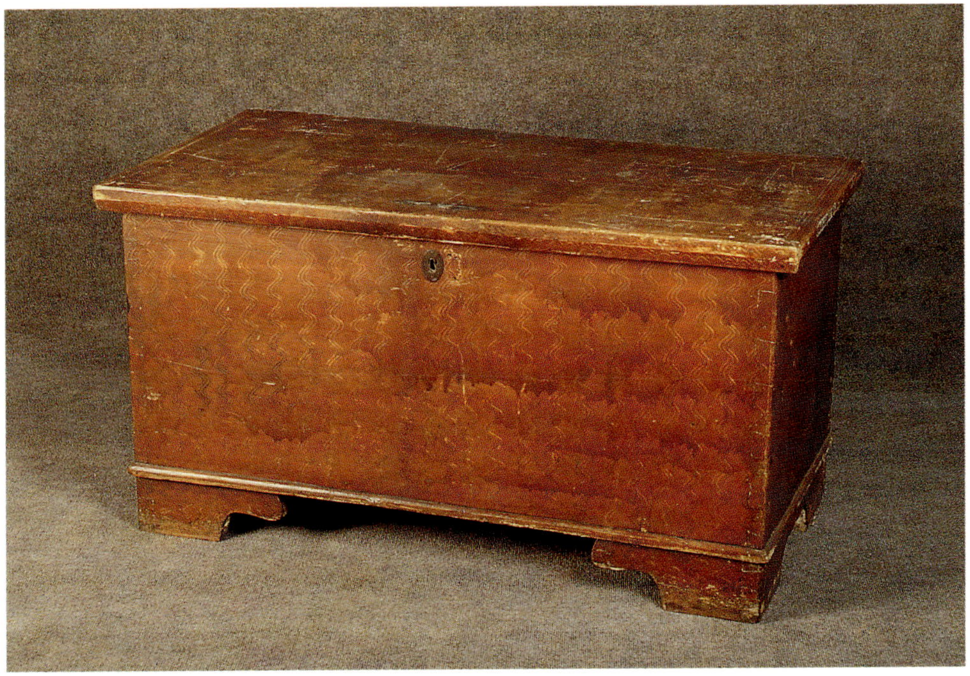

German painted blanket chest with red/ brown stain and squiggled wood grain lines of contrasting lighter color, resting on bracket feet $650.

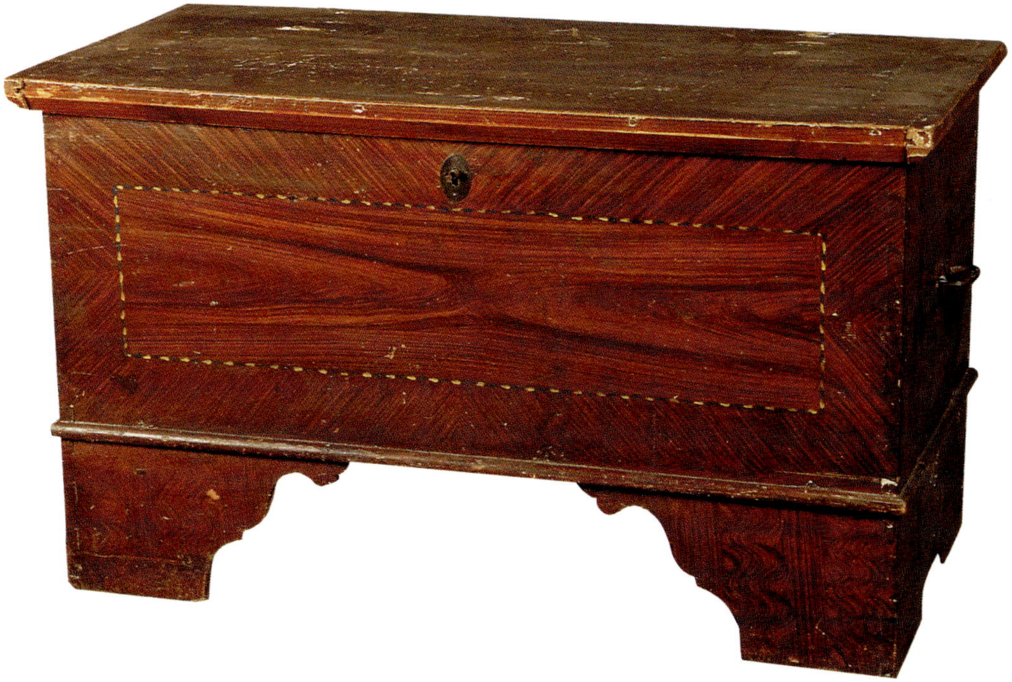

Grain painted blanket chest with a hinged top and iron side handles, the front painted with a simulated flame grain decoration, thin base molding, and deep bracket feet. $395.

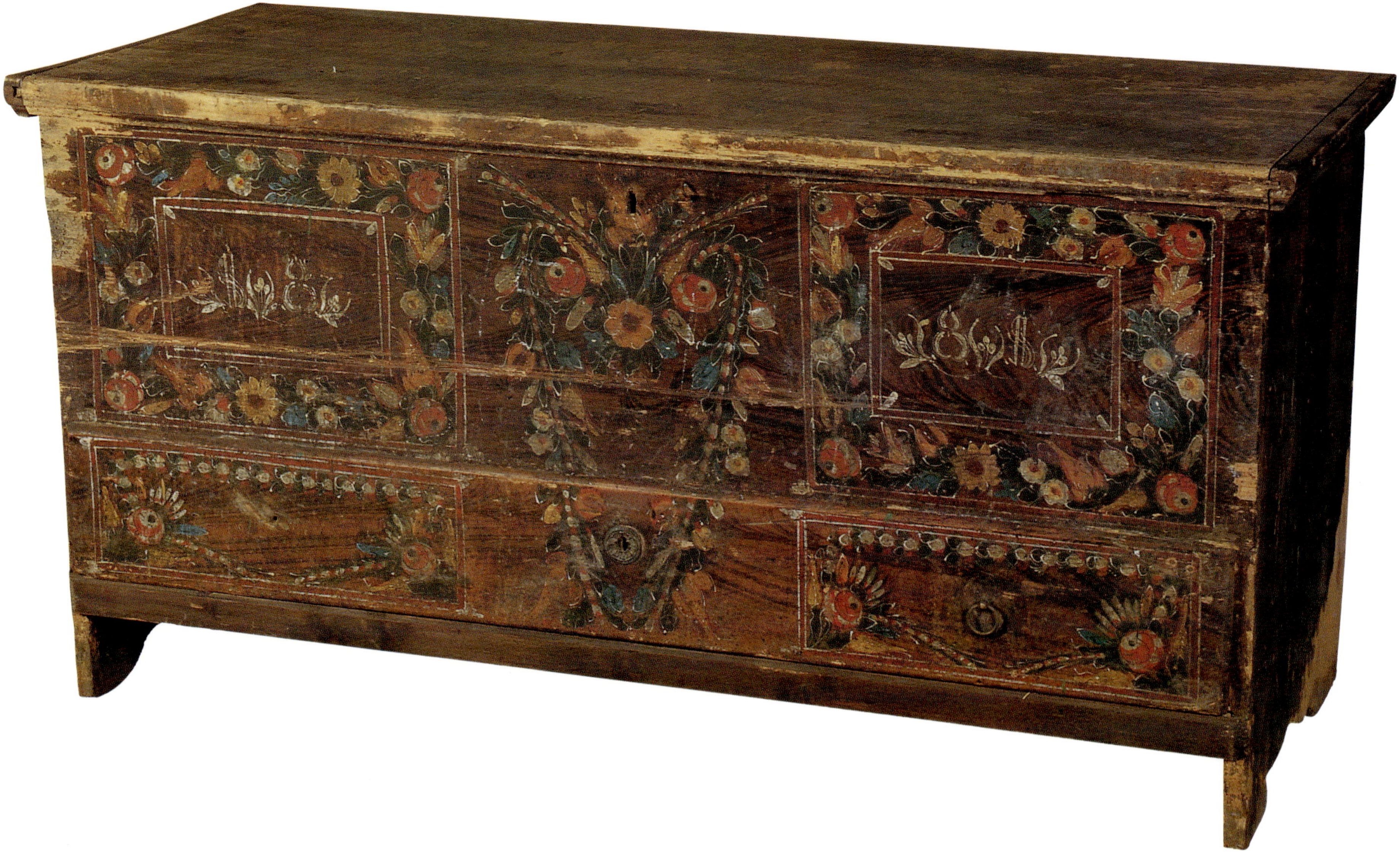

Painted blanket chest with brown/red background decorated with original floral design. The side boards continue to form the feet. $895.

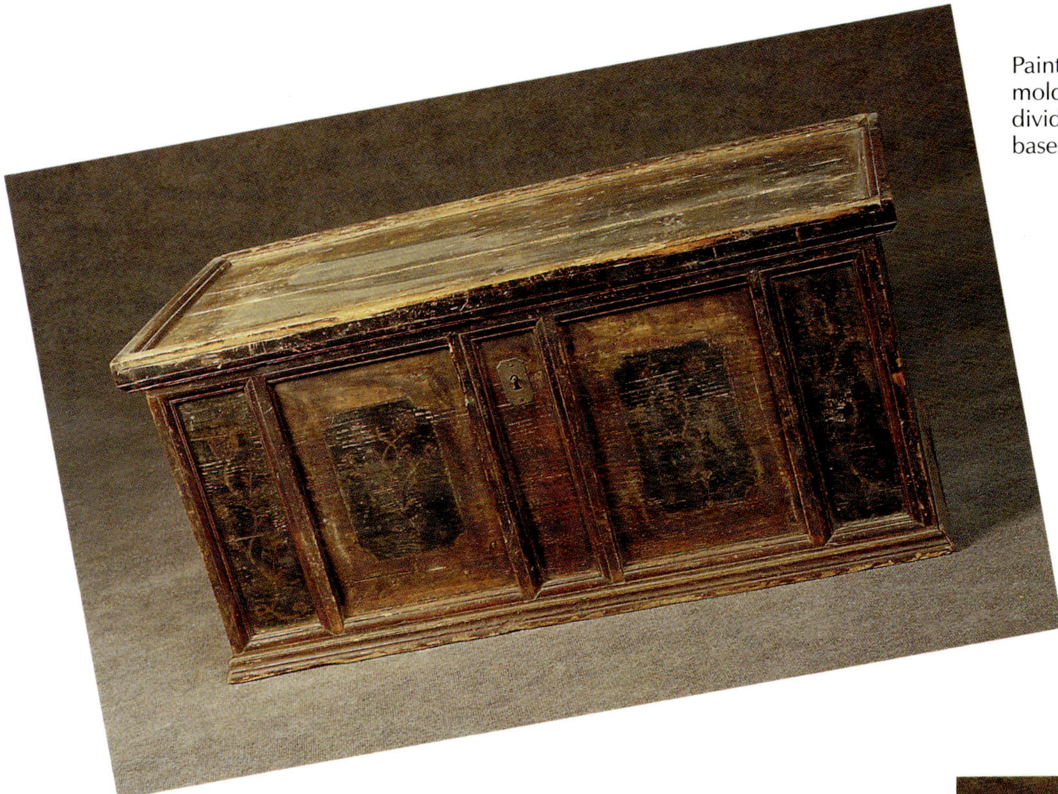

Painted blanket chest, top recessed with an applied molding over the painted front in five sections divided by moldings, the case resting on a stepped base molding, Rococo style. $675.

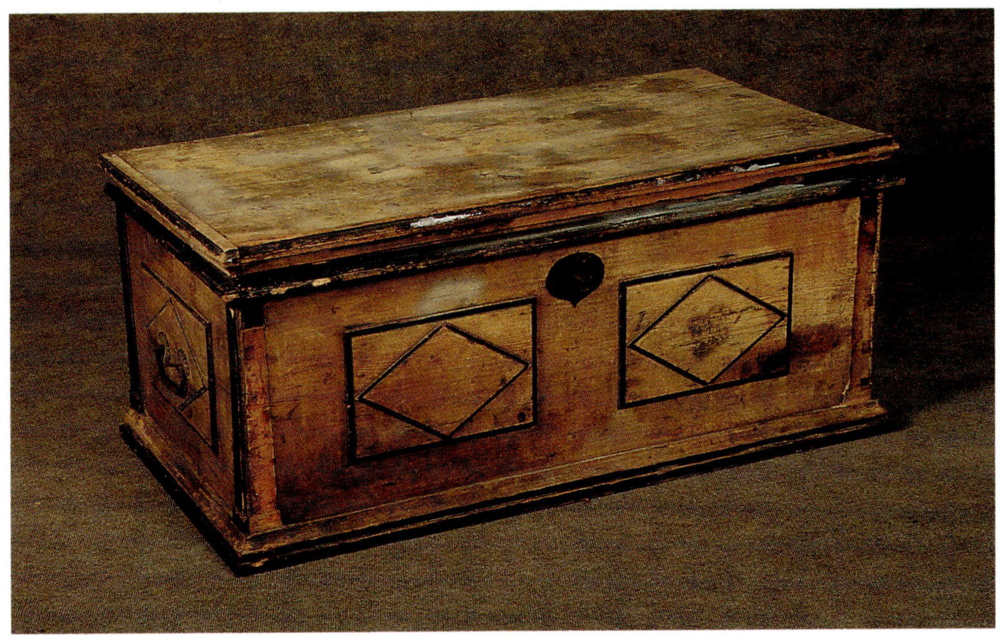

Painted blanket chest with old yellow surface, black borders, and raised panel outlines. $695.

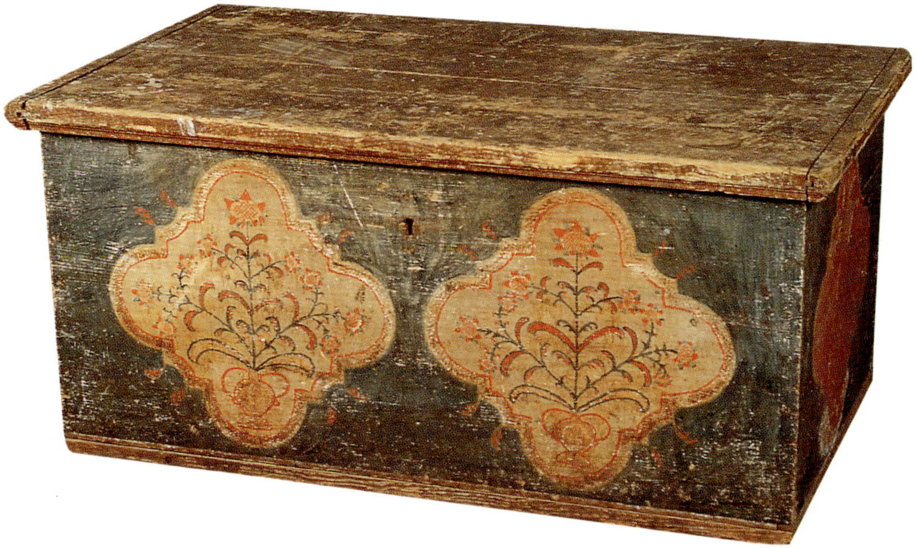

Painted blanket chest with hinged lid and front painted green with two contrasting quatrefoil panels ornamented with floral decoration. The base molding rests on the floor. $895.

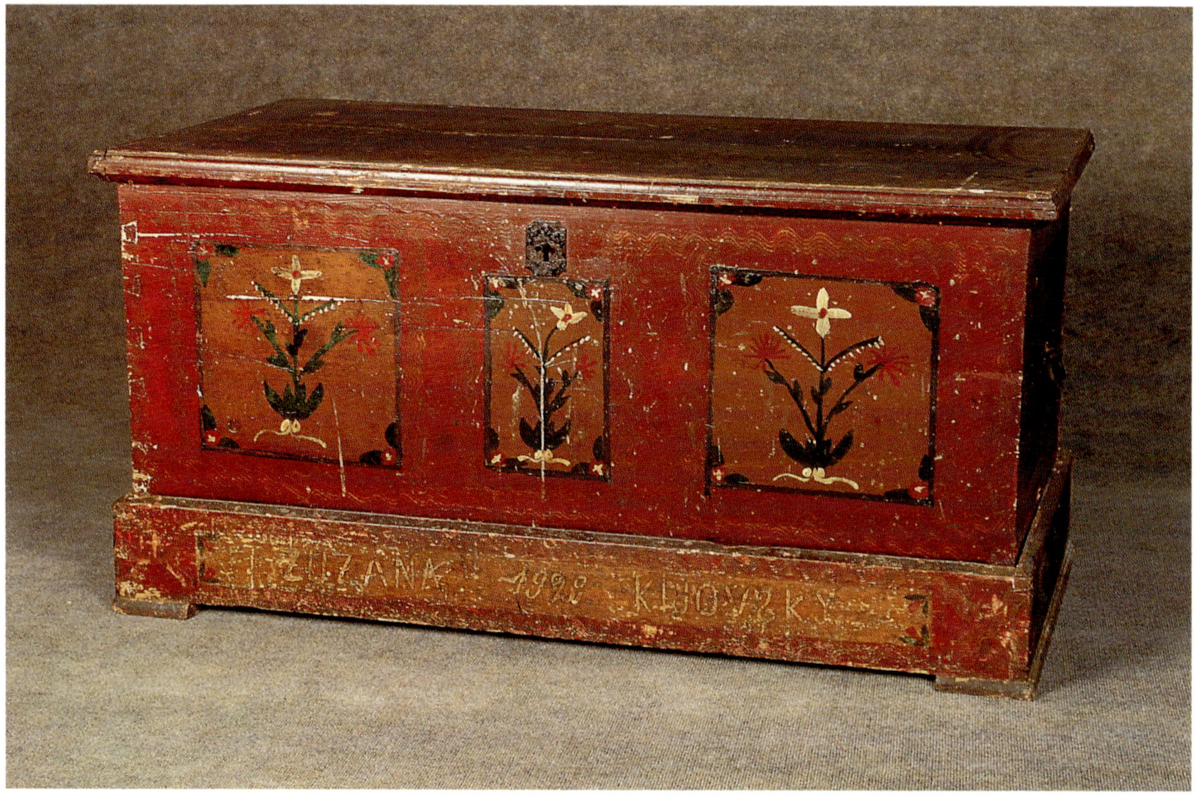

Painted, two-part, Czechoslovakian blanket chest with separate base and three rectangular front panels with floral decoration, dated 1928. $695.

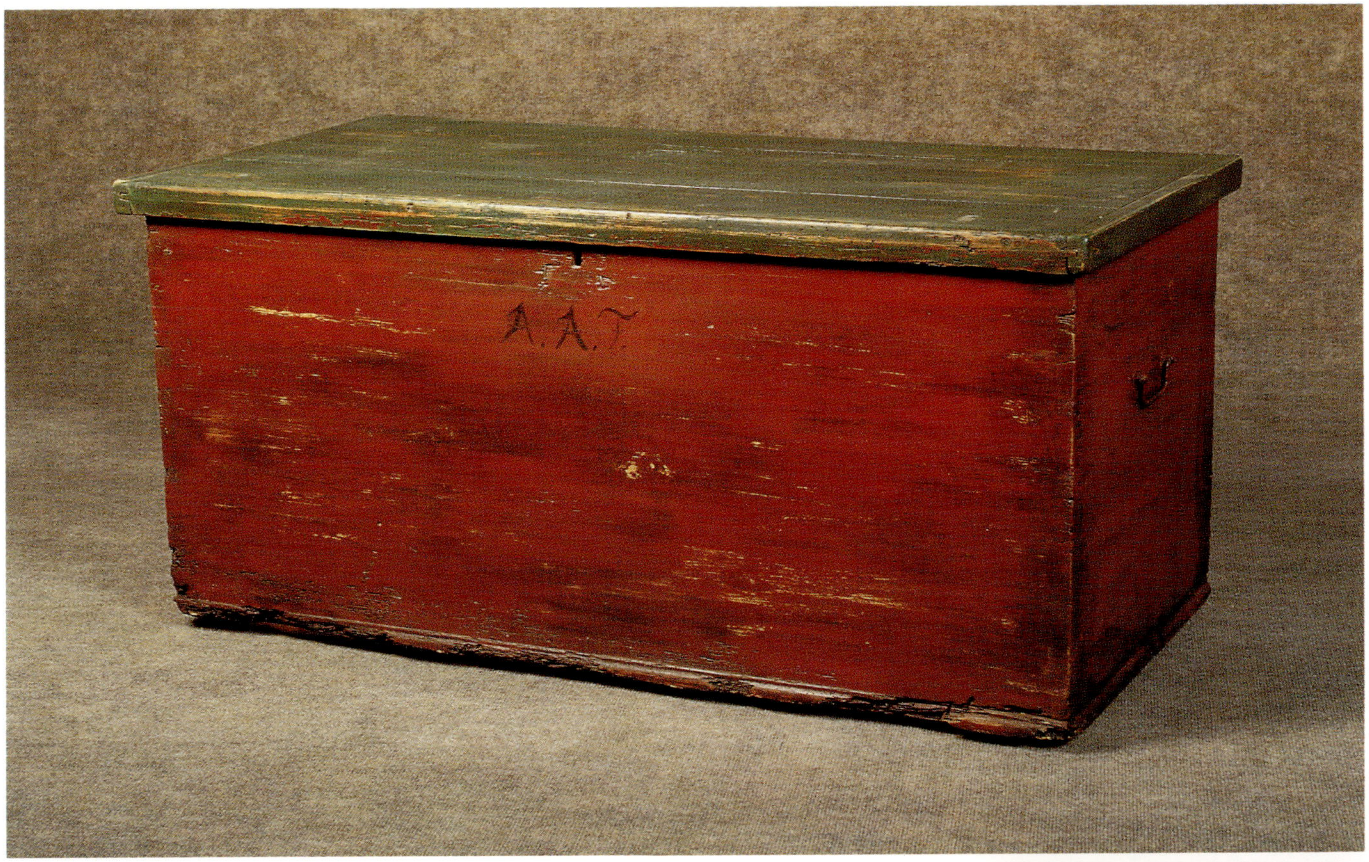

Blanket chest with green painted top and red painted bottom, with painted initials "AAF."

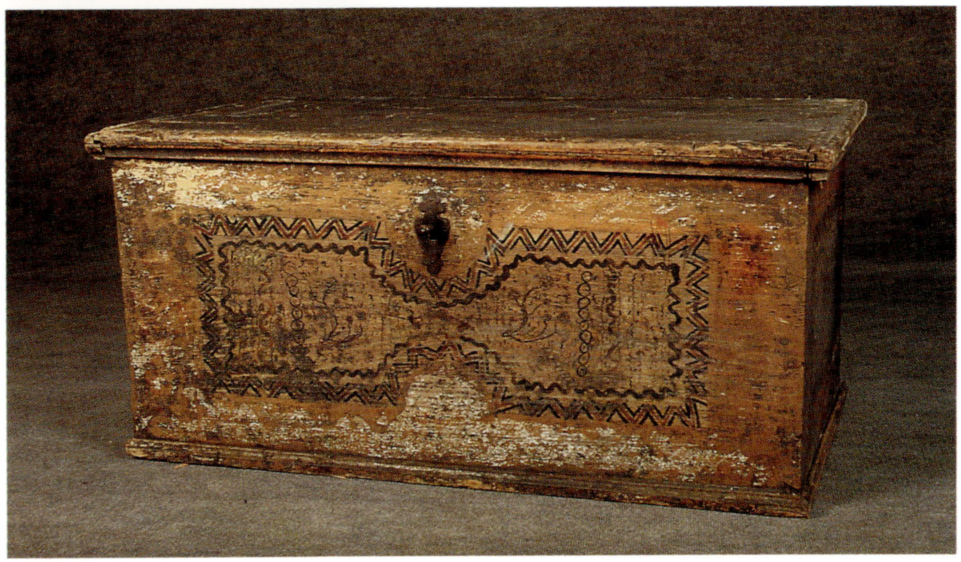

Blanket chest with hinged top, old paint and primitive painted front panels with geometric borders, base with molded trim.

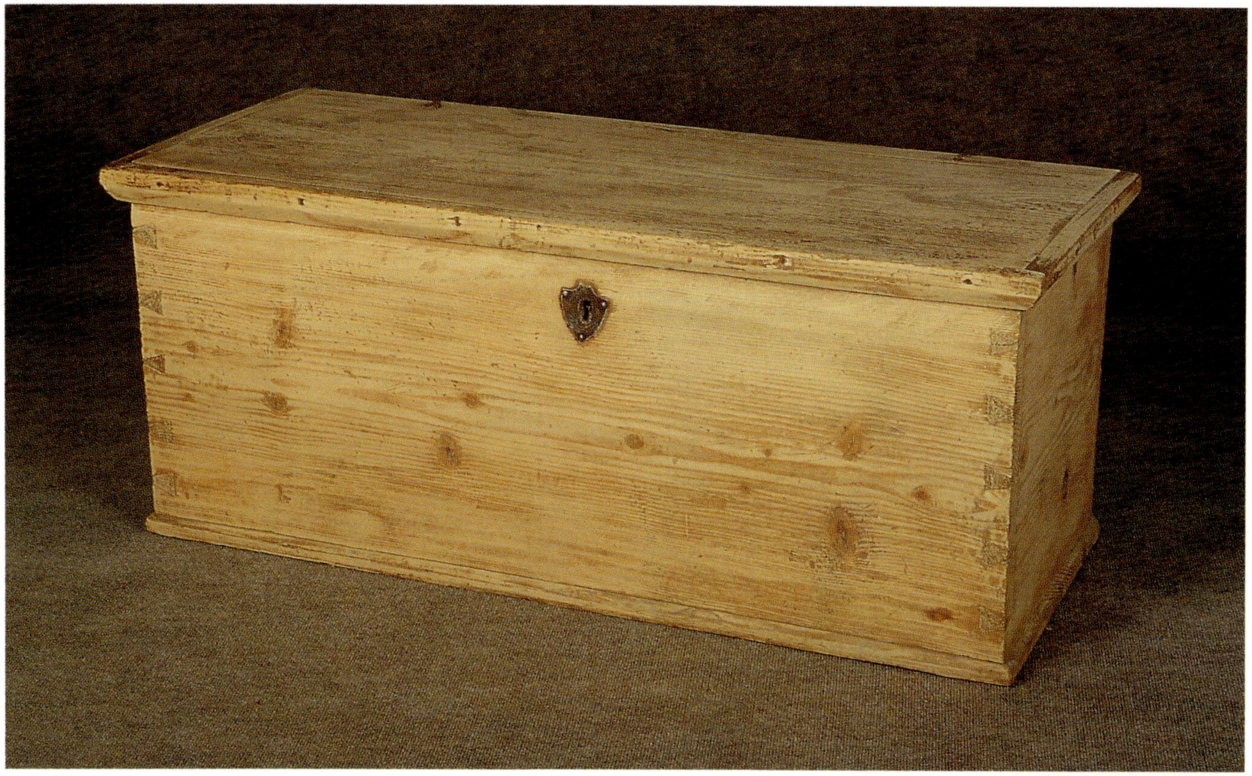

Blanket chest with molded edge to the hinged top and dove-tailed corners, pine wood and plank base. $450.

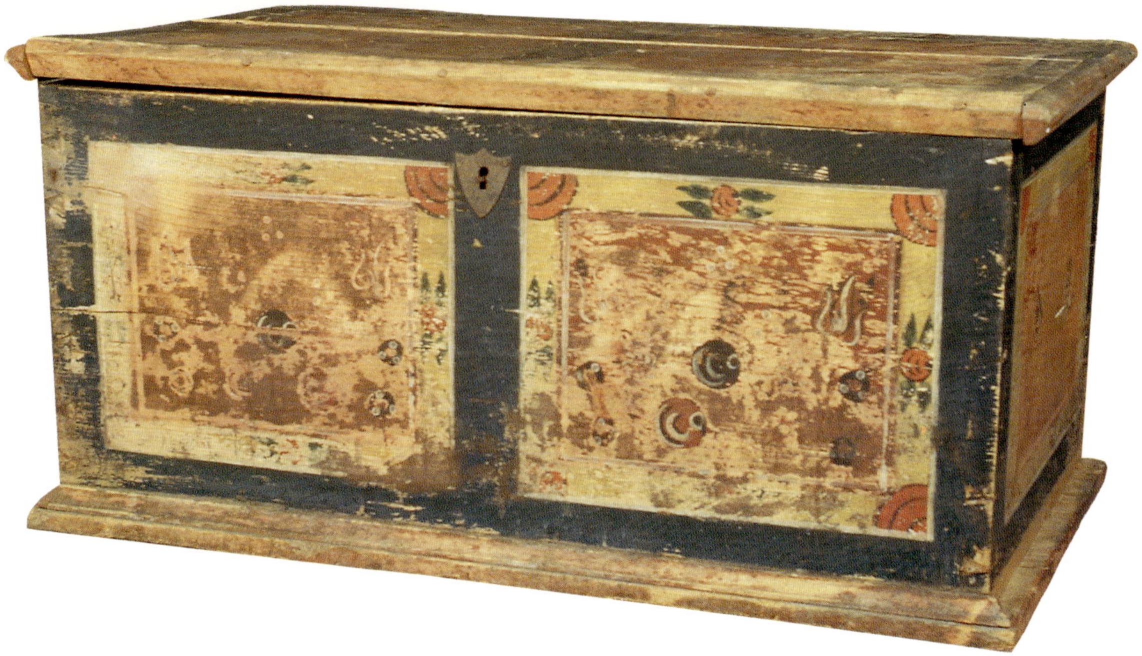

Blanket chest with much of the original paint remaining. Green background with floral painted front panels and base molding.

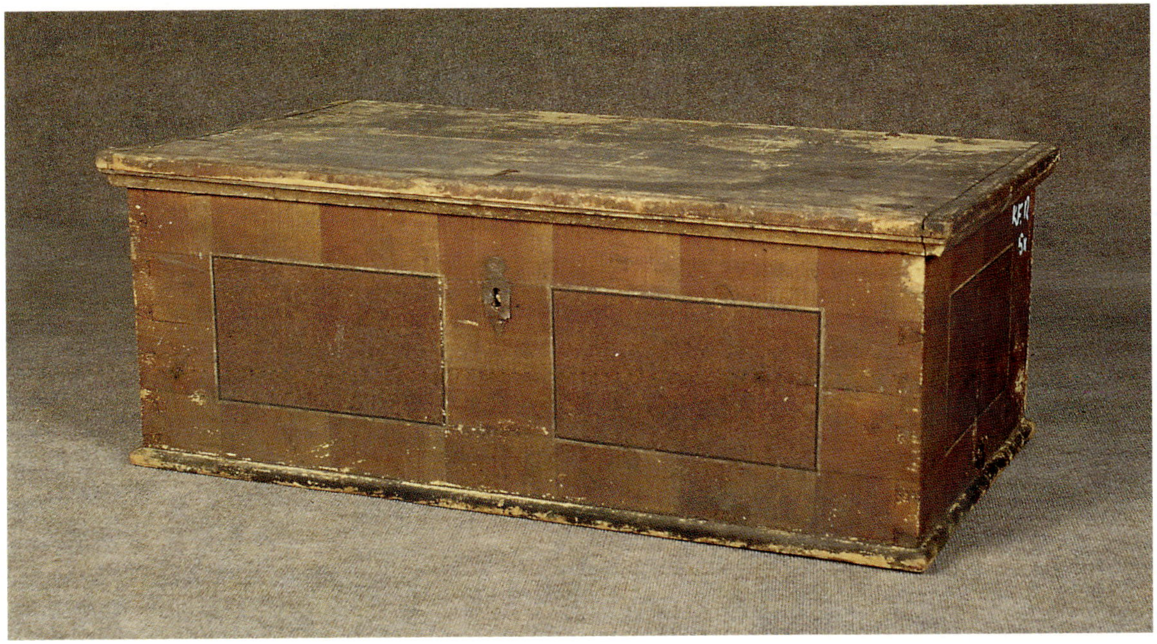

Blanket chest with hinged and molded top, painted brown surface with contrasting brown panels, dove-tailed corners and base molding.

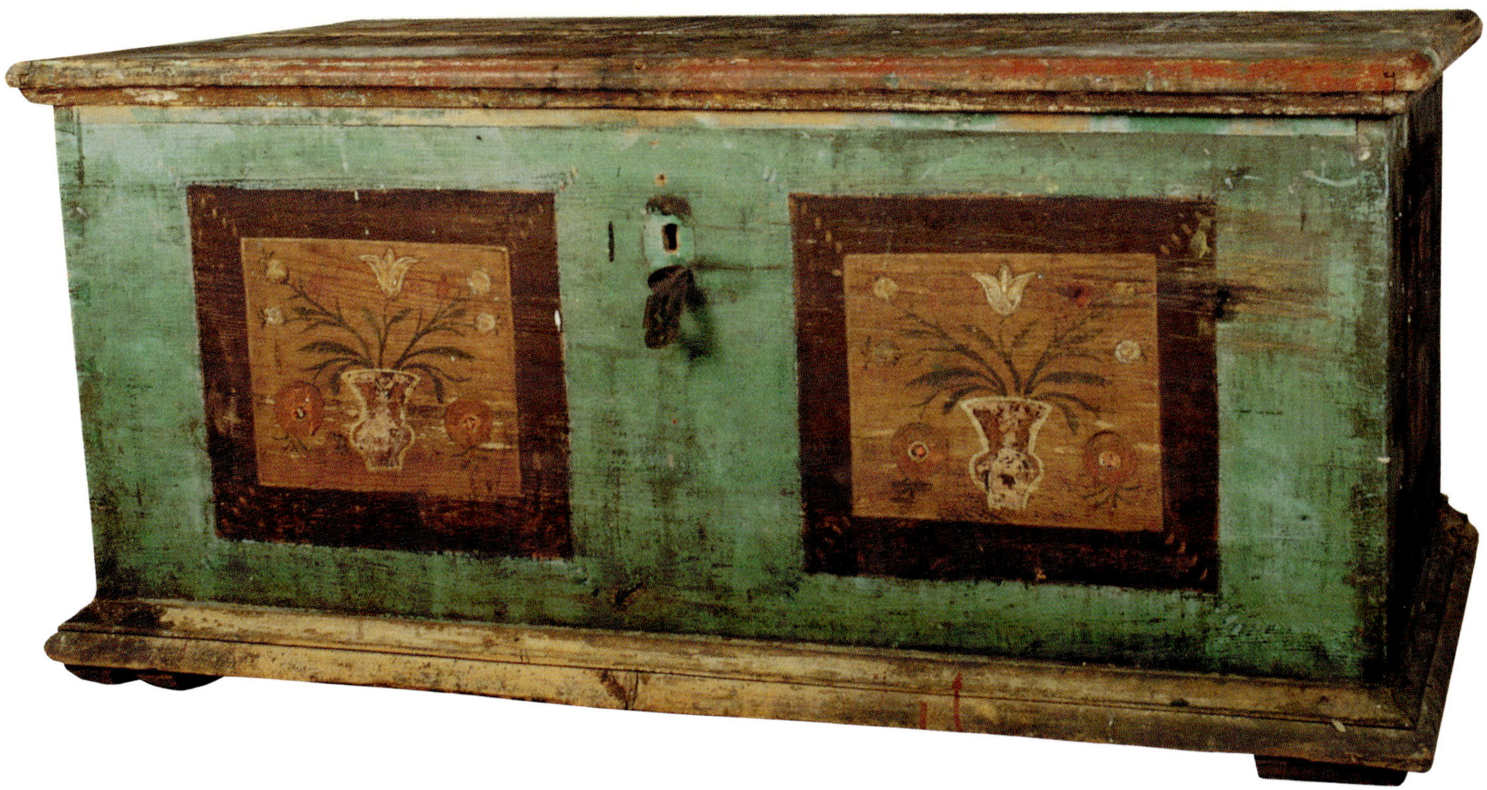

Blanket chest with light green background, floral painted front, and contrasting base molding.

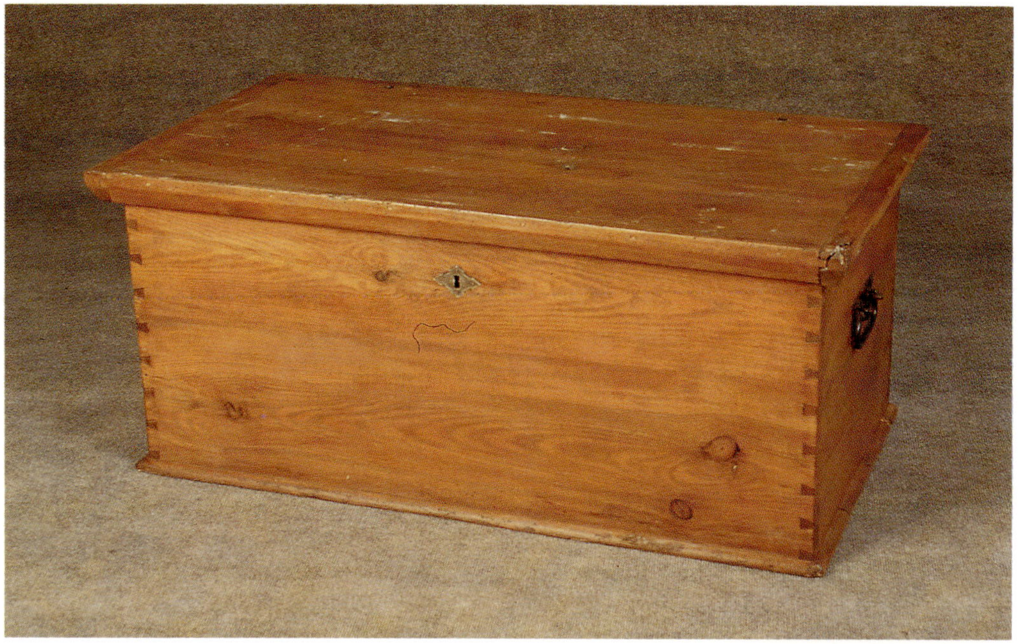

Blanket chest with molded edge to the hinged top, dove-tailed corners, and iron side handles, molded base. $450.

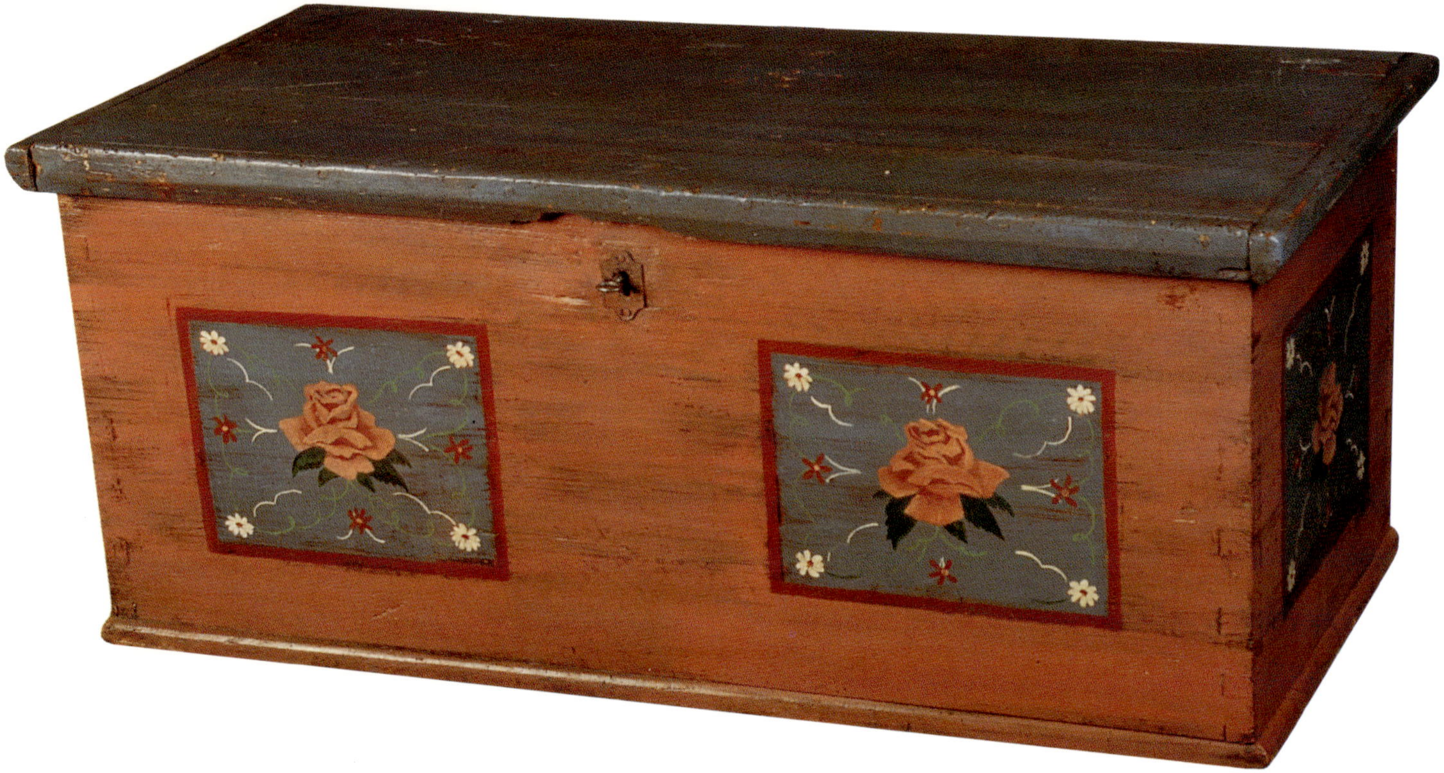

Painted blanket chest with a gray/blue top and red body ornamented with two rectangular gray/blue panels and floral decoration. The base molding rests on the floor. $450.

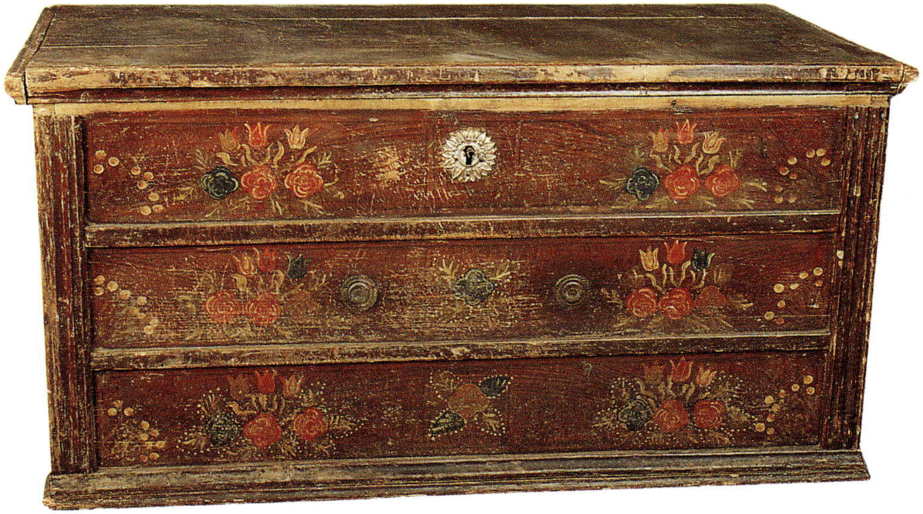

Painted blanket chest with brown painted background, three front panels divided by horizontal moldings and decorated with floral sprays. $595.

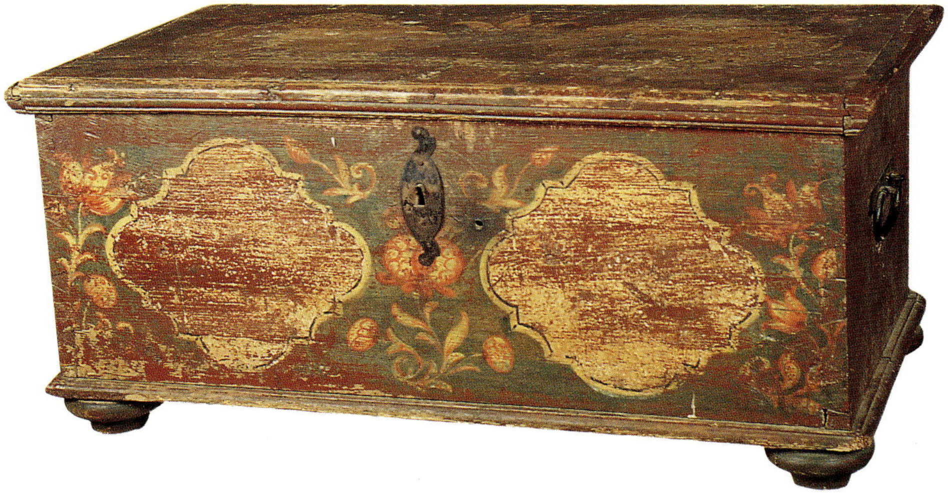

Painted and decorated blanket chest with hinged lid, floral sprays, and two contrasting front panel serpentine reserves.

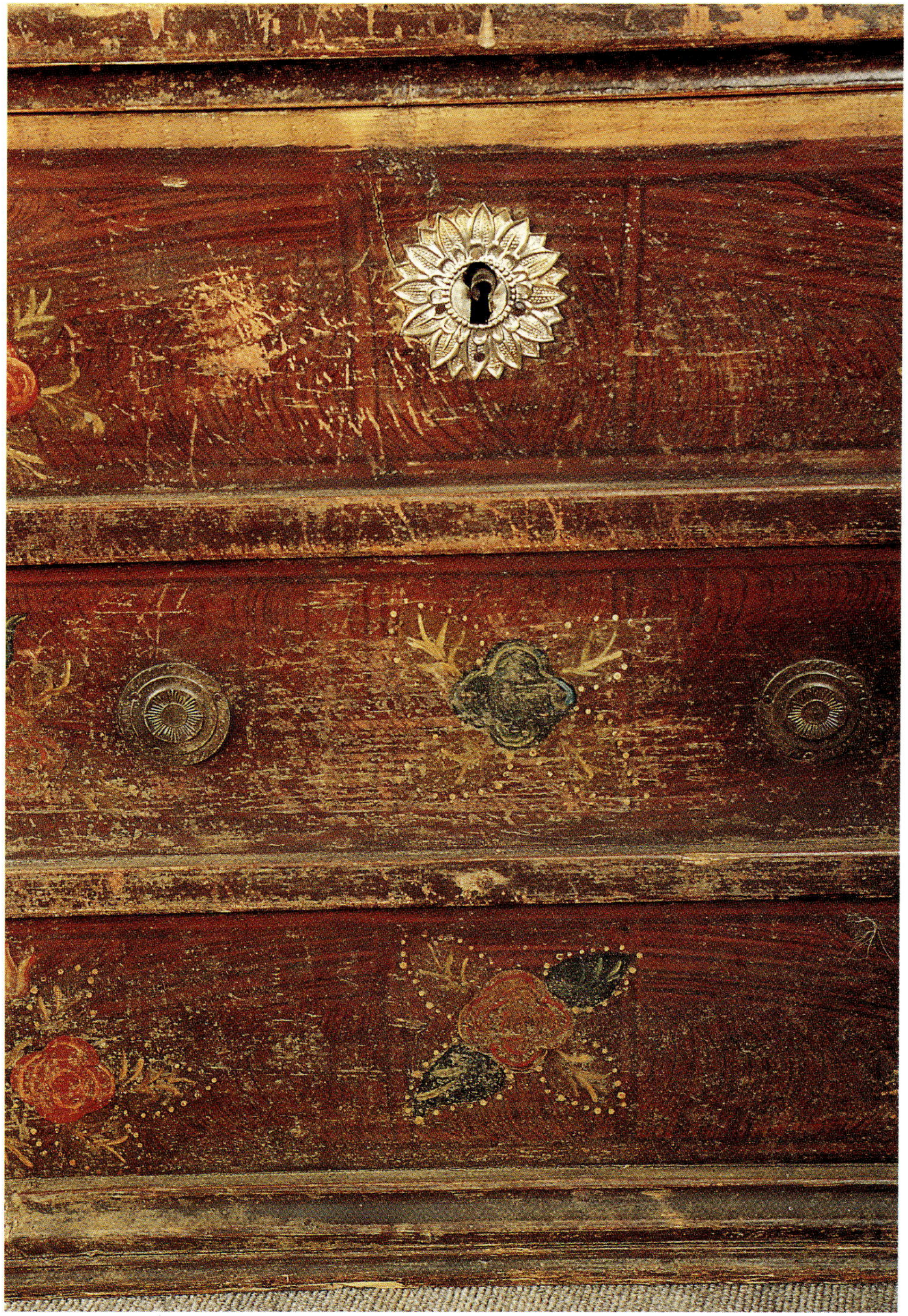

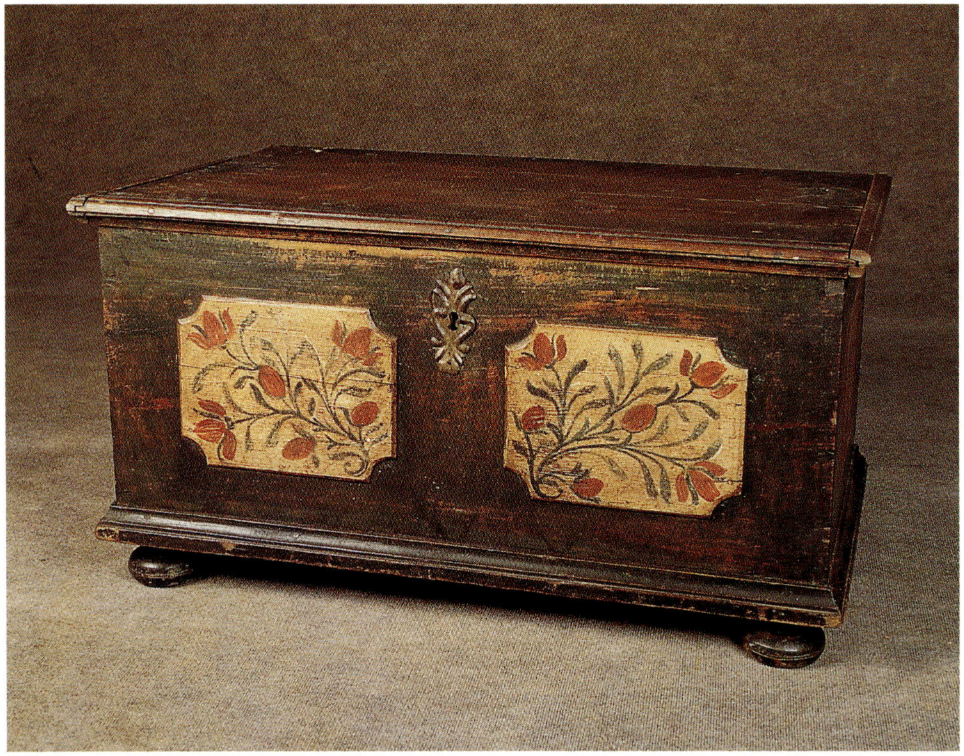

Painted blanket chest with hinged lid, interior till box, front escutcheon, and two raised panels with cut corners and painted floral decoration resting on a base molding and bun feet. The lid is supported on long iron strap hinges. $895.

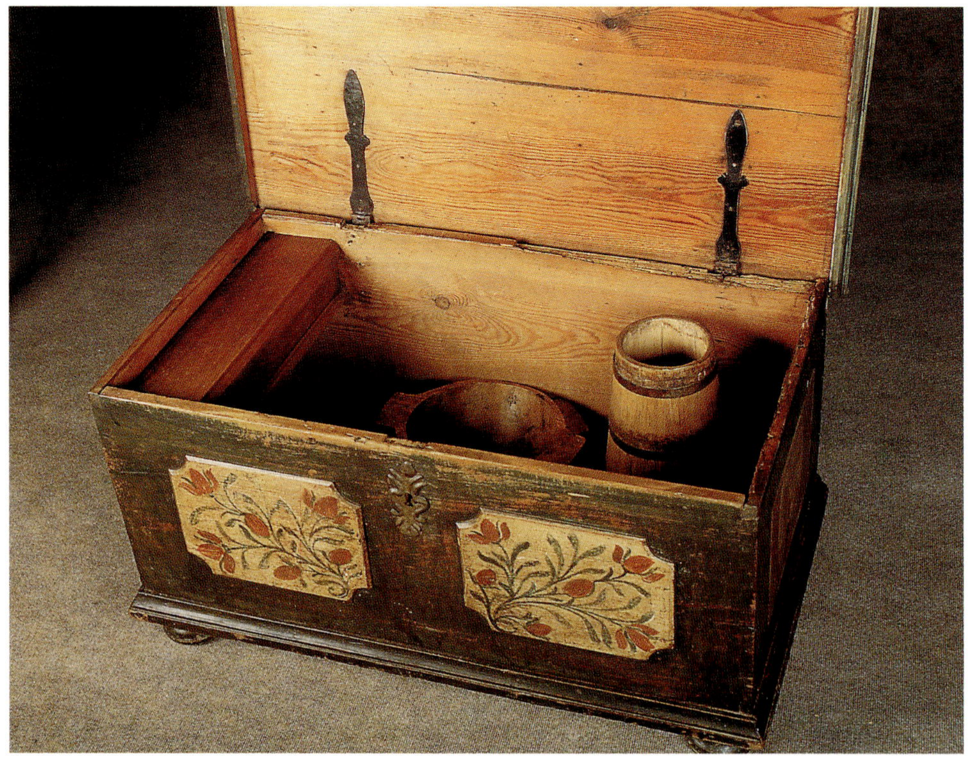

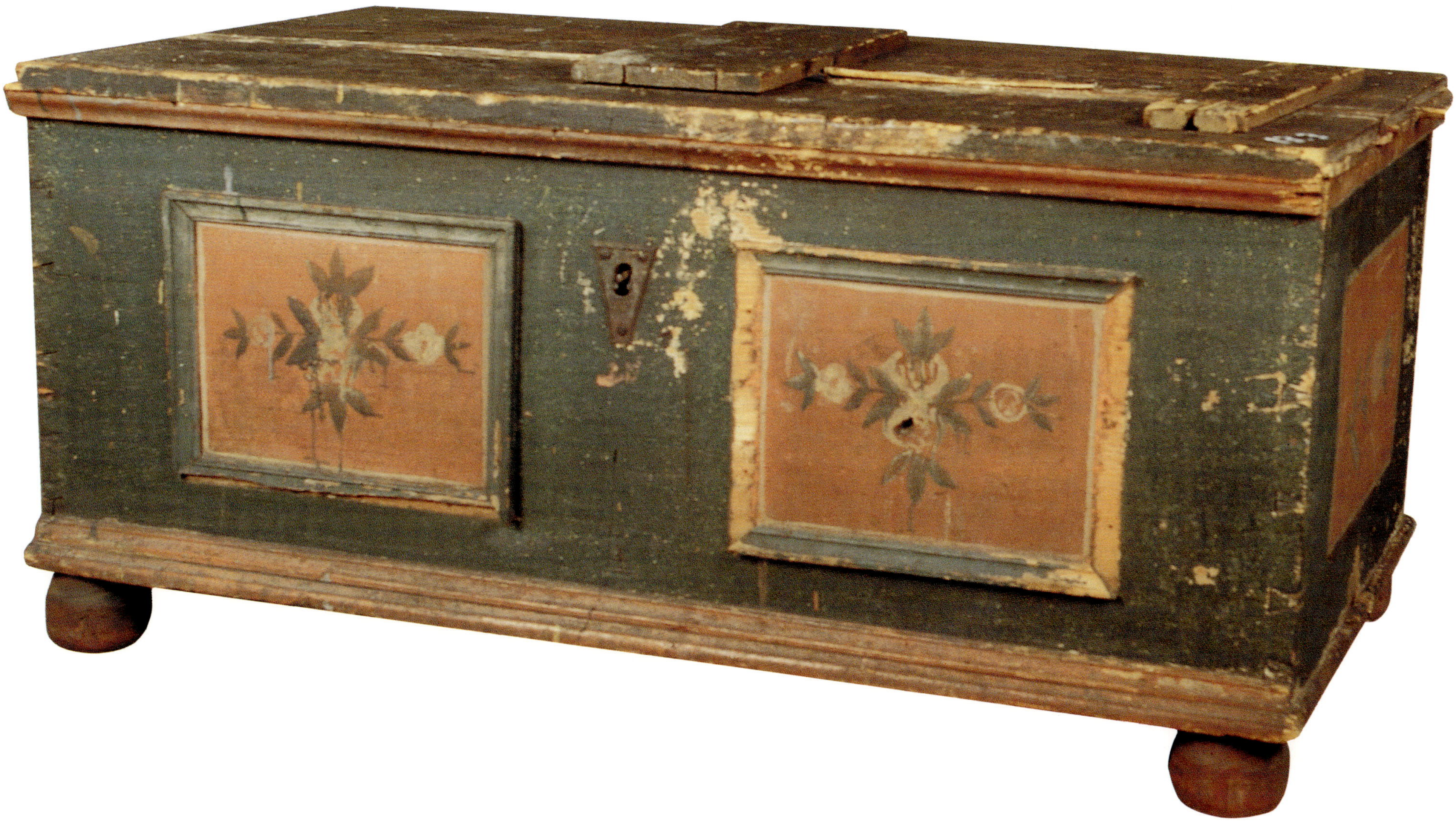

Painted blanket chest with braced hinged top and two red panels on front with applied molded frames, floral decoration, and green background, resting on round feet.

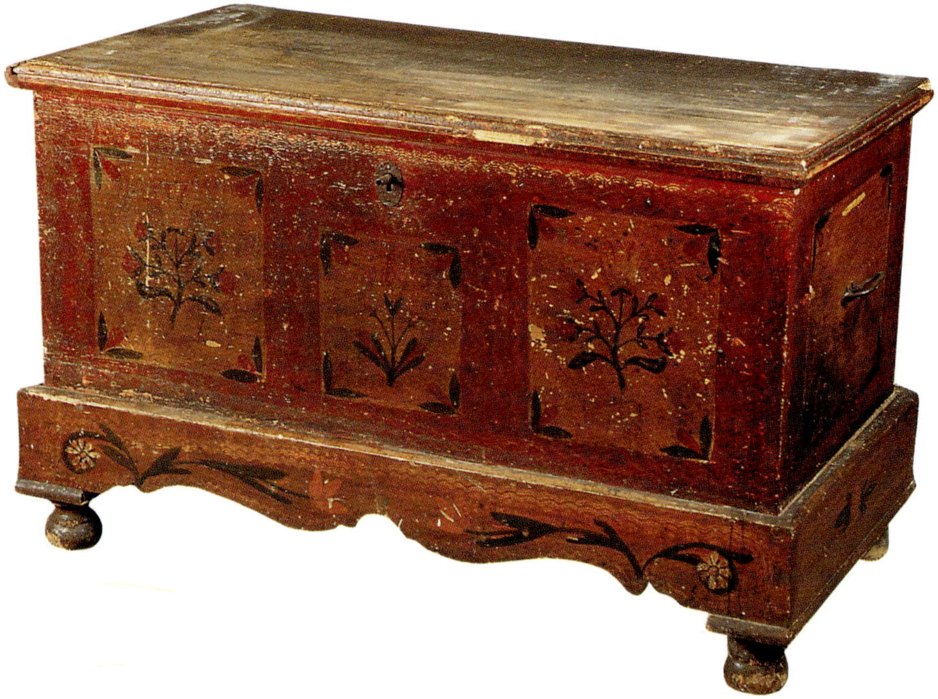

Large painted blanket chest with red background and three front panels of floral decoration. A separate scalloped and floral decorated deep base molding rests on turned feet. $695.

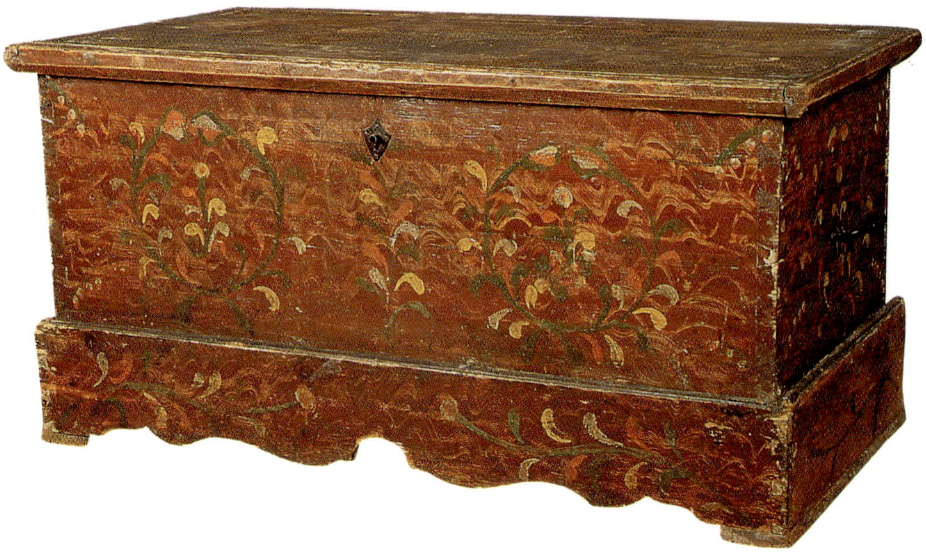

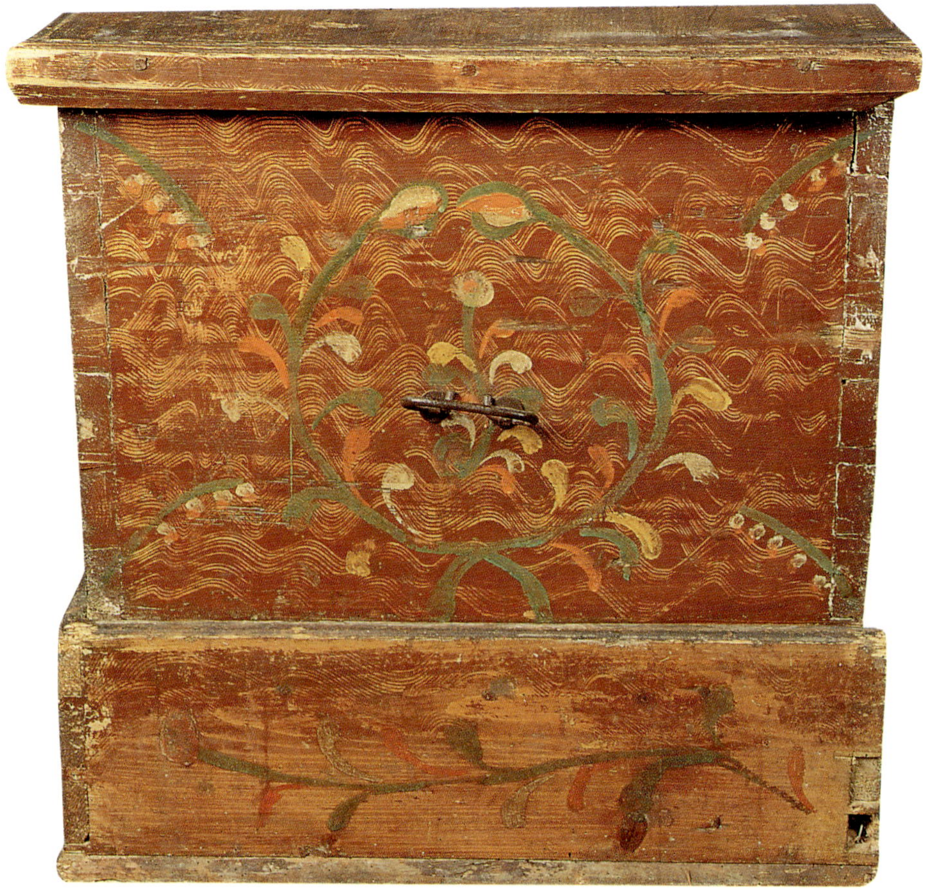

Czechoslovakian two-part blanket chest with red painted background and floral decoration. The case rests on a separate deep base molding with scalloped front edge. $795.

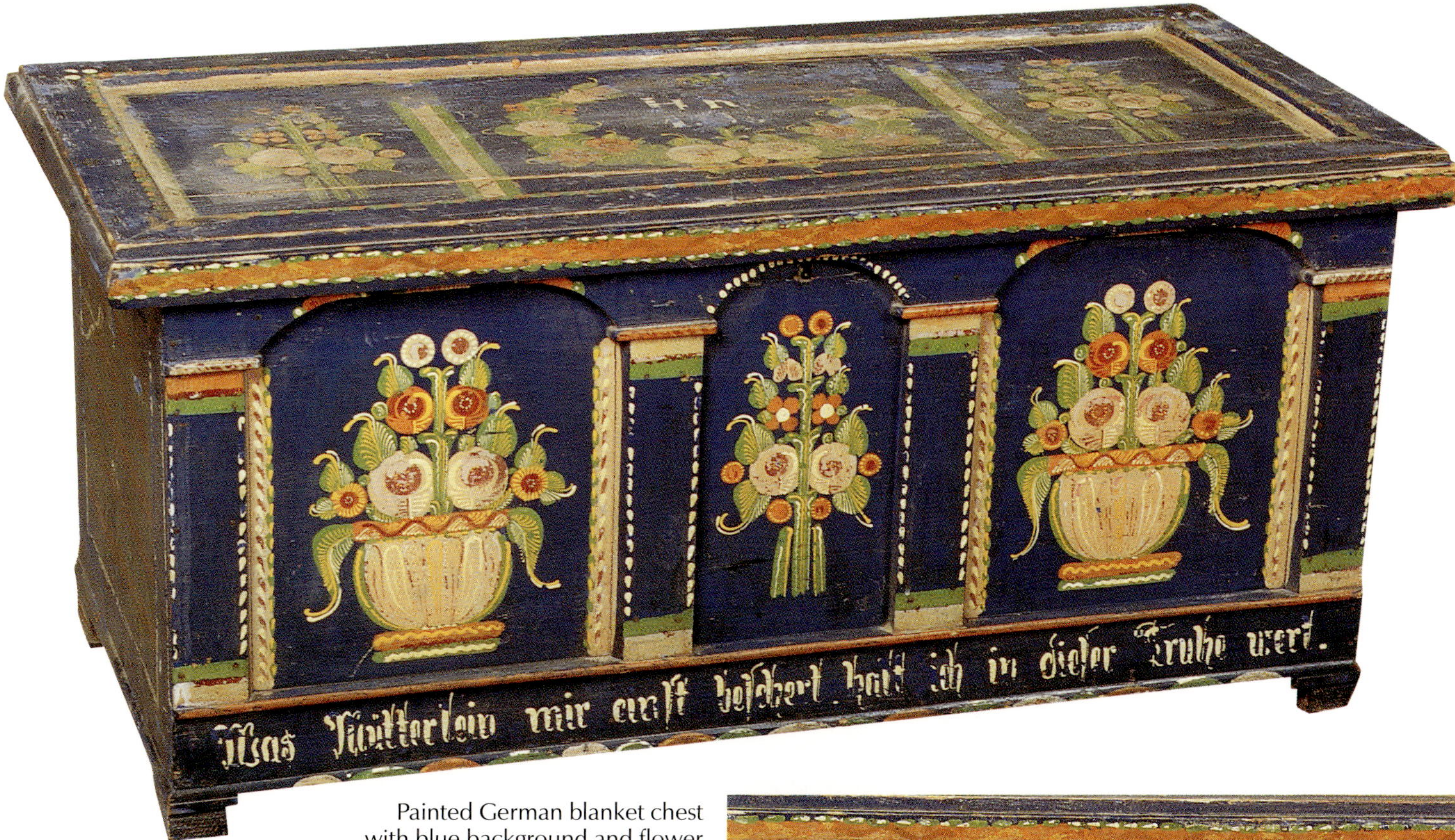

Painted German blanket chest with blue background and flower bouquet decorations on the top and front. Inscribed in German and dated 1910, 39" wide. $625.

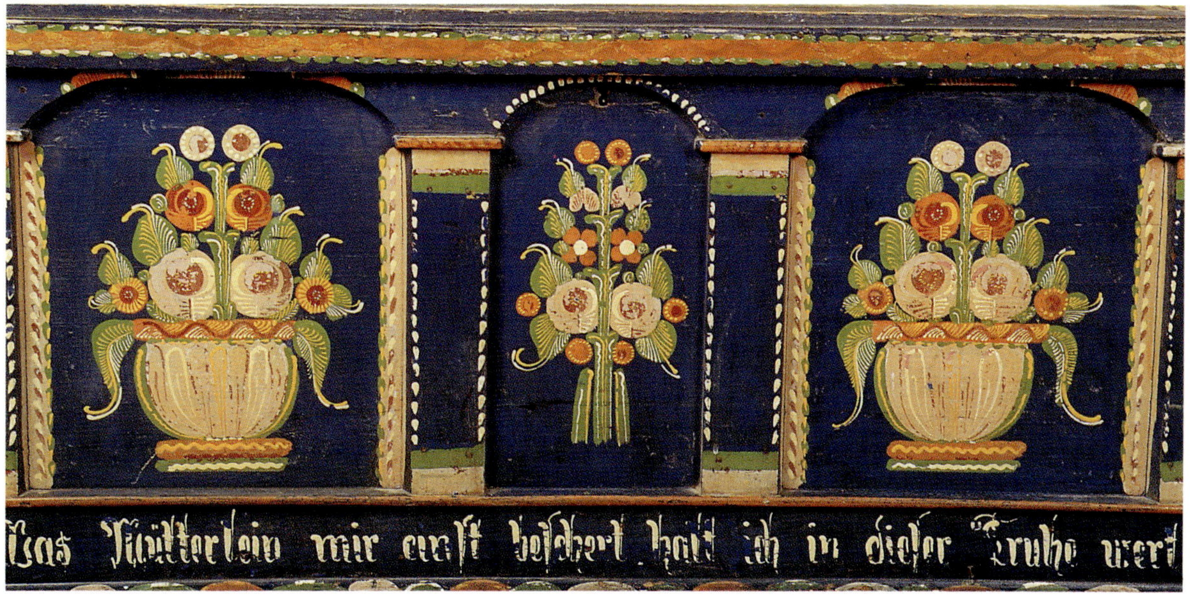

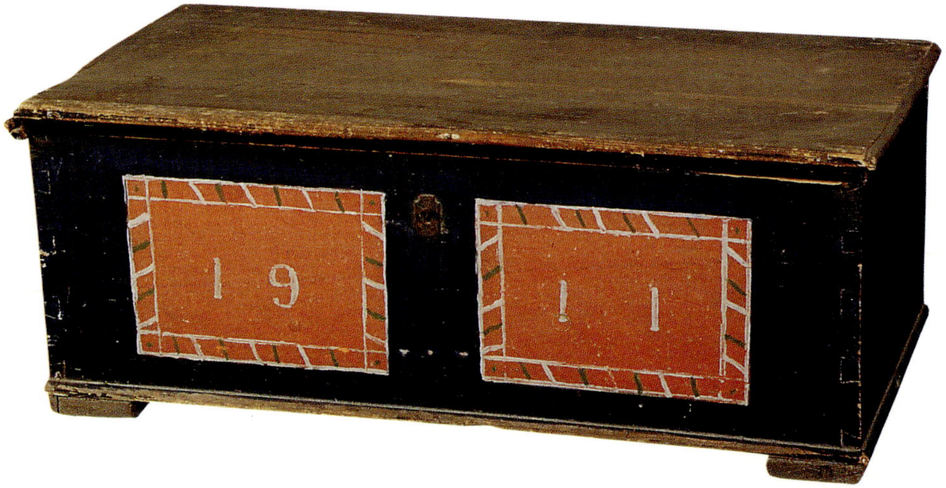

Blanket chest with a scrubbed top. Sides painted deep blue with two front panels of red, dated 1911. The base molding rests on block feet. $595.

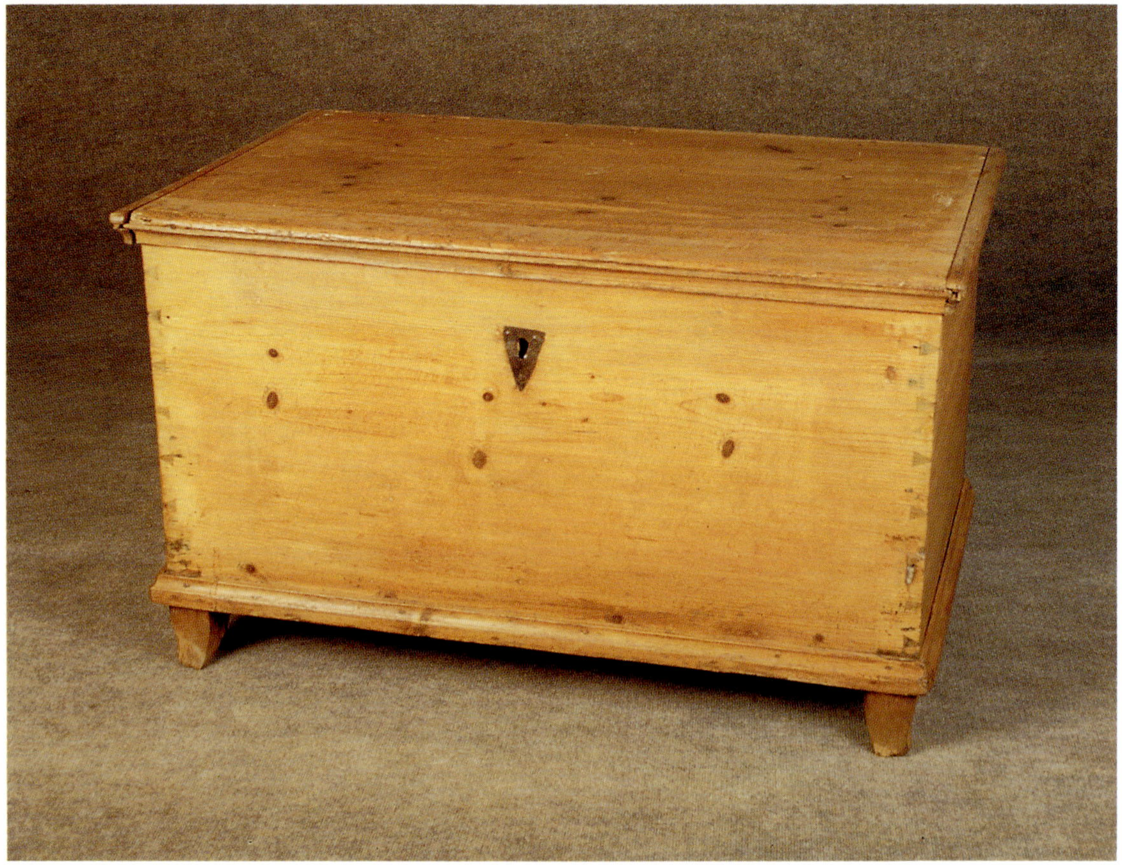

Blanket chest with a molded edge to the hinged top, dove-tailed corners, and a molded base on tapering squared legs. $450.

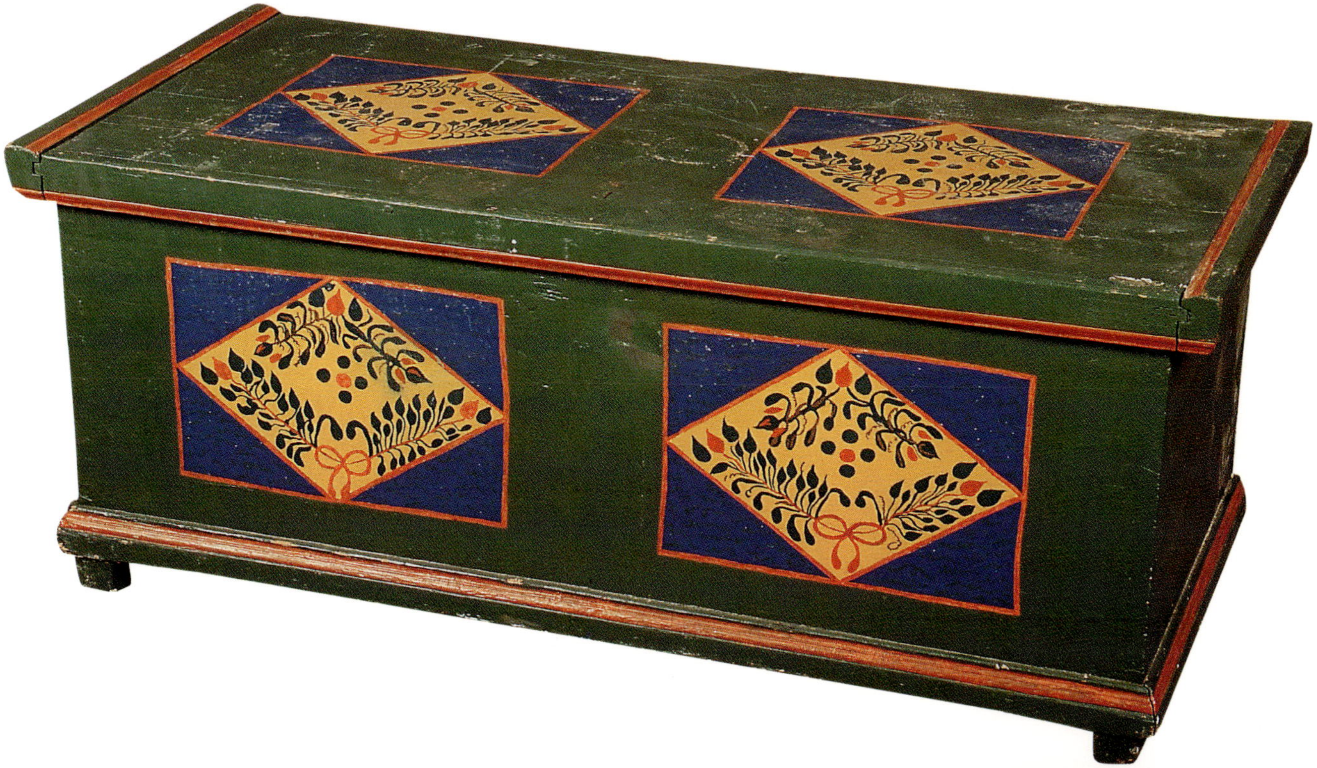

Blanket chest with brightly painted diamond panels of floral decoration on a green background, straight feet. $695.

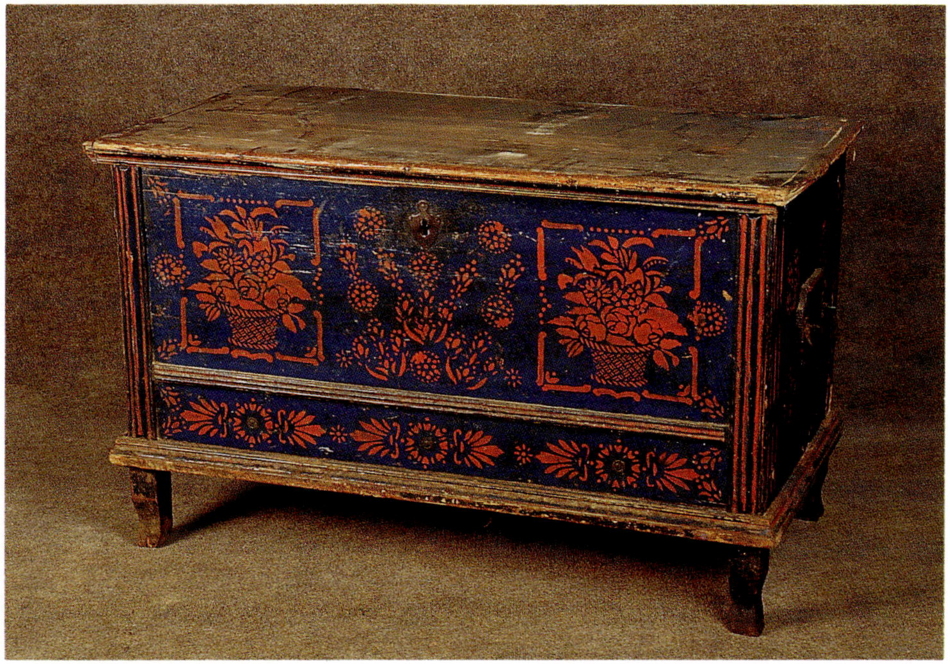

Blanket chest with a hinged top and blue painted background with orange stenciled floral decoration on the front and sides. A false drawer in the front is above a base molding and square shaped feet. $695.

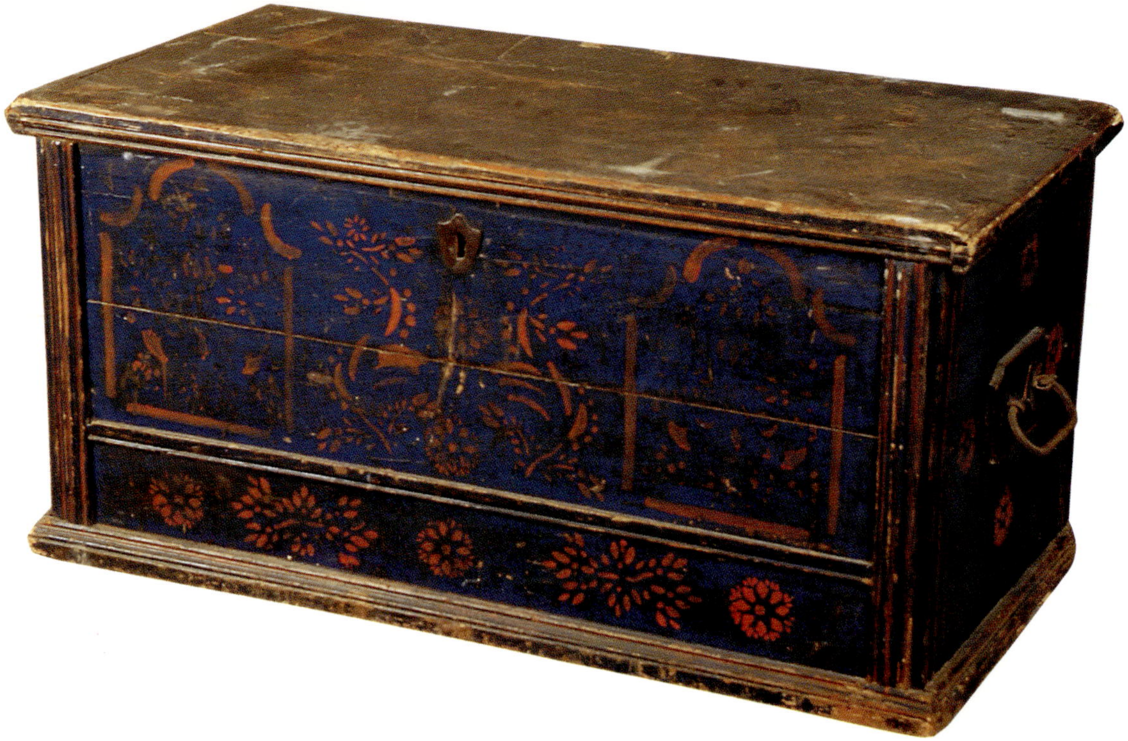

Painted blanket chest with deep blue background and orange floral decoration above a base molding that extends to the floor. Iron side handles are mounted on applied, shaped panels.

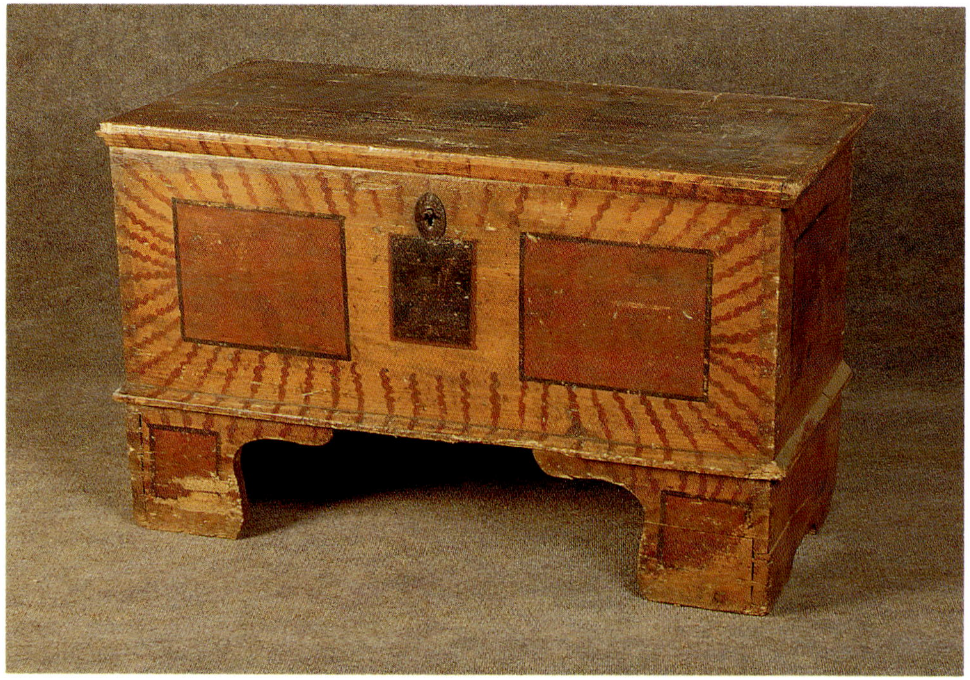

Painted blanket chest with two red panels and radiating red lines on an orange/brown background which extends over the base molding, side boards, and deep bracket feet. $595.

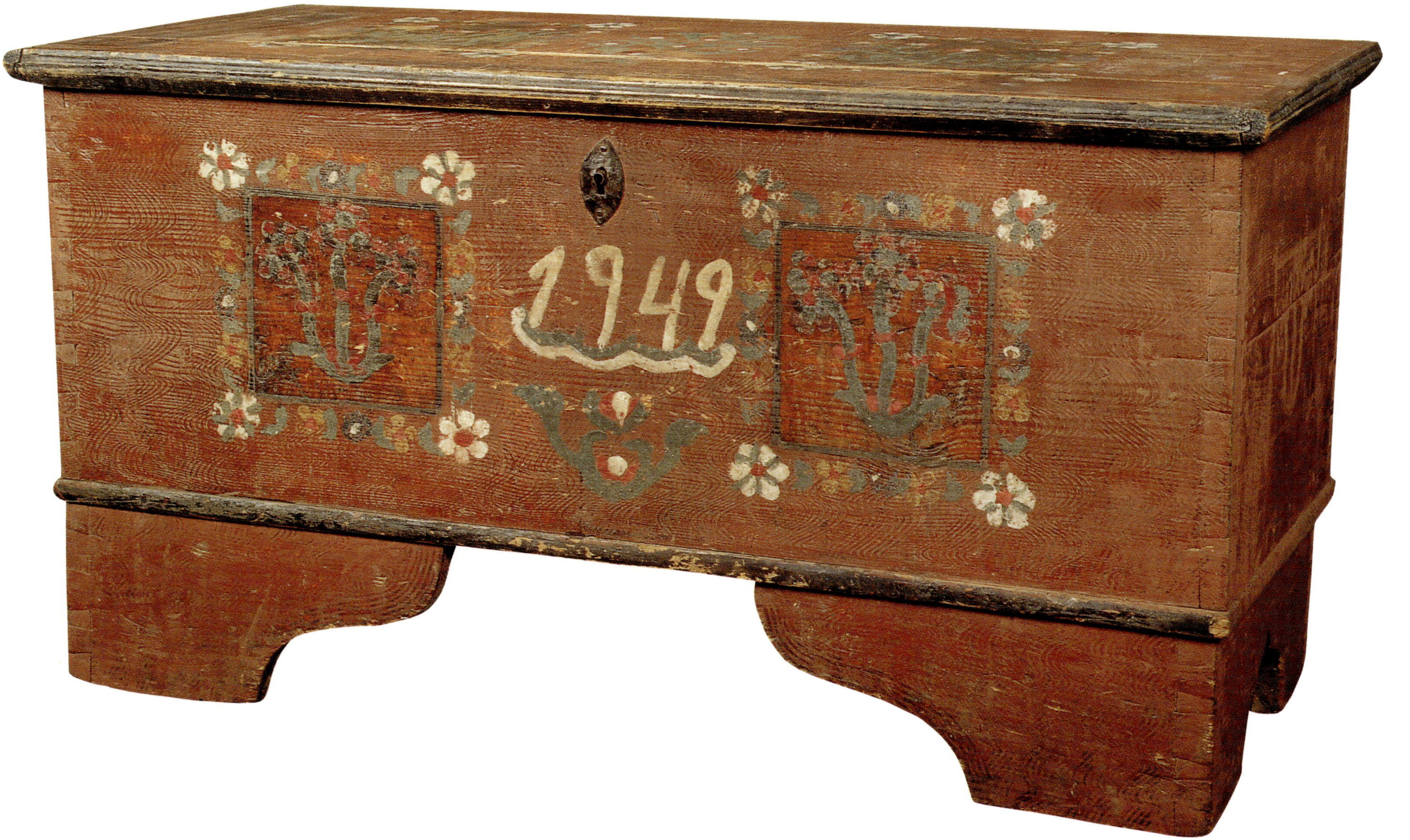

Red painted blanket chest of red painted background and two floral clusters on the front, white corner flowers, and the date 1949 (probably repainted), originally c.1870-80. $695.

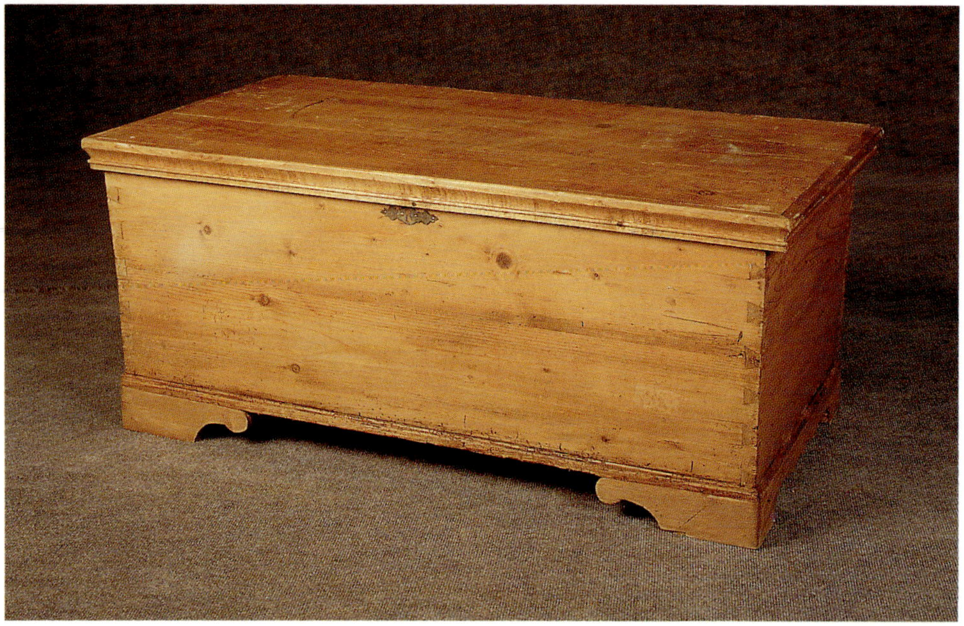

Small pine blanket chest with hinged lid and front escutcheon, resting on scrolled block feet. $425.

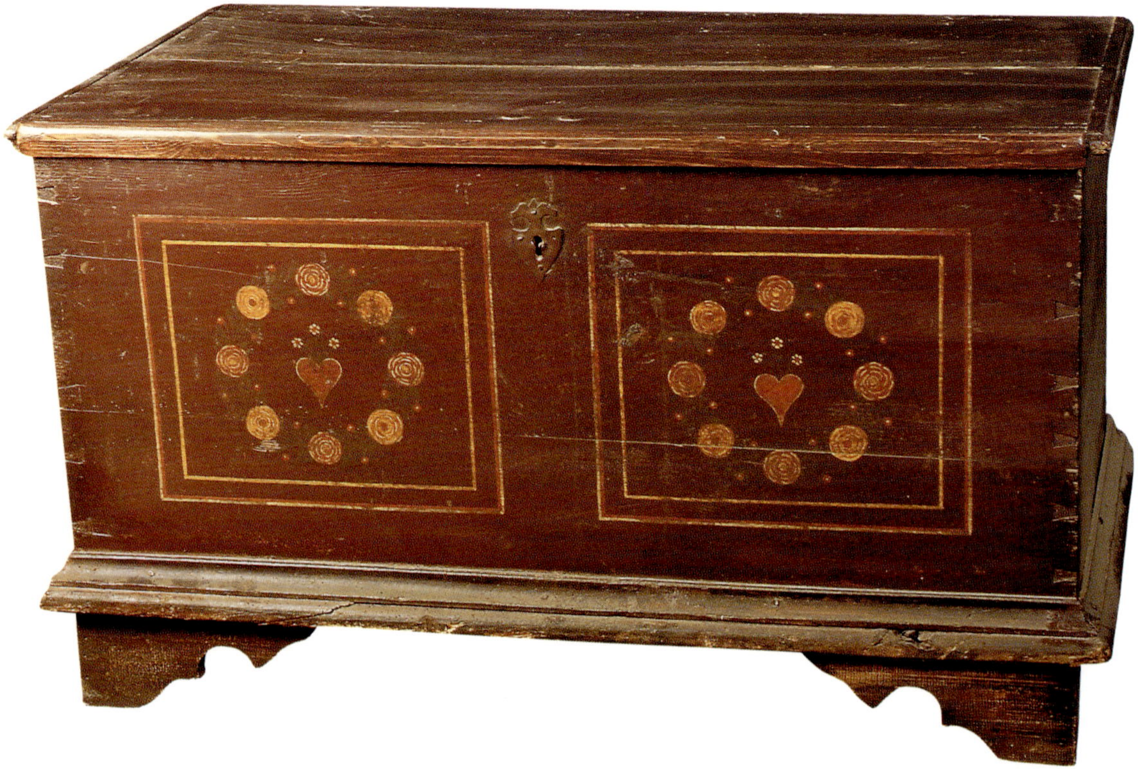

Blanket chest with hinged flat lid, brown background, and two rectangular panels with floral decoration. The deep base molding rests on shaped bracket feet. $695.

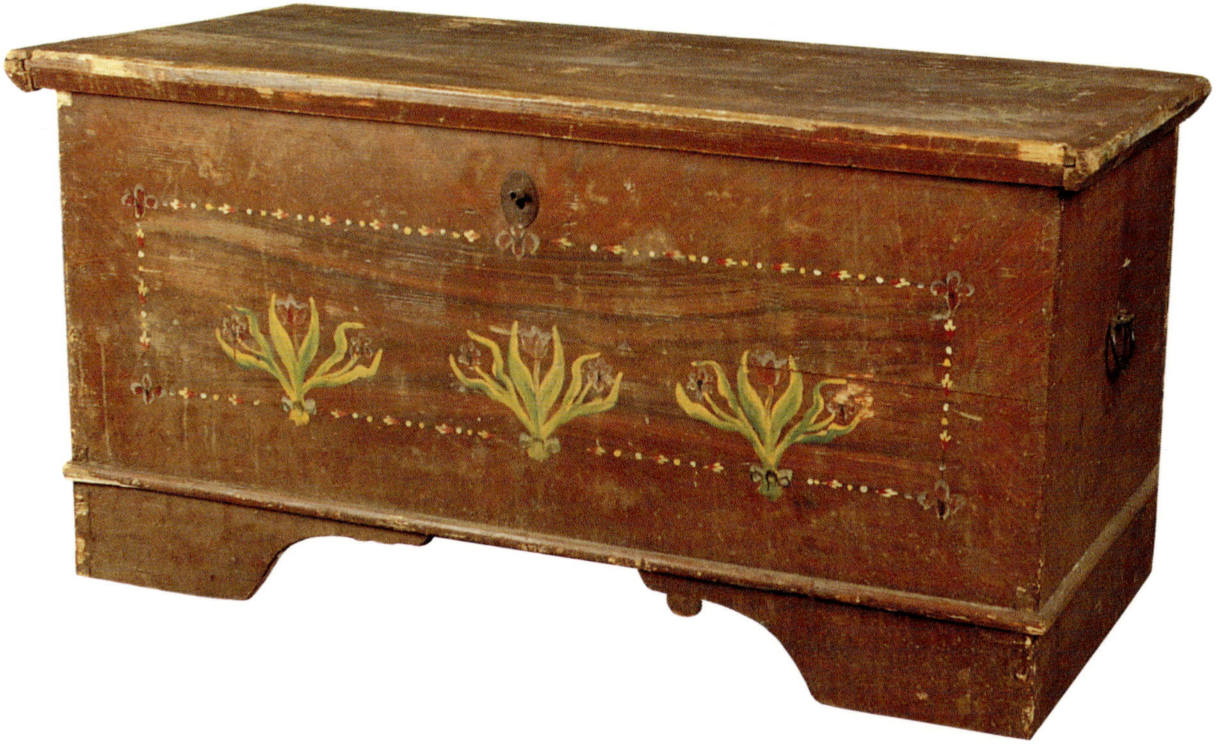

Blanket chest of pine with a hinged overhanging top, brown/red background with three bunches of painted flowers in the front panel, and bracket feet. $350.

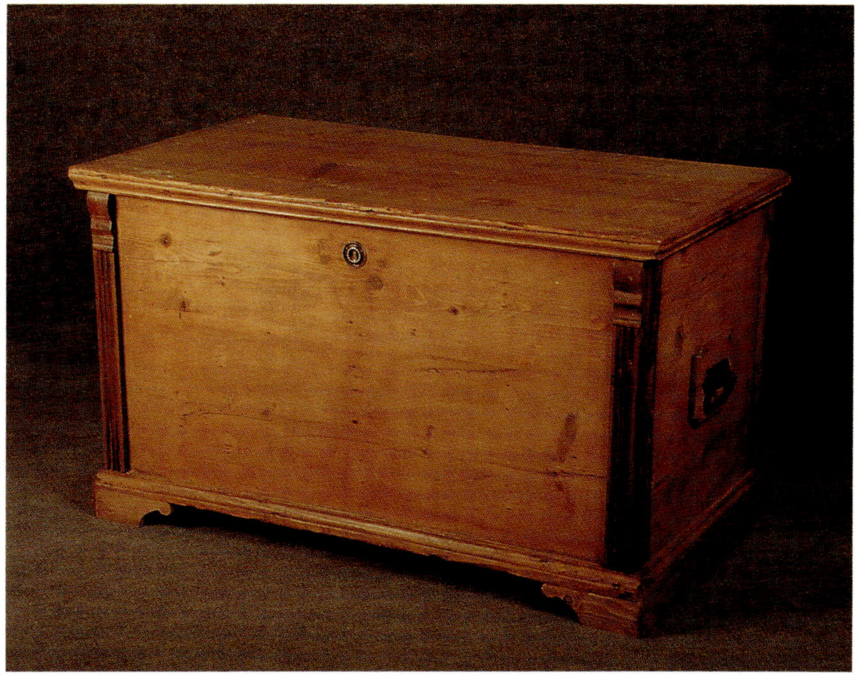

Deep blanket chest with rectangular molded top over two applied reeded and scrolled stiles and a base molding on bracket feet, Arts & Crafts style. $475

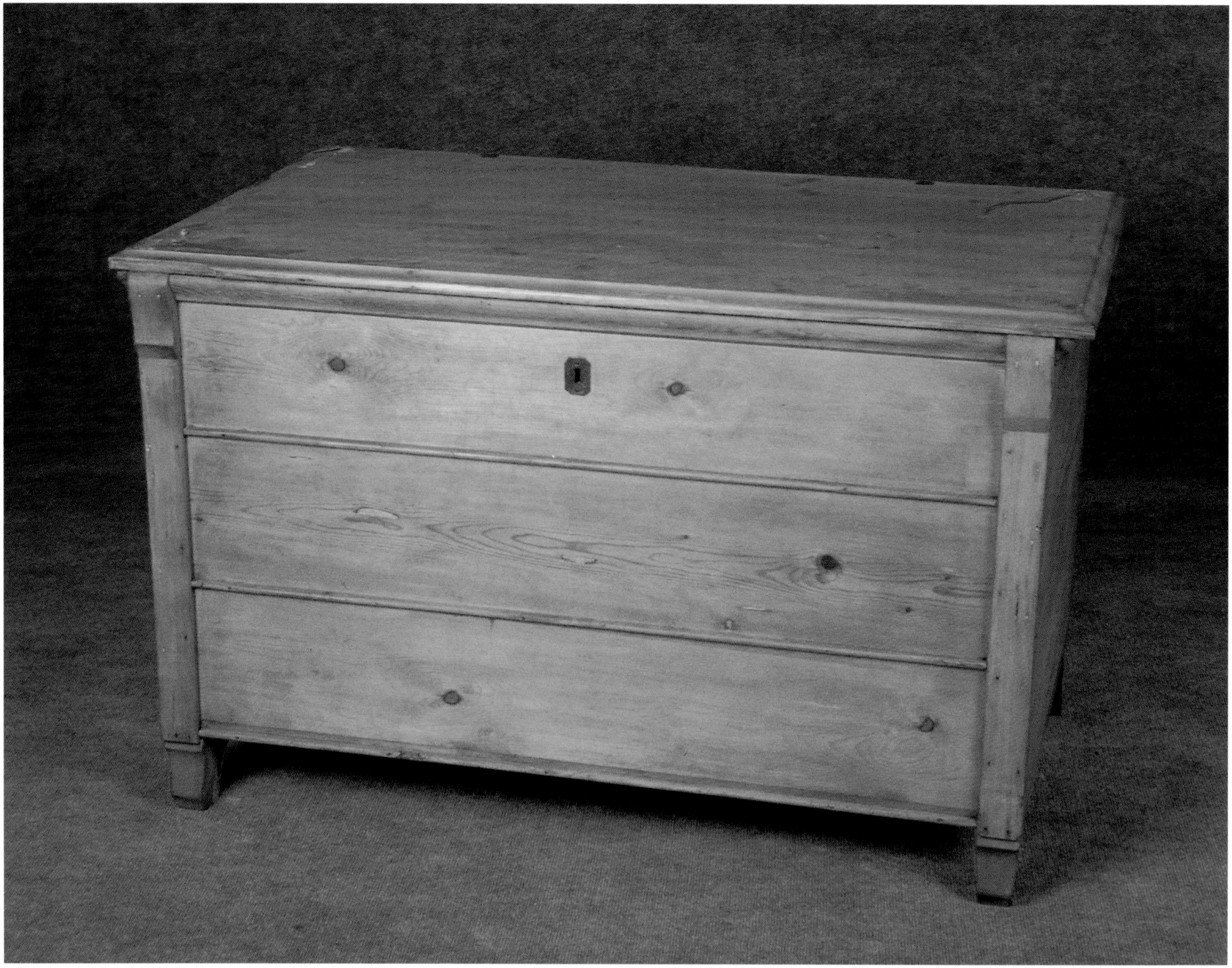

Blanket chest of pine with three horizontal panels on the front and metal escutcheon. The stiles are flat. Inside, a till box is on the left side, Arts & Crafts style. $525.

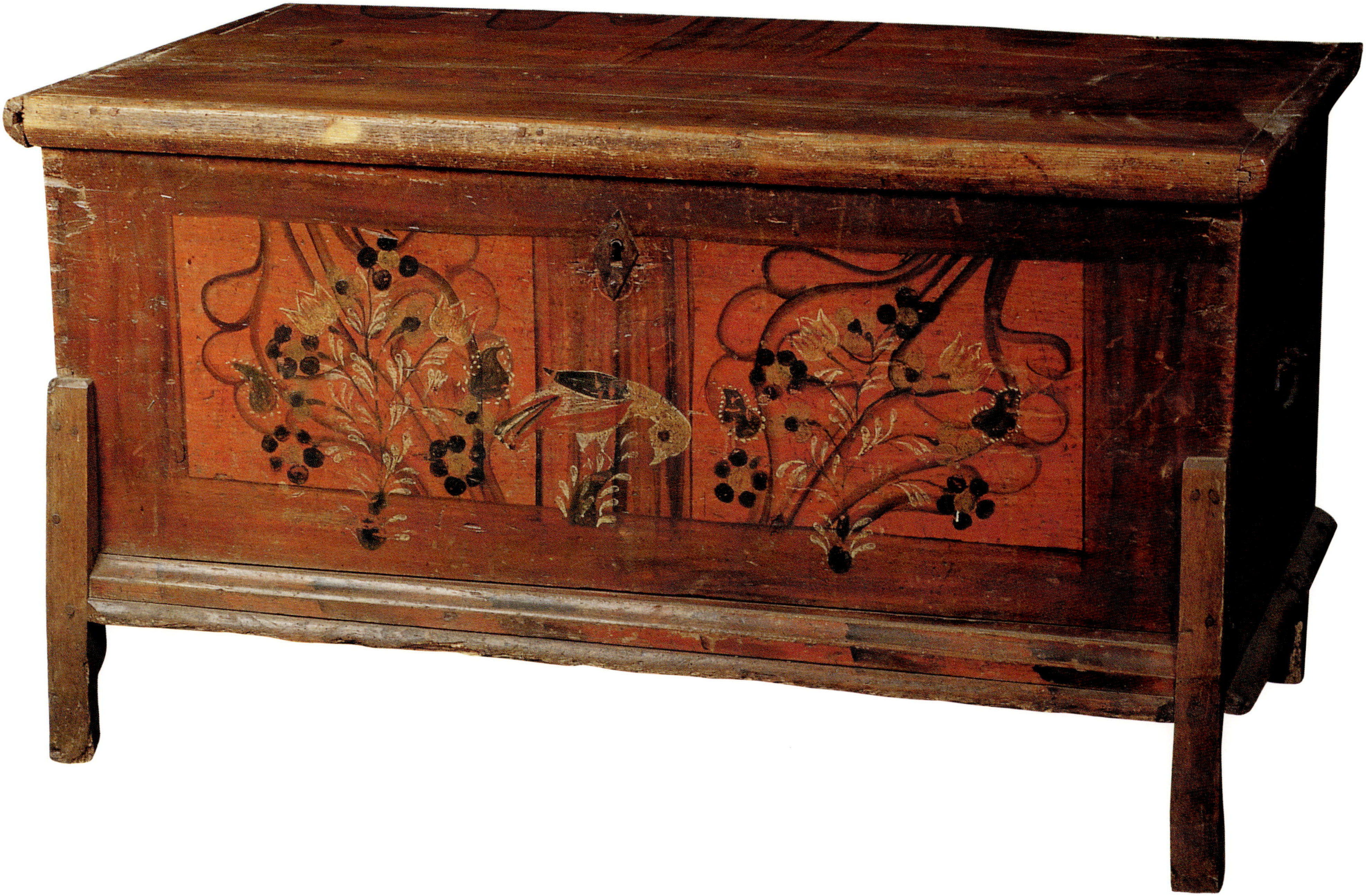

Painted blanket chest with red/brown background and front rectangular panels with floral decoration and bird painted in the center. Applied stiles form the legs. $795.

Solid-door Cabinets and Wardrobes

Single-door Cabinets

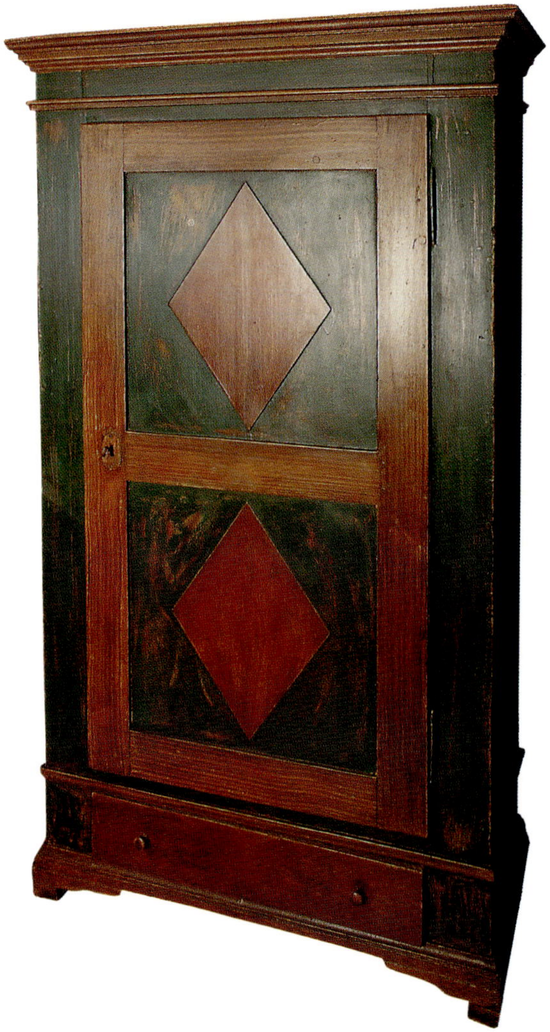

German, painted, single door cabinet with a straight molded cornice over a door with two red raised diamond designs on green recessed panels. Below is a single drawer with two wooden knob pulls. The case rests on bracket feet. $1295.

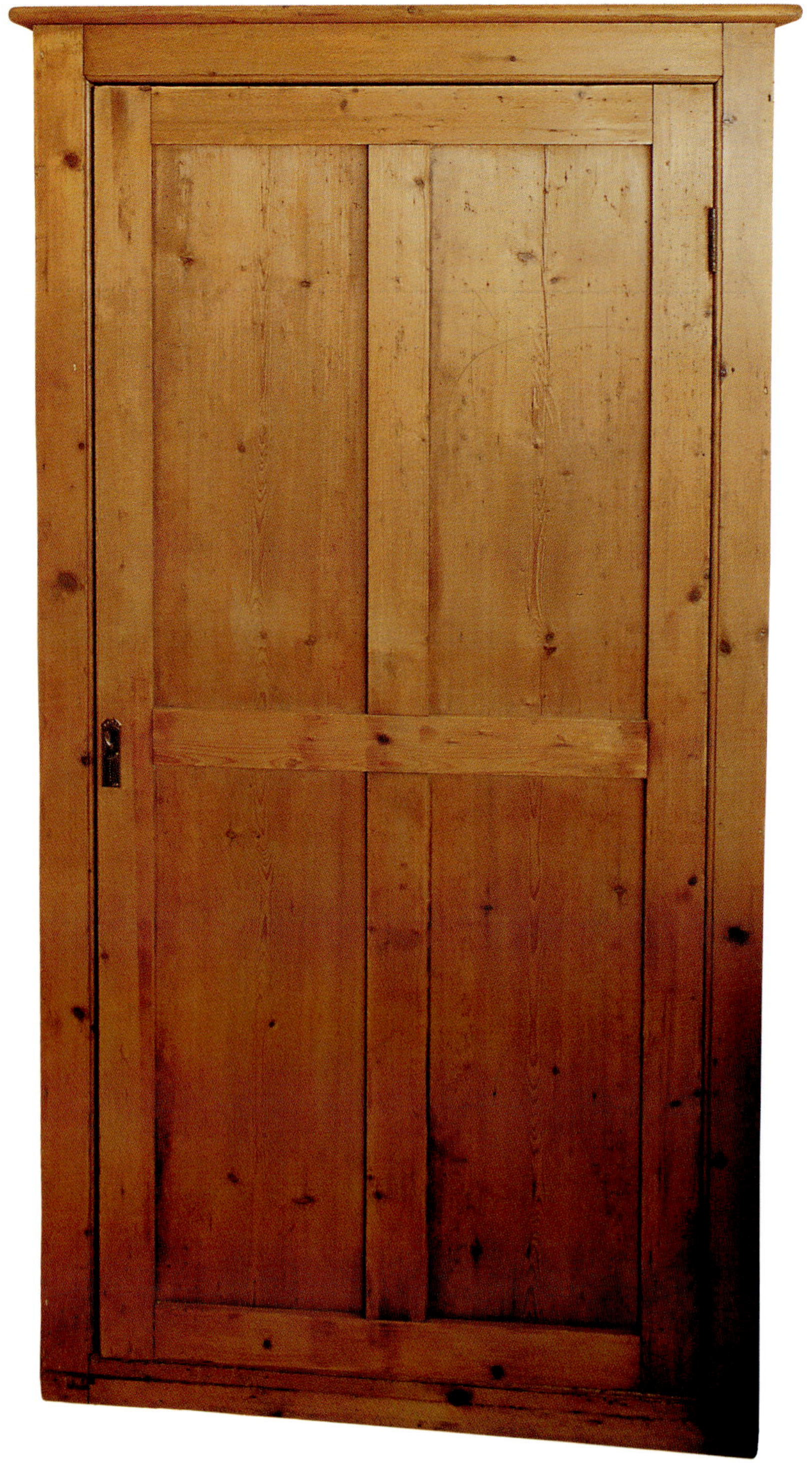

Irish corner cabinet of pine with a single door of four recessed panels and a molded base. $1475.

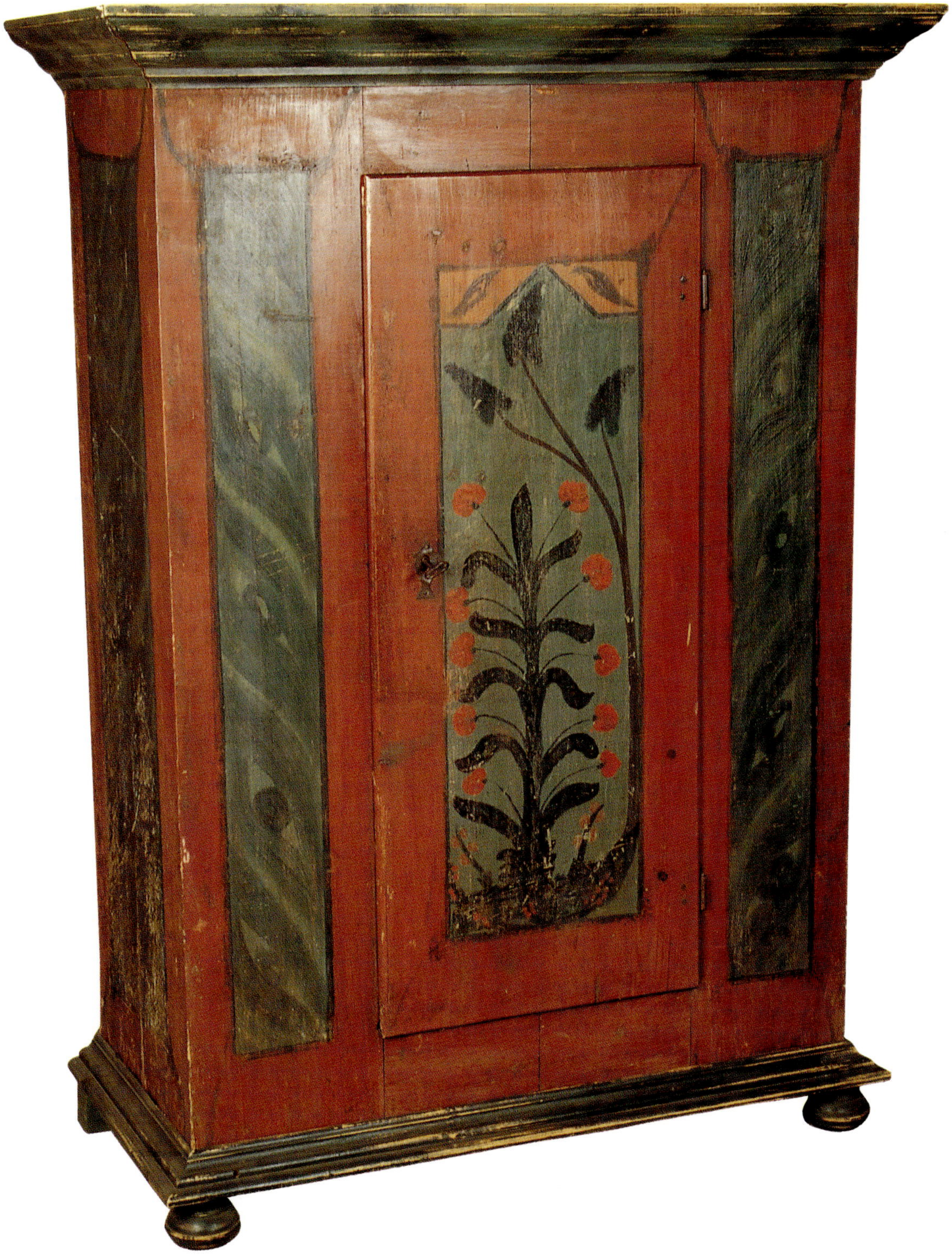

Three-piece painted wardrobe with separate overhanging cornice painted green with shading, case painted red with marbleized side panels, and single door painted with floral decoration, all resting on a separate base of green painted molding, bun front feet, and blocked back feet. $4850.

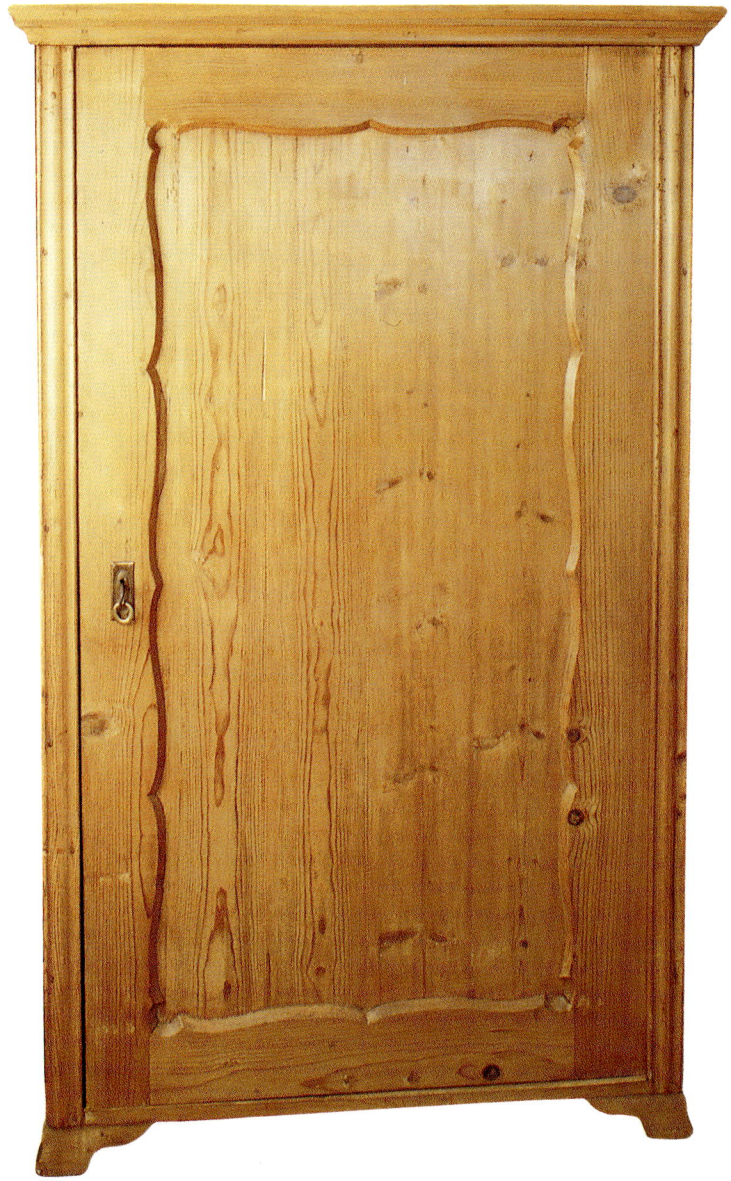

German wardrobe with straight cornice over a single door with scalloped frame and metal escutcheon. The simple base rests on small bracket feet. $995.

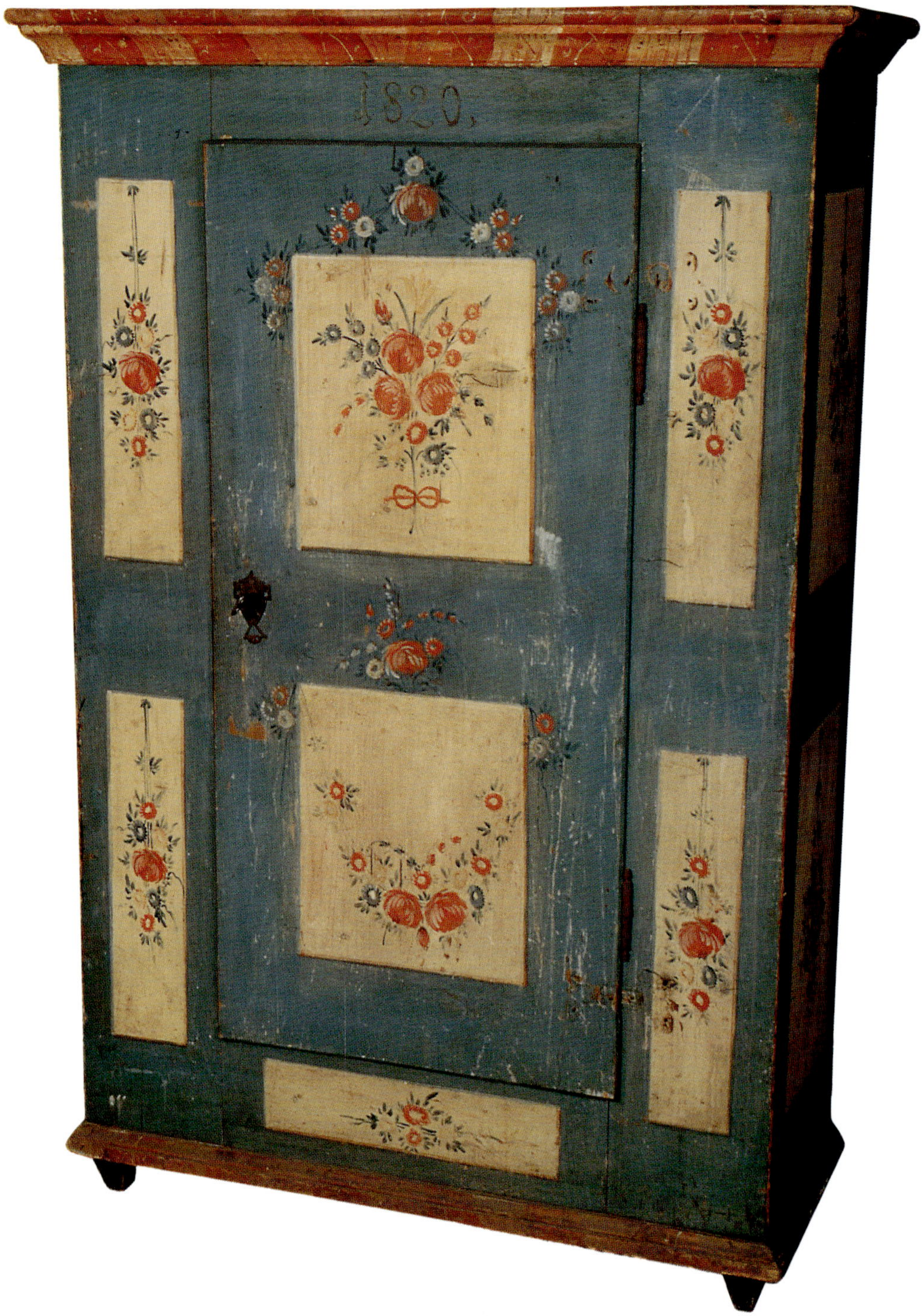

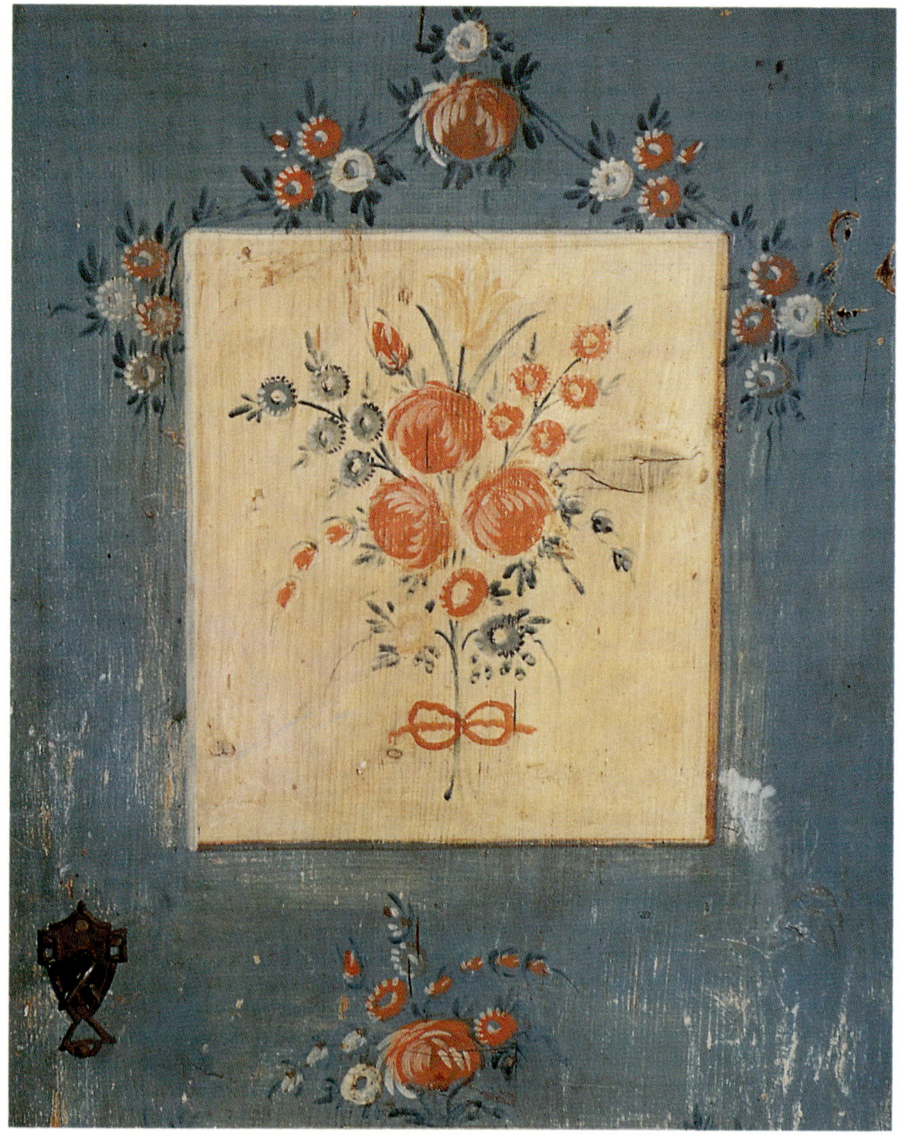

German wardrobe with original blue painted background and white panels with floral decoration, a single door, applied base molding, and tapering short feet, Empire style, c.1820. $6895.

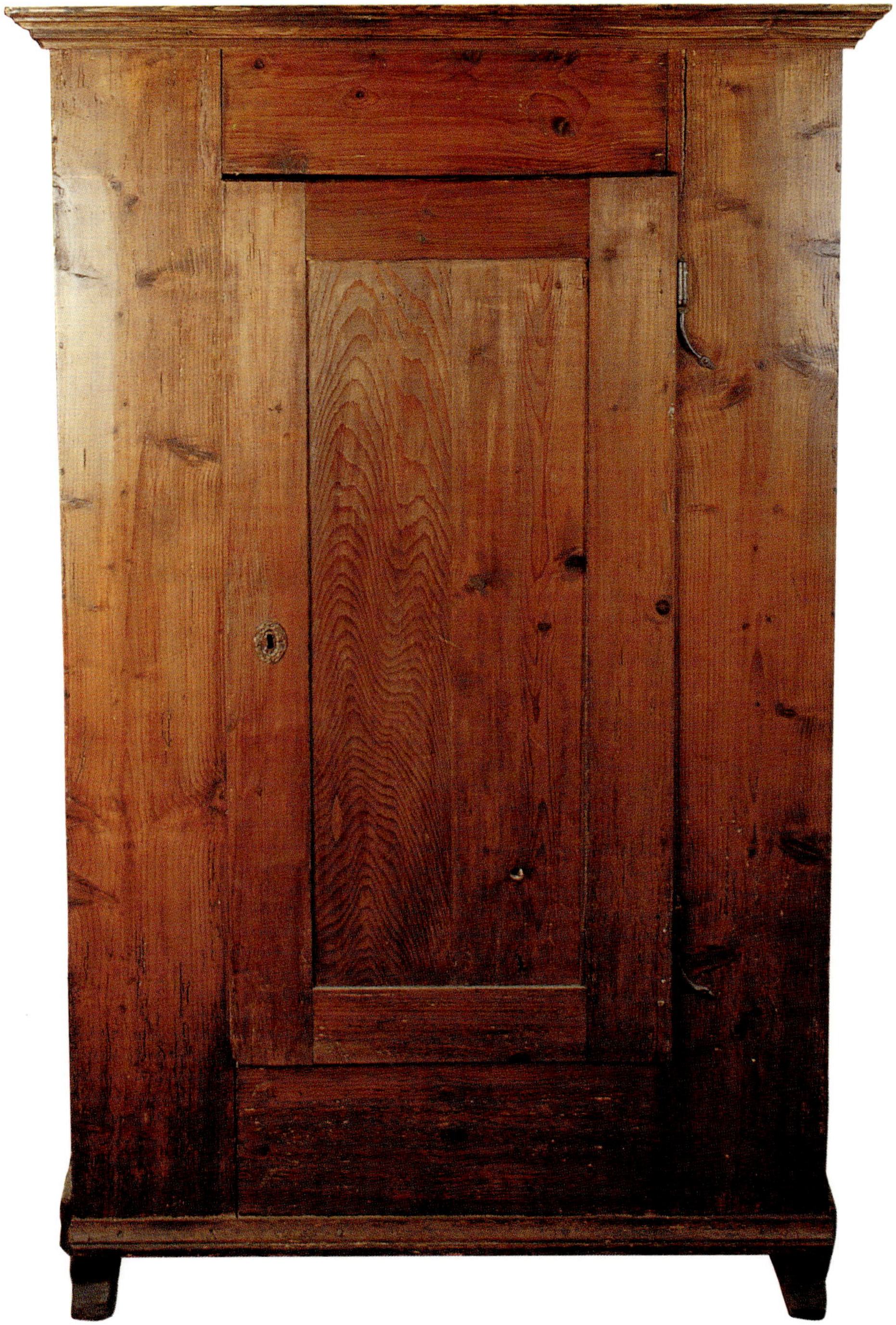

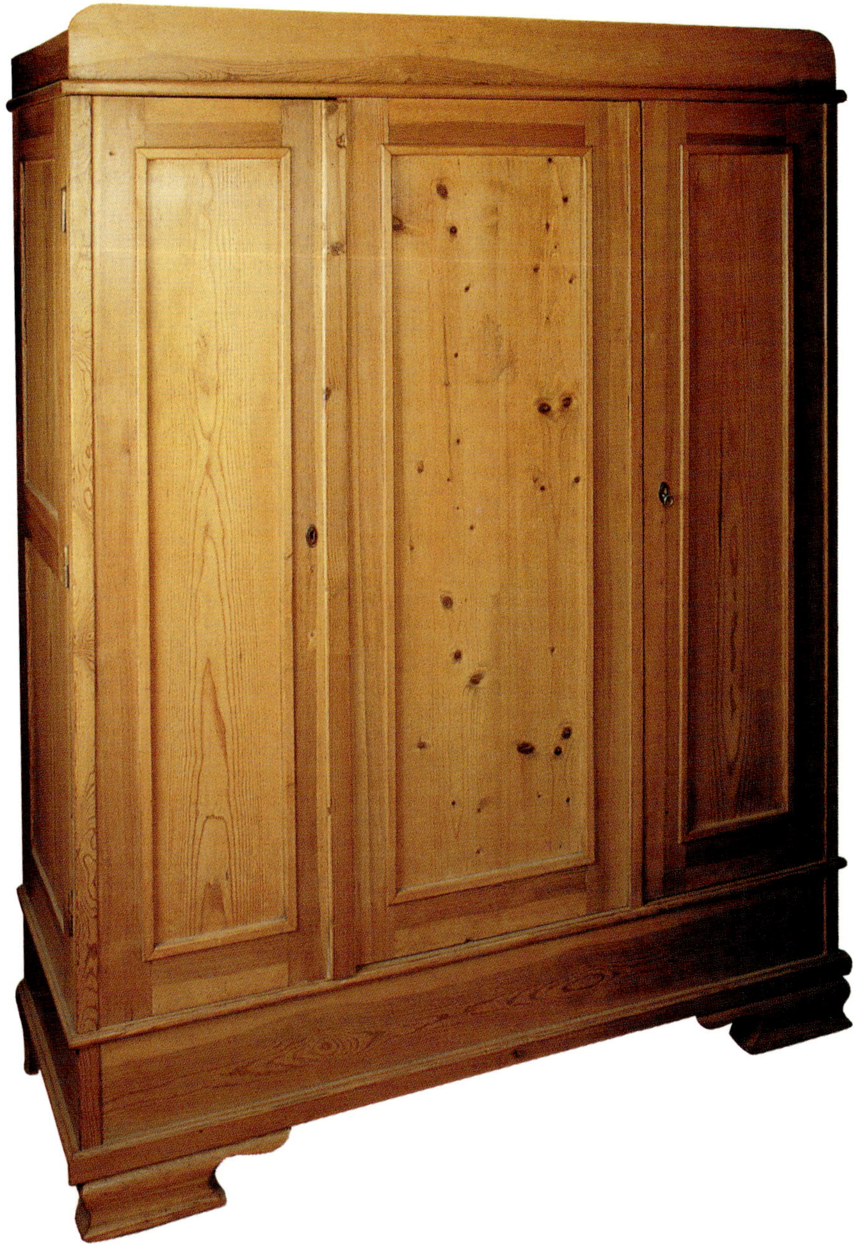

Left: German wardrobe of dark stained pine with rat-tail hinges supporting the single, recessed panel door. An applied base molding rests on trestle feet. $950.

Right: German wardrobe with raised flat cornice over a single, recessed paneled door and flanking fixed panels. A straight base rests on ogee bracket feet. $1595.

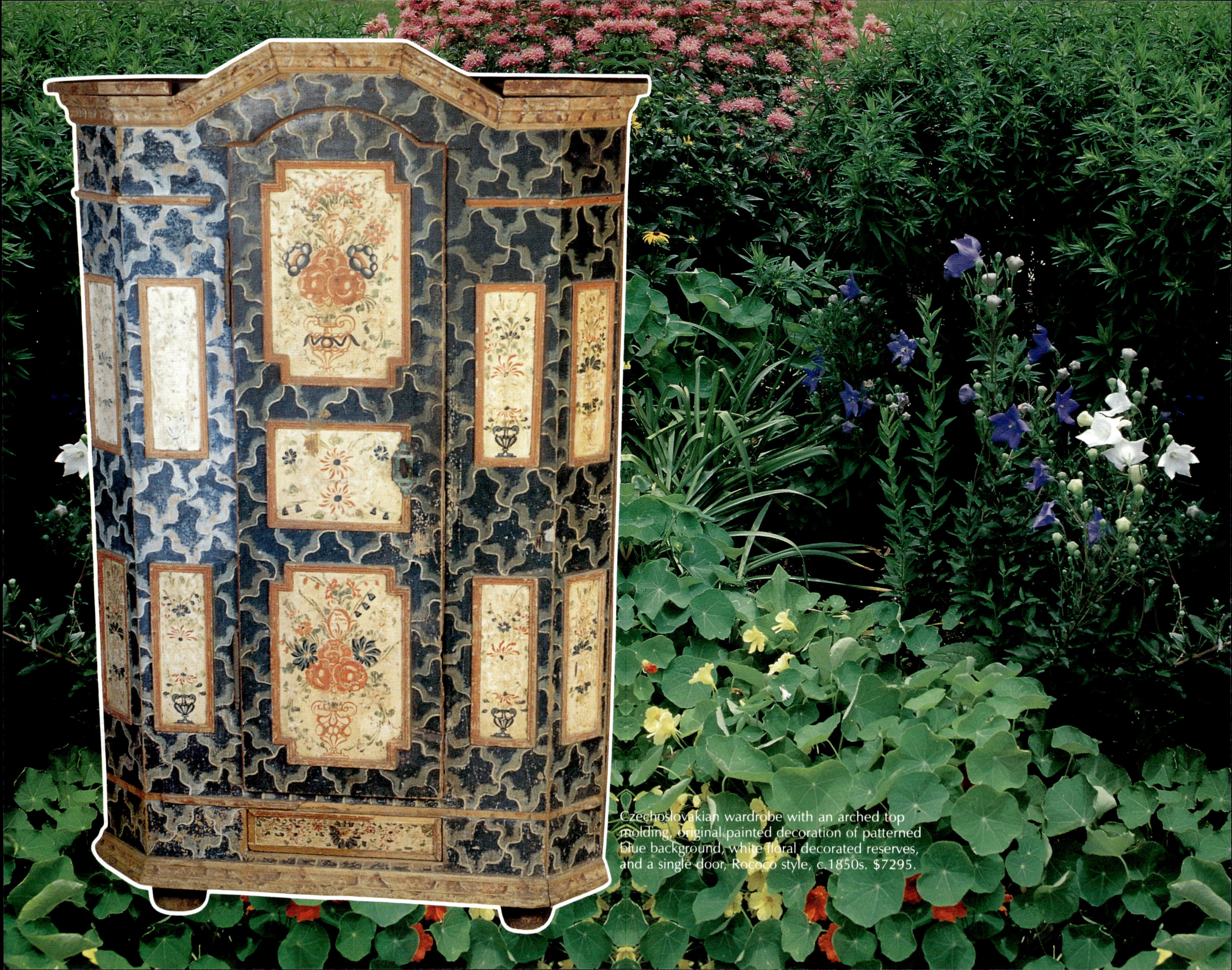

Czechoslovakian wardrobe with an arched top molding, original painted decoration of patterned blue background, white floral decorated reserves, and a single door, Rococo style, c.1850s. $7295.

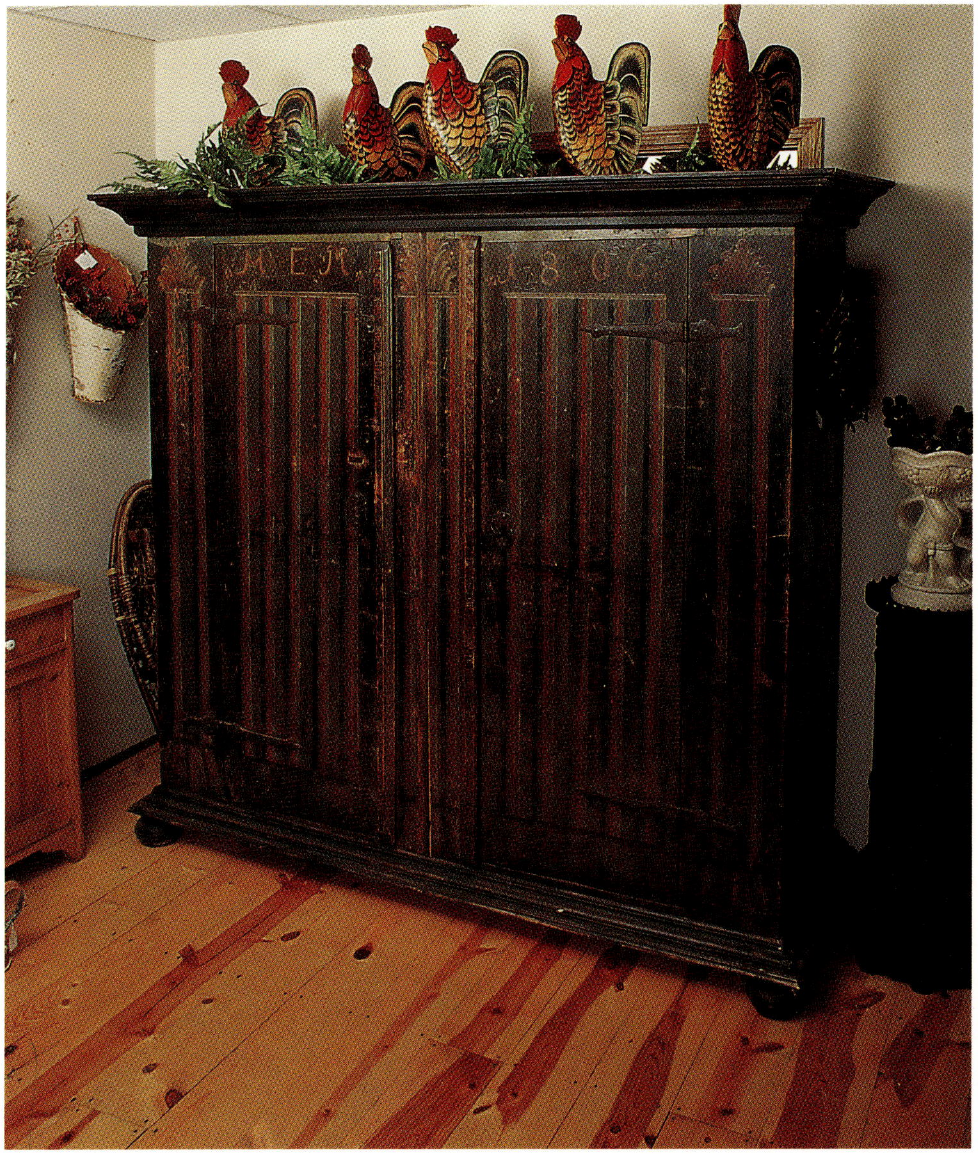

German Baroque style, large painted wardrobe with striped decoration on the front and sides, dated 1806. The case has two doors with iron strap hinges and rests on bun feet. $6500.

Baroque style painted wardrobe with arched front case, two doors painted in panels with floral bouquets. $4395.

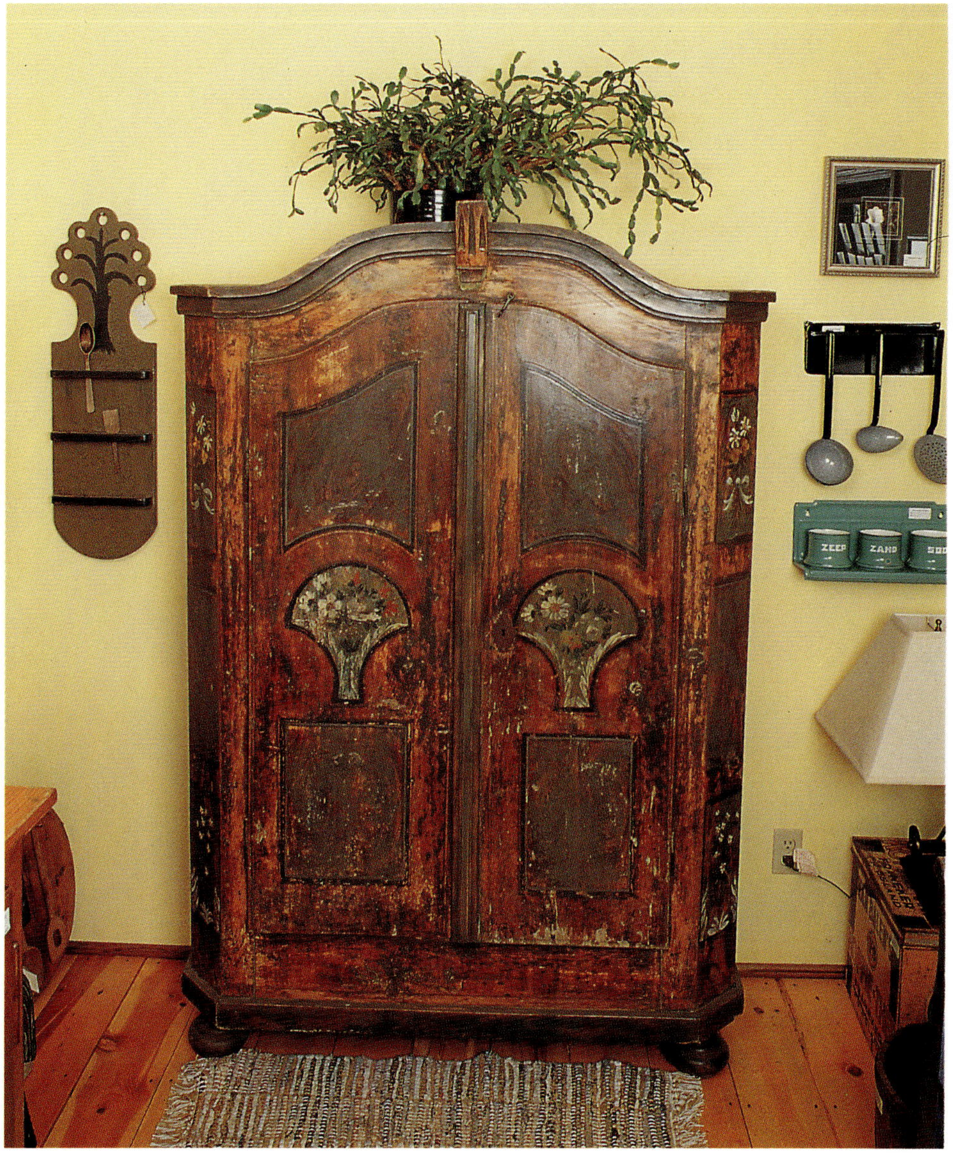

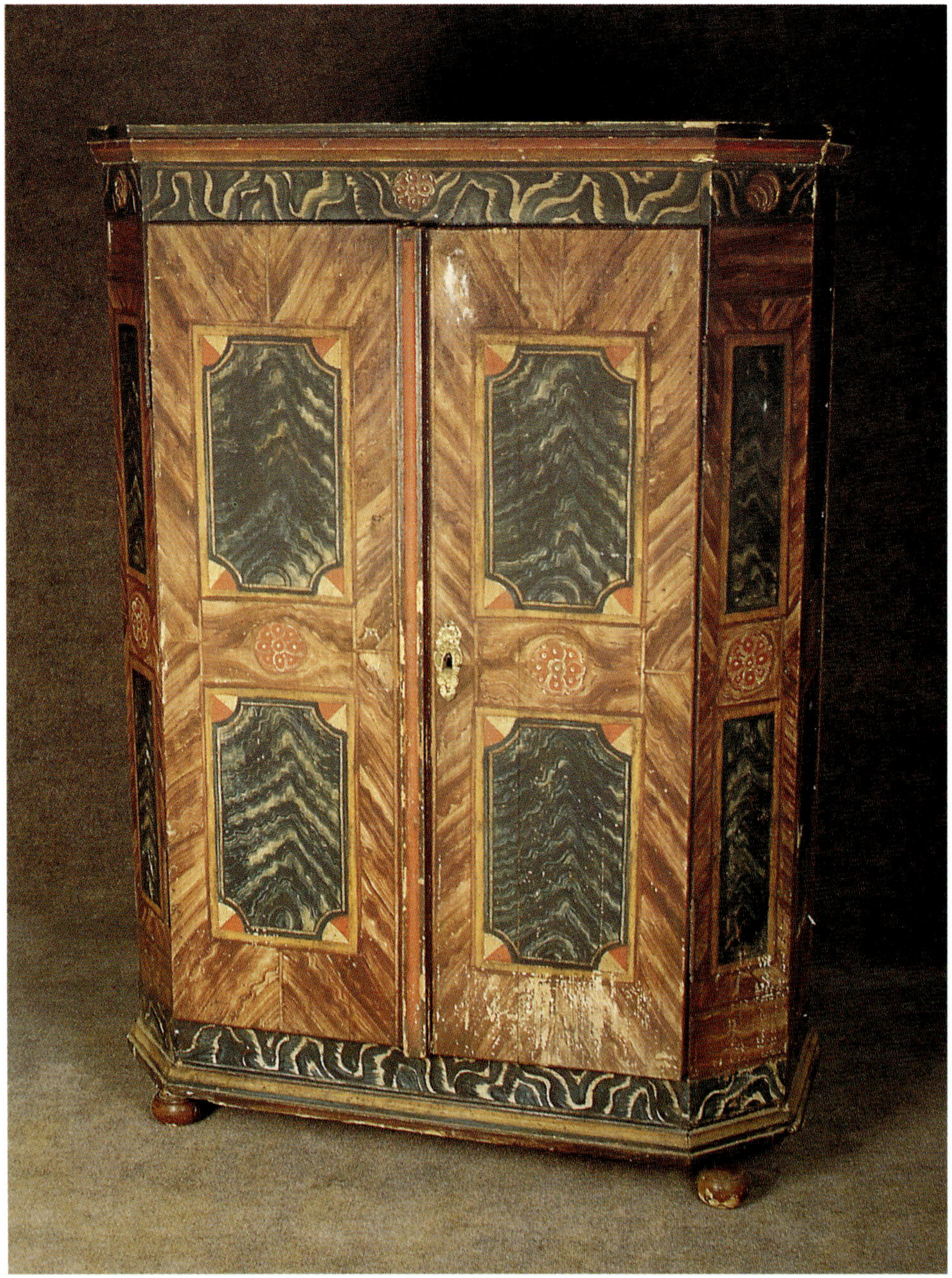

German wardrobe with original painted surface, two hinged doors, and turned feet, c.1830s. $7395.

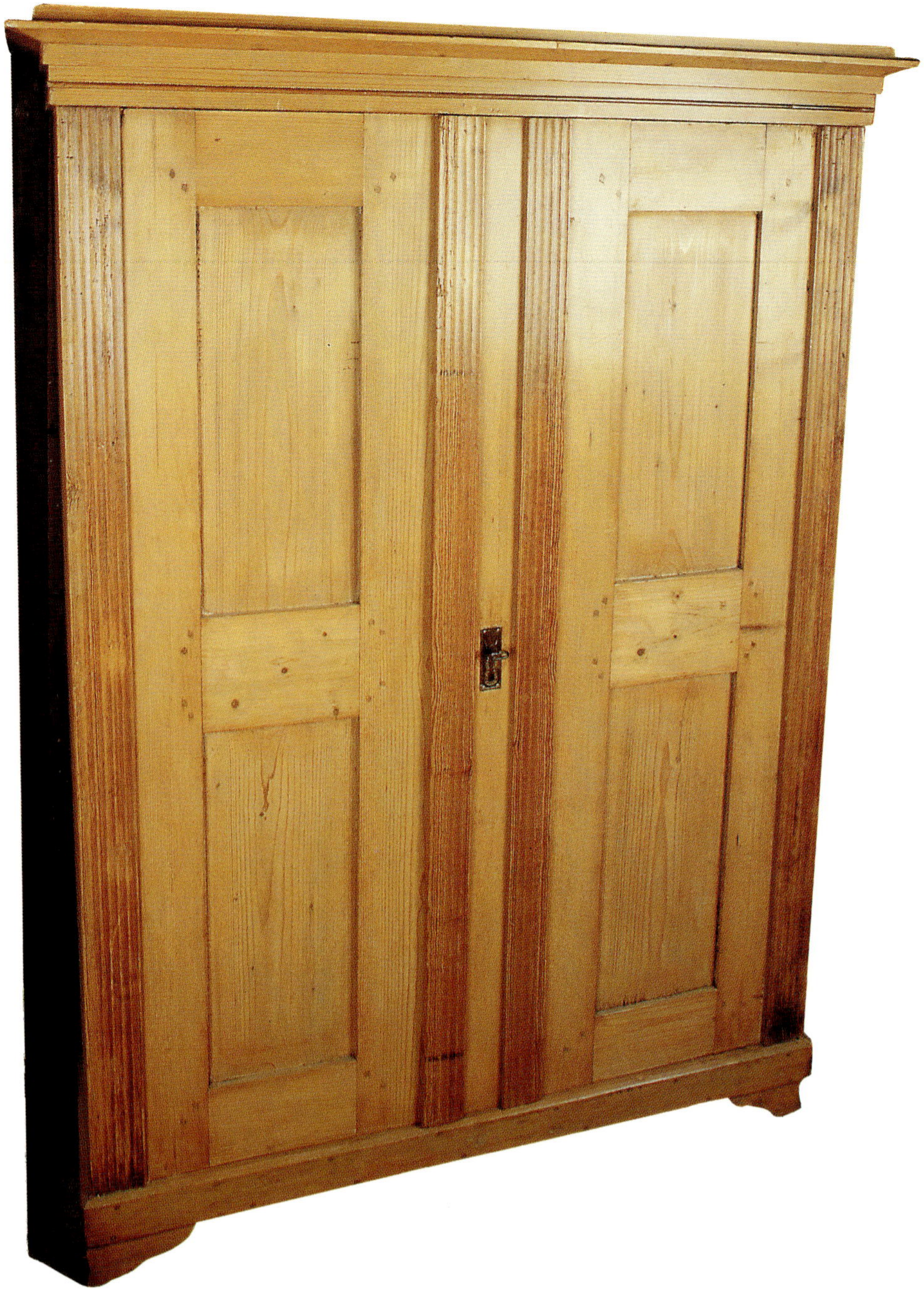

German wardrobe with straight cornice over two rectangular paneled doors and fluted stiles, a base molding and bracket feet, Empire style. $1295.

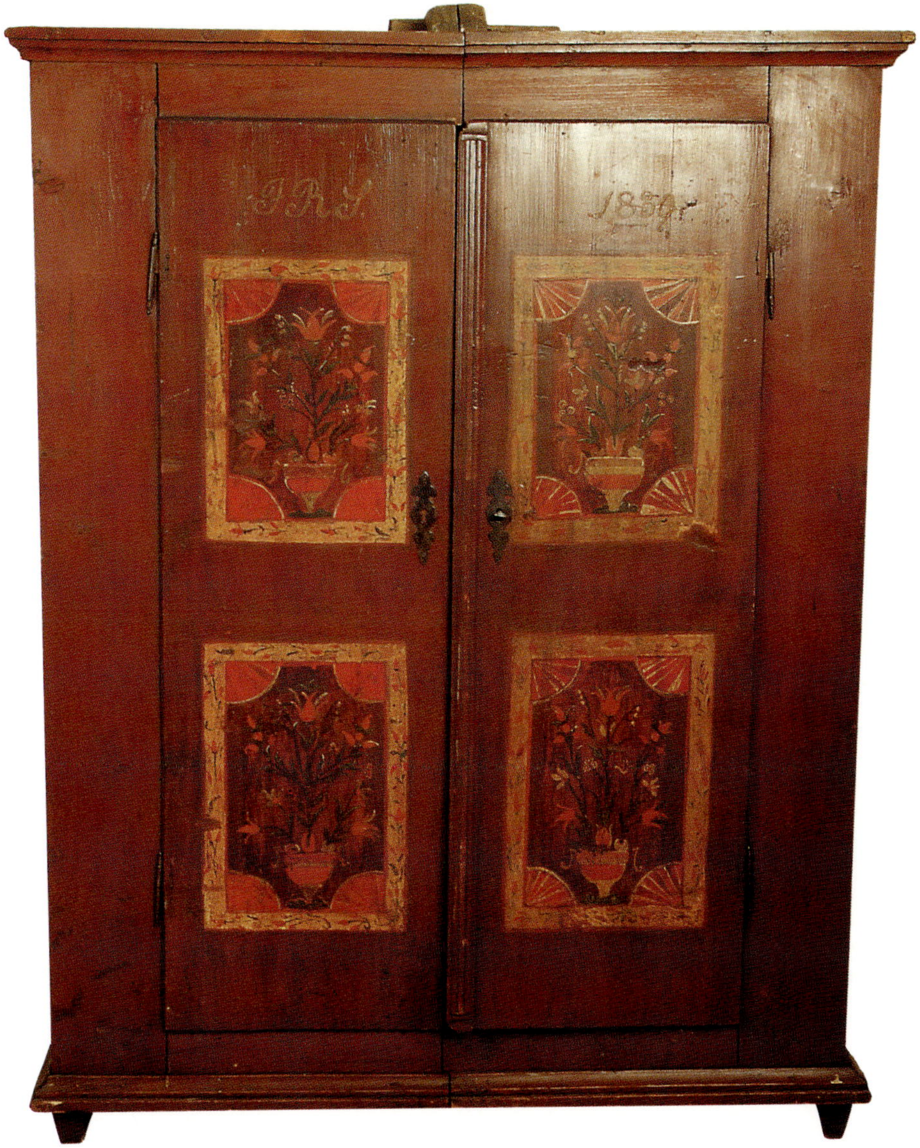

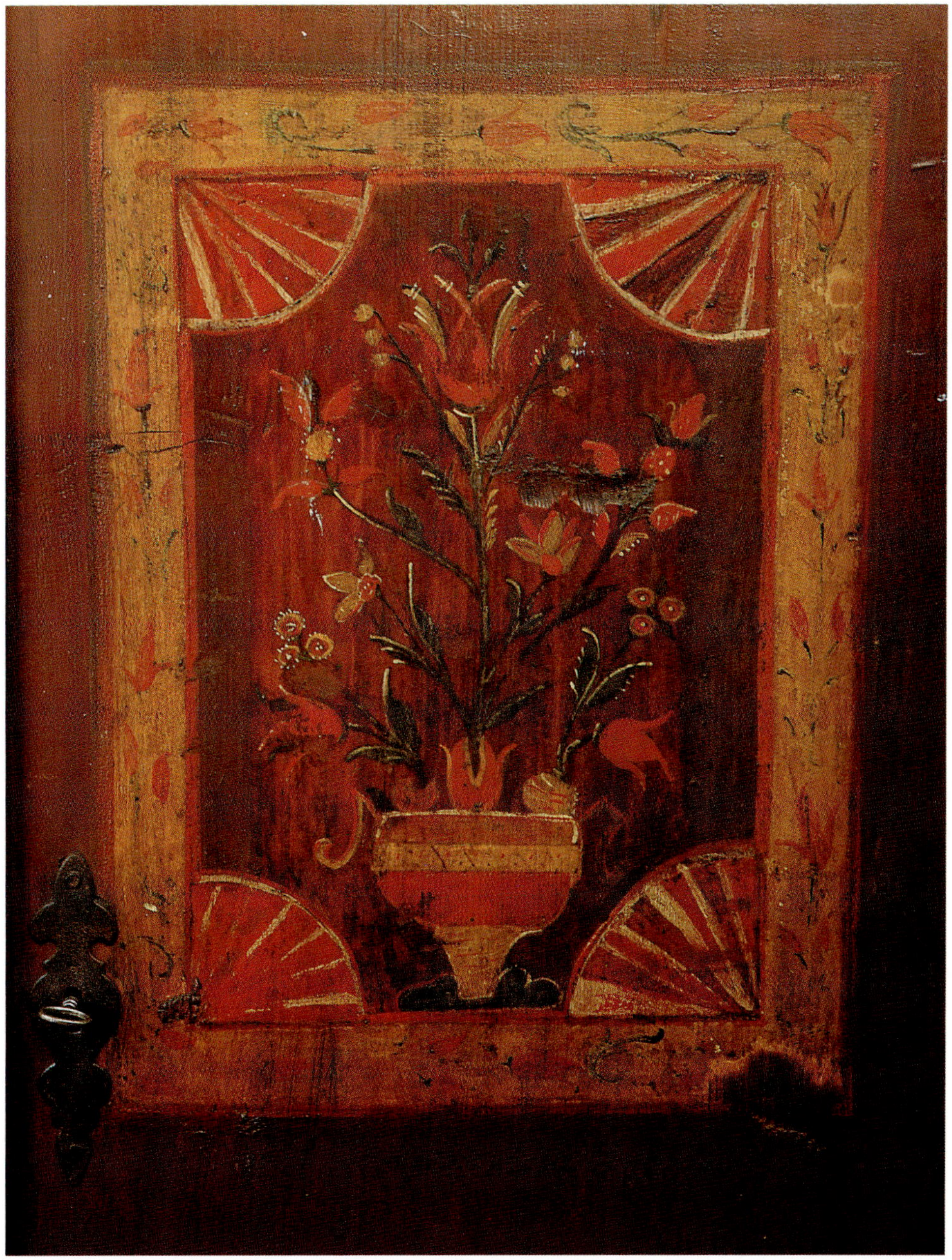

German painted wardrobe with red background on two doors, each with two rectangular panels decorated with floral bouquets and inscribed "FRS 1839." The applied base molding rests over tapering square feet.

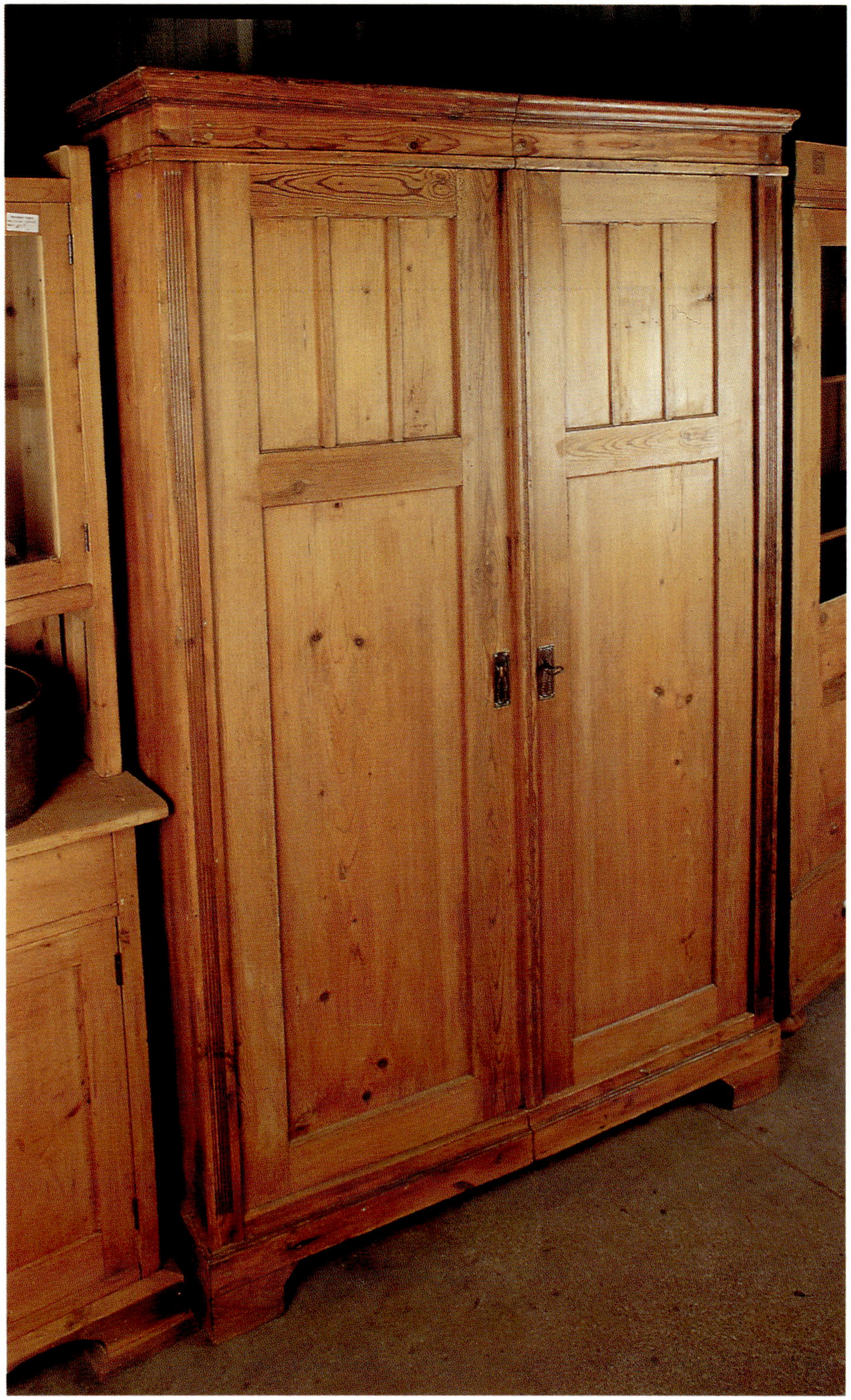

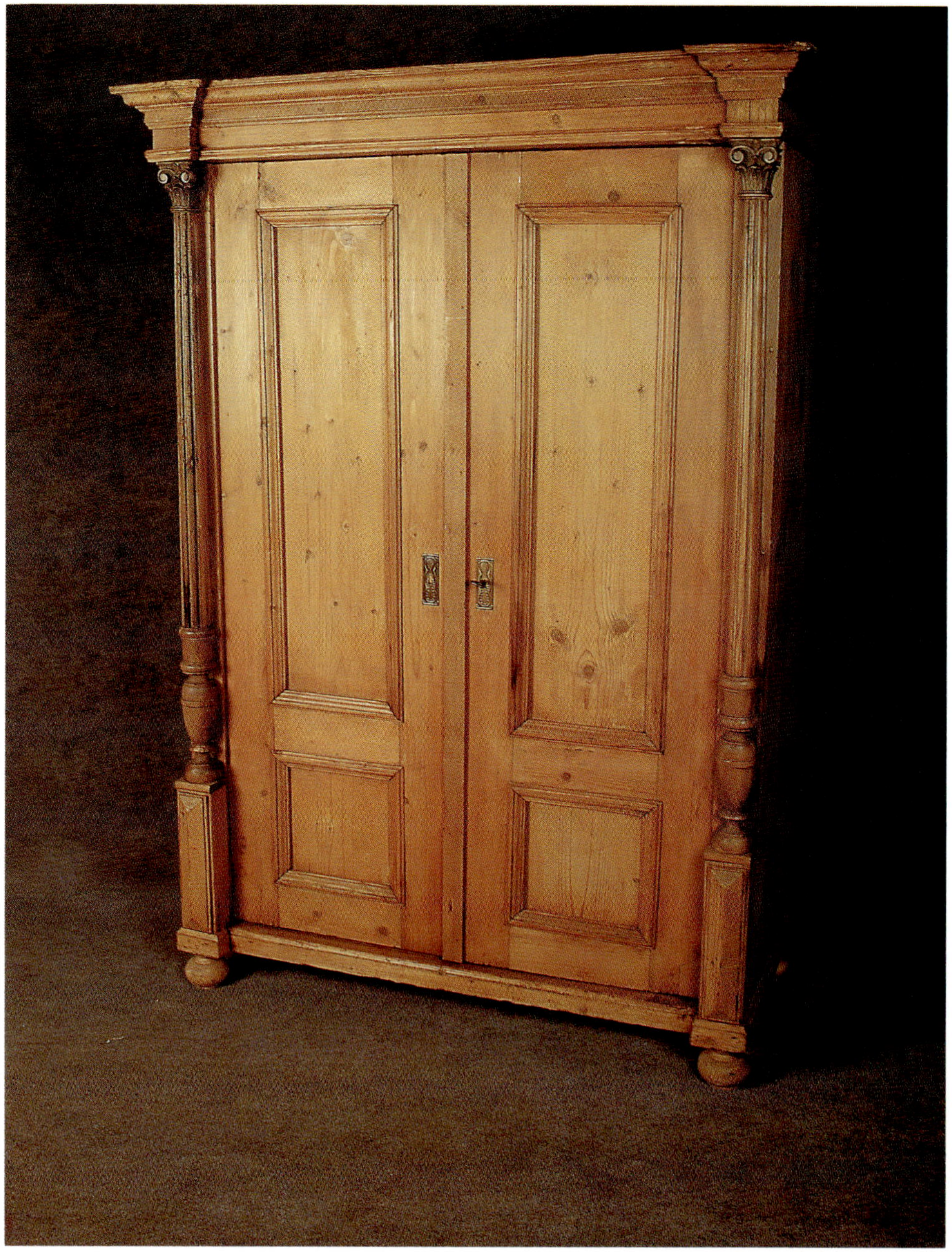

Left: A two-door wardrobe with straight cornice and plain frieze over two doors with applied blind panels, metal escutcheons, and reeded stiles over bracket feet. $995.

Above: Two-door wardrobe from Eastern Germany or Czechoslovakia with a straight cornice stepped forward above the side columns, doors with two recessed panels, narrow base molding rests on bun feet, Renaissance Revival style, c.1880. $1495.

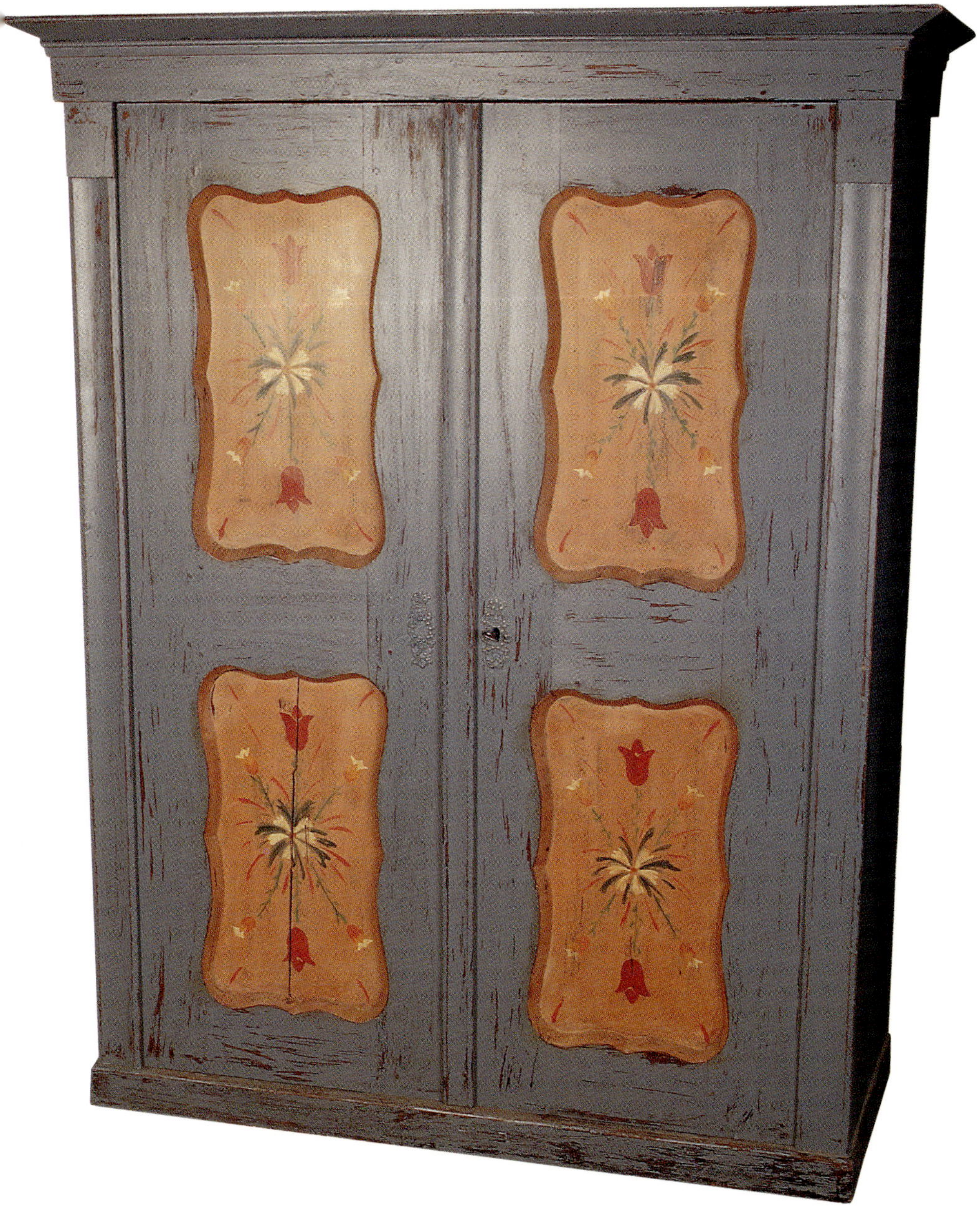

German wardrobe with repainted surface of blue background and four recessed panels with floral decoration on the two hinged doors. $1395.

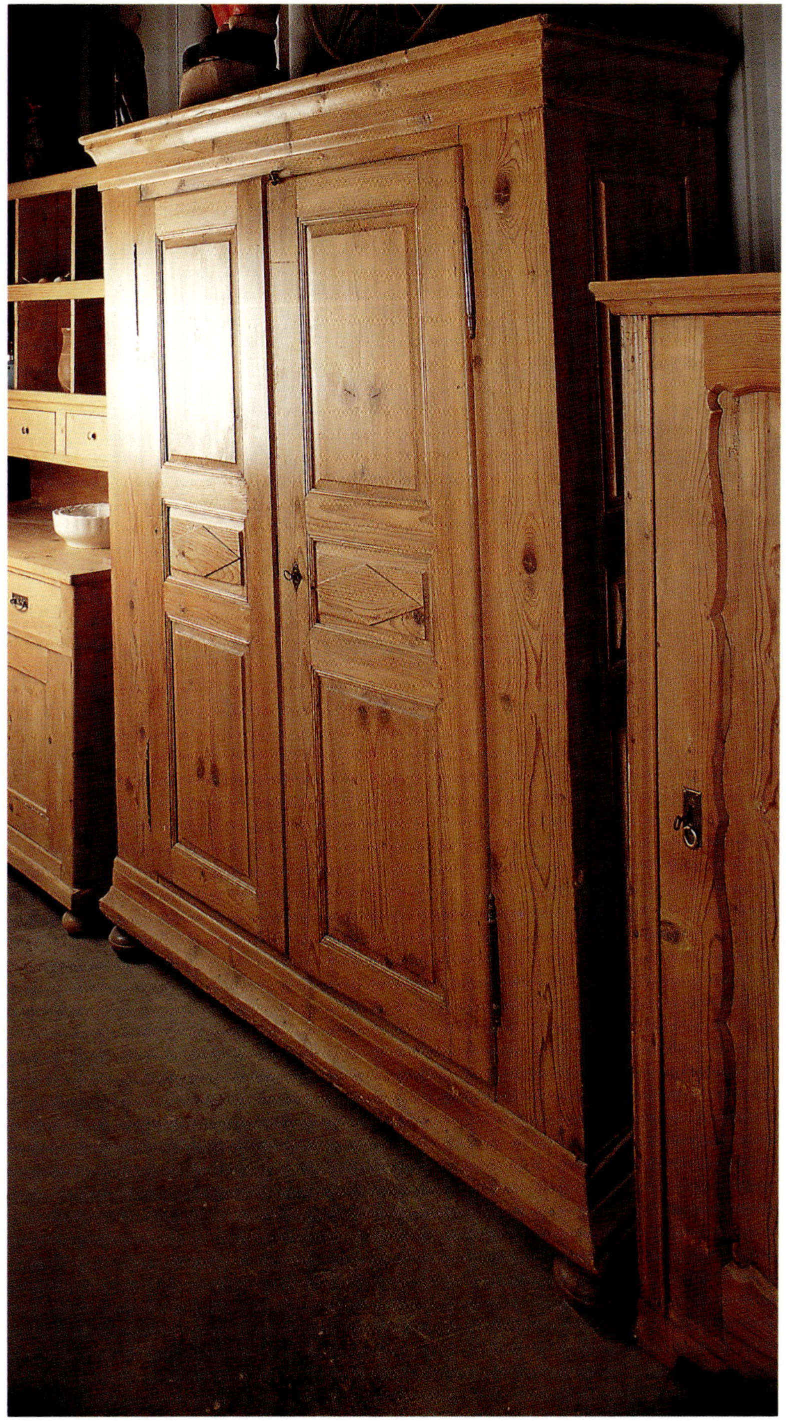

French wardrobe with straight complex molded cornice over two doors with three raised panels including a raised diamond at center. The case rests on a strong base molding and bun feet. $2995.

Two-door Cabinets with Drawers

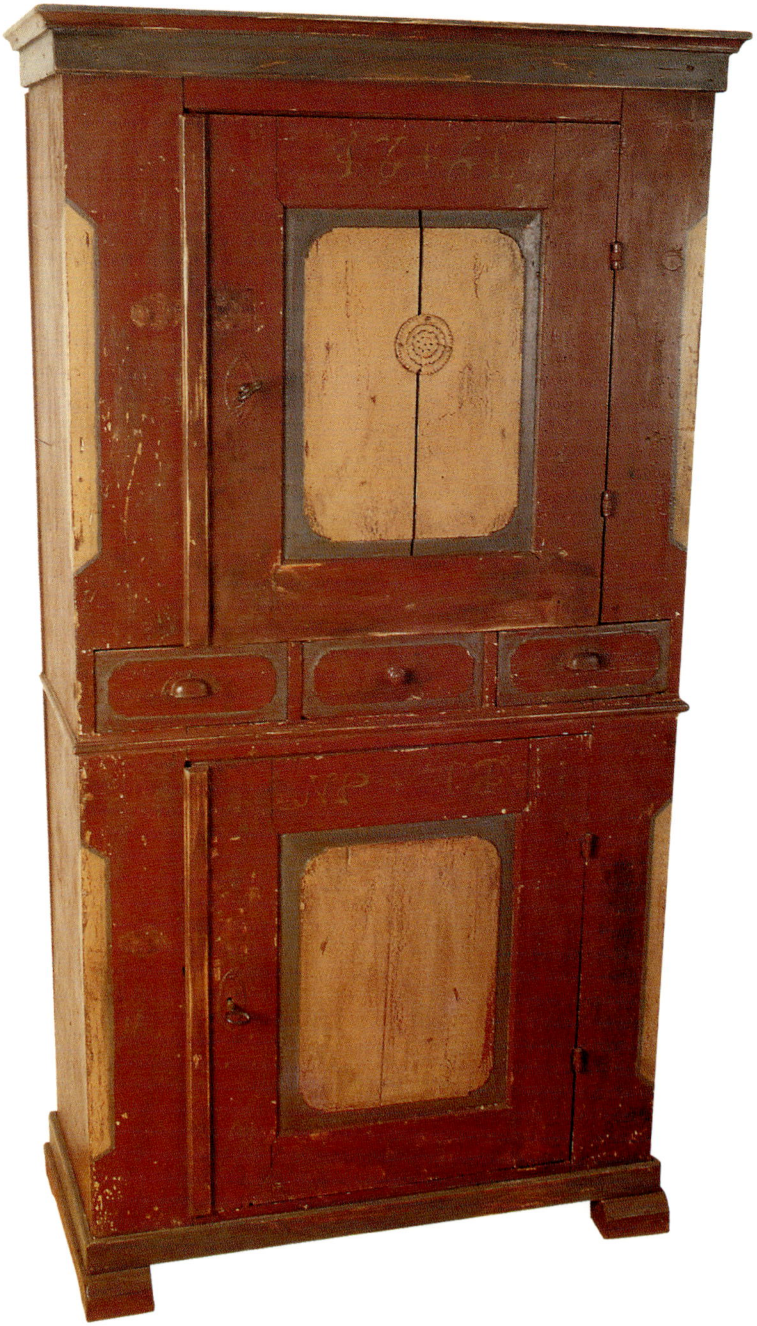

German Baroque painted spice cabinet dated 1761 with applied molding above a raised panel door with a pierced metal plate at the center, and three small drawers below. The bottom case has a single raised panel door above an applied base molding and trestle feet. $4495.

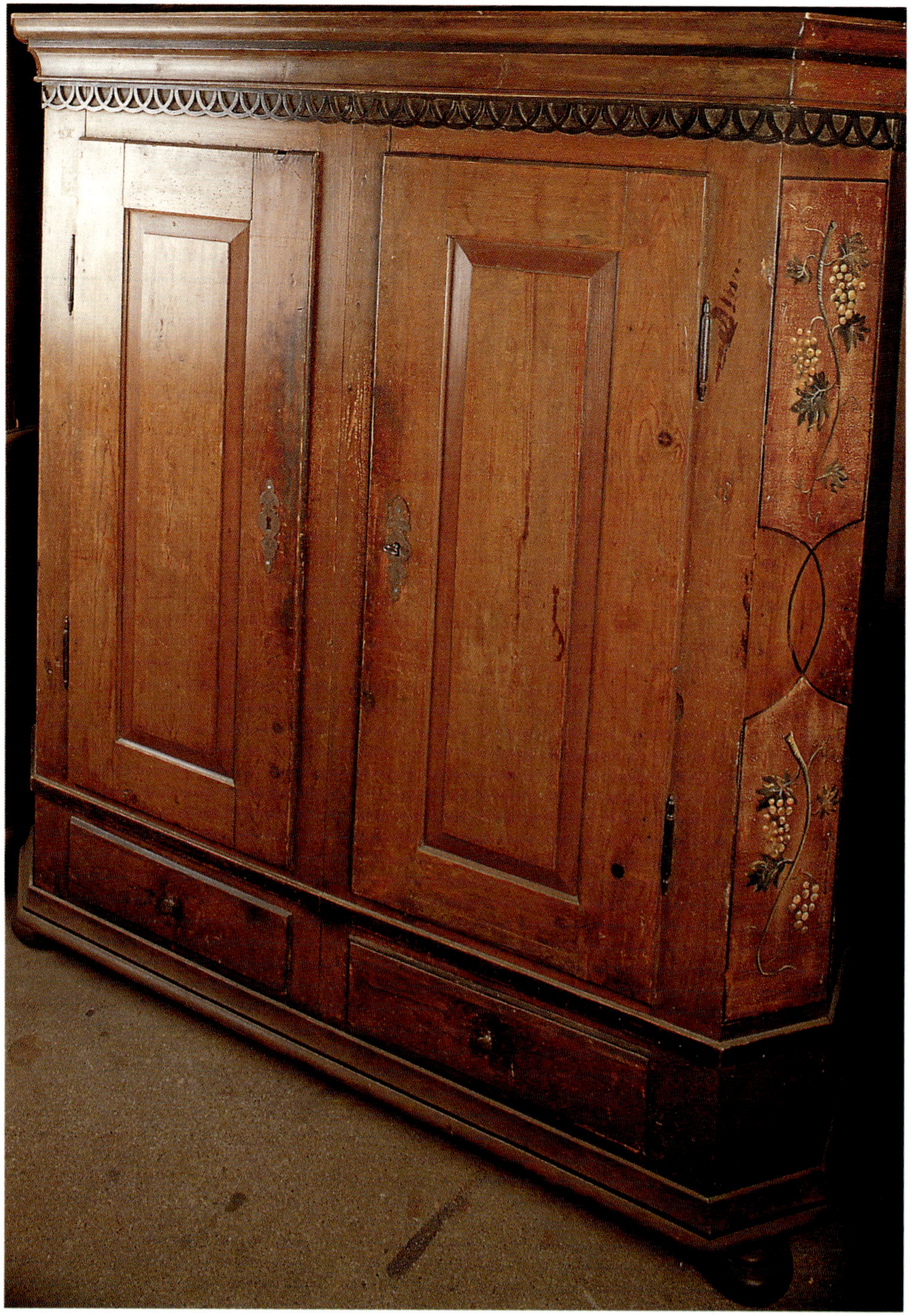

German Baroque two-door wardrobe with a straight cornice and concave frieze over an applied open scalloped molding. Two raised paneled doors and two drawers in the base rest over a base molding and bun feet. $3250.

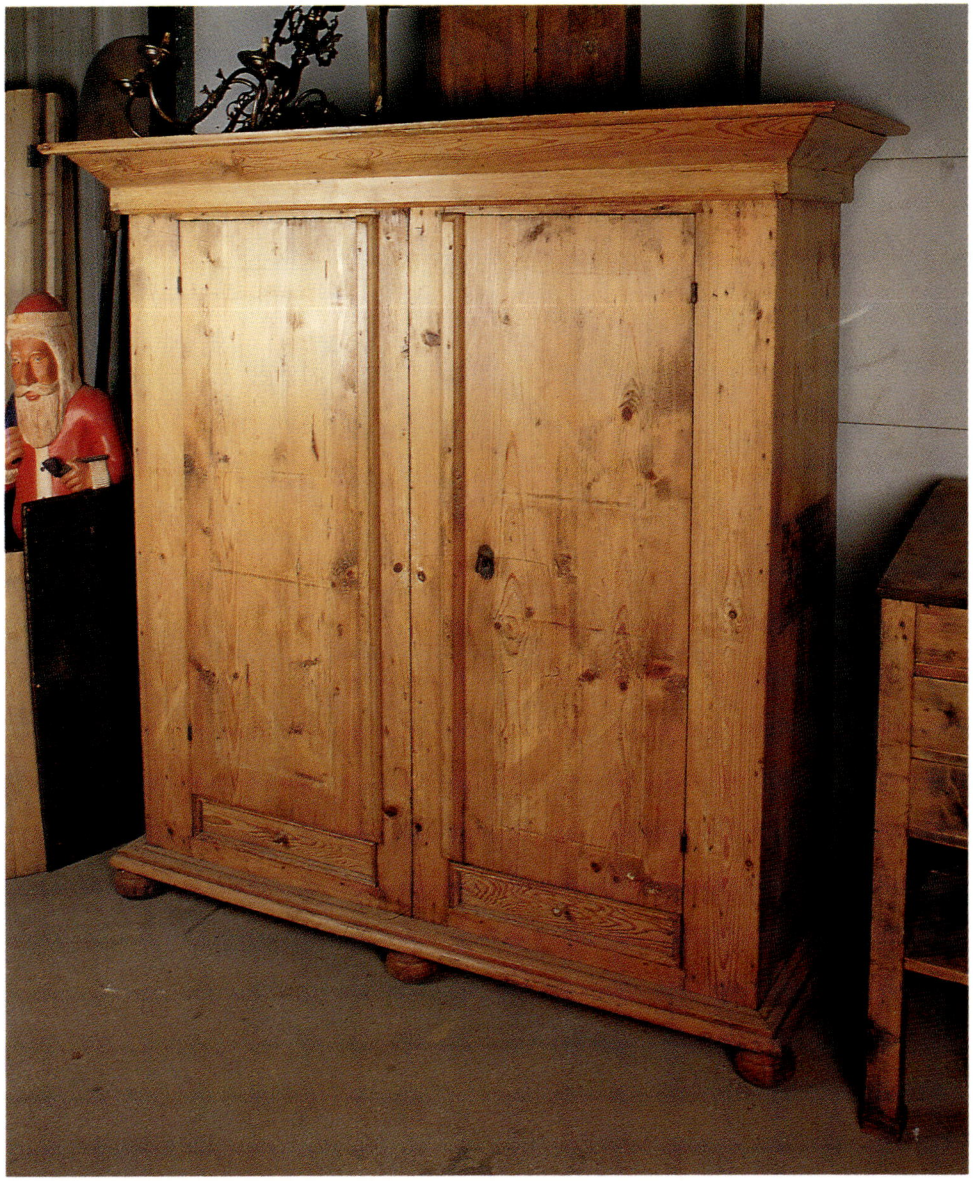

Large German two-door wardrobe of pine with deep overhanging cornice molding over solid plank doors, two drawers with peg knobs, a thin base molding and bun feet, Louis XVI style, c.1780. $3750.

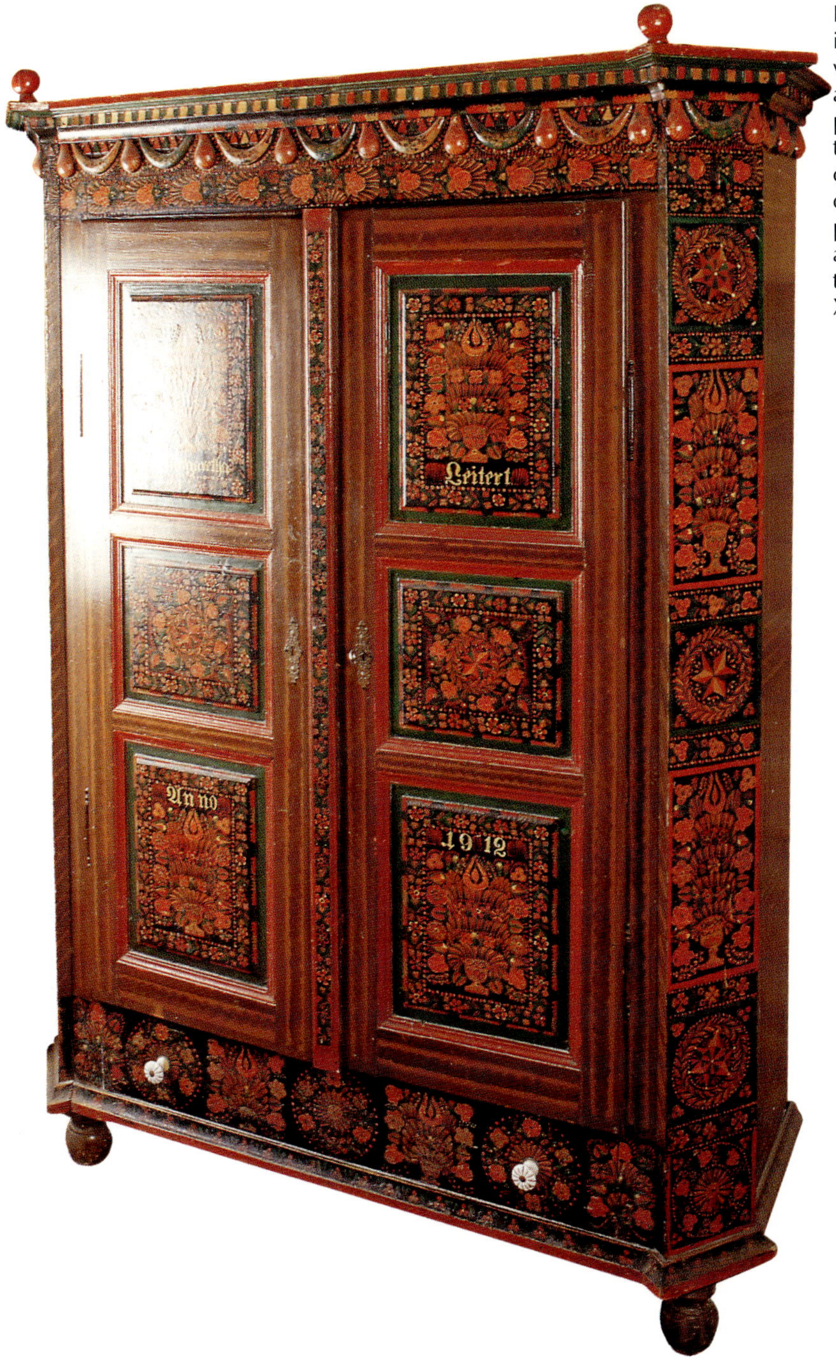

Painted Hungarian wardrobe with lively orange and green painted decoration of great complexity. Two doors with raised panels hang over a long drawer and turned feet, Louis XVI style. $5995.

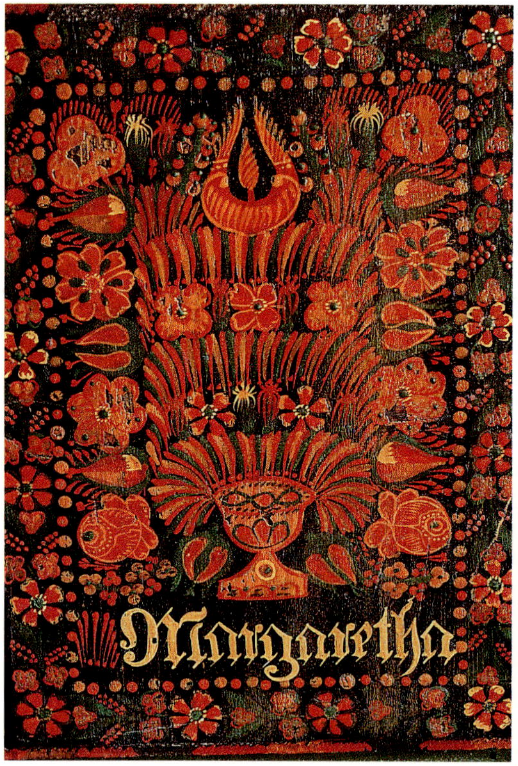

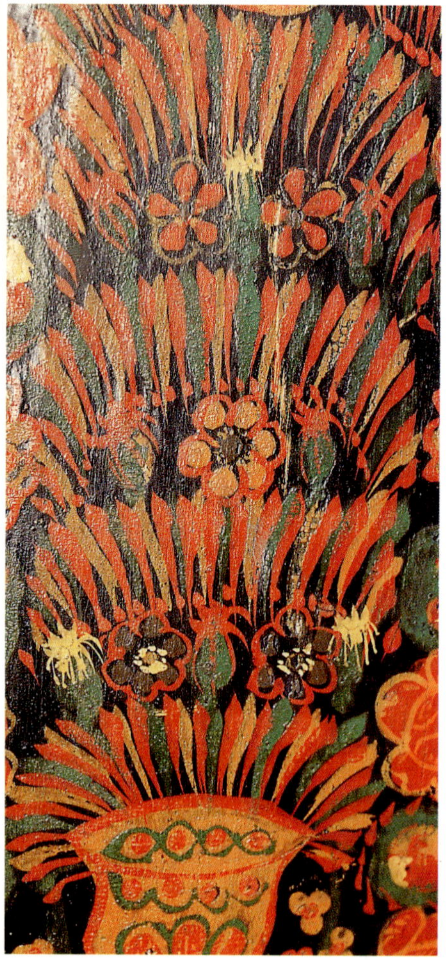

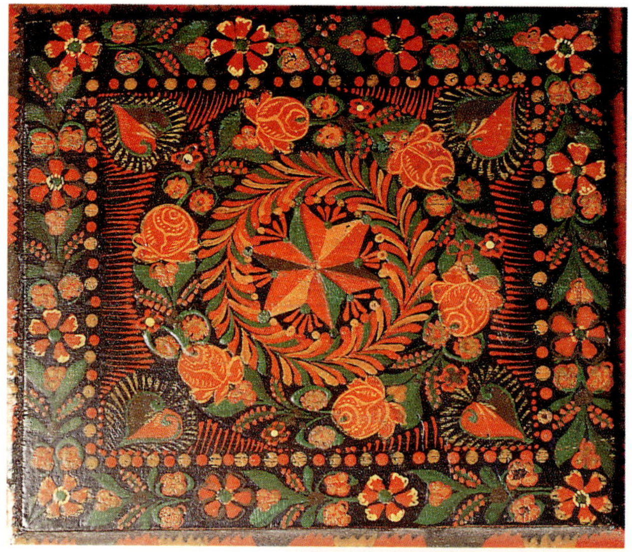

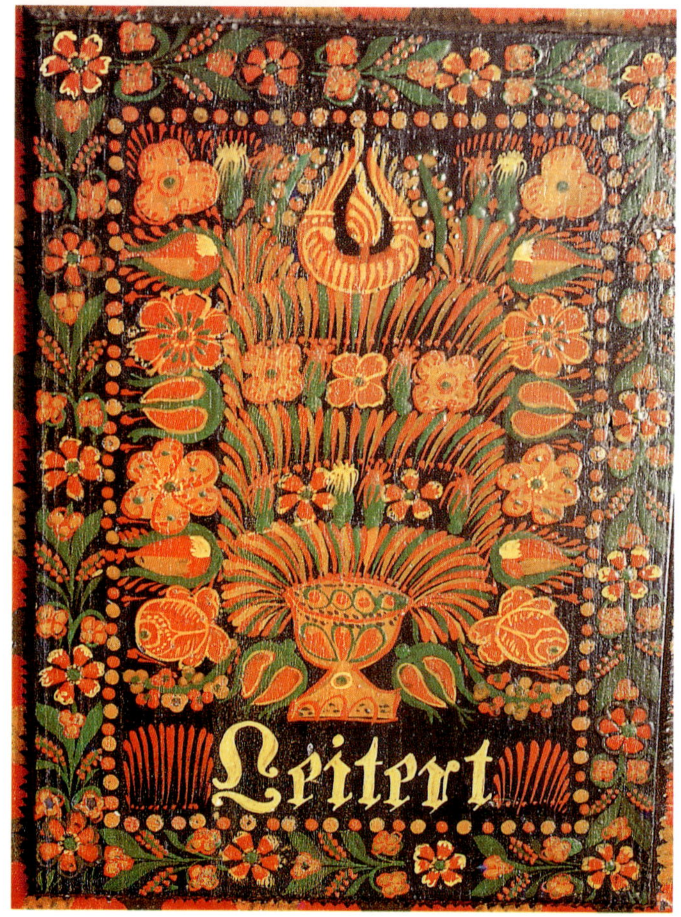

Close-ups of photo on previous page right.

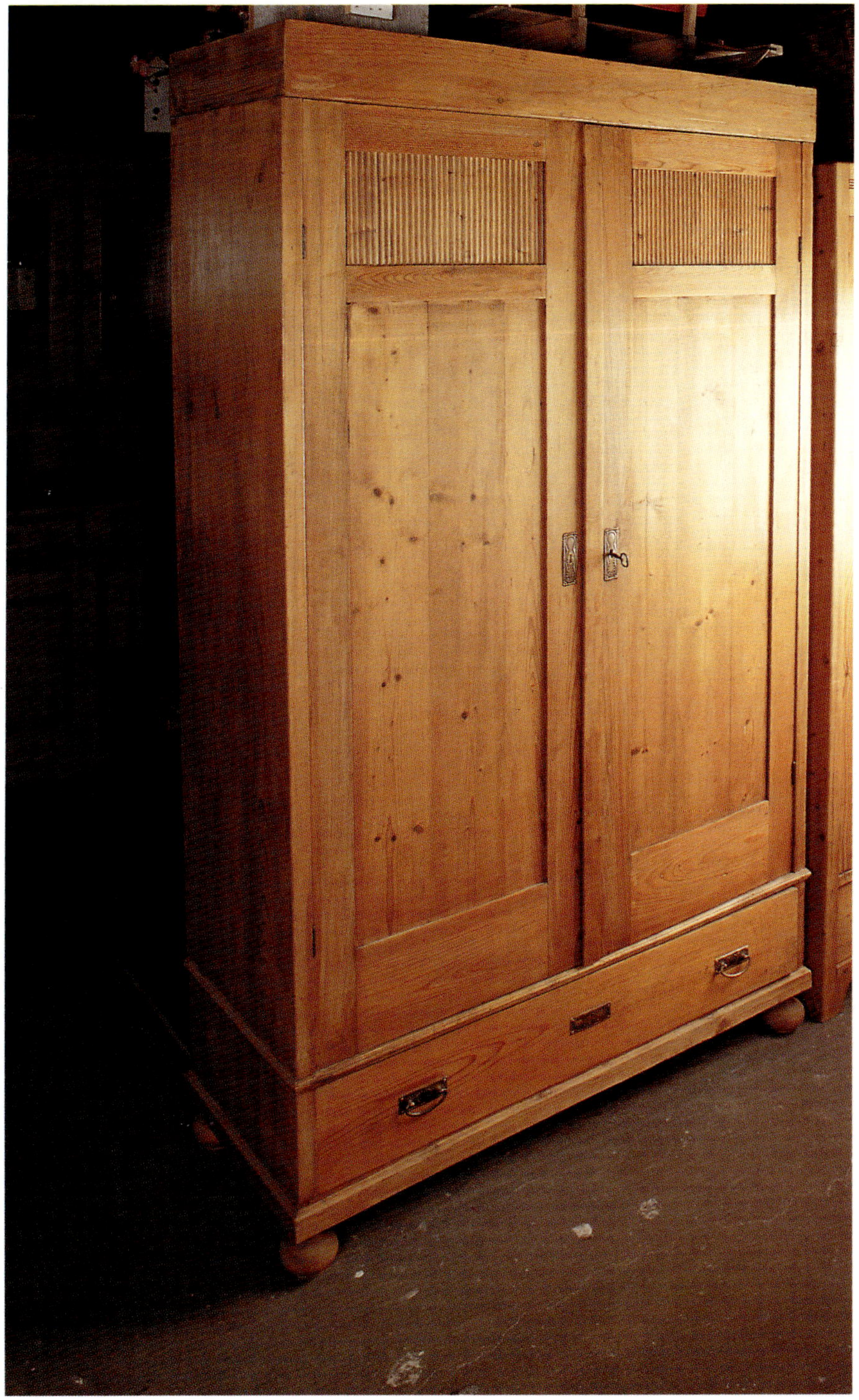

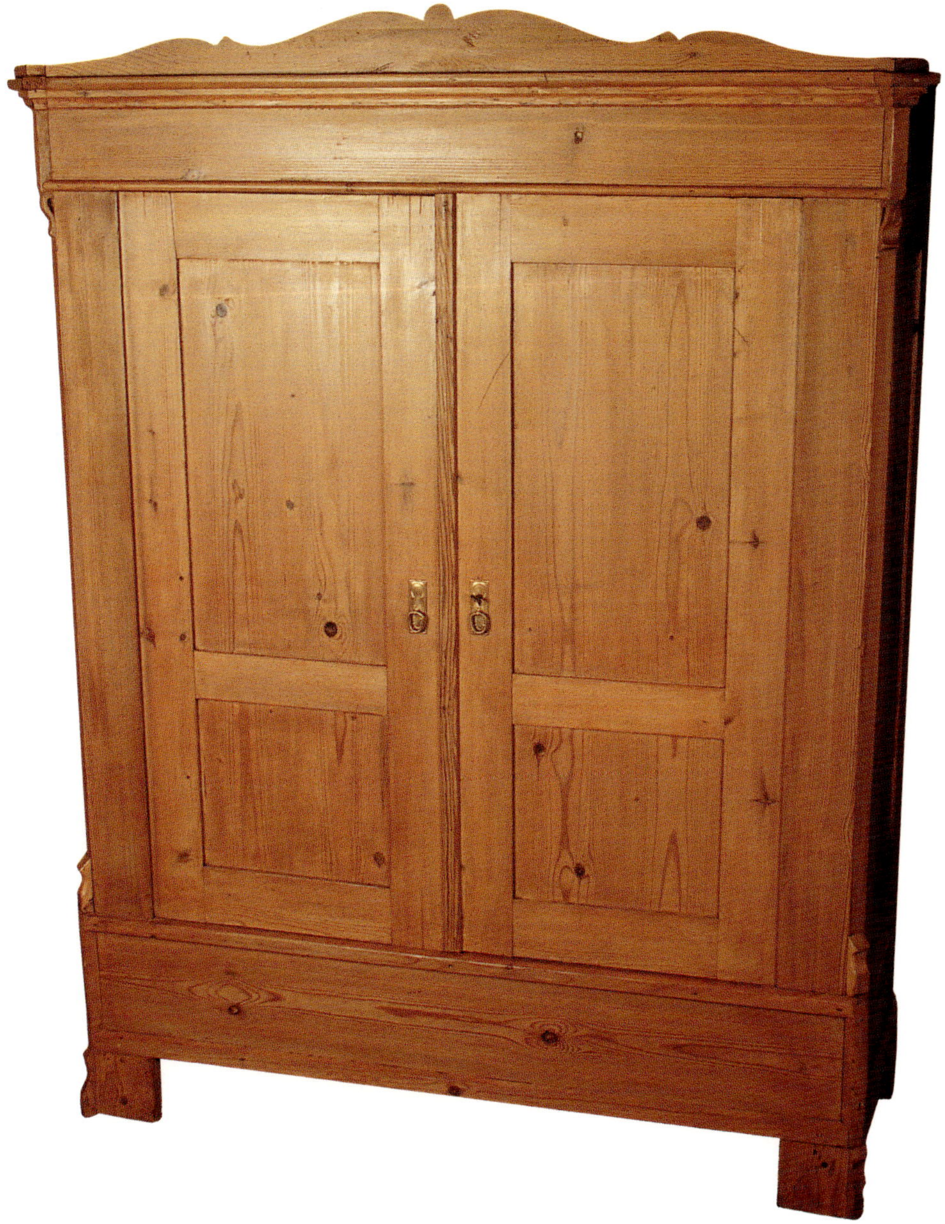

Left: Hungarian two-door wardrobe with straight deep cornice over two doors with reeded panel above recessed panels, metal escutcheons and a long drawer in the base with straight molding, and bun feet. $995.

Above: German, two-door wardrobe with shaped cornice over a plain frieze and two double paneled doors, solid base, and canted corners that continue into the legs. $2495.

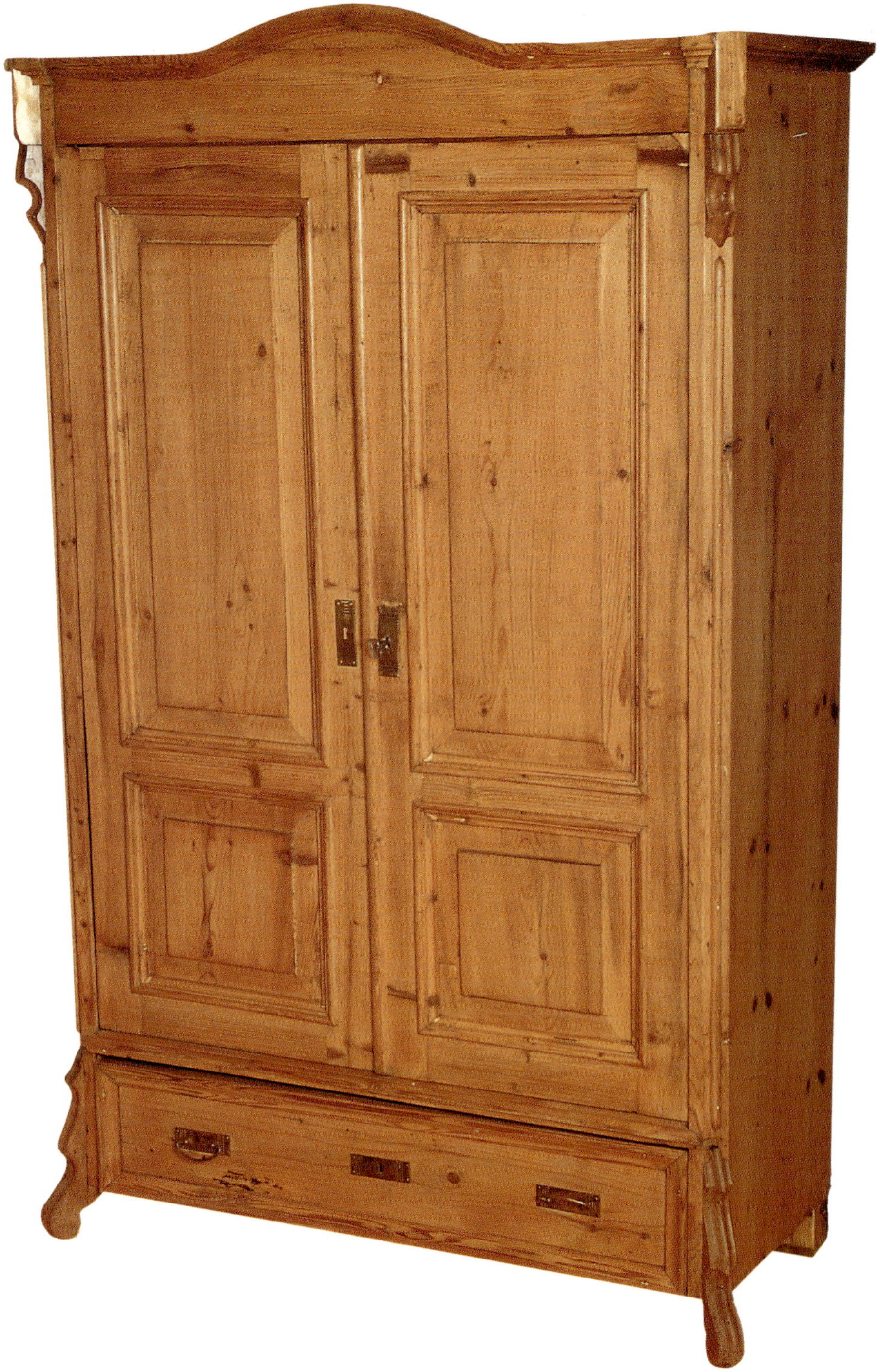

German two-door wardrobe. $1195.

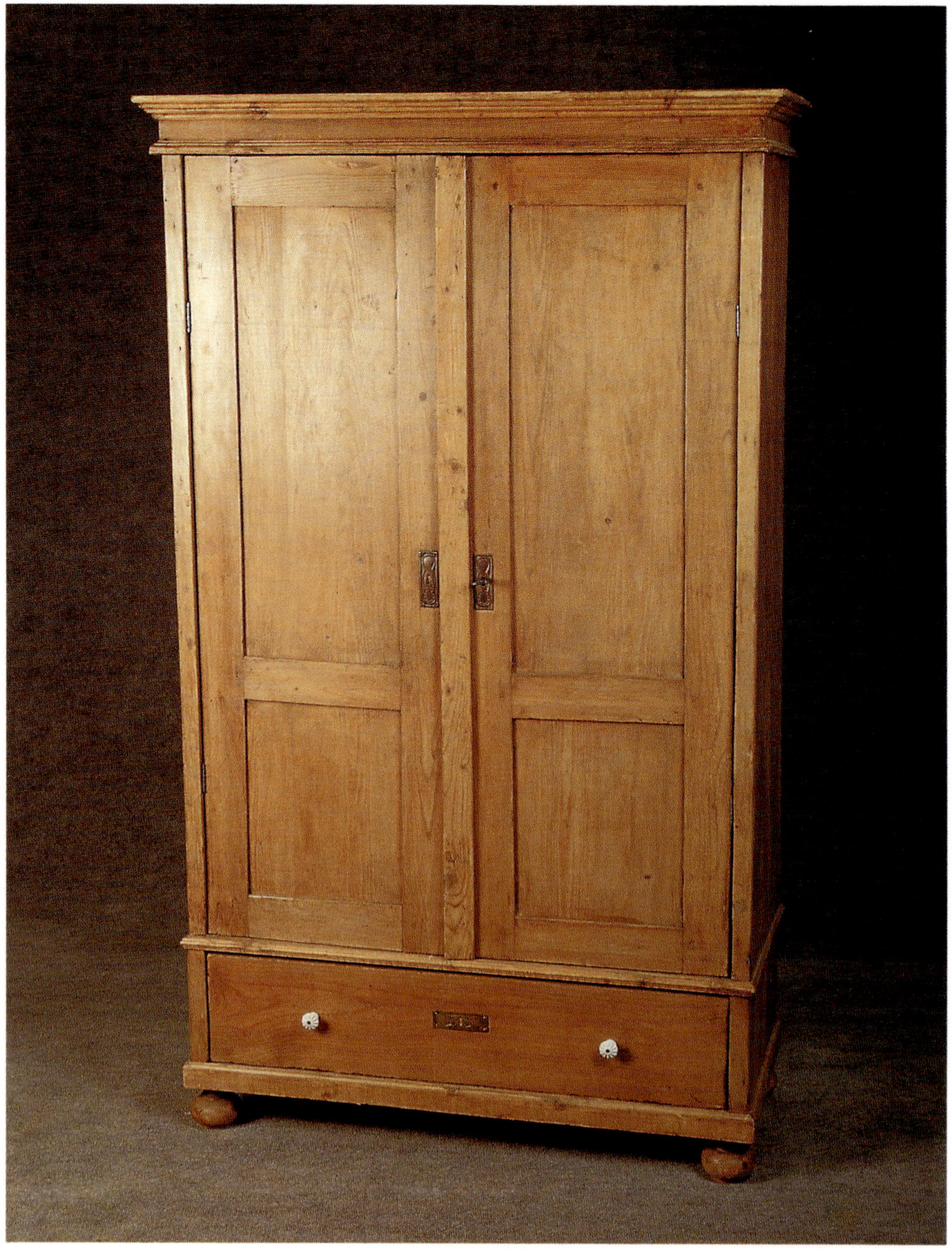

One-piece painted wardrobe with a straight cornice molding over two doors with two recessed panels and metal escutcheons on each and in the base a single drawer with two white porcelain knobs. The straight base molding rests on four bun feet. $995.

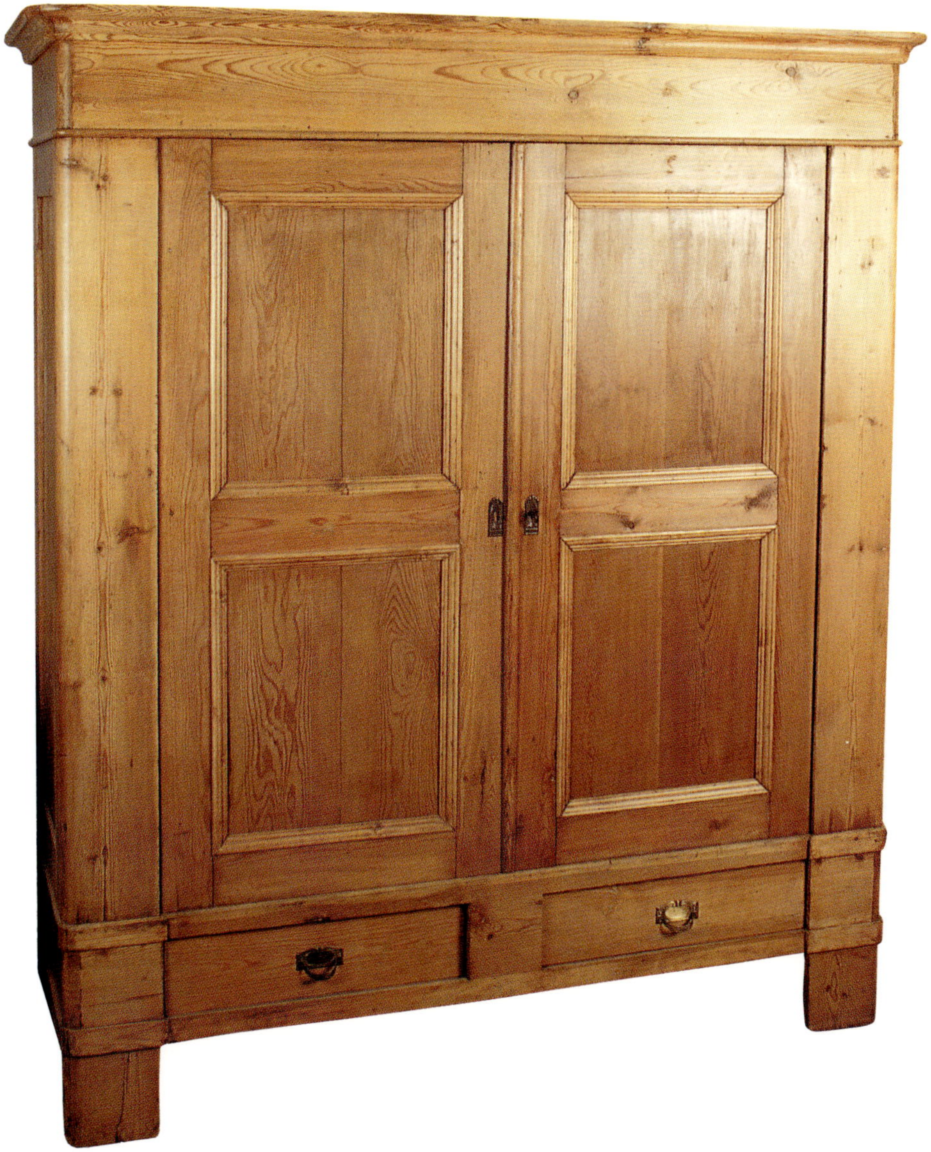

Large German two-door wardrobe with rounded corners. A deep cornice molding is above two double recessed panel doors and two plain drawers in the base on straight bracket feet. $2995.

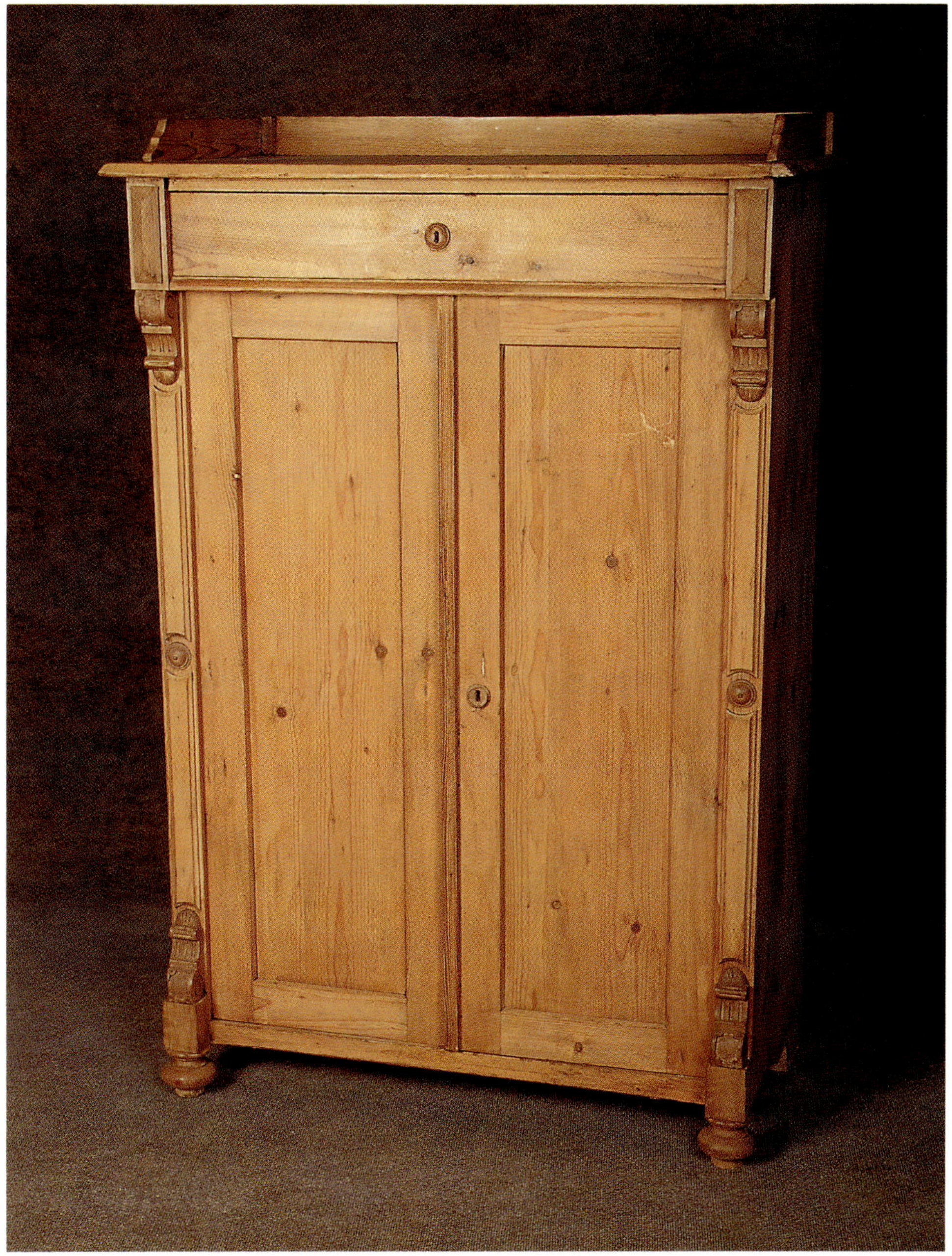

Straight cabinet with rectangular top, raised back, and side pieces, single top drawer, and two tall, recessed paneled doors flanked by decorated stiles, Renaissance Revival style. $1095.

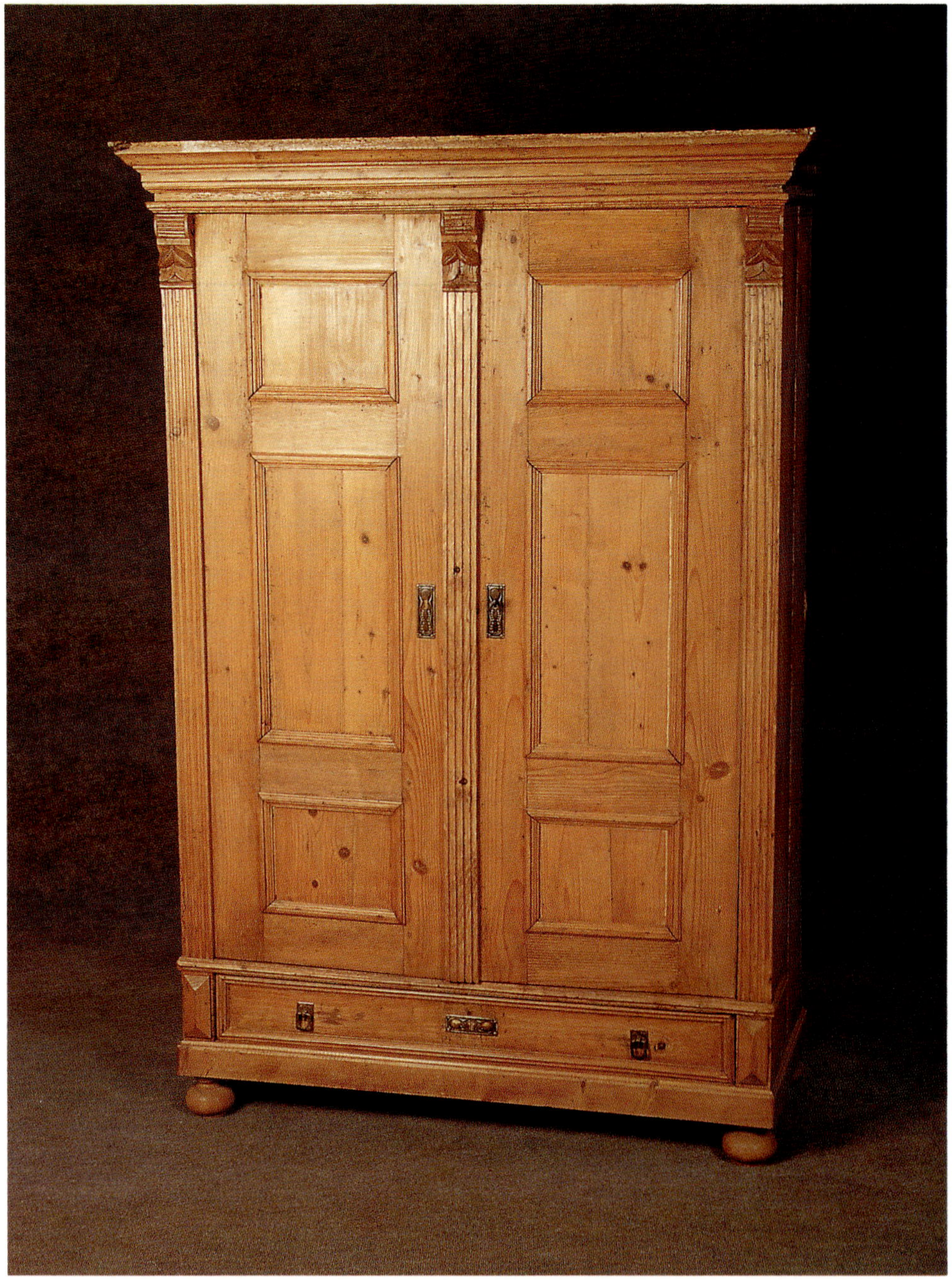

One-piece pine wardrobe with molded cornice overhanging two doors each with three recessed panels, the stiles and between the doors are fluted with carved cornice volutes. The base has a single drawer with metal escutcheon and pulls, all resting on a molded base and bun feet, Renaissance Revival style. $1095.

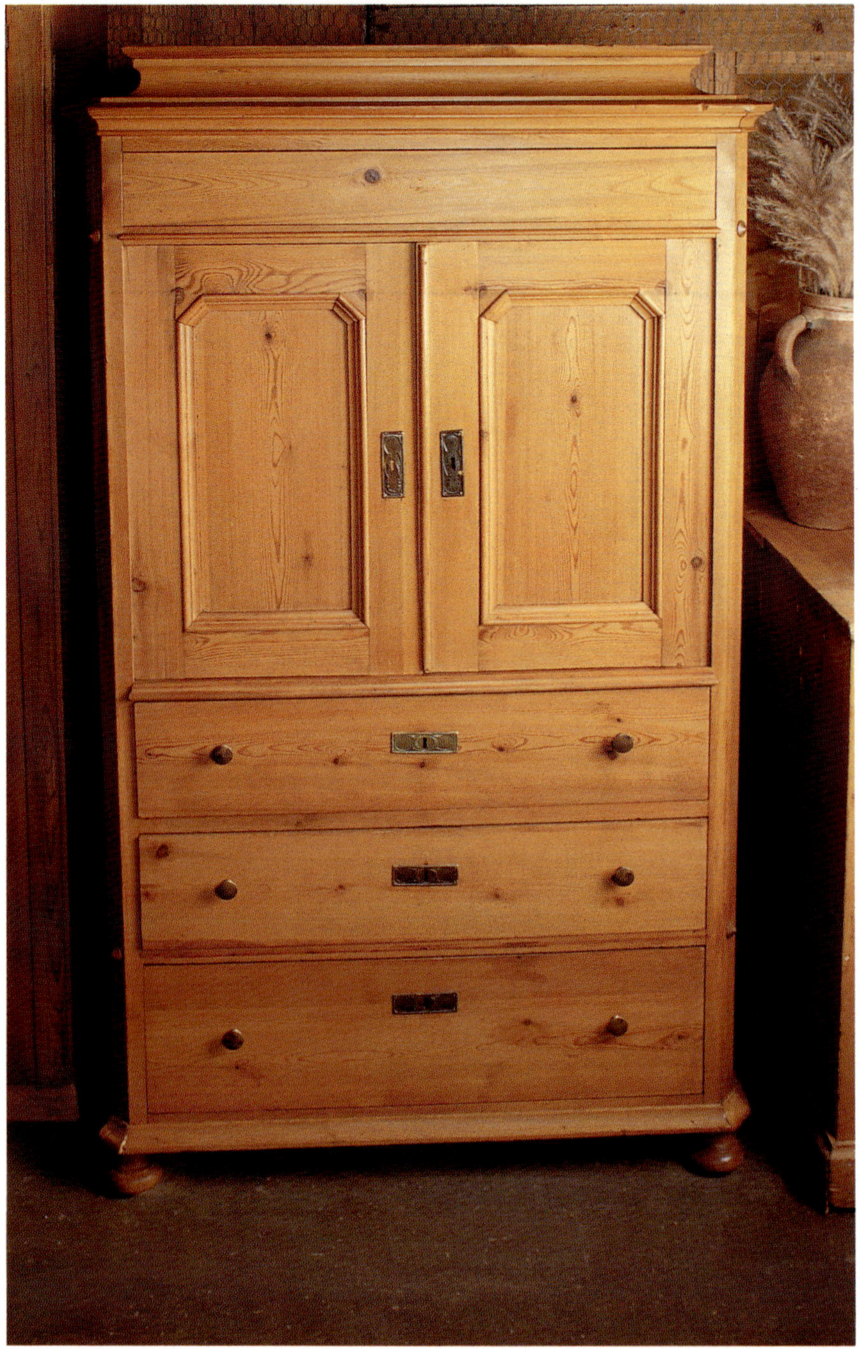

Two-door cabinet with raised molding on the top and a complex cornice over canted corners with applied turnings, deep frieze, and two recessed paneled doors with cut upper corners and three long drawers and bun feet. $2495.

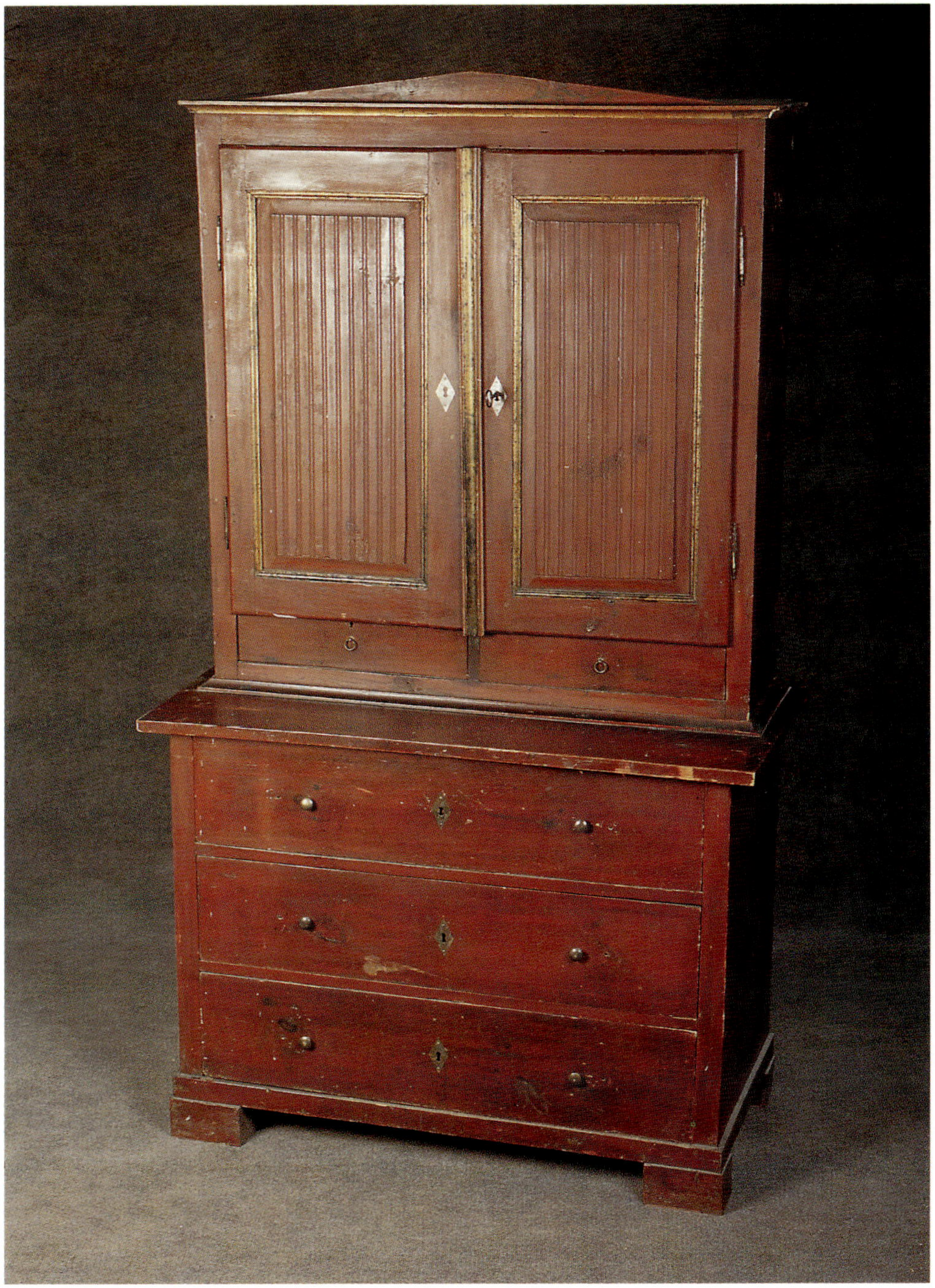

German painted cabinet with a two-part top with peaked crest over two recessed and ribbed paneled doors and three drawers. $3695.

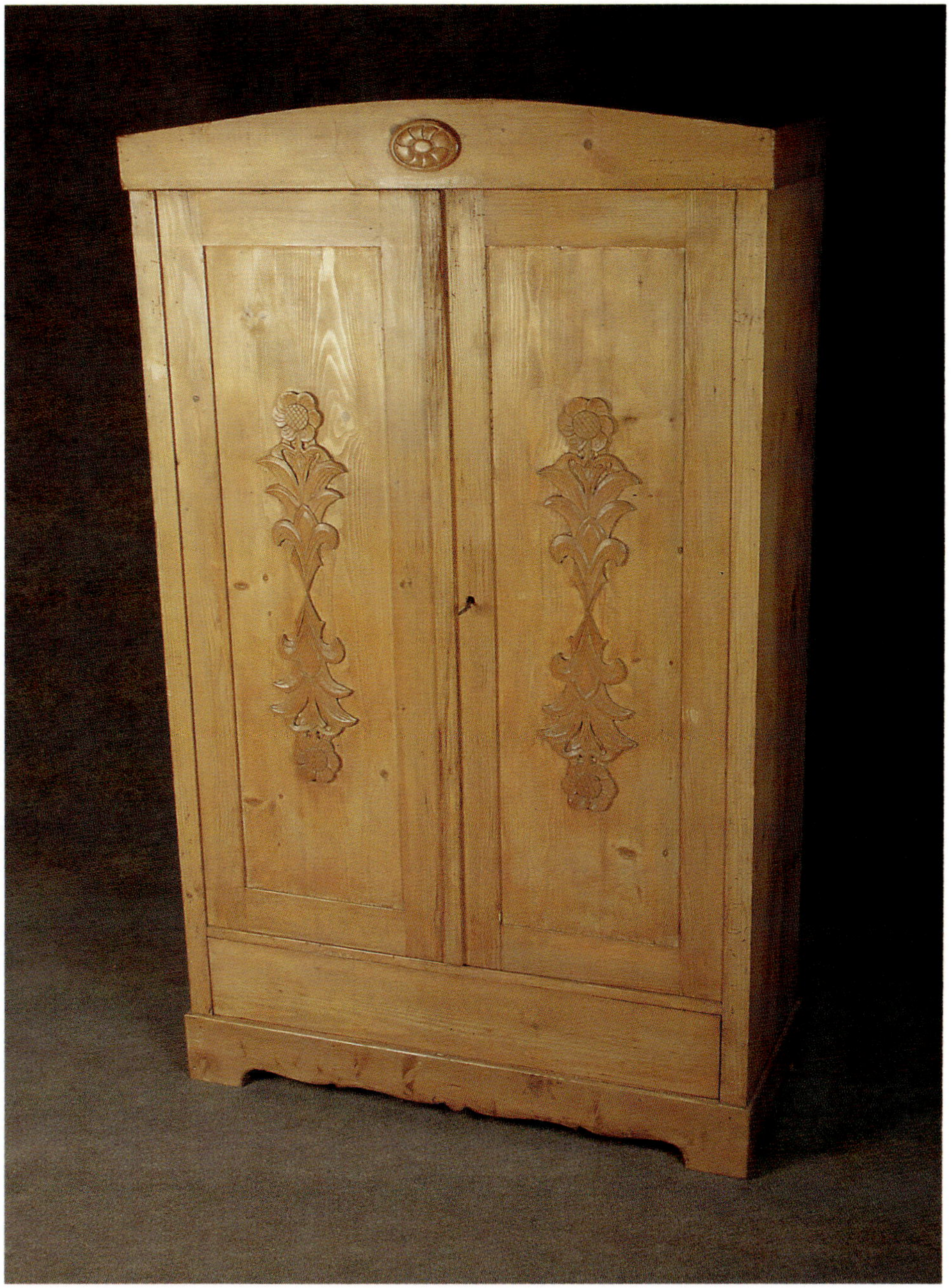

Pine wardrobe with a gently arched cornice with applied oval carving over the case with two recess-paneled doors with floral relief carved decoration. The base has a single drawer above the scalloped base. $995.

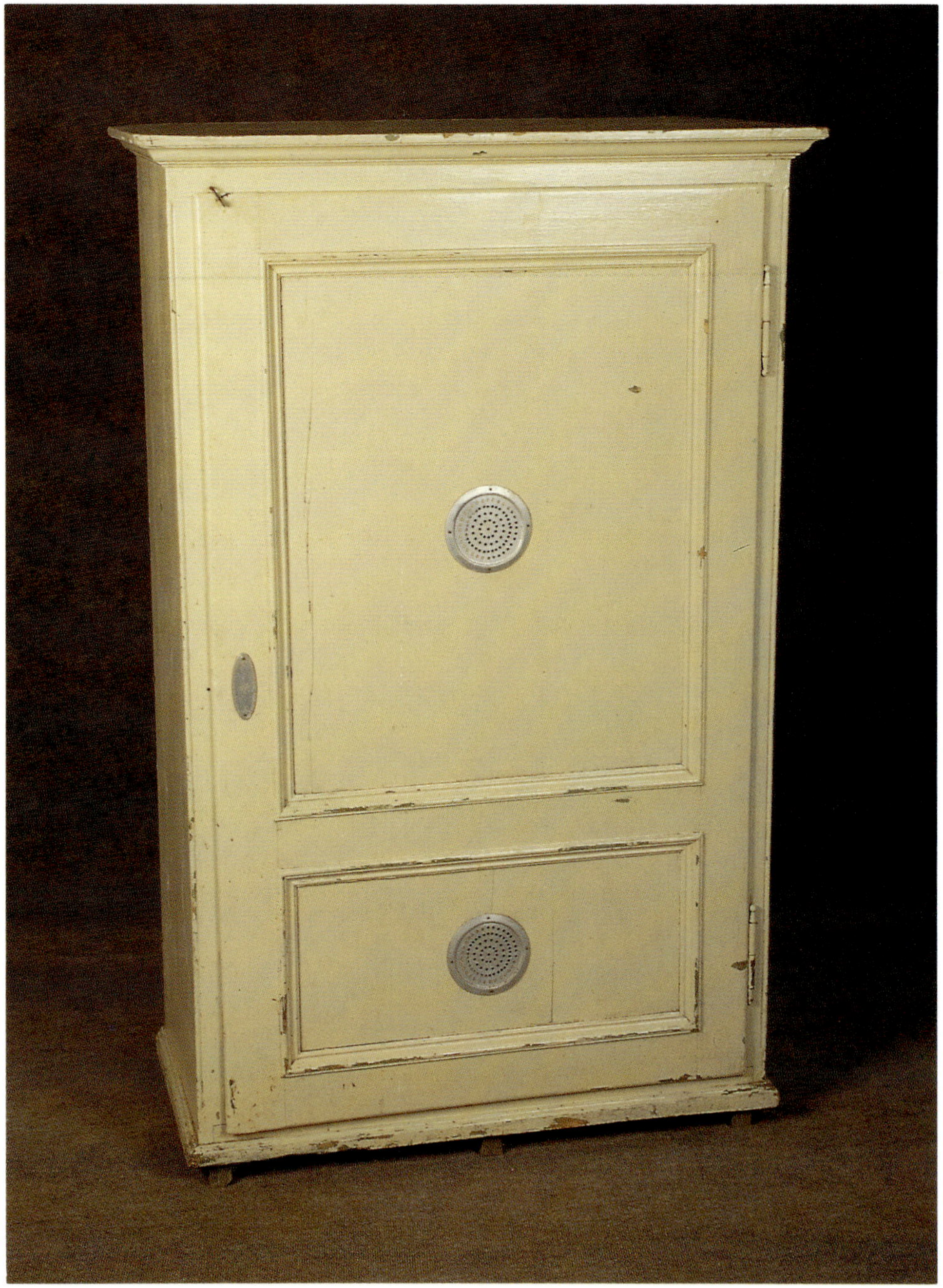

White painted "spice cabinet" with three shelves and four drawers inside, door with two pierced round metal inserts, on a base molding and block feet. $795.

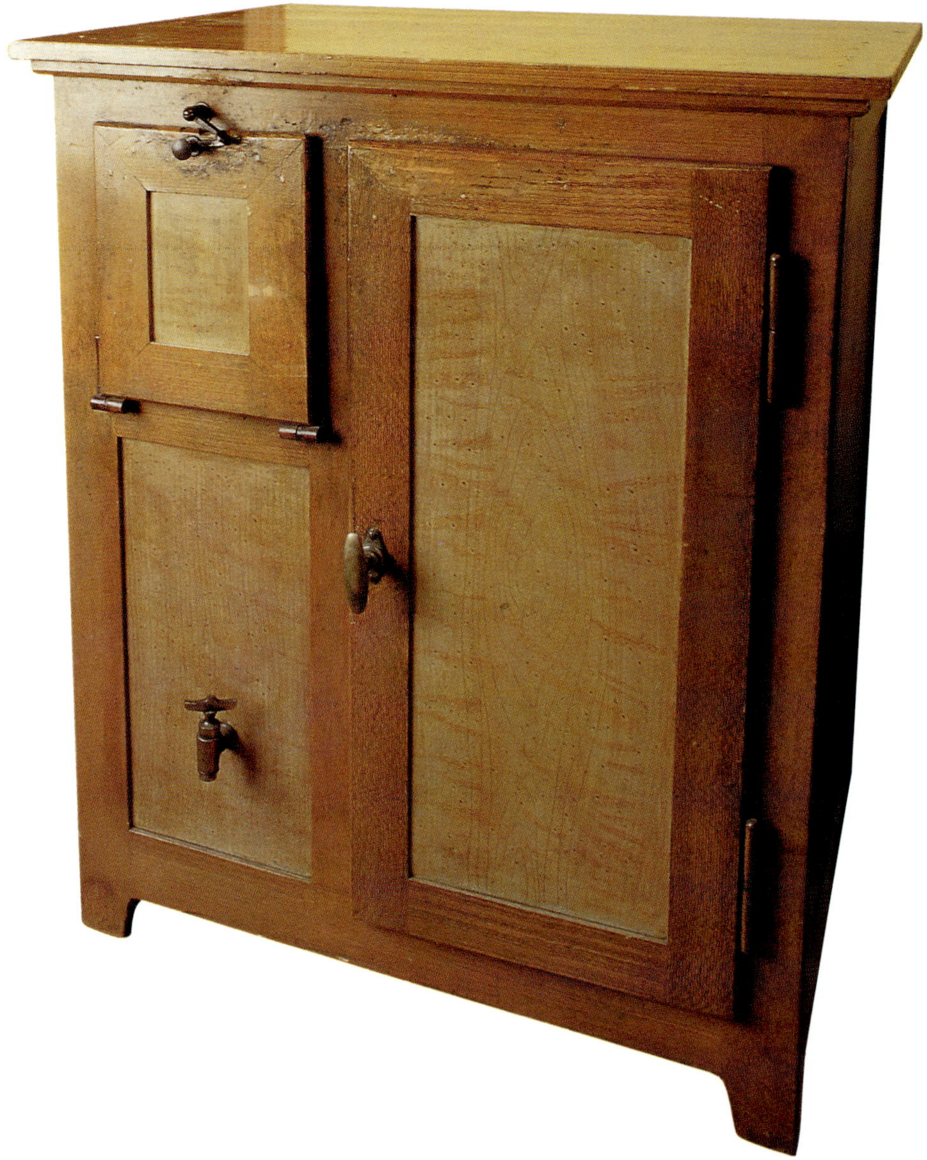

German ice box with grain painting. $1250.

Three-door Cabinet

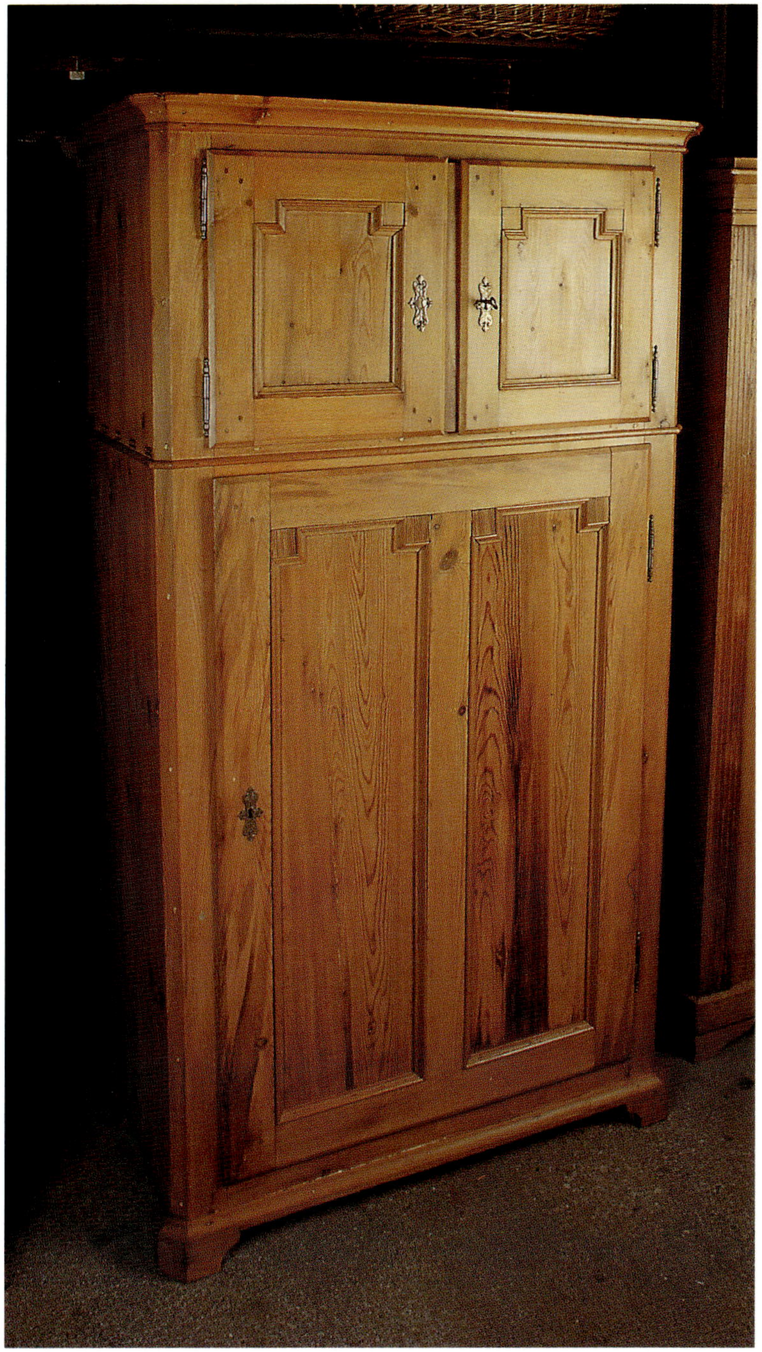

Danish cabinet with straight cornice over the case with canted corners and two small over one long rectangular paneled doors and bracket feet. $2495.

Four-door Cabinets

Two-part painted wardrobe with a straight cornice molding over a deep frieze and two recessed and molded panels enclosing shelves. The separate base section has two drawers with metal pull plates over two doors matching those of the top section. The stiles on both parts are canted and the straight base rests on straight feet. $1295.

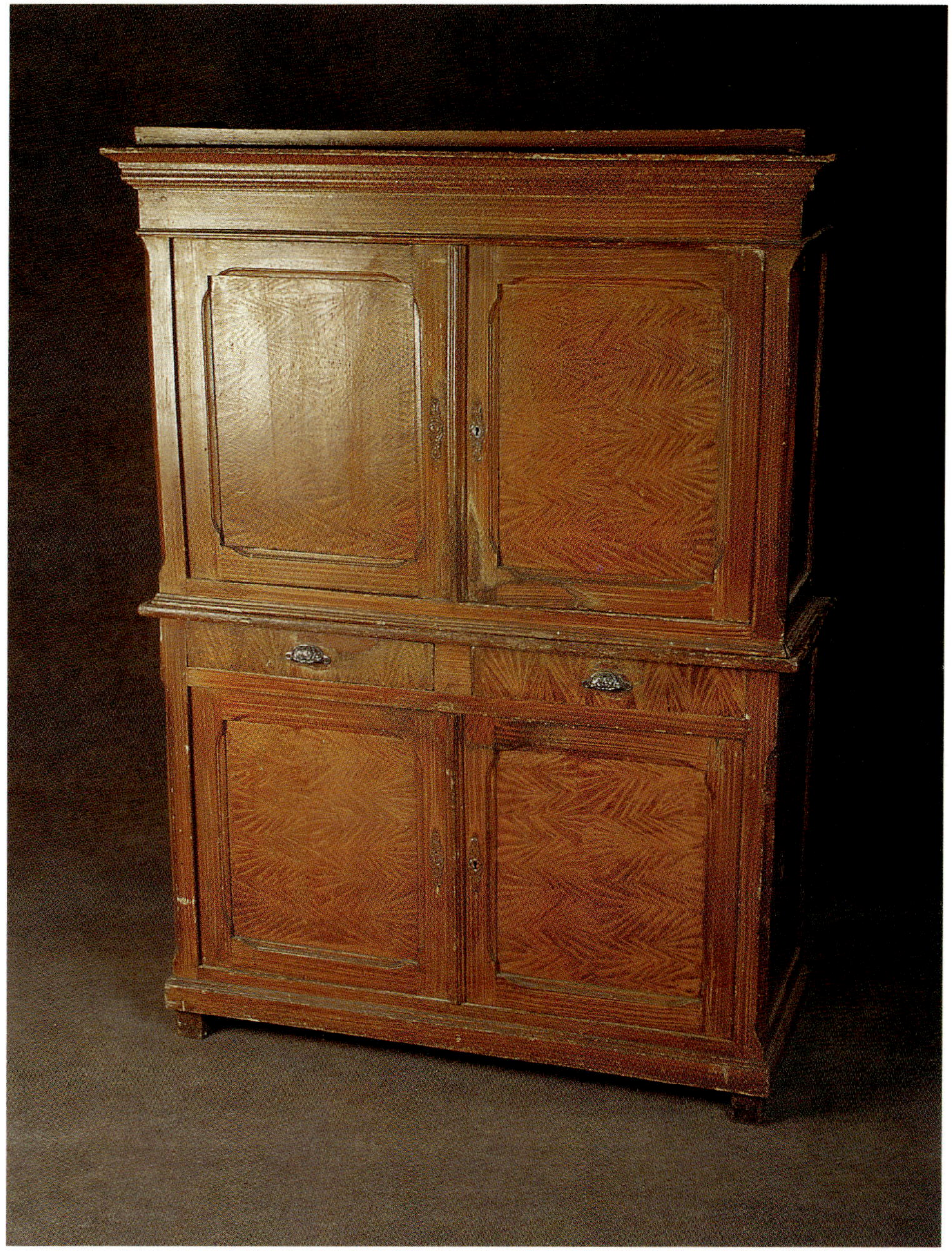

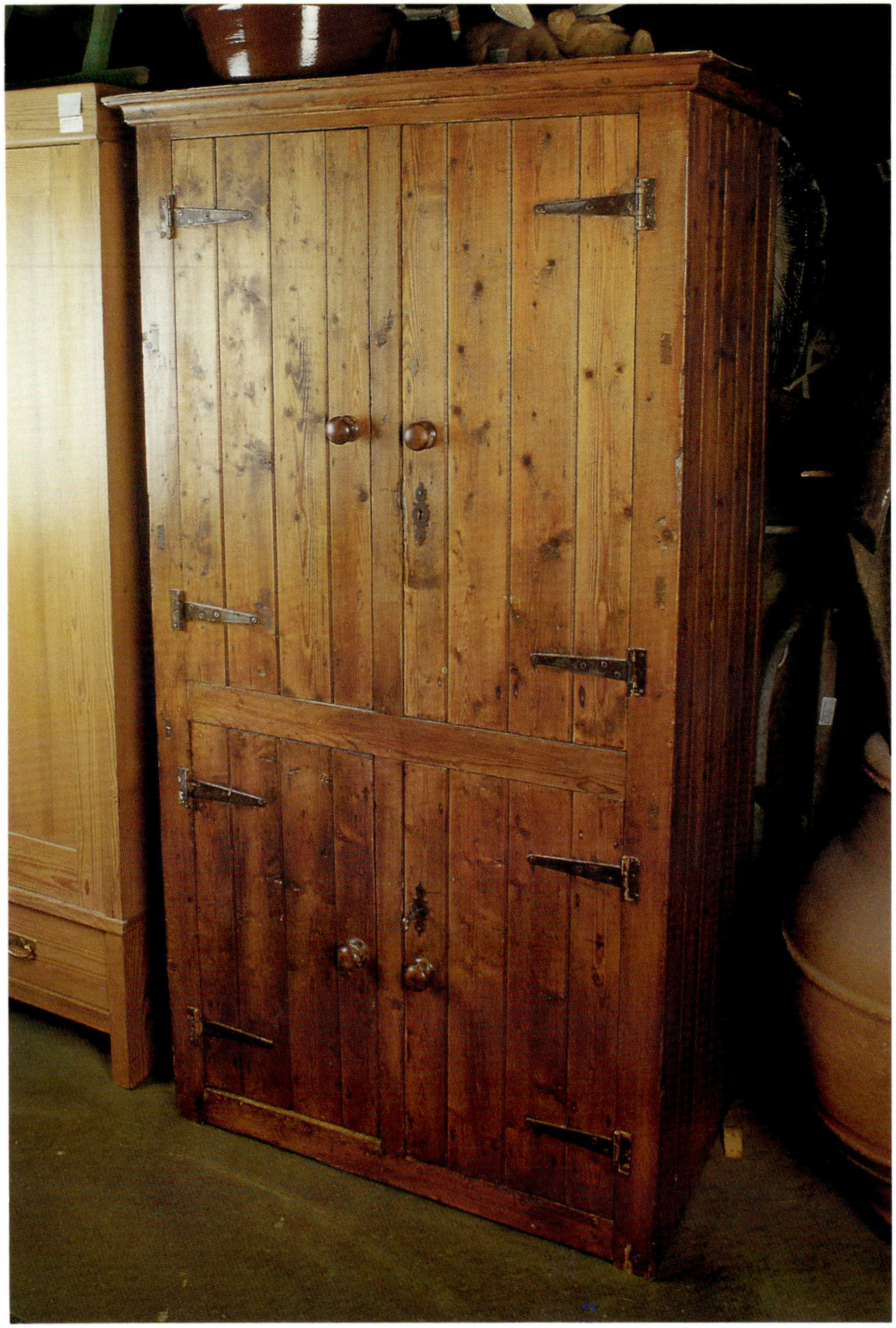

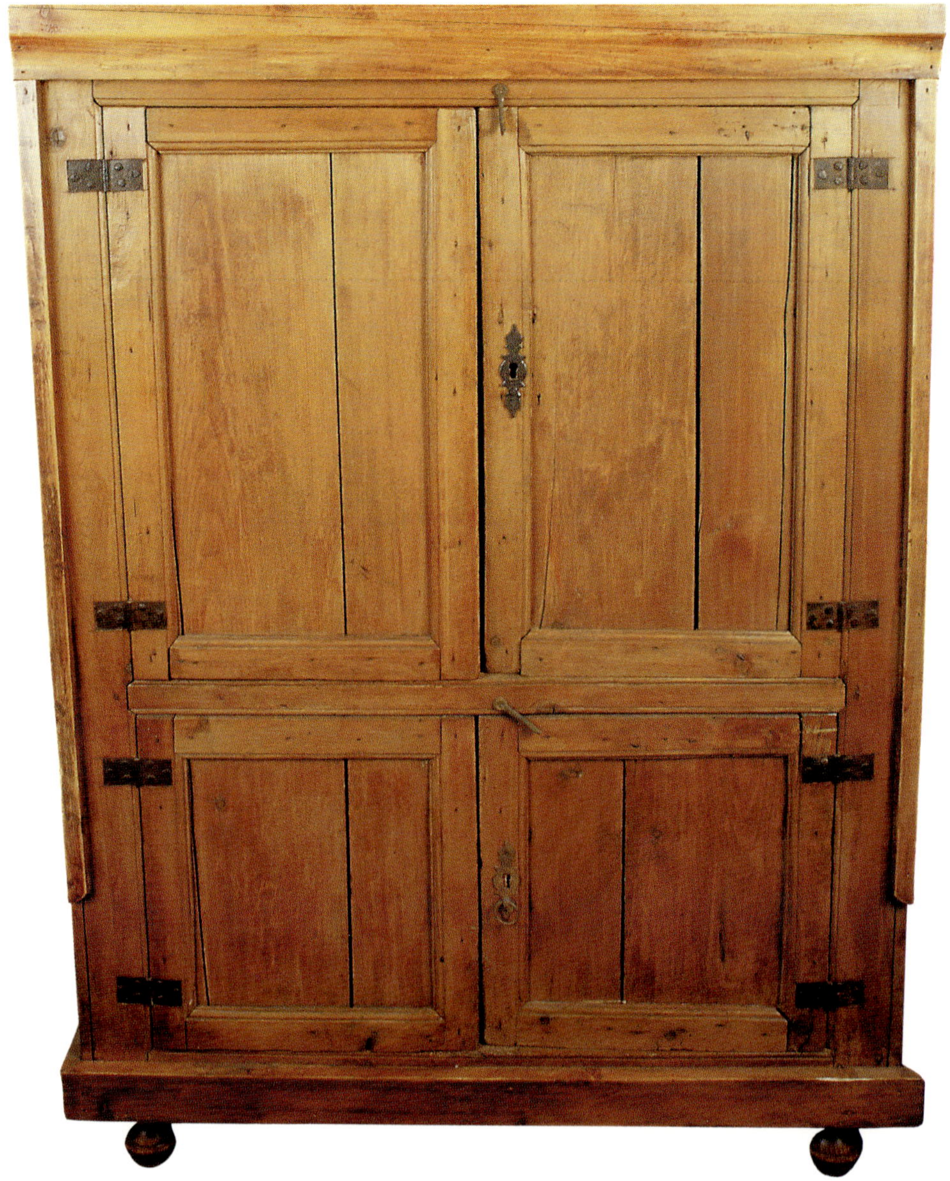

Irish four-door cabinet with straight cornice molding and four rectangular panel doors with iron hinges and escutcheons, resting on a base molding and bun feet. $795.

Four-door cabinet of multi-board construction, with long iron hinges, wooden knob pulls, and the stiles continuing to the floor.

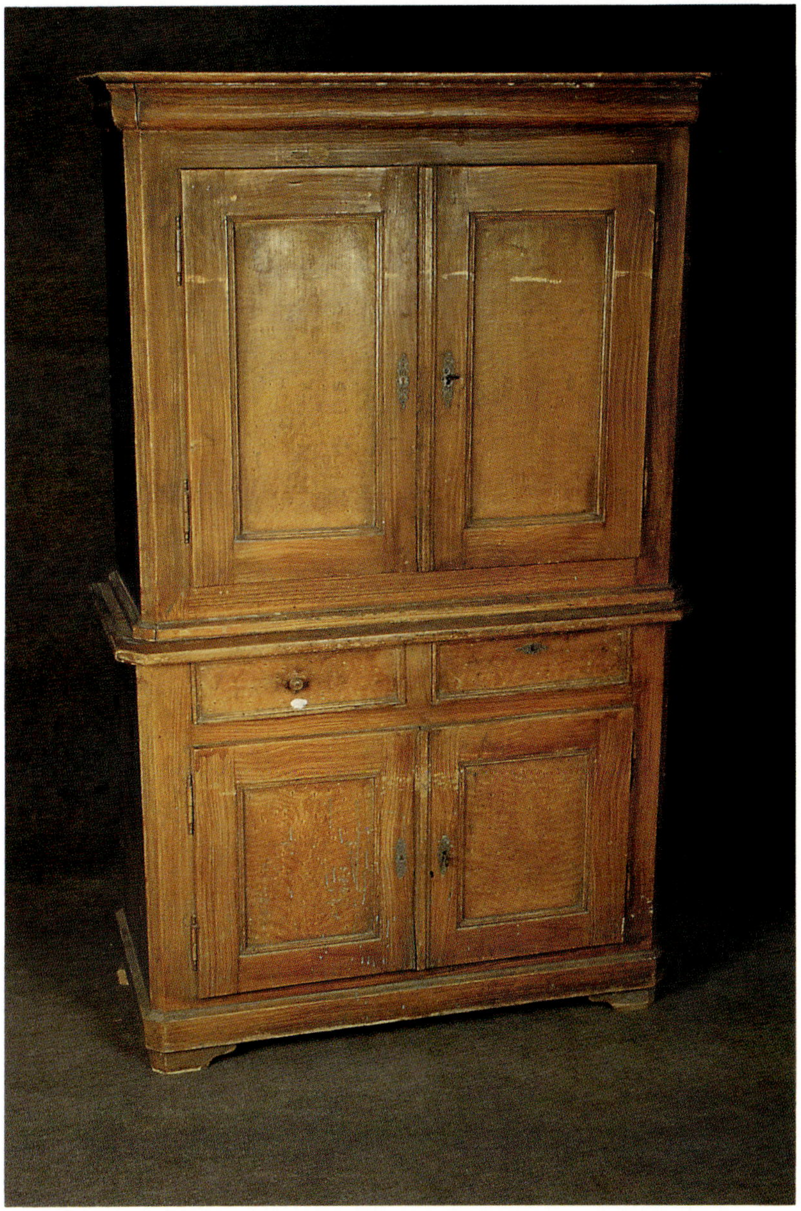

Two-part, French cabinet, c.1875, with original brown grain painted surface. The upper section with a scroll molding and canted corners above two recessed paneled doors. The base section extends beyond the top and has two drawers above two recessed paneled doors, a base molding, and shaped bracket feet. $1895.

Six-door Cabinet

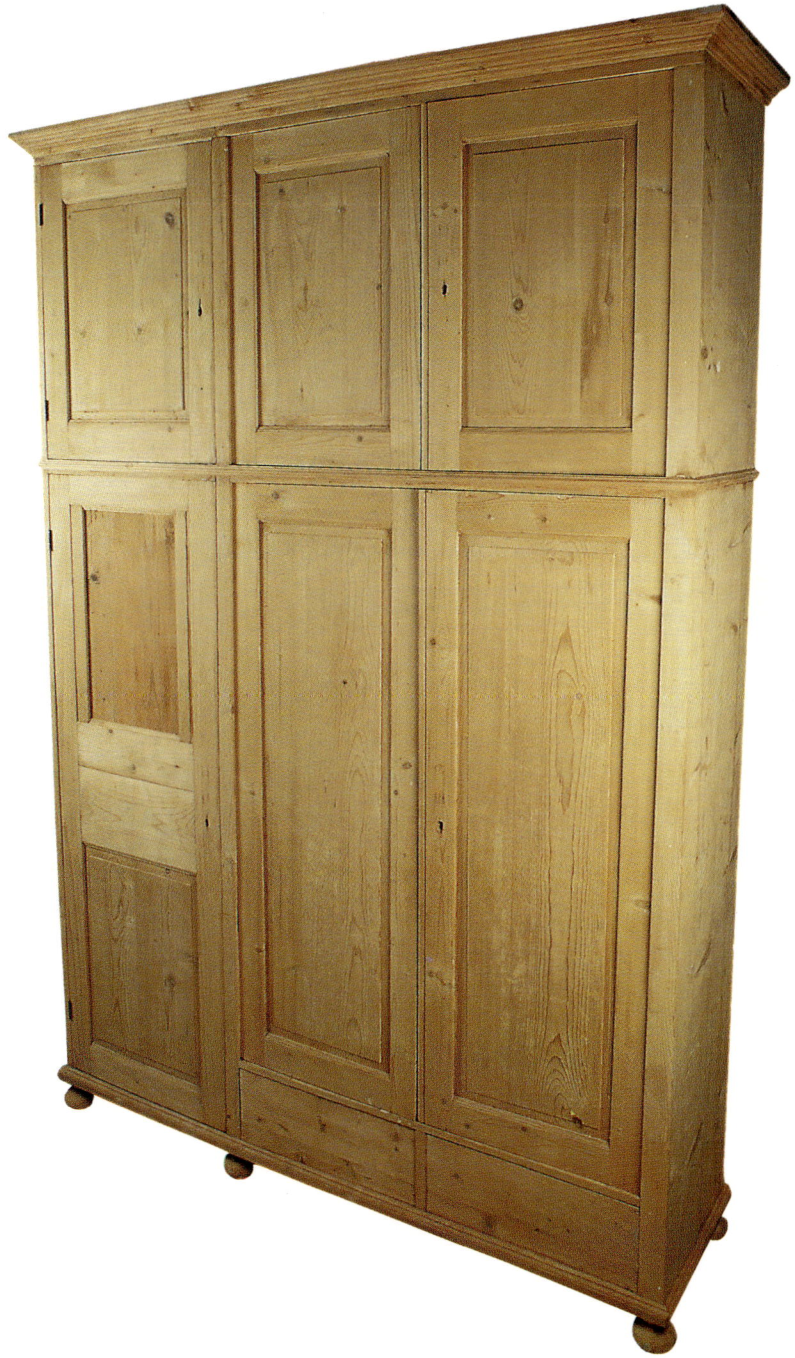

Large, one piece, pine wardrobe with an upper section of three paneled doors over a lower section of three doors of non-matching design, enclosing shelves. The big case rests on bun feet. $5495.

Glass-door Cabinets

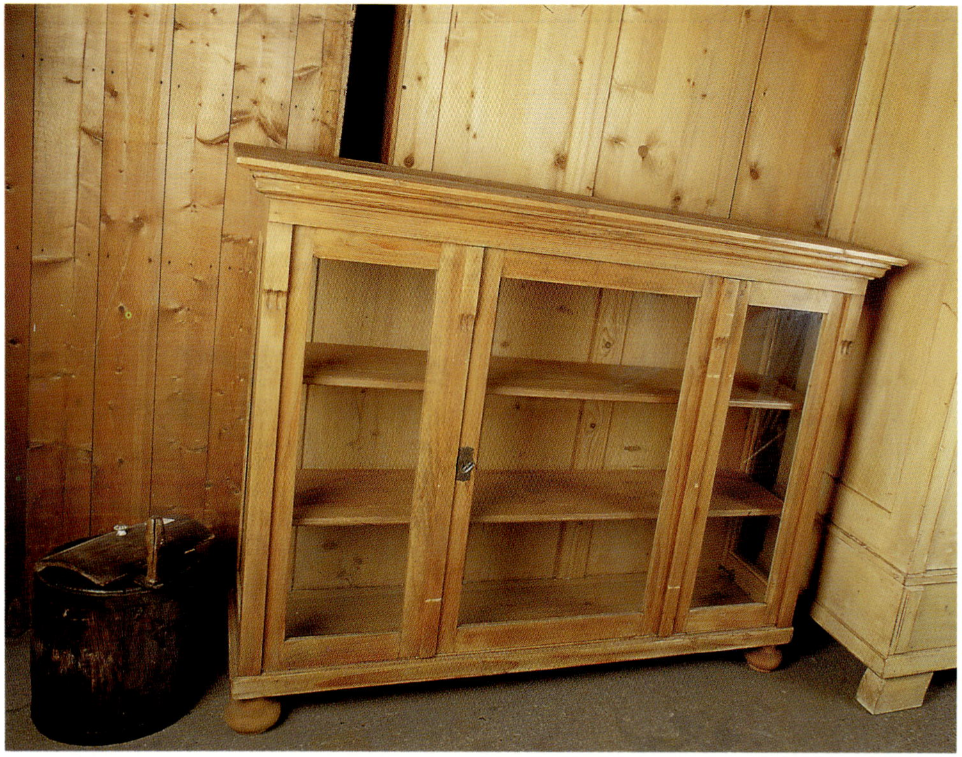

Pine bookcase/cabinet with straight top and cornice molding and shaped stiles over a case with glass sides and front panels enclosing three shelves. The base molding rests on bun feet.

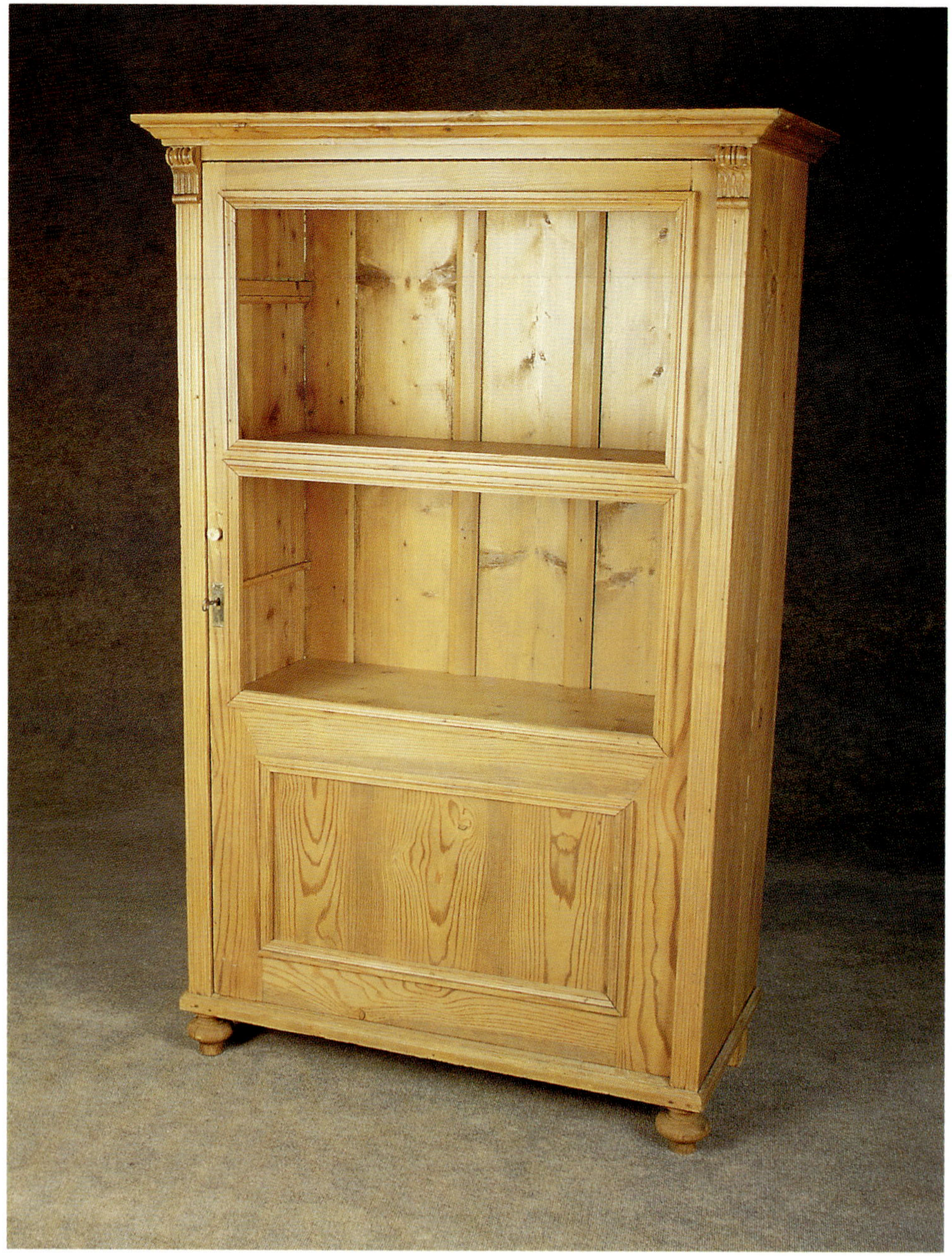

Pine open cabinet with overhanging molded top, two open shelves, and a paneled door.

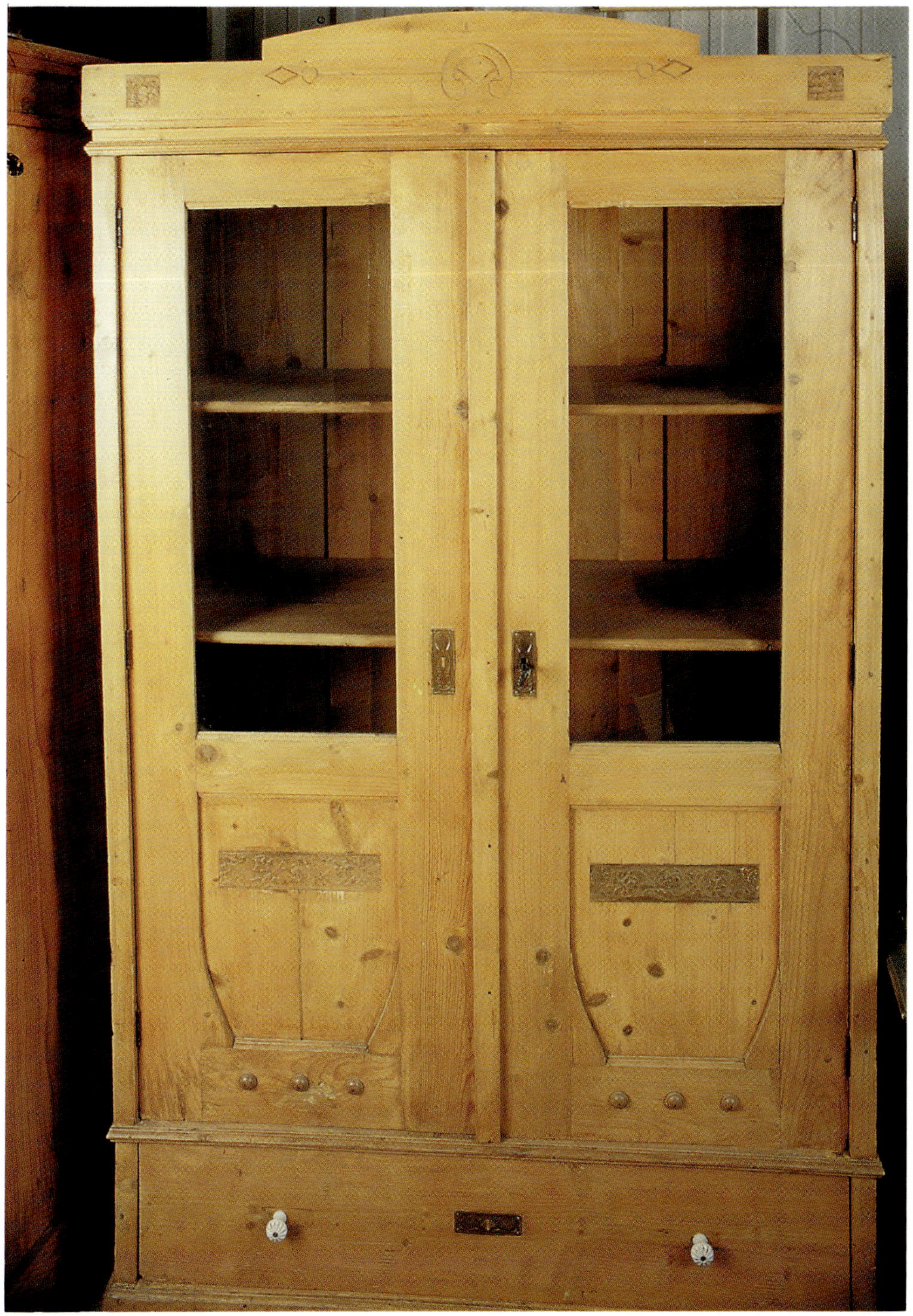

Hungarian Art Nouveau cabinet with incised arched pediment and two carved rectangles over two glazed doors with applied carving below. The base has a single drawer with two white porcelain knobs and a metal escutcheon. The base molding rests on bun feet. $1185.

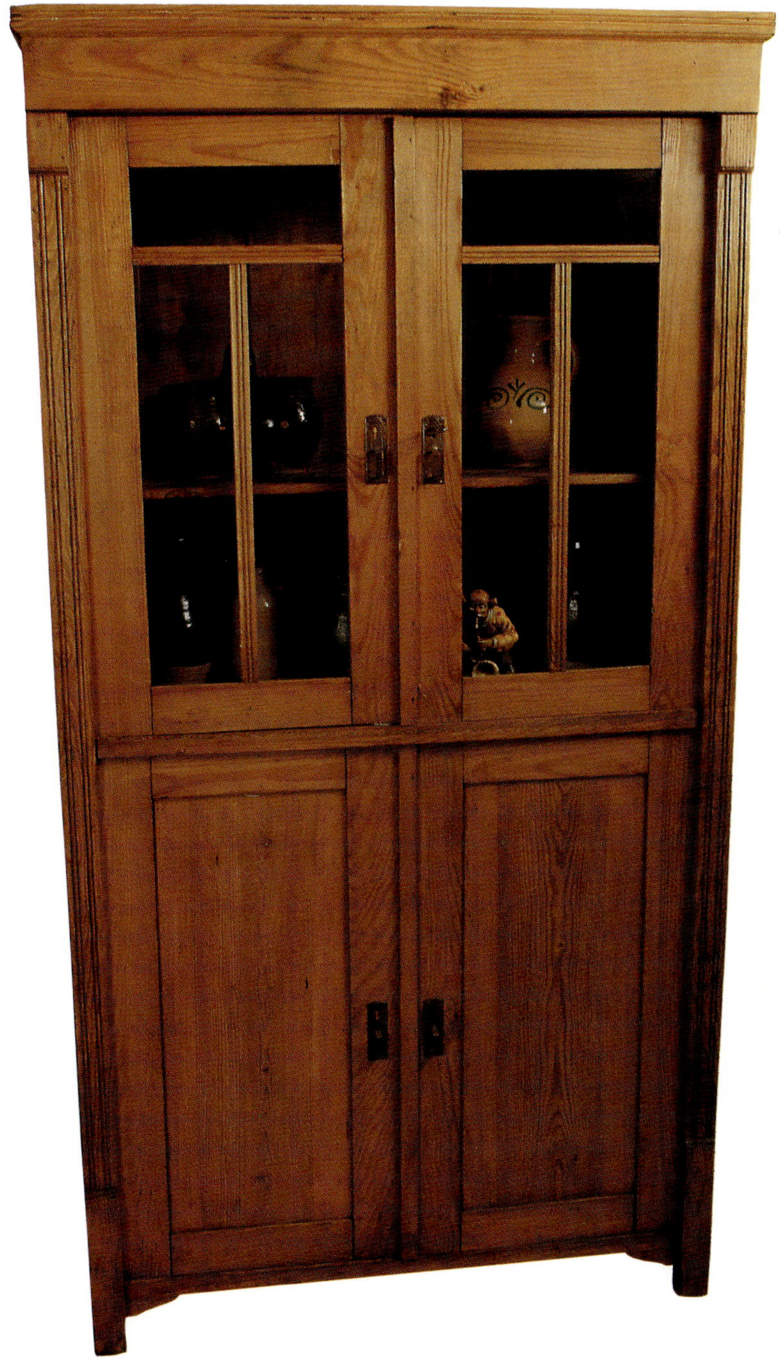

German flat cabinet with straight cornice and two glass paned doors over two recessed paneled doors. The stiles are ribbed and continue down to form the feet. $1595.

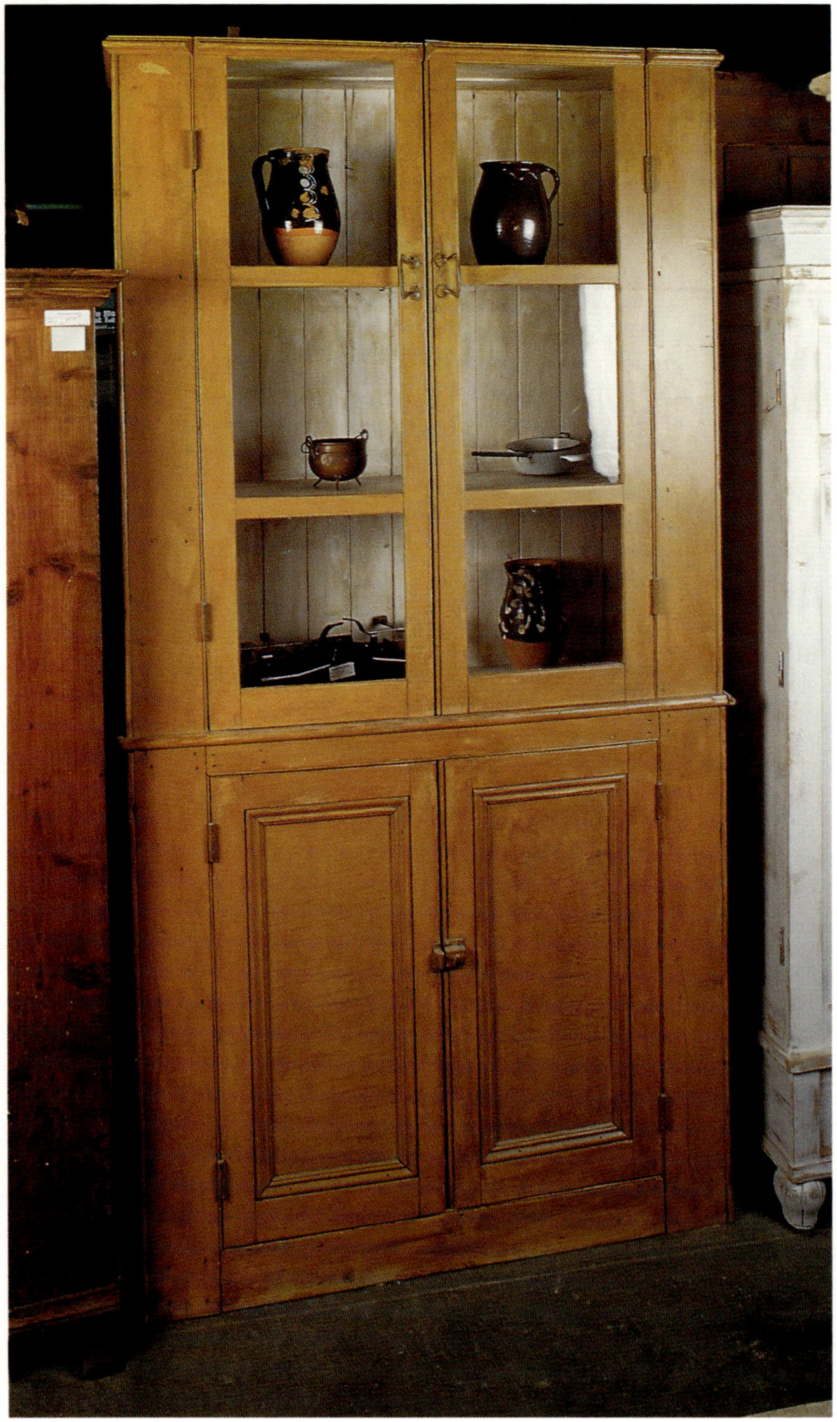

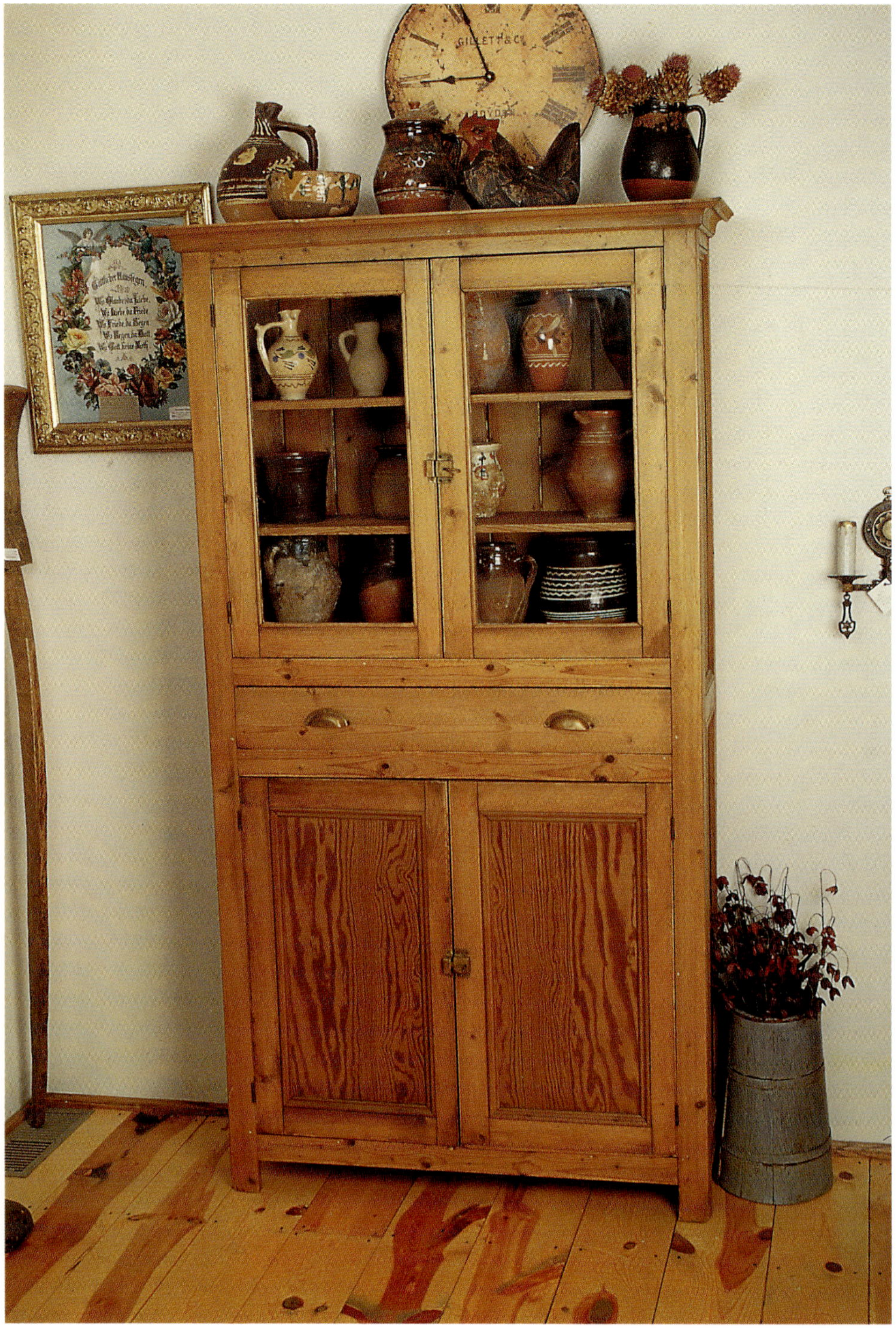

Left: Irish cabinet painted yellow with thin straight cornice over two doors with three glass panes in each, enclosing shelves. The lower cabinet has two recessed paneled doors on a straight base molding. $1395.

Right:
Irish glass display cabinet, c.1880s. $1285.

Cabinets with Shelves

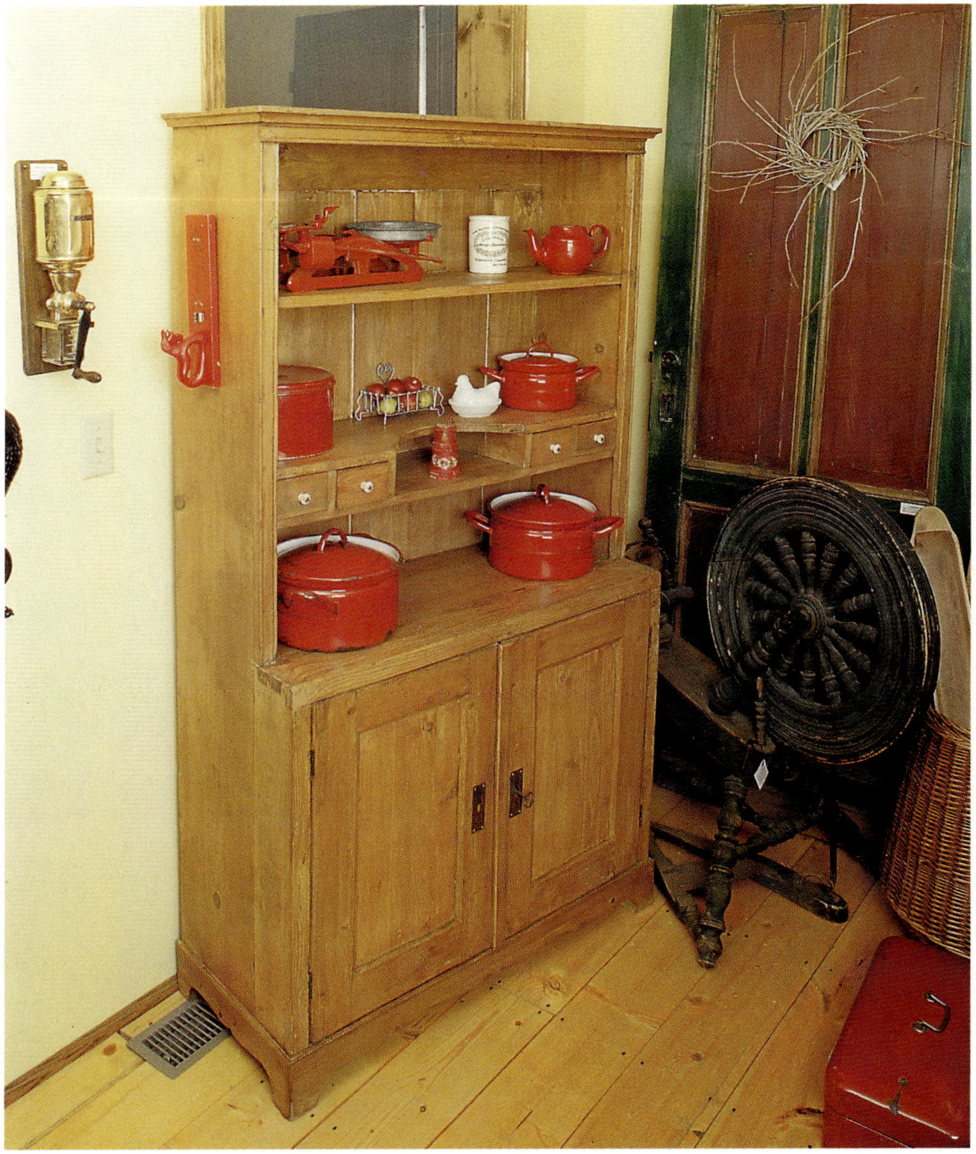

Open cabinet with straight shelf over a shaped shelf and four small drawers with white porcelain knobs. The lower section with two recess paneled door over a scalloped skirt and bracket feet.

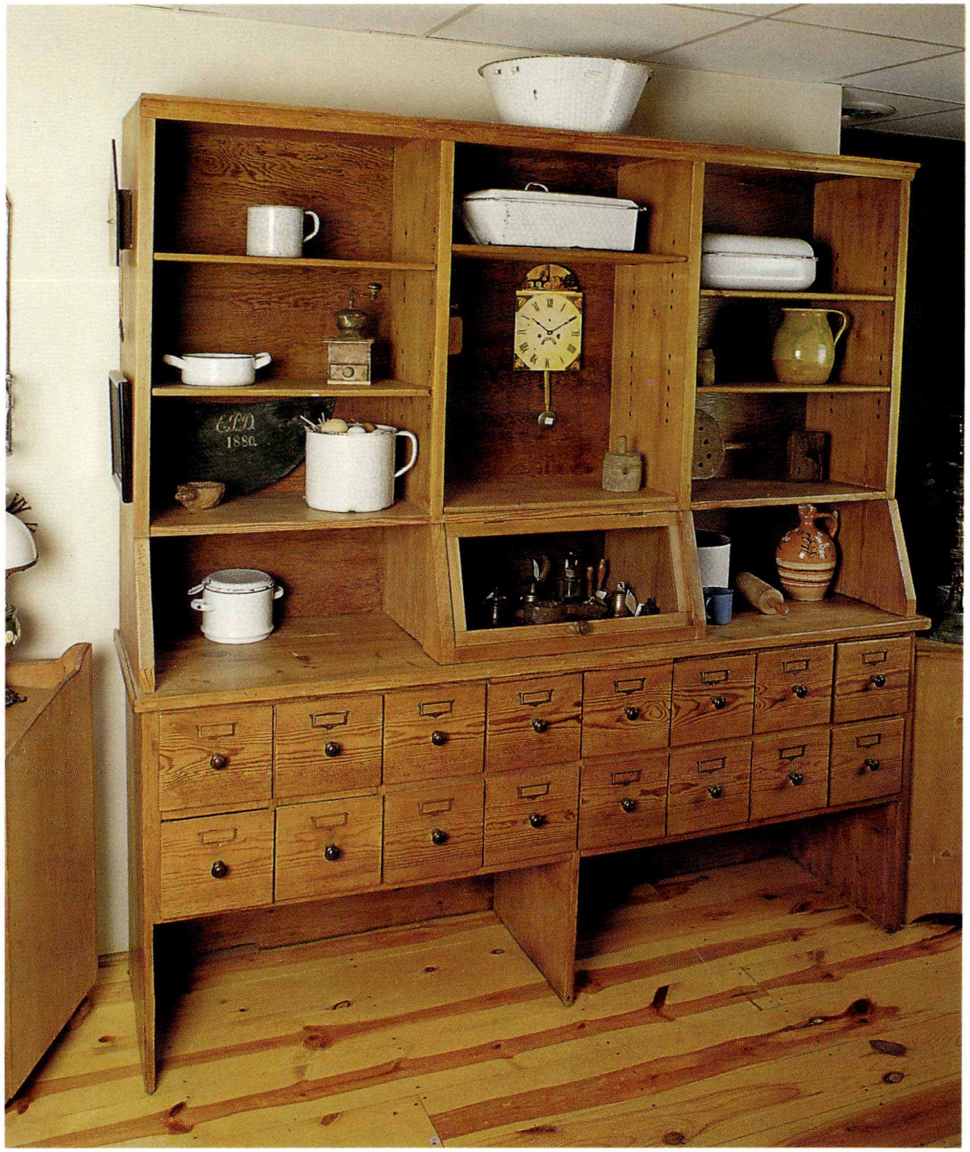

German cabinet for a retail shop with many small compartments in the base and three sections of open shelves in the top. $4295.

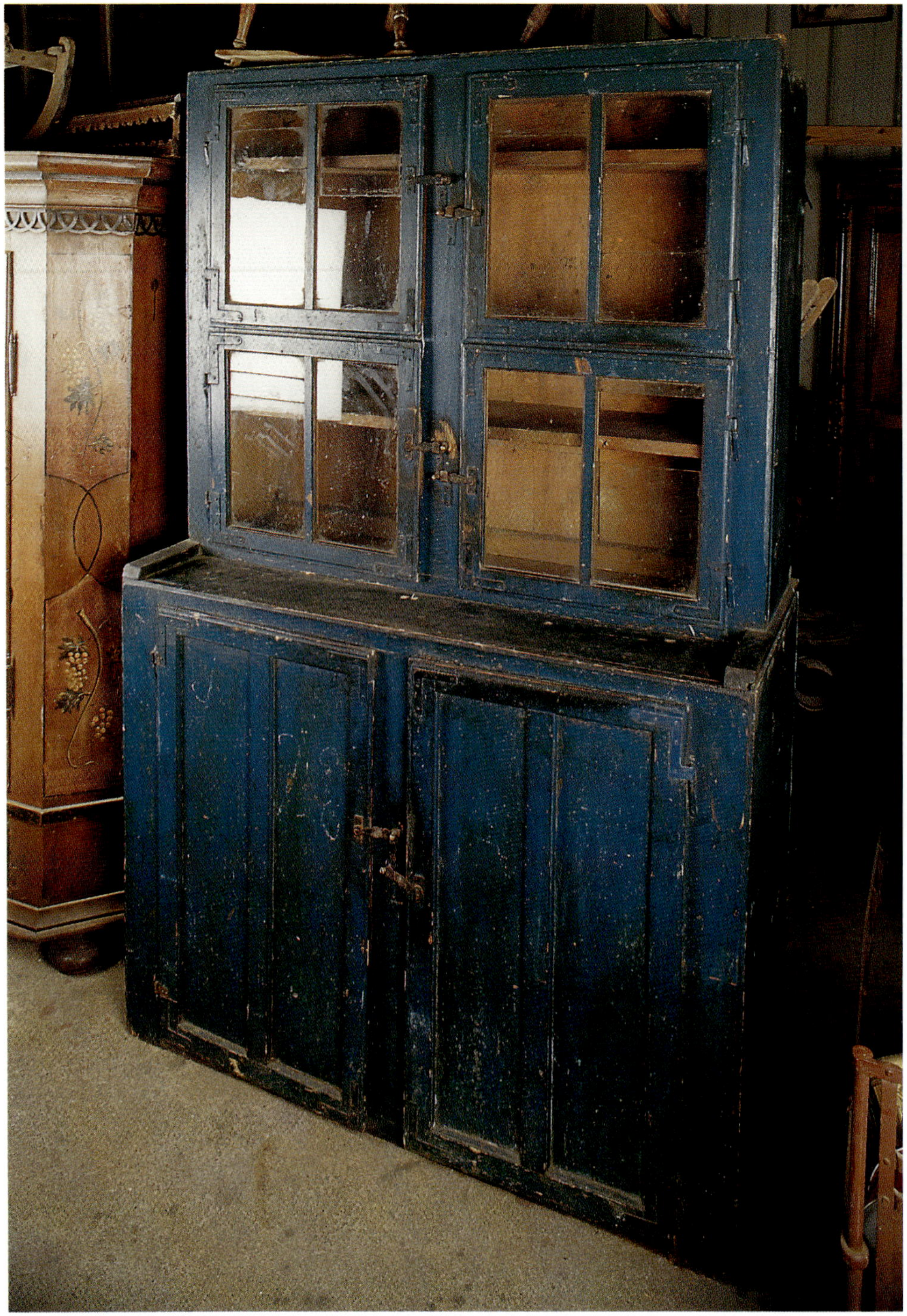

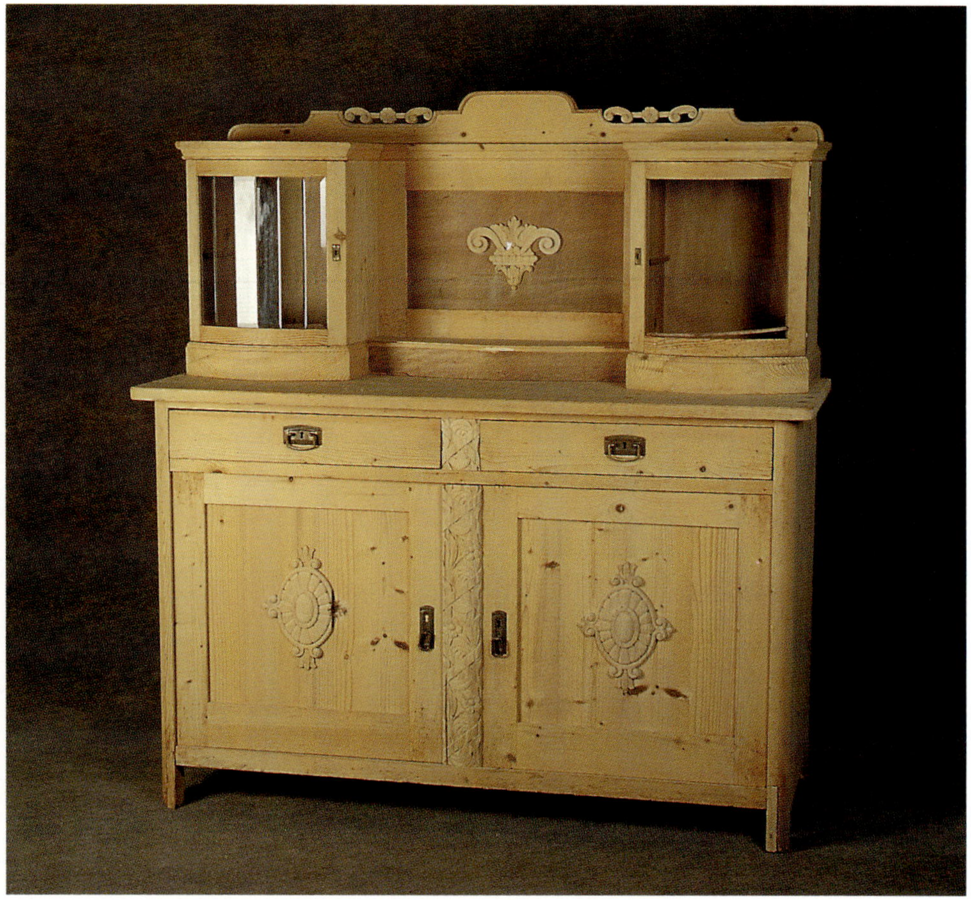

Pine buffet with a shaped crest on the backboard and two attached side cabinets with leaded glass doors glass missing on one side and a central wood panel with applied scroll carving. The projecting lower case has two drawers over two recess paneled doors with applied carved wood cartouche and metal escutcheons. The stiles extend to form the feet.

Two-part Russian painted cabinet with blue paint, a straight cornice over four glazed doors (the glass is pieced) enclosing shelves. The projecting lower case has two paneled doors. There is no base molding, c.1850s. $1695.

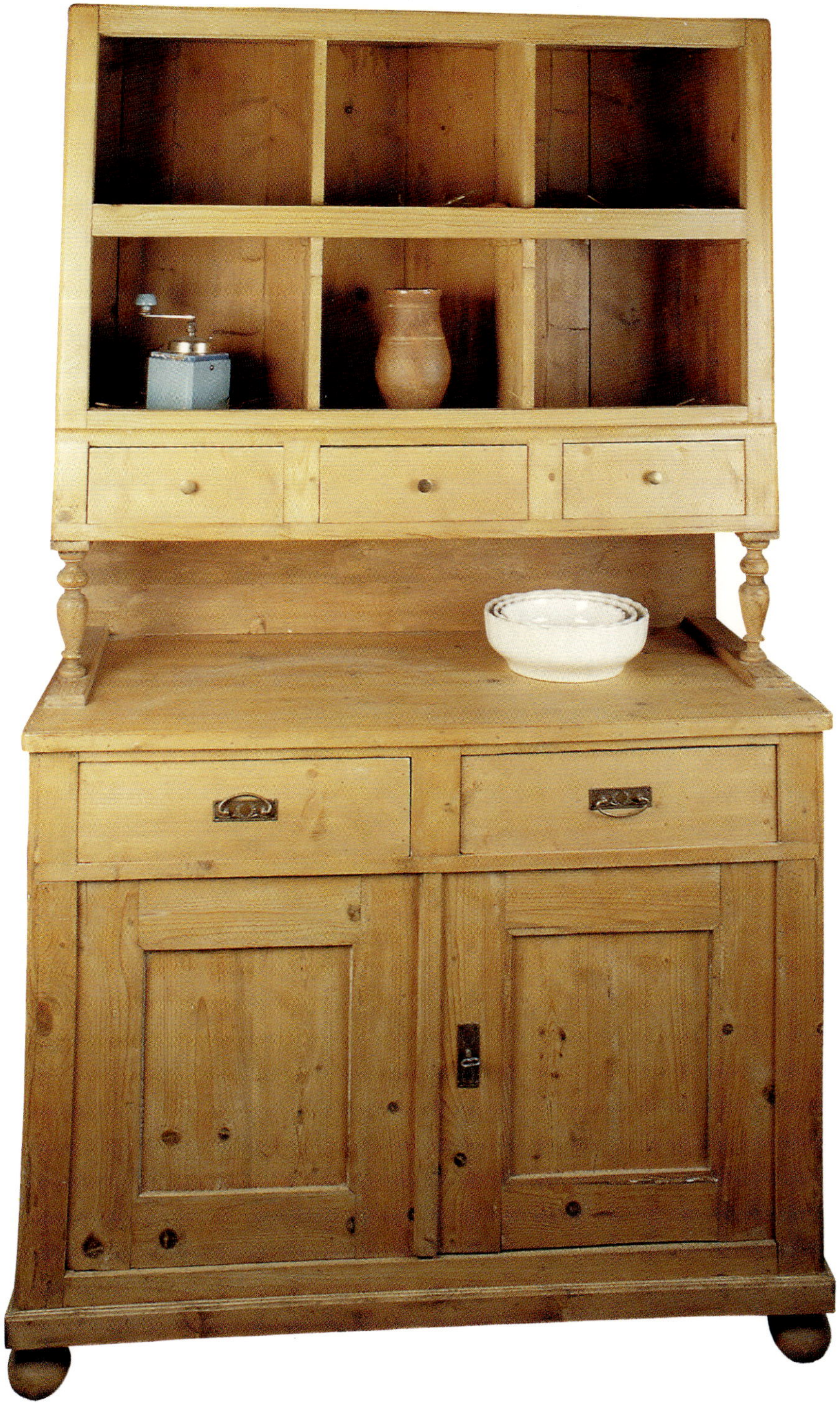

German cabinet with straight cornice over six open shelves and three drawers over an open shelf with two turned supports for the upper section. The base projects with two drawers and two rectangular paneled doors, all resting on a straight base molding and bun feet. $1425.

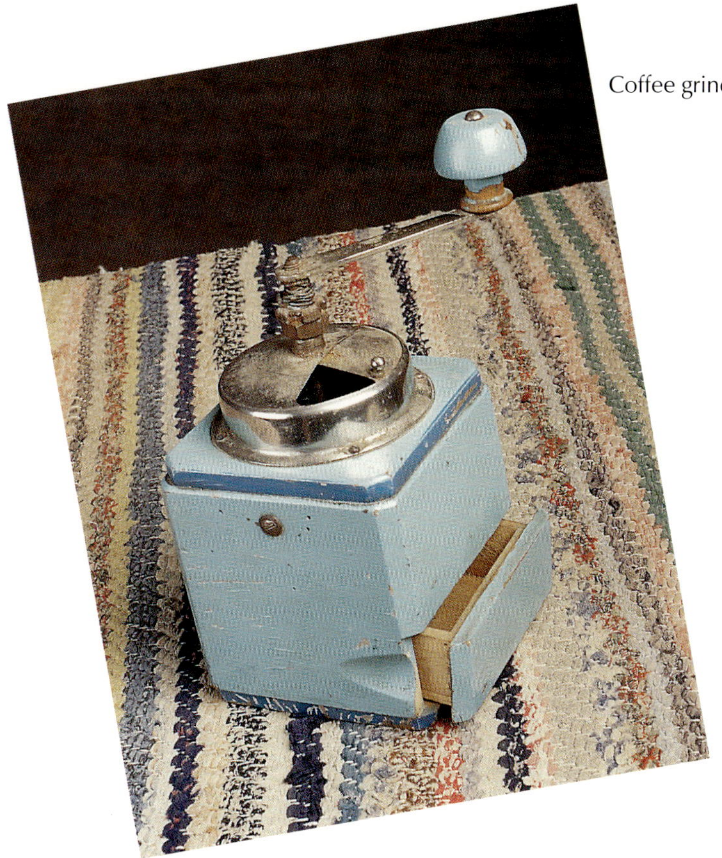

Coffee grinder

Left: Undecorated cabinet with two glazed doors above an open shelf and two drawers above two recessed- panel doors, French, Arts and Crafts style, c.1880.

Right: Two-part French cabinet with a straight cornice over two glazed doors enclosing two shelves and an open shelf with turned front corner supports. The lower case has three drawers with wooden knob pulls over two recessed-panel doors, a straight base molding, and turned front feet.

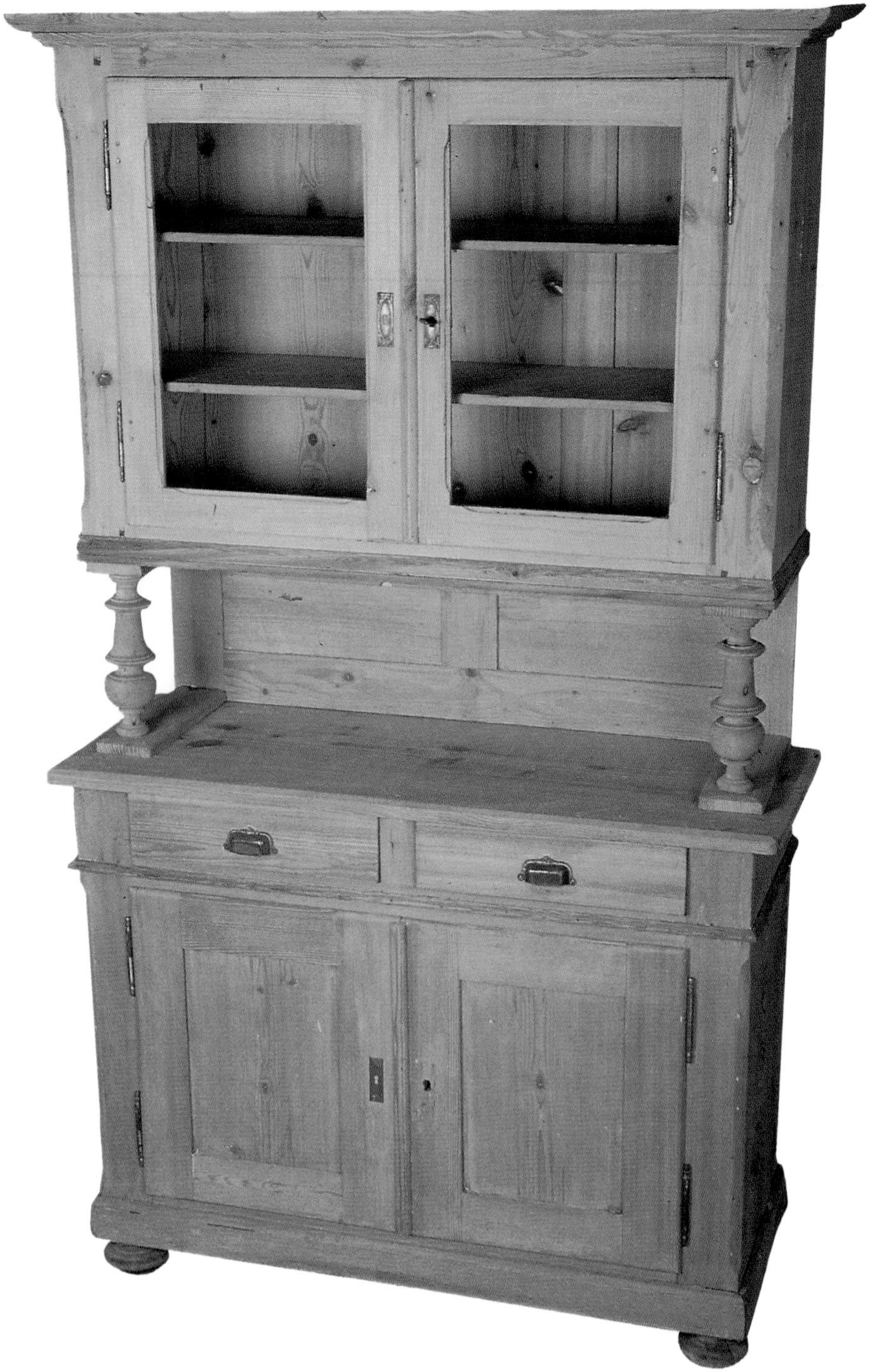

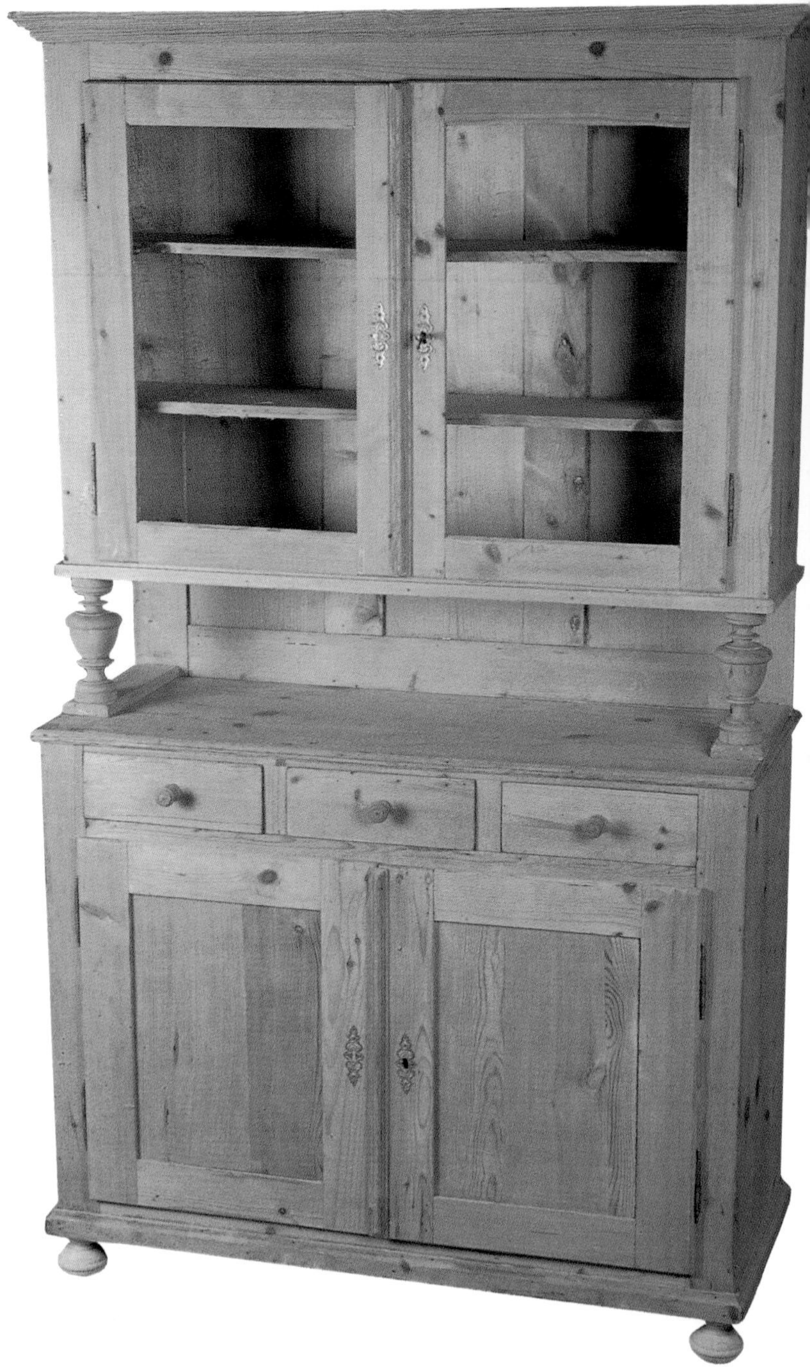

Irish cabinet with tongue and groove joined pine boards, a straight cornice molding, and four doors. $1295.

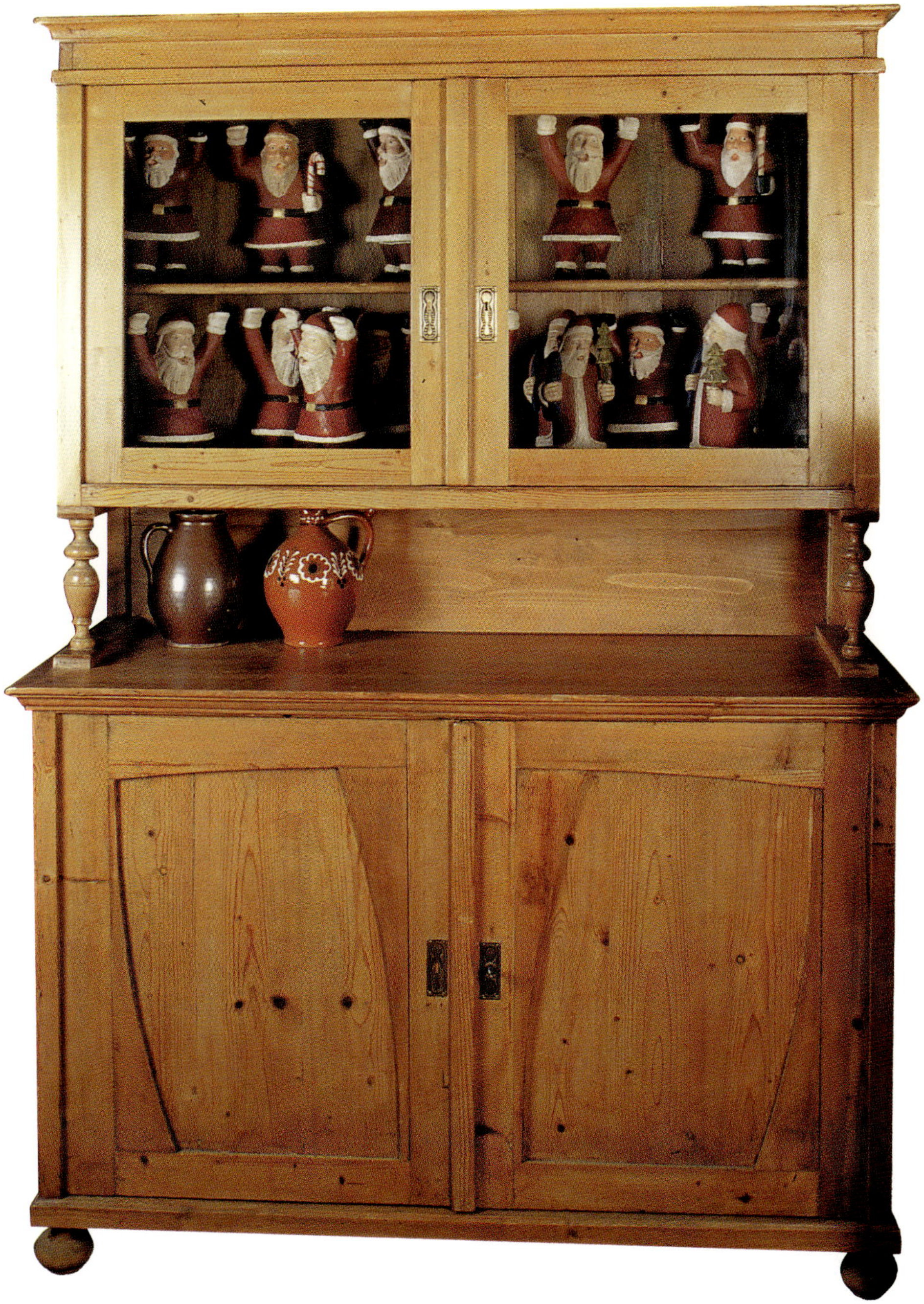

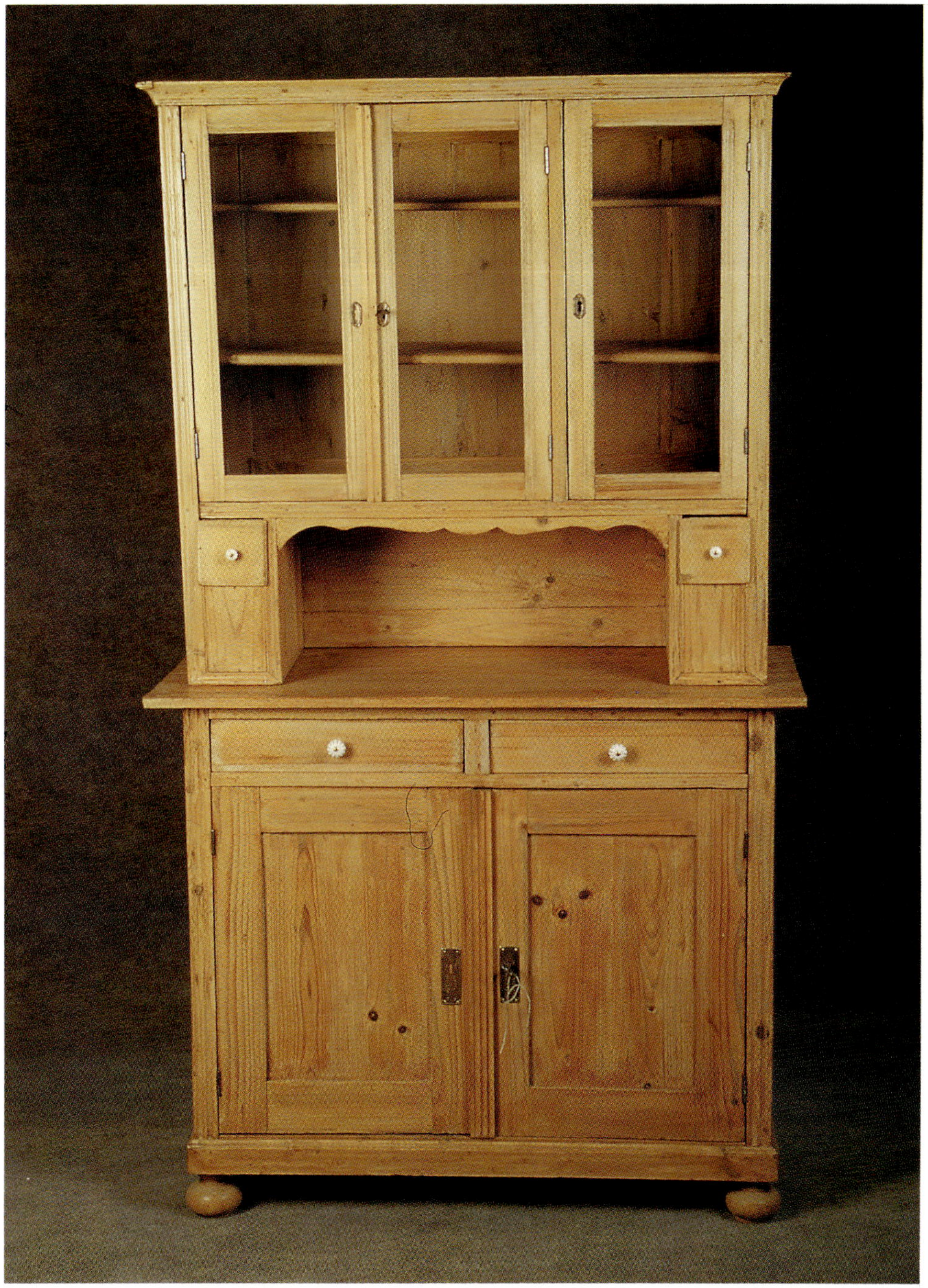

Two-part pine cabinet with a straight cornice molding over three glazed doors enclosing shelves and with two small drawers flanking an open shelf with nicely scalloped flat cornice. The lower cabinet has two drawers with white porcelain pulls over two paneled doors with metal escutcheons, all resting on a straight base molding and four bun feet. $1195.

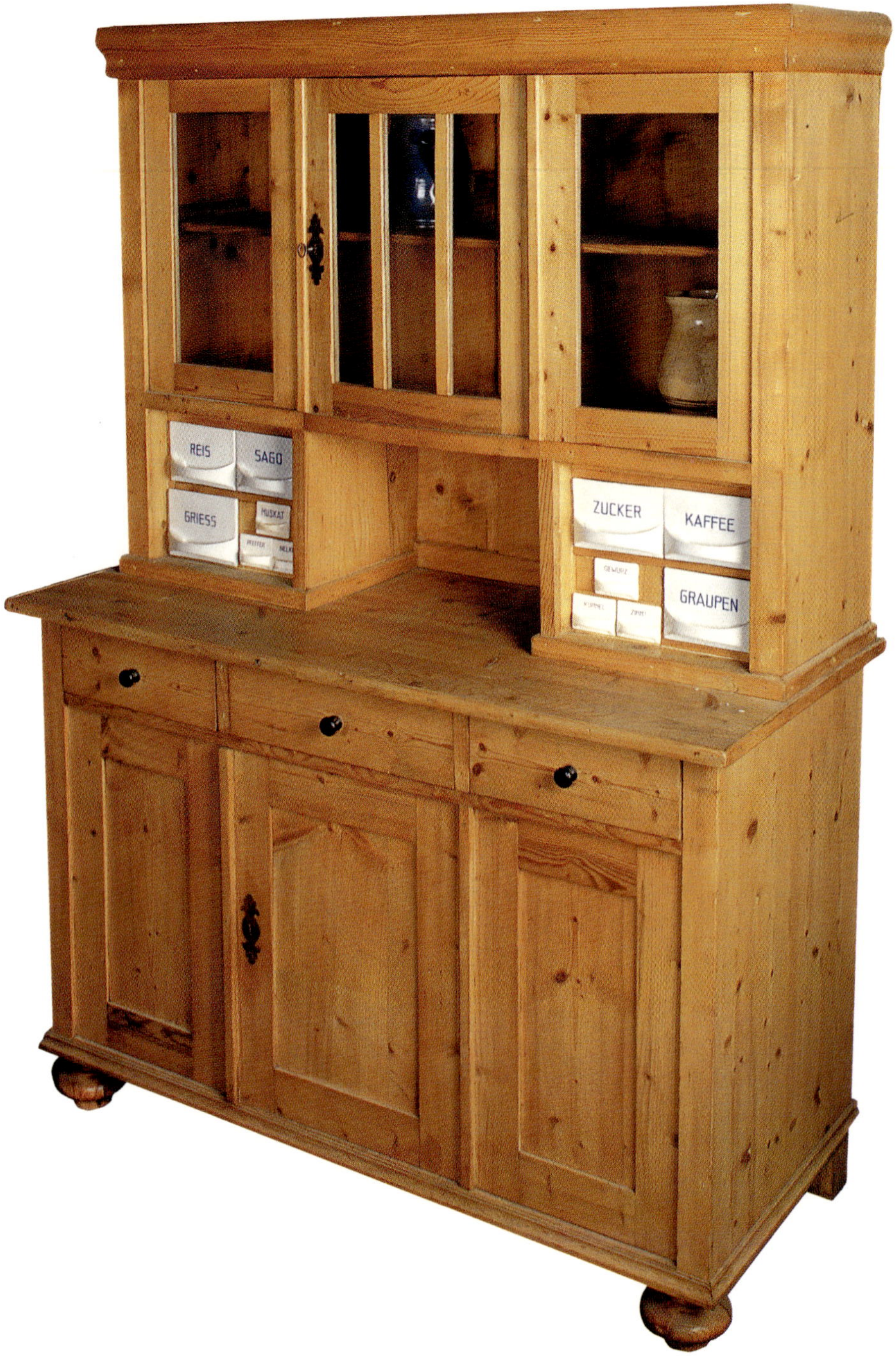

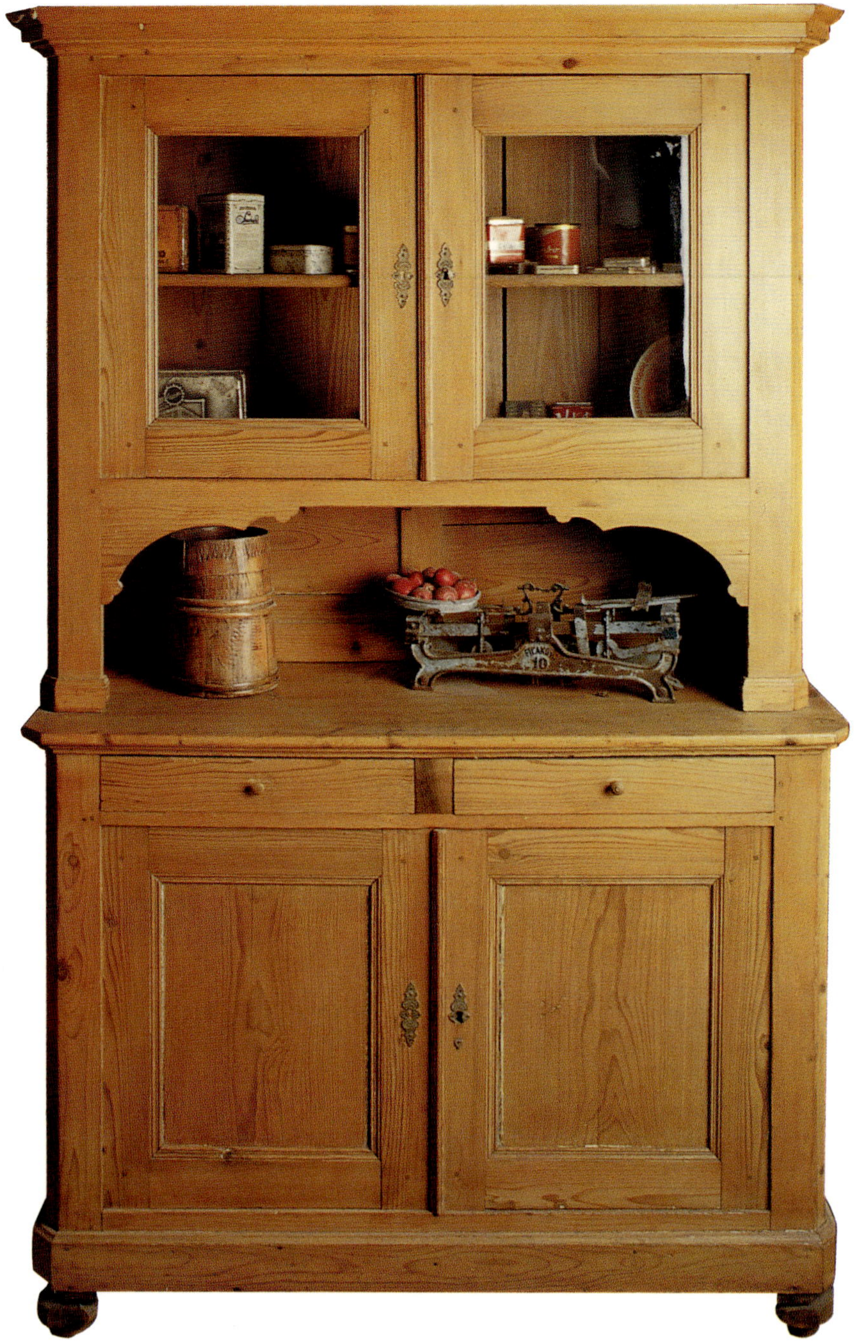

Left: Glass-front cabinet with twelve porcelain spice boxes. A straight ogee cornice rests over three glazed doors enclosing a shelf, the center door convex, and the side cabinets with porcelain boxes lettered with spice names. The lower cabinet has a projecting case of three drawers over a single door and two fixed, recessed panels. The base molding rests on bun feet. $2195.

Right: French cabinet with straight cornice molding over canted corners and two glass doors enclosing a shelf and an open shelf. The base projects with cut corners and two drawers over two recessed-panel doors. The straight base molding rests on blocked feet. $1495.

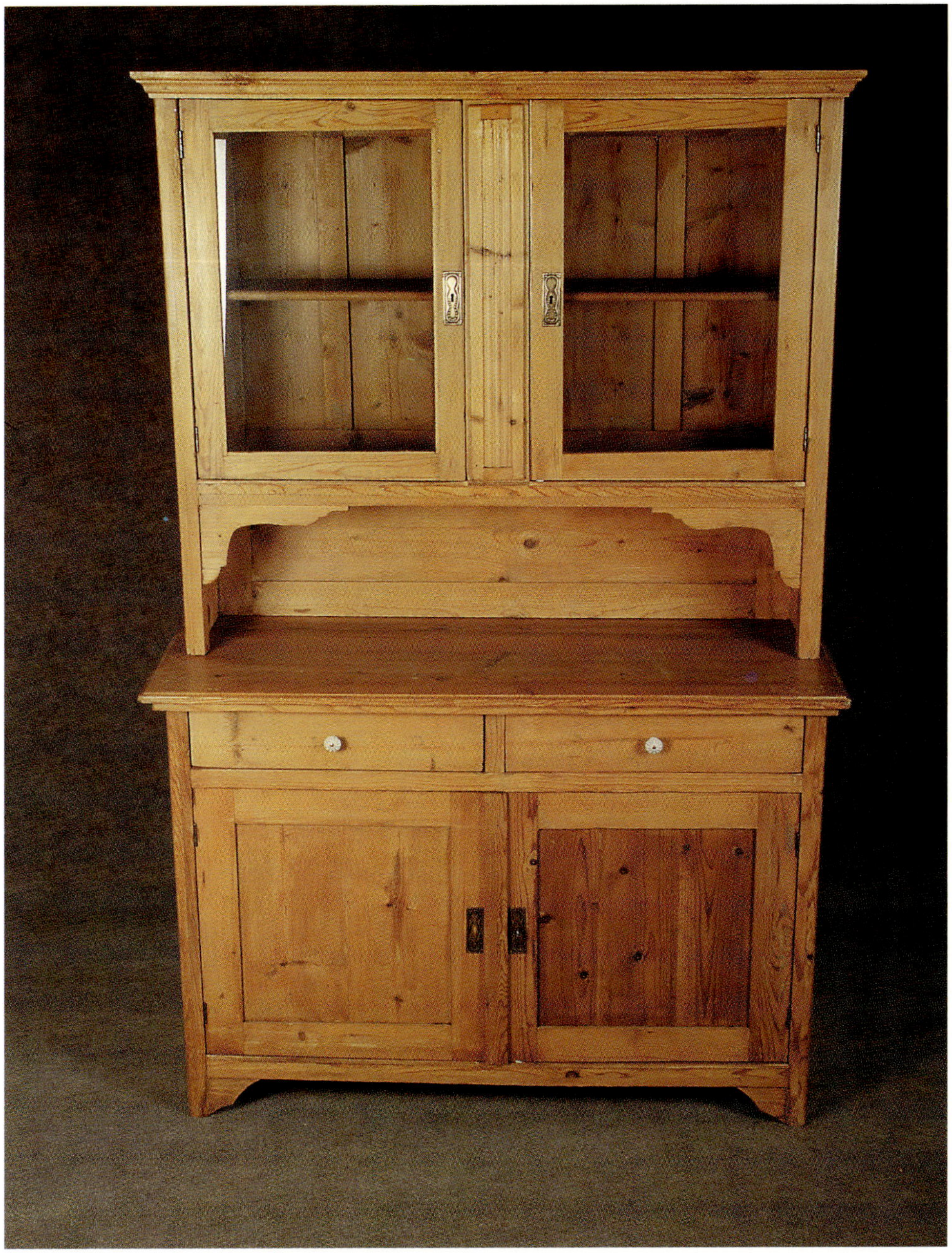

Two-part pine cabinet with straight cornice molding over two glazed doors enclosing shelves and below an open shelf. The lower case has two drawers with white porcelain pulls and two recessed panel doors with brass escutcheons, all resting on a straight molding and stiles forming the feet. $1195.

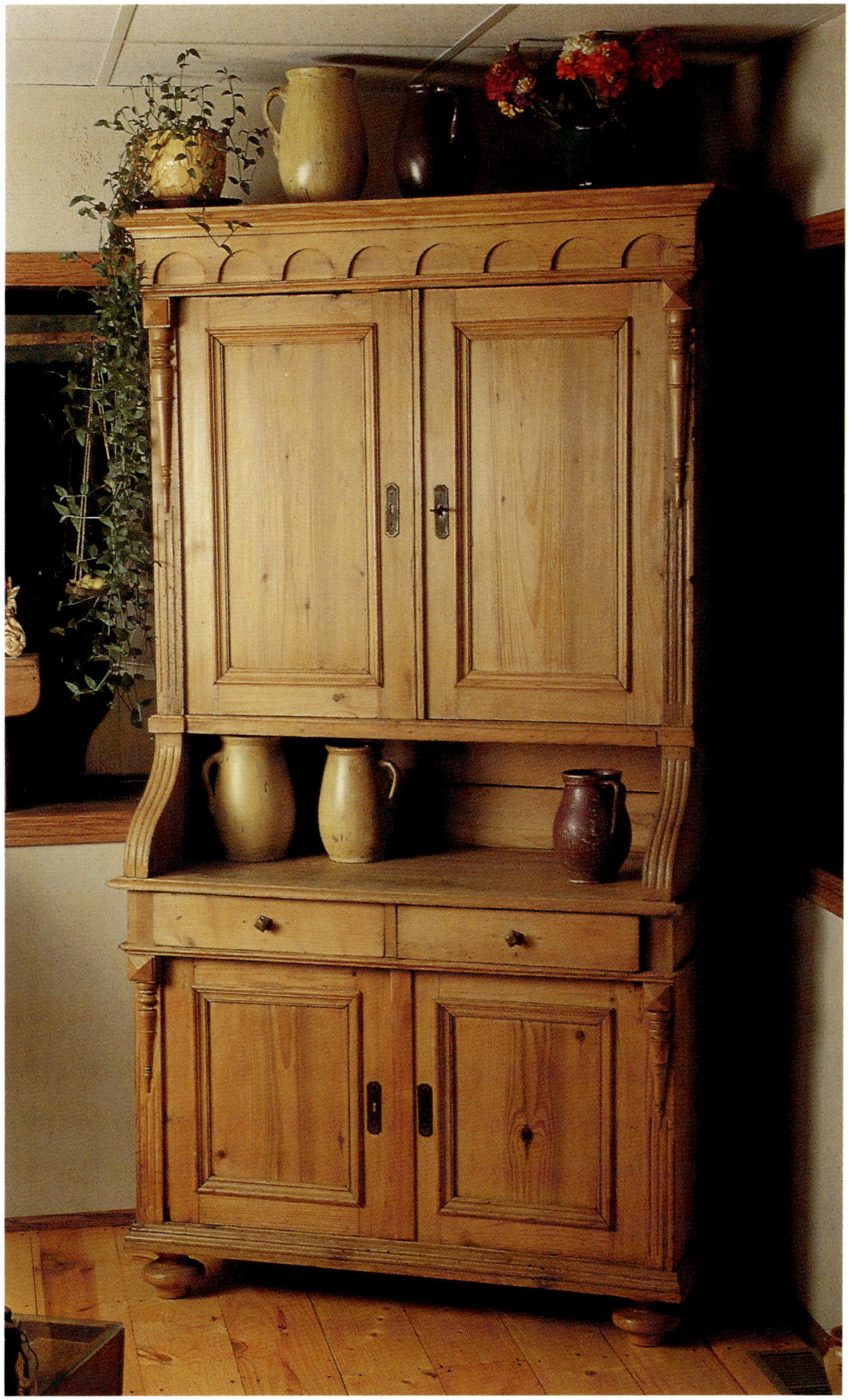

Right: German cabinet with an applied arched frieze over two recessed-panel doors, an open shelf, and two recessed paneled doors, all resting on bun feet. $1495.

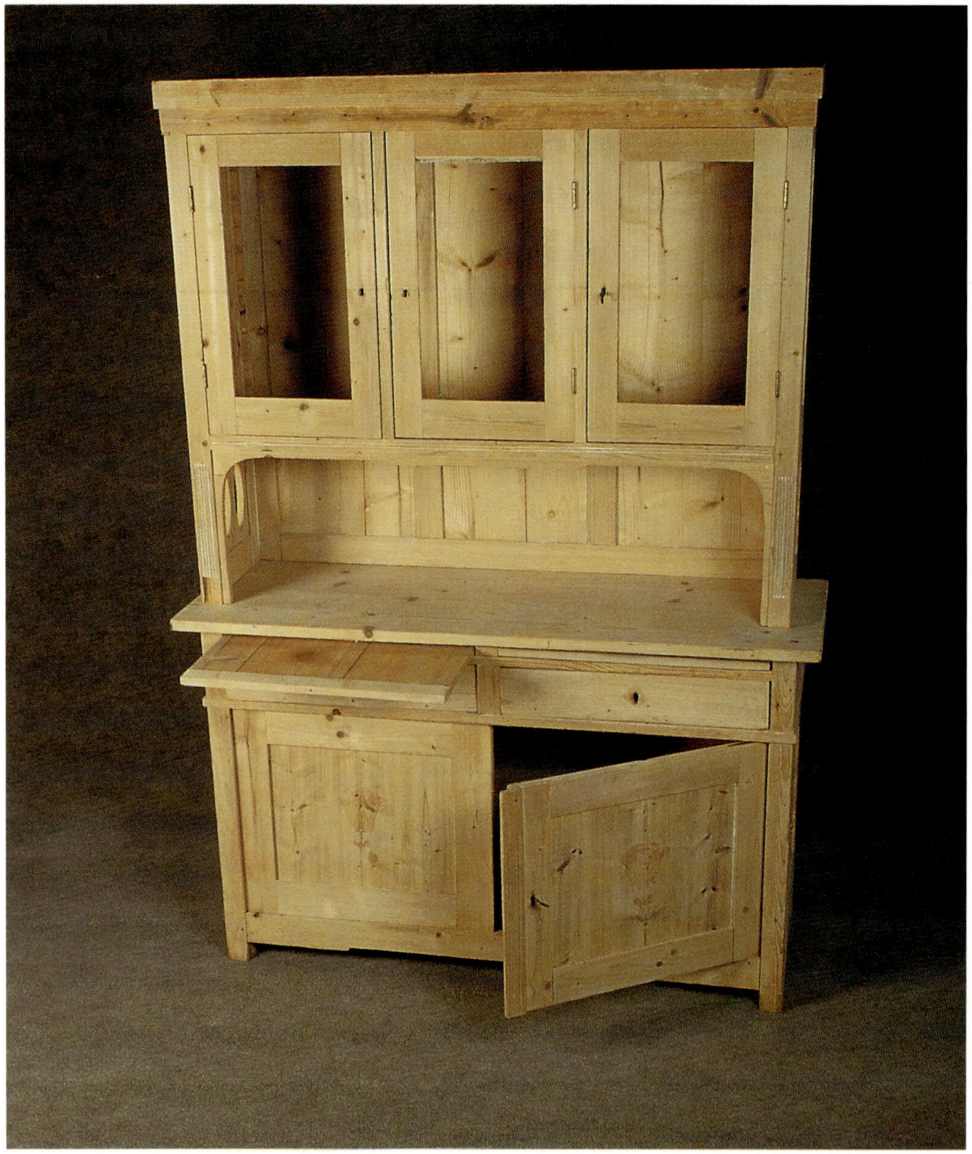

Two-part cabinet with a straight cornice over three glazed doors, glass missing, enclosing two adjustable shelves and below an open shelf. The base section has two small drawers over two pull-out dough boards and two doors enclosing shelves.

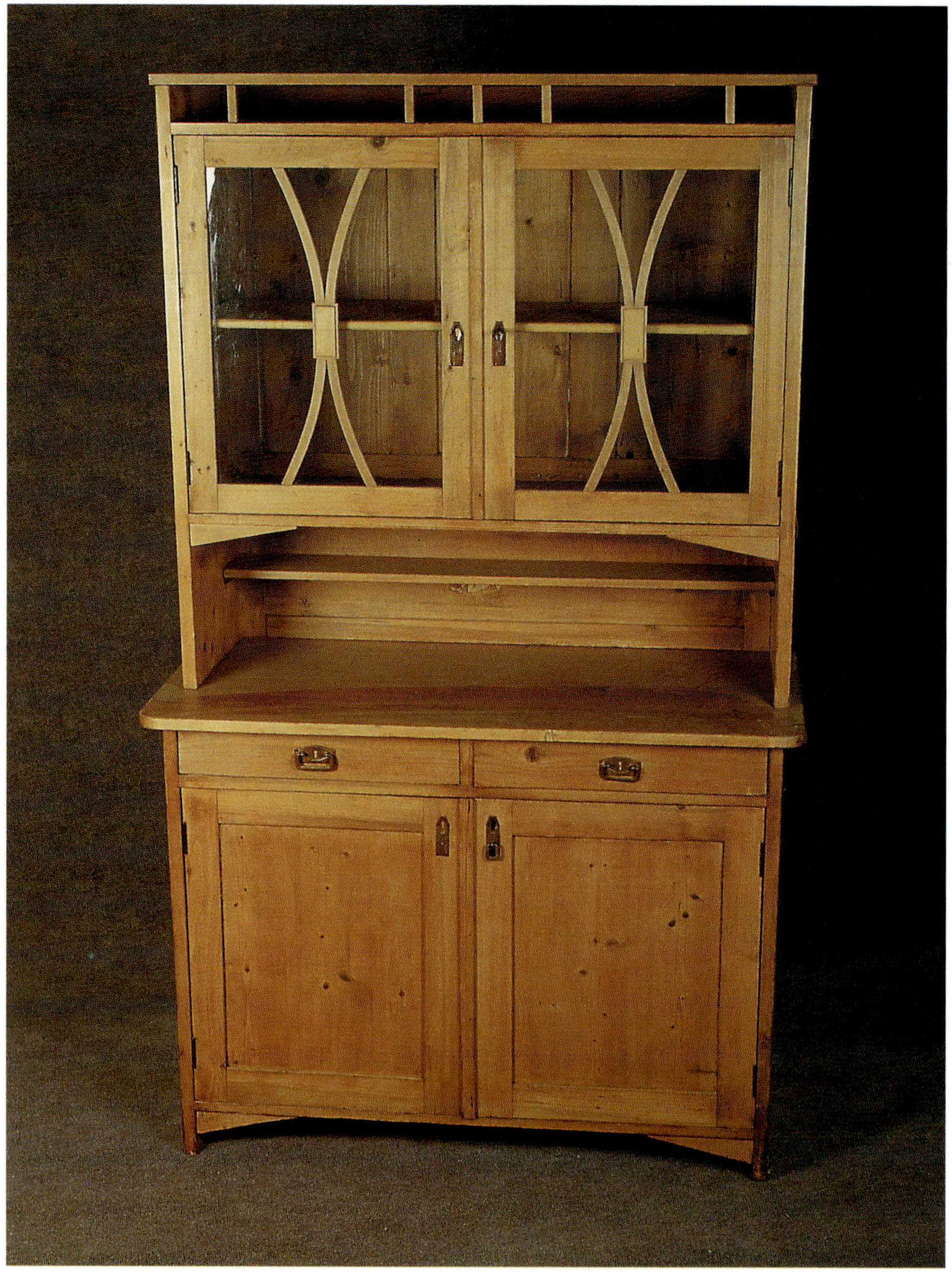

Two-piece flat cabinet with open frieze above two glazed doors enclosing shelves. An open shelf rests above a protecting top of the lower case where two drawers with metal handles rest over two recessed-panel doors, all supported by the stiles that continue to form the feet. $1425.

Left: Cabinet with straight cornice over three glazed doors, two canted, enclosing two shelves. An open shelf and two drawers are over two recessed-panel doors, a scalloped skirt, and blocked bracket feet.

Right: Irish cabinet with straight cornice molding over two doors with glazed fronts enclosing two shelves, and open shelf and projecting lower case with two recessed-panel doors and a straight base molding. $1395.

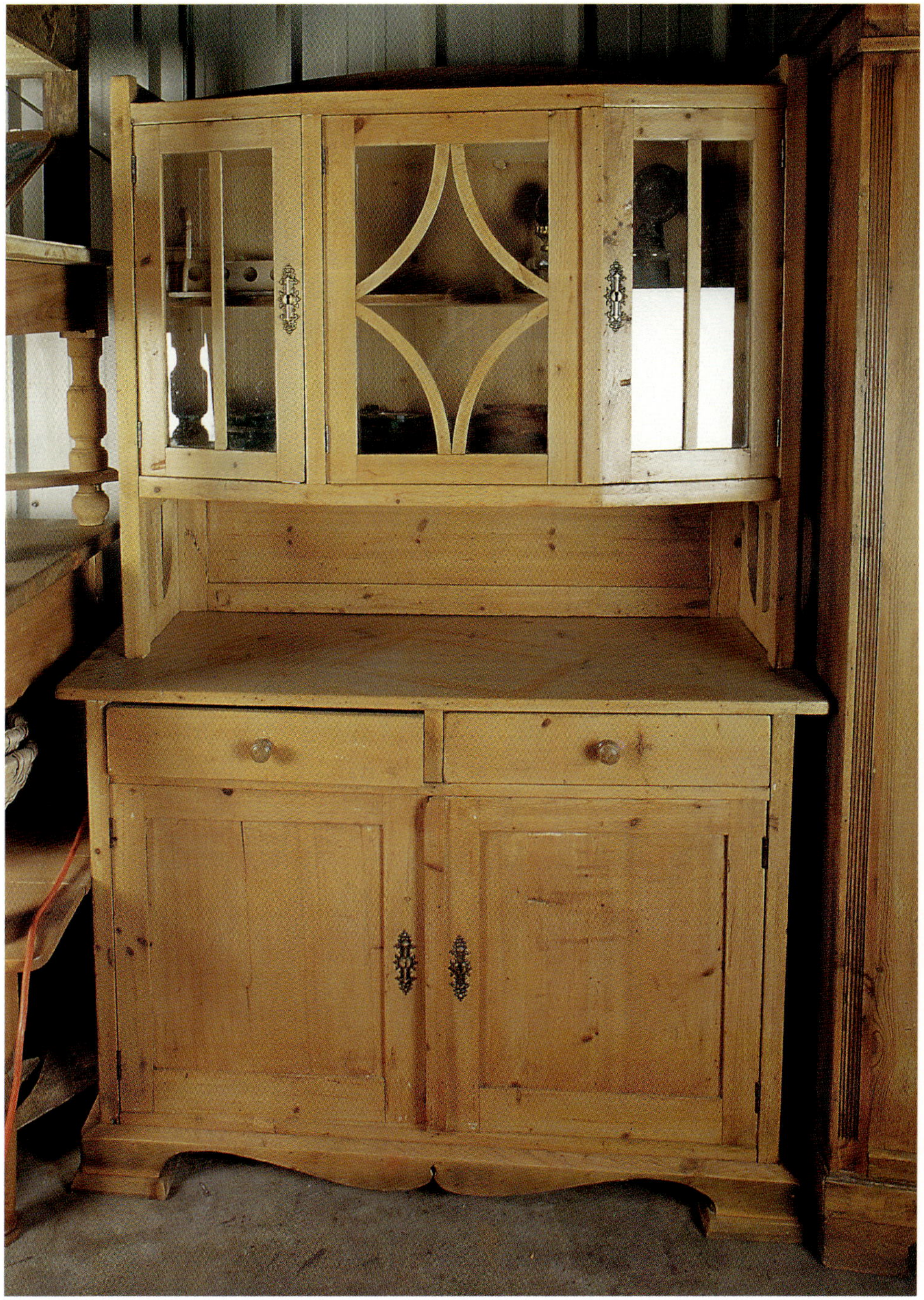

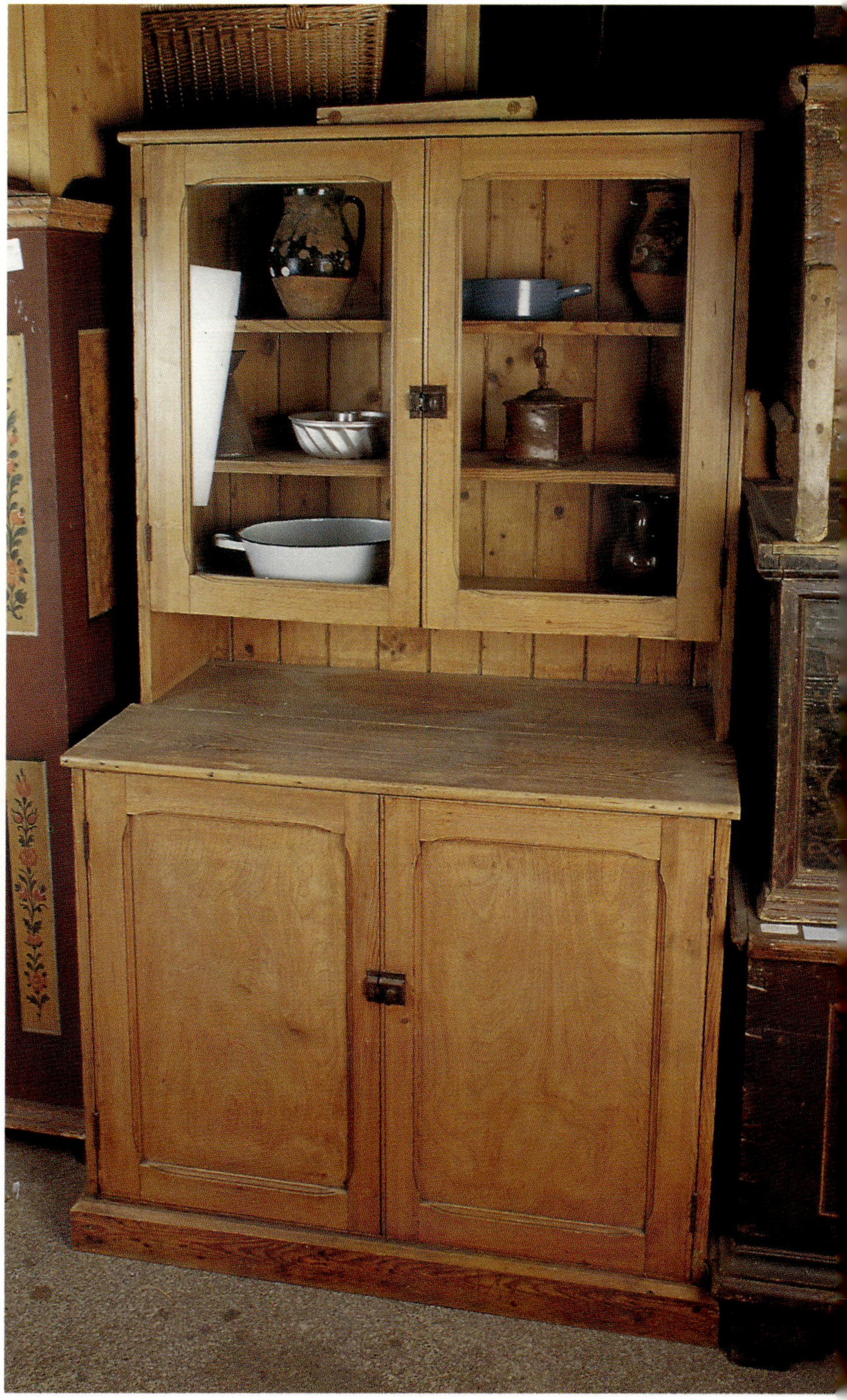

Low Cabinets

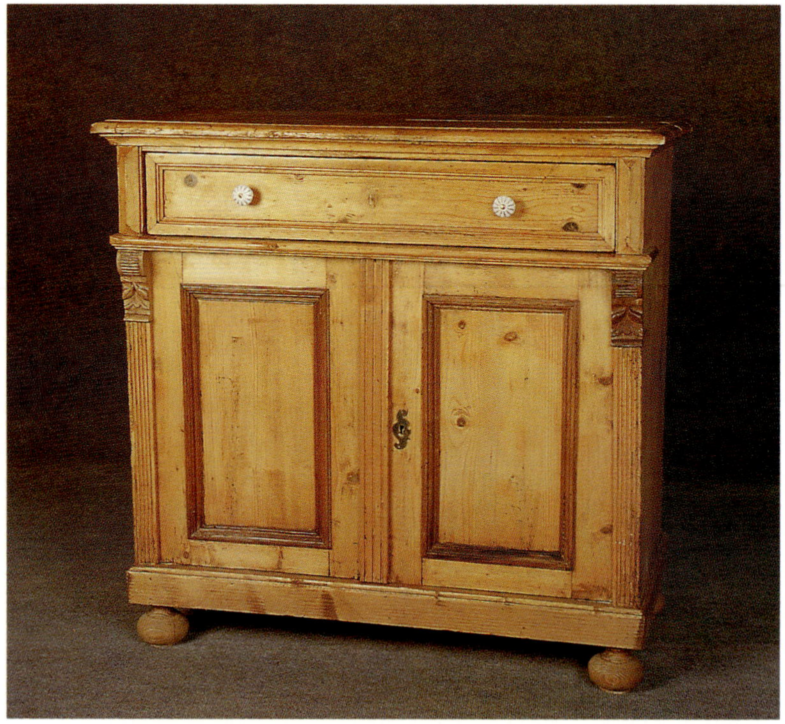

Pine cabinet with a drawer over two recessed-panel doors and molded base resting on bun feet.

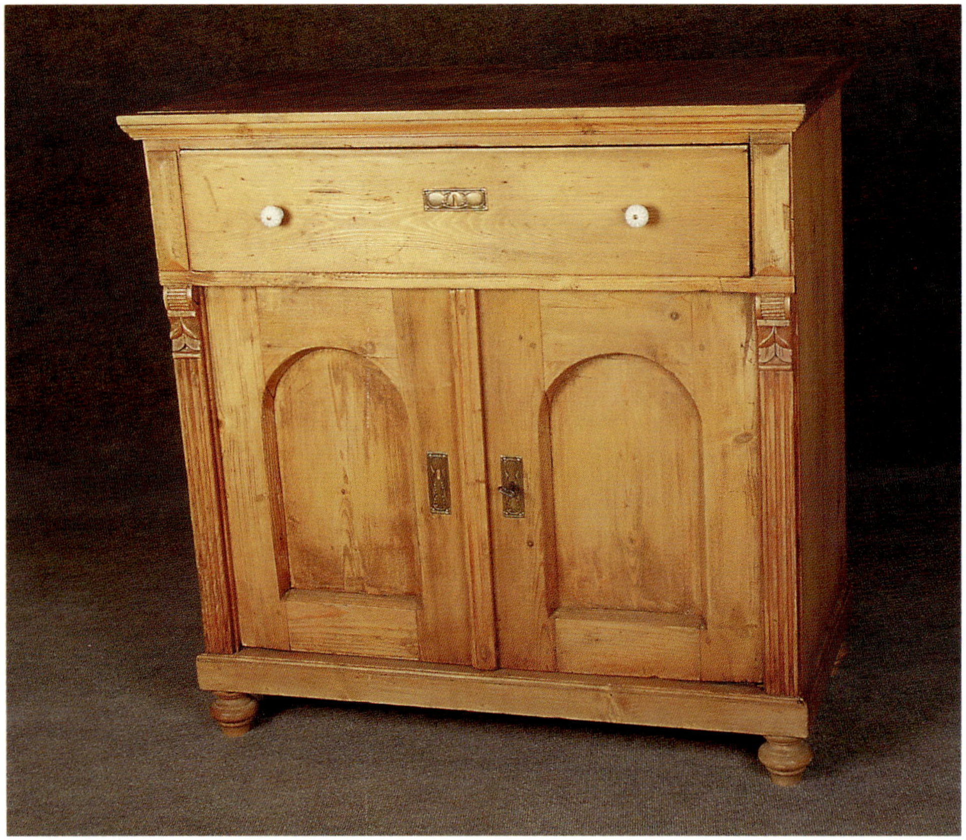

Pine cabinet with molded top support over a single drawer with metal escutcheon and two porcelain knobs over two arch recessed-panel doors and ribbed stiles, standing on turned feet.

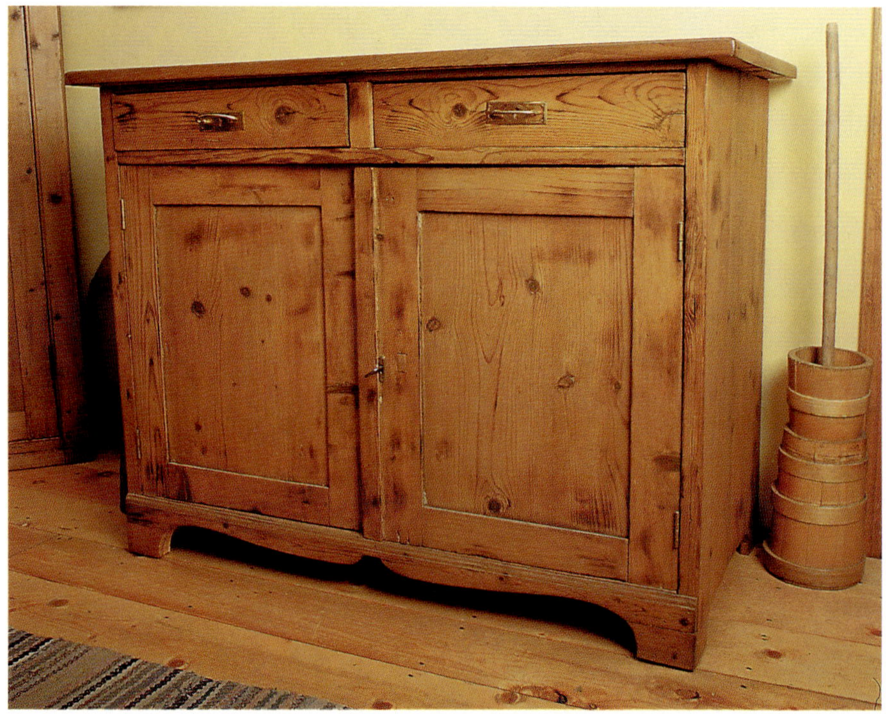

German cabinet with rectangular top overhanging two drawers with brass pulls and two recessed panel doors with metal escutcheon over bracket feet. $775.

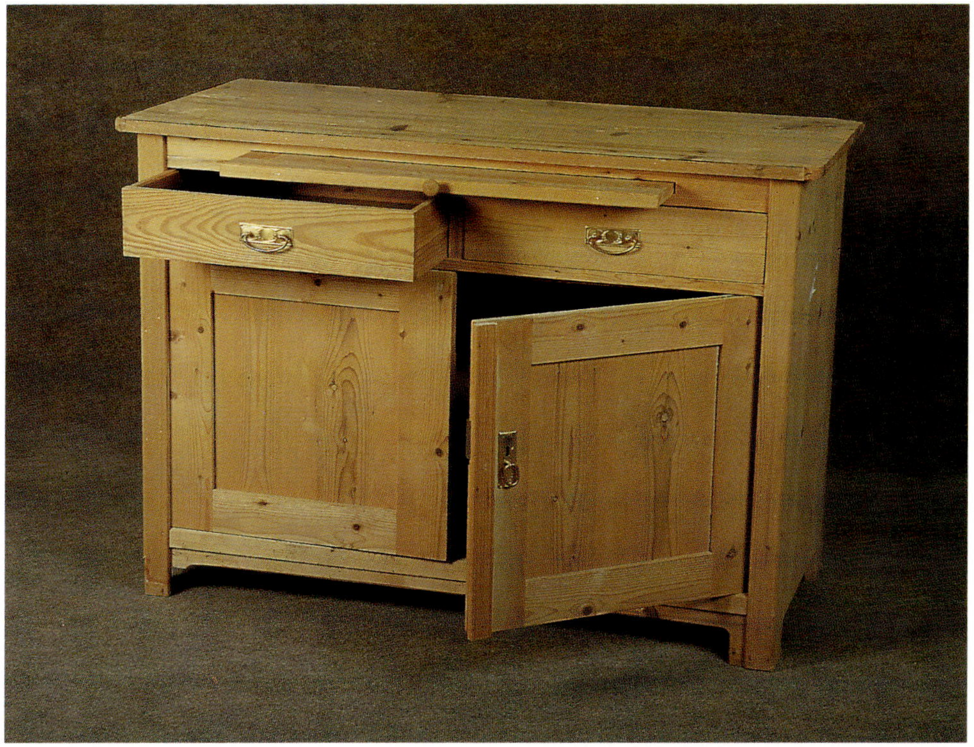

Pine cabinet of drawers with a sliding dough board, two short drawers, and two recessed-panel doors enclosing a shelf. The case rests on a straight base and the stiles form the feet.

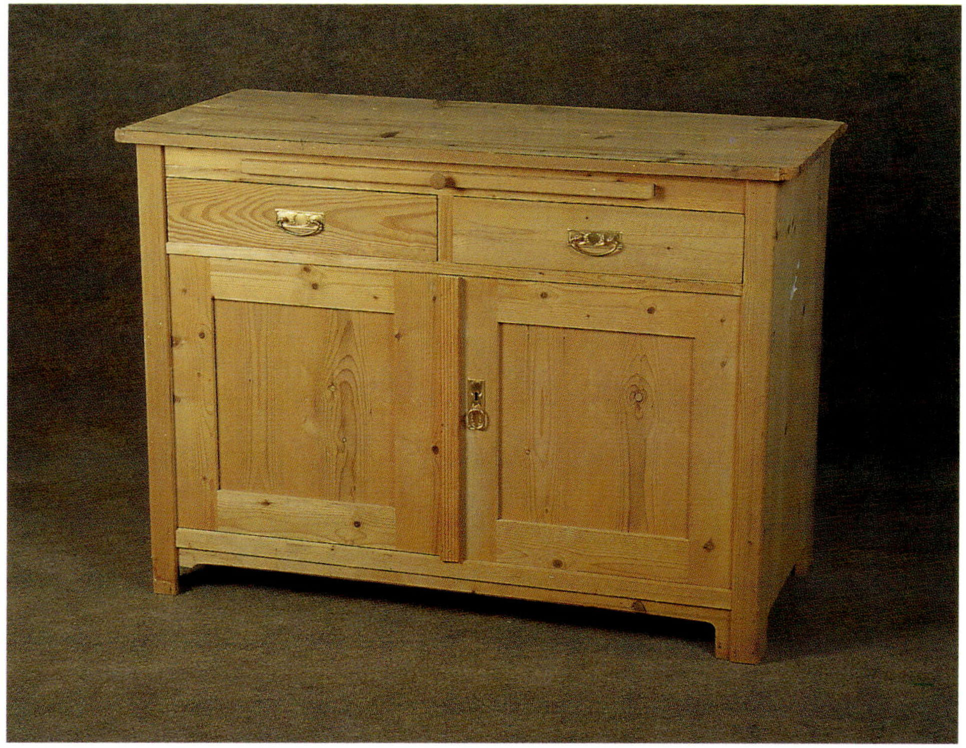

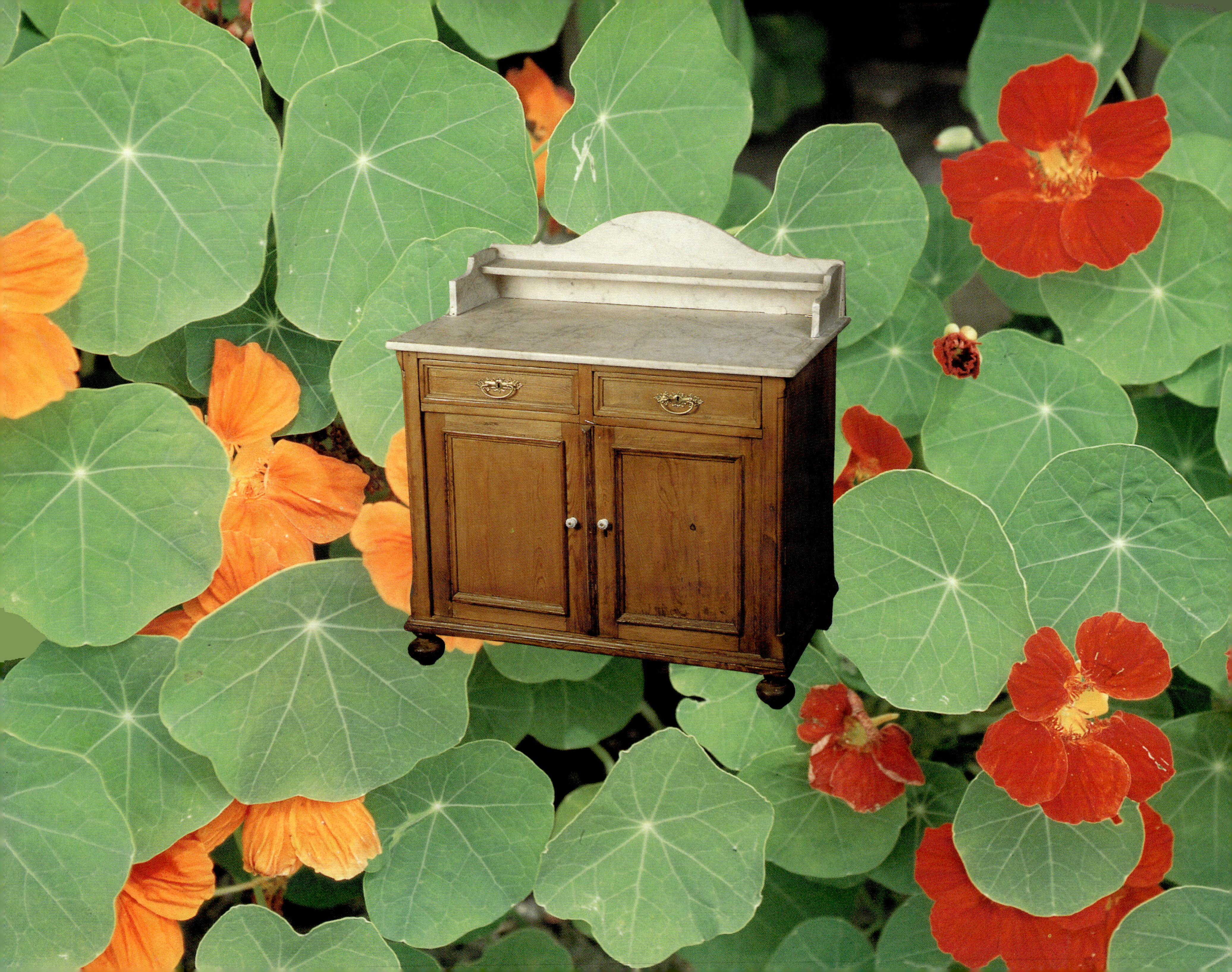

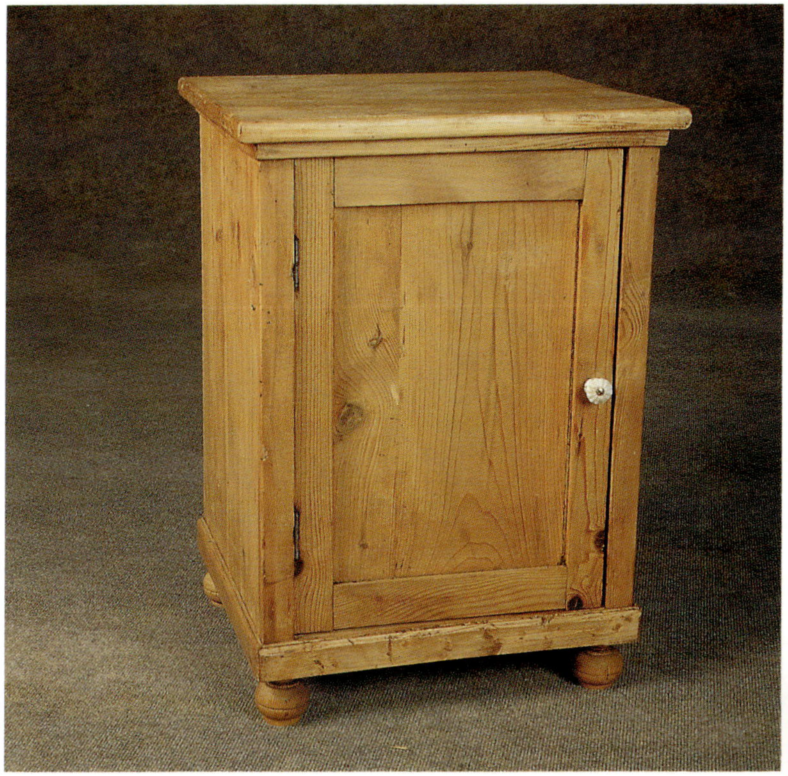

Cabinet with single hinged and recessed-panel door with white porcelain knob. $150.

Pine cabinet with a flat rectangular top and open shelf with scalloped cornice over two recessed-panel doors with metal escutcheons, fluted stiles, and a base molding on bun feet. $650.

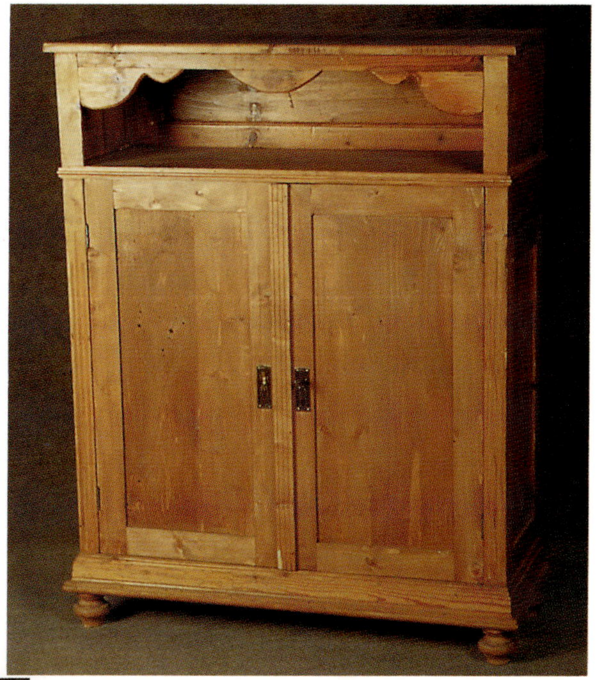

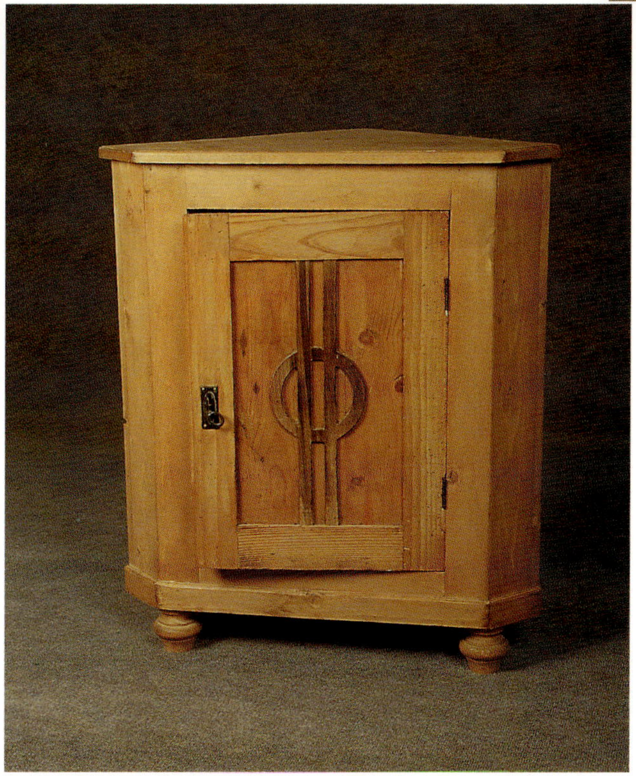

Corner cabinet with a recessed-panel door with applied molding decoration, iron escutcheon and lock, and turned legs $375.

Opposite page: Marble top dry sink with two drawers with brass pulls over two recessed-panel doors with white porcelain pulls, resting on a base molding and bun feet.

Chests of Drawers

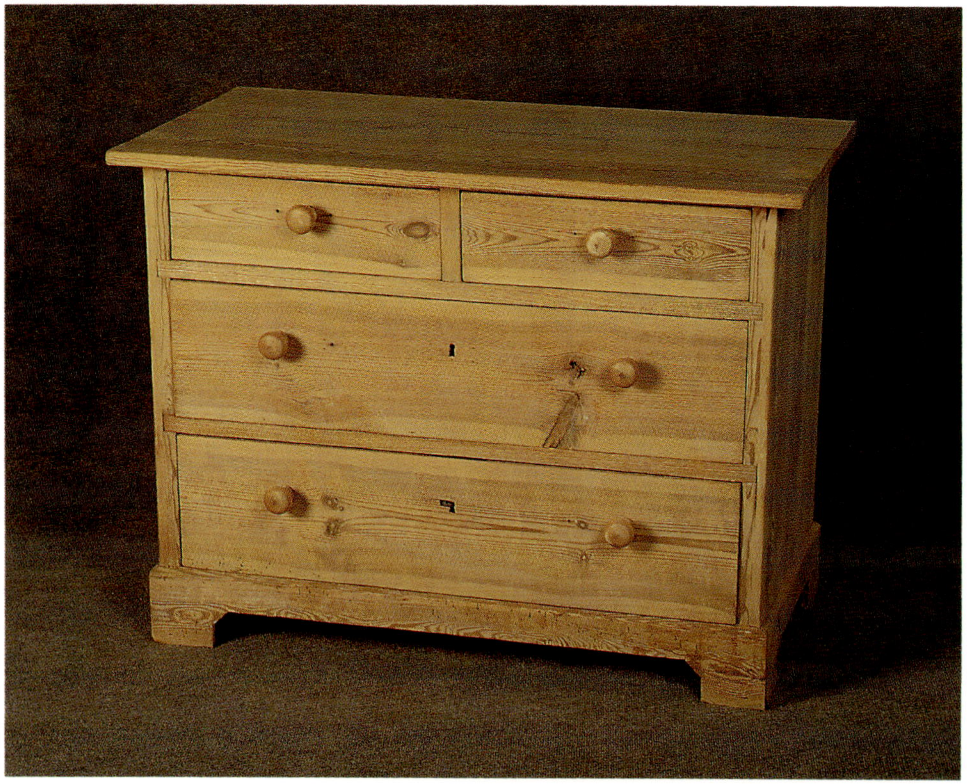

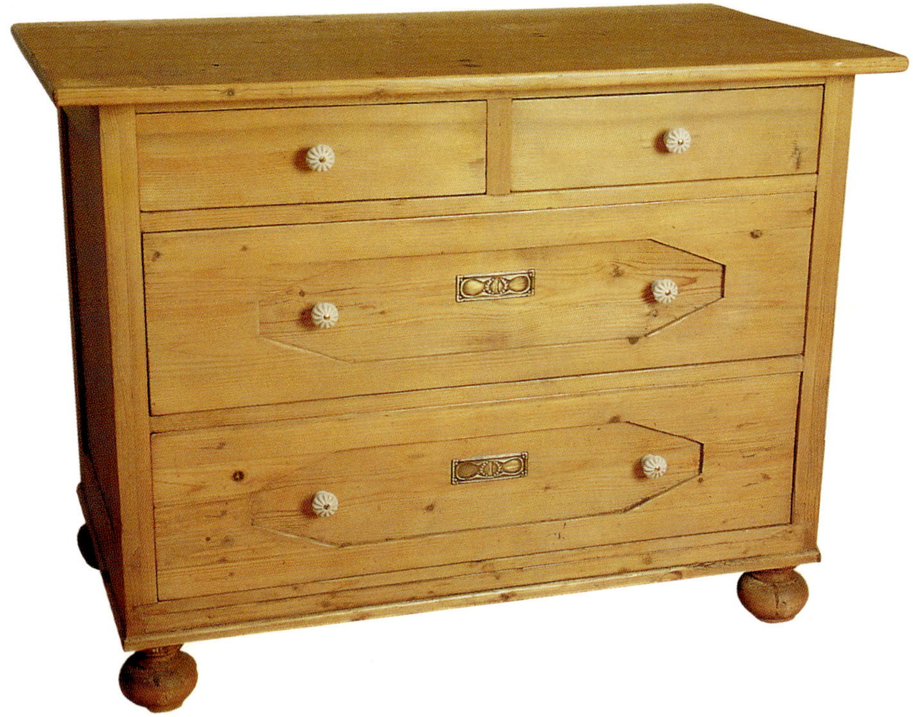

Above: Pine chest of two small drawers over two long drawers with wooden knob pulls resting on a solid base and bracket feet. $695.

Top right: Chest with two short drawers over two long drawers with recessed central panels and white porcelain knobs and resting on bun feet. $695.

Bottom right: German blanket chest painted green with black trim, rectangular top, three drawers with wooden knobs, ribbed stiles and bracket feet. $895.

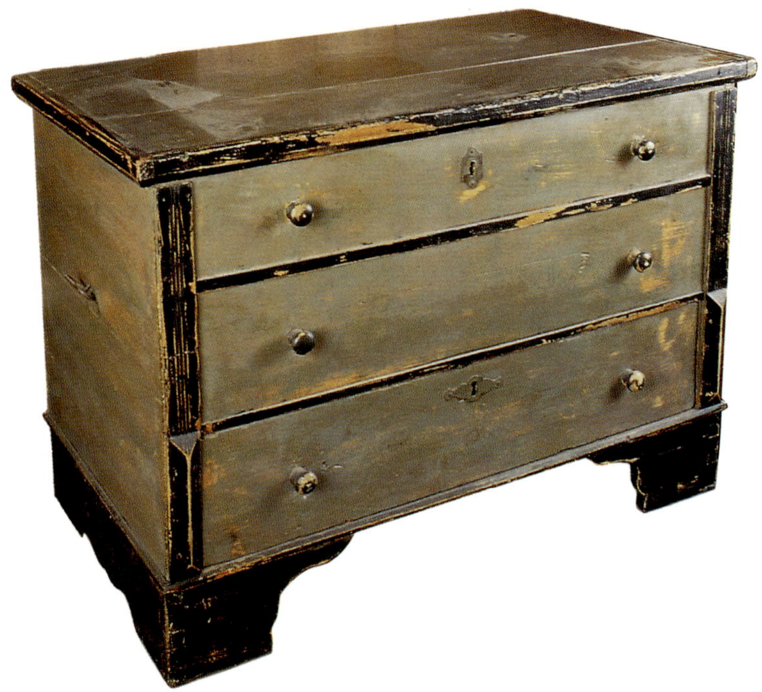

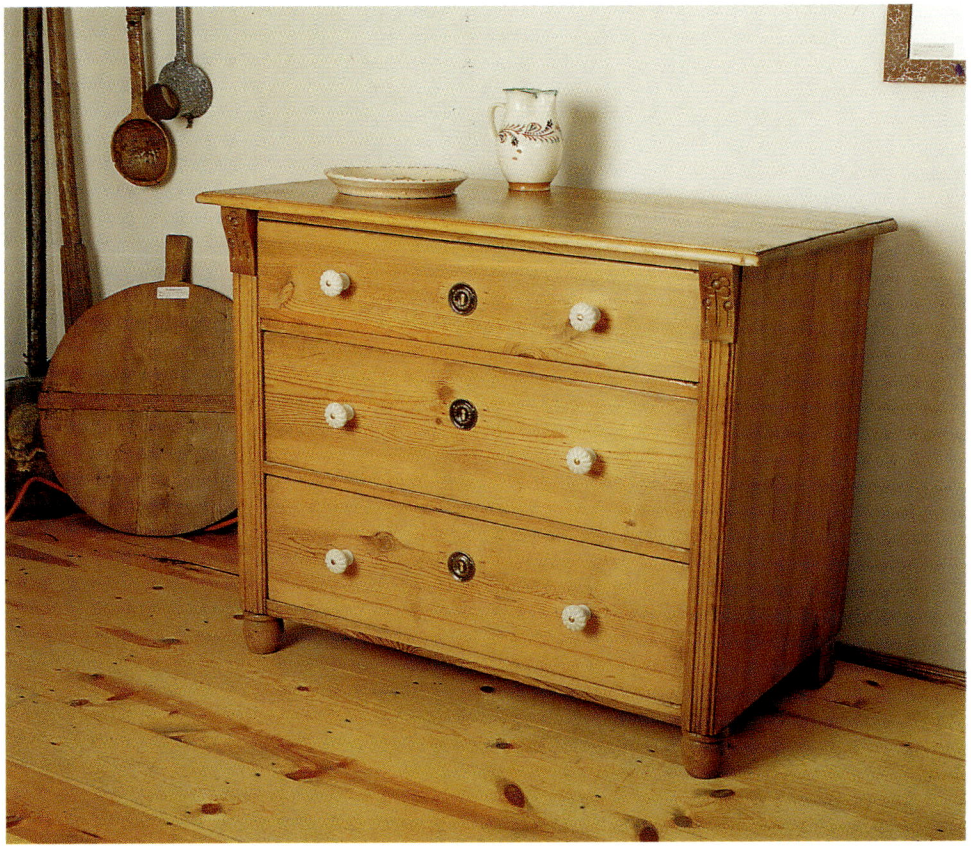

Pine chest of three drawers with white porcelain pulls and metal escutcheons. The stiles are ribbed with applied carved capitals and the case rests on front feet and blocked back feet.

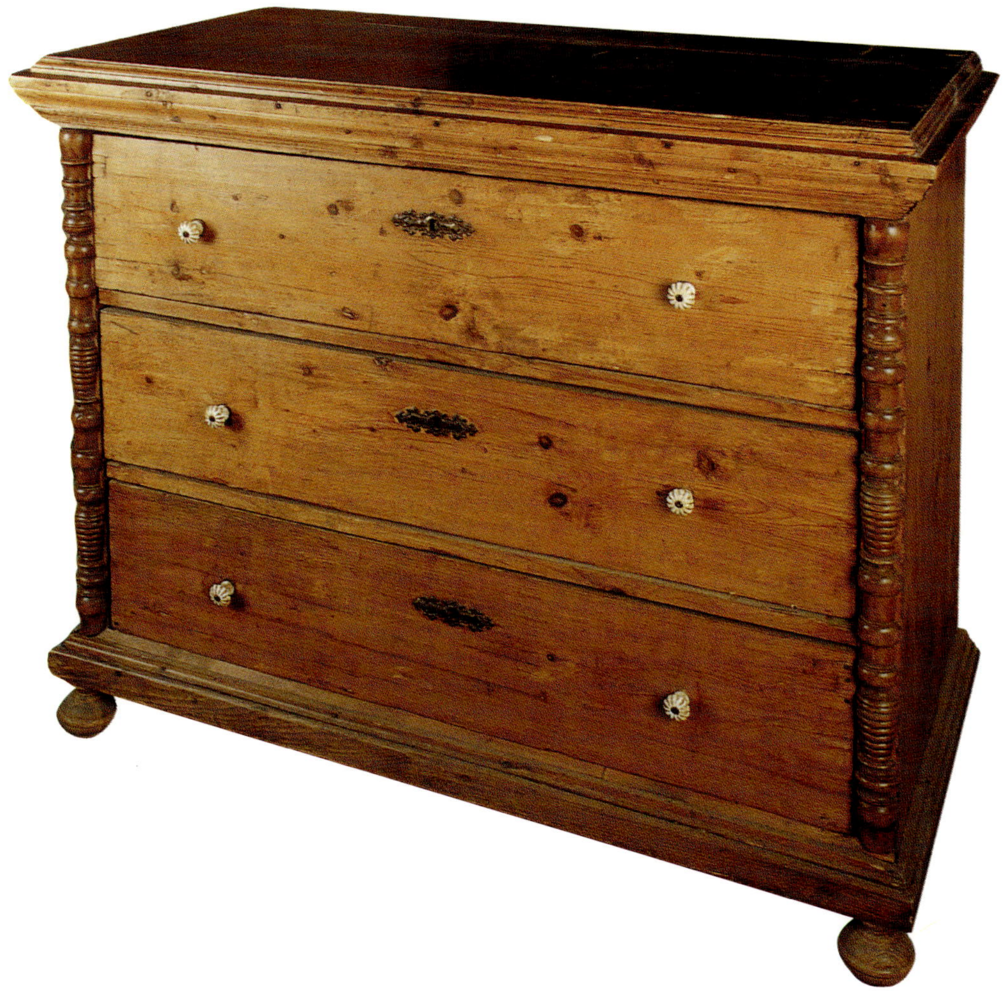

Dresser with raised rectangular top over three large drawers with white porcelain pulls and applied half turnings on the stiles. The base molding rests on turned front feet and blocked feet. $950.

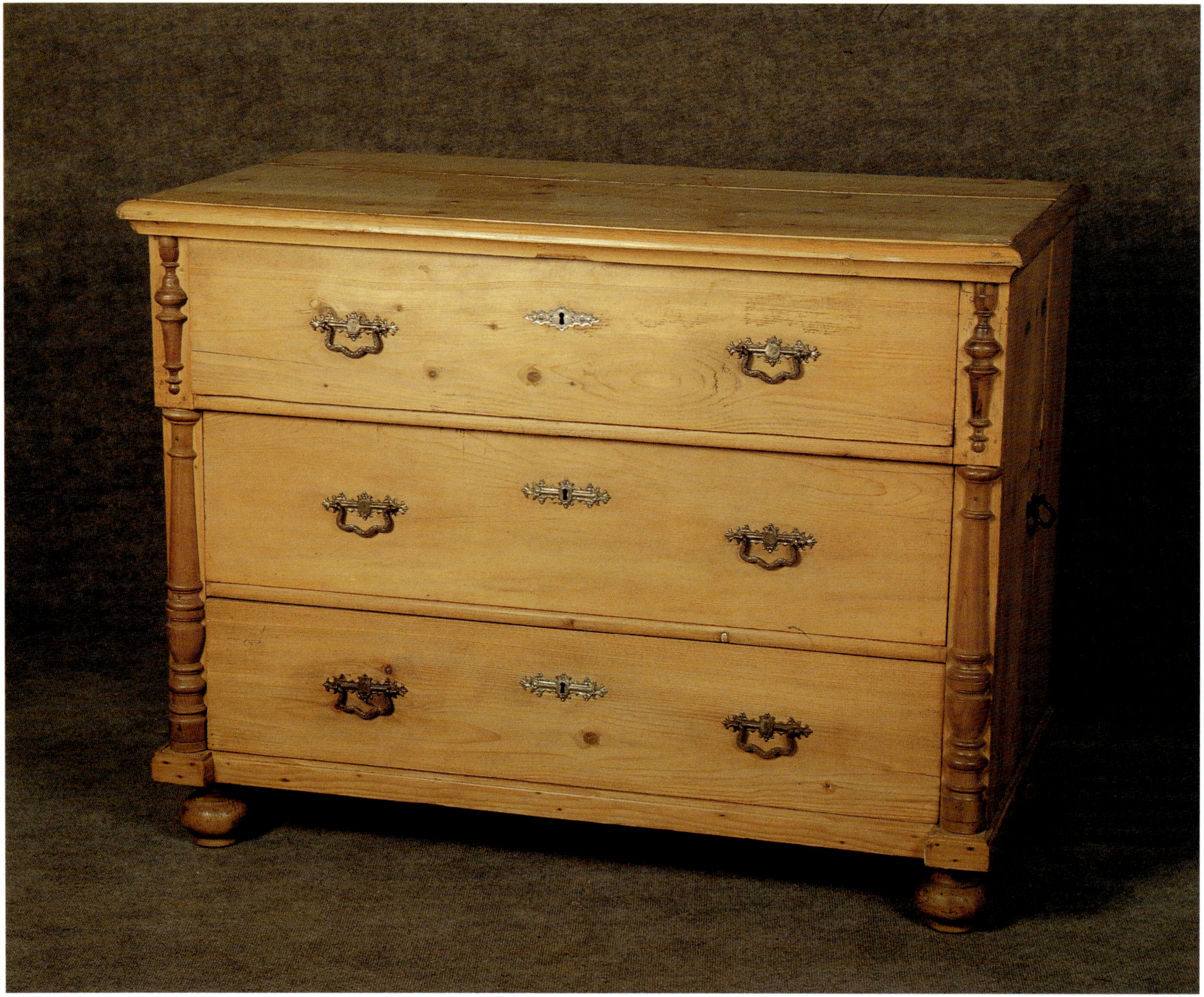

Pine chest of three drawers with applied half-turned decoration to the stiles, each drawer with a metal escutcheon and handles, all resting on turned feet. $895.

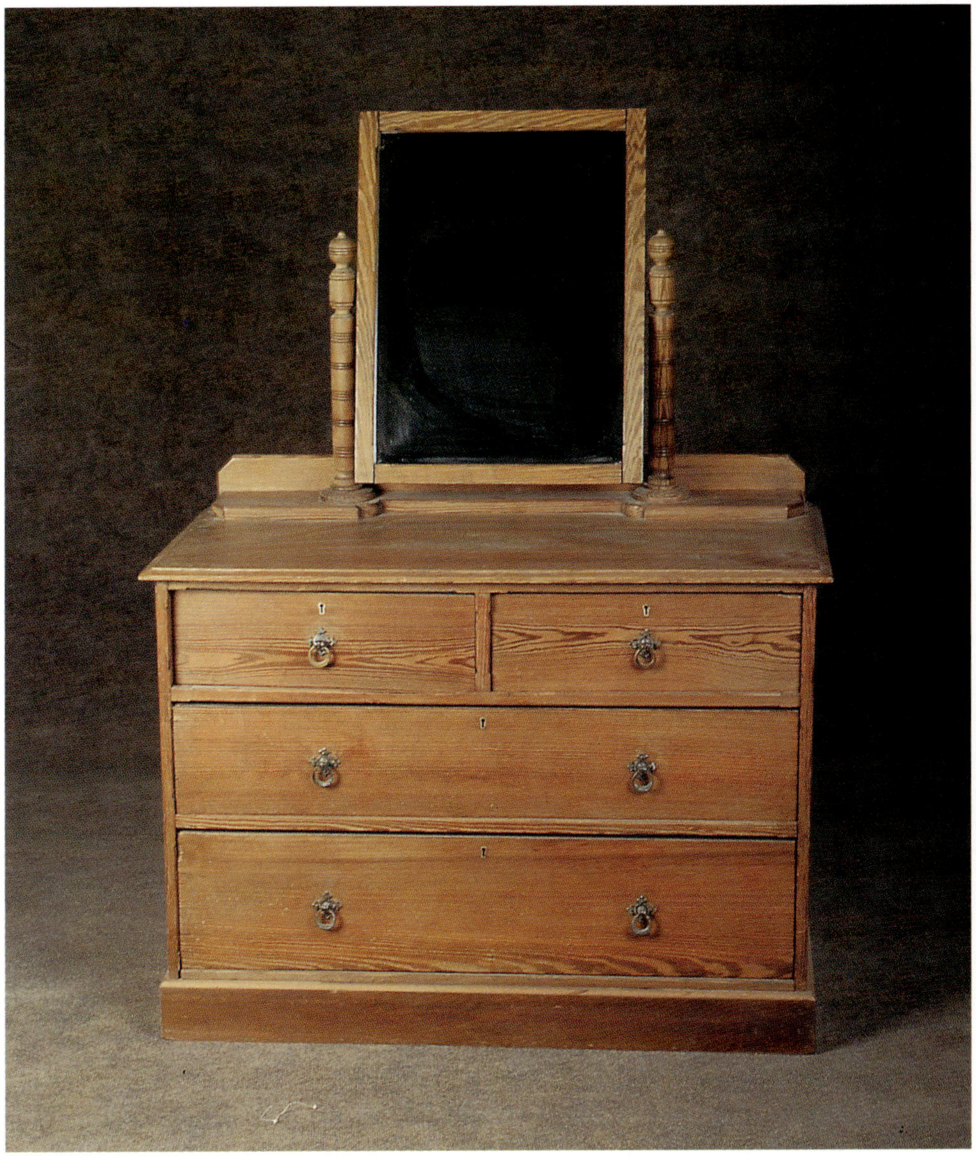

Irish vanity with rectangular mirror between turned supports resting above the case where two small drawers rest over two long drawers on a straight base molding. $795.

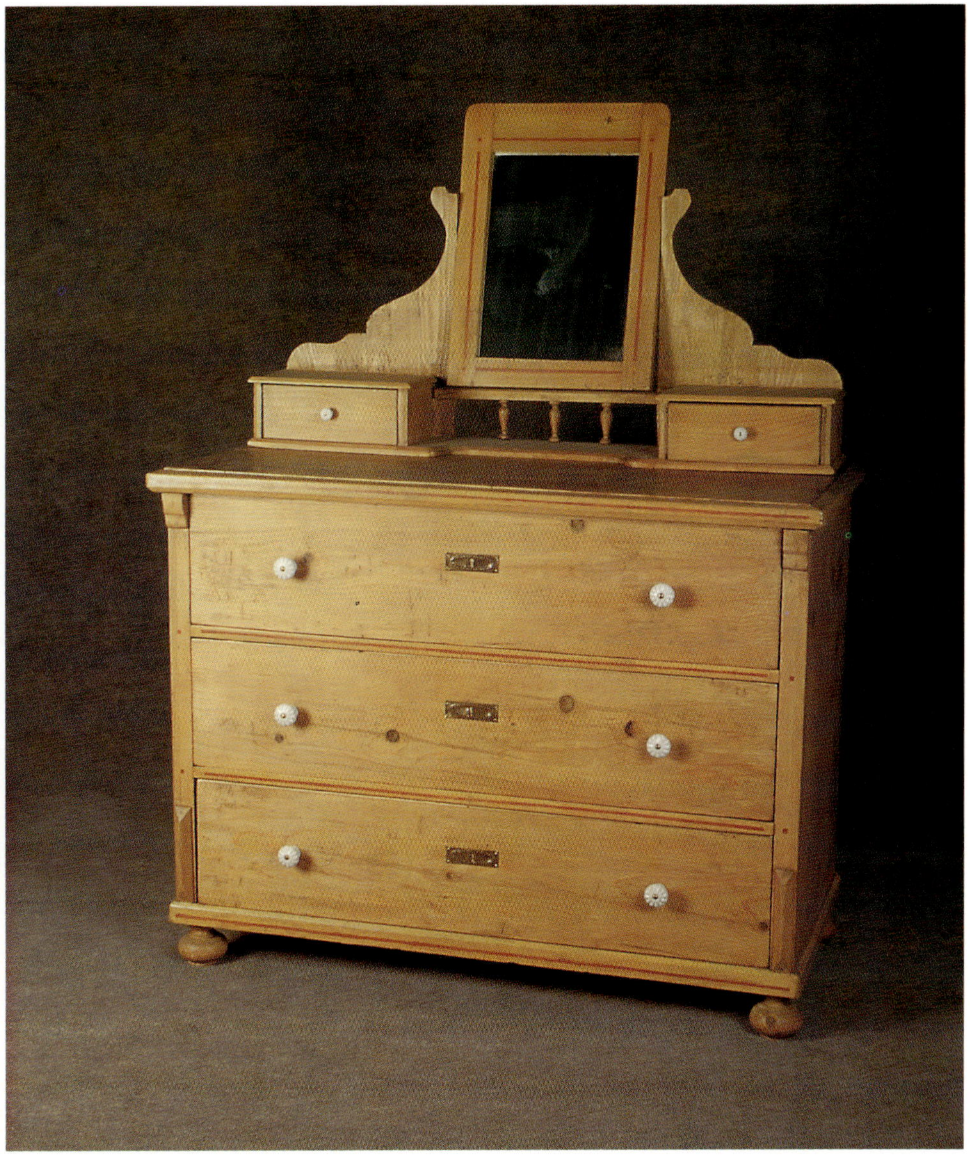

Chest of three drawers with a separate unit on top composed of an adjustable mirror flanked by two small drawers. The rectangular top overhangs the case and the stiles have applied details to the top and base. Horizontal planes are painted yellow with a red line, and the case rests on a base molding and bun feet. $985.

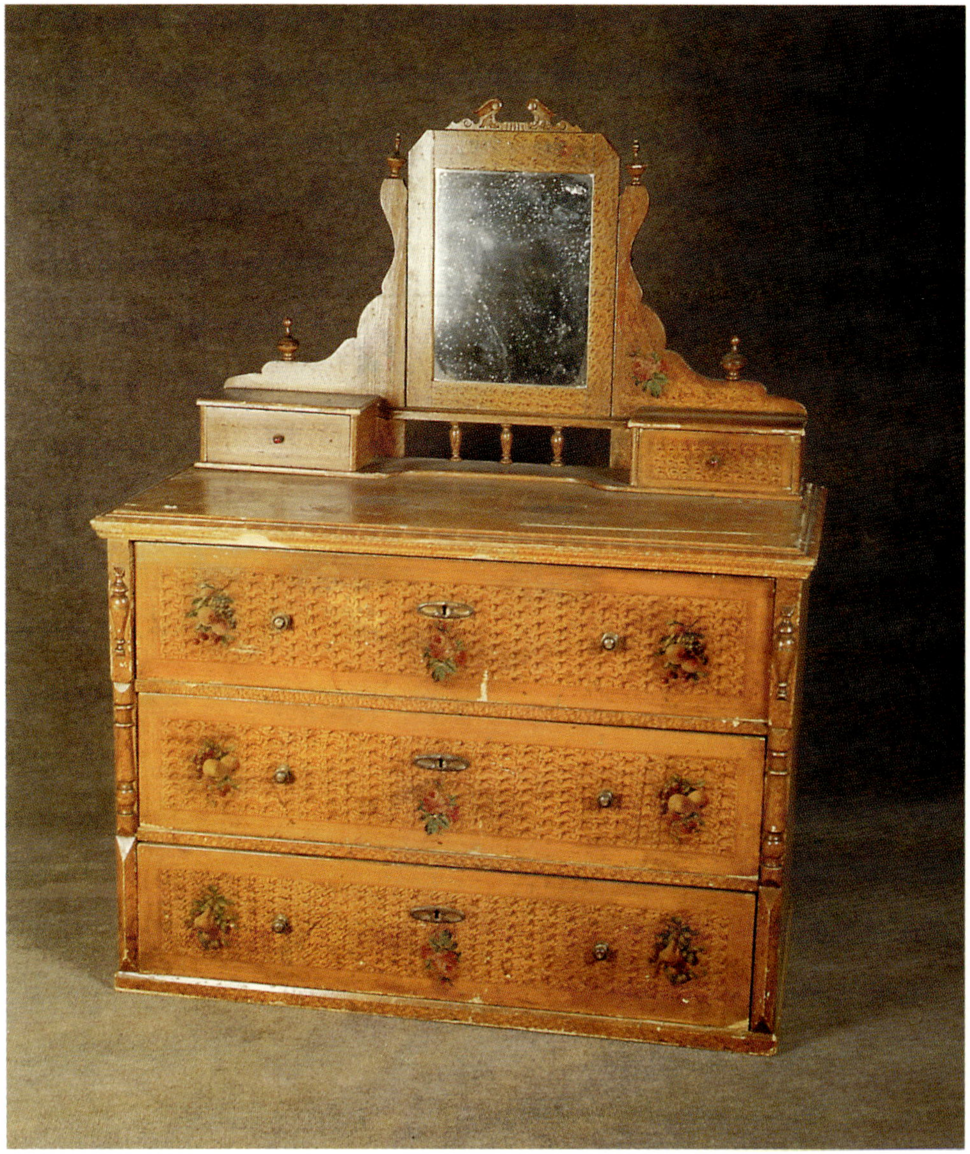

Painted chest of drawers with a separated top section comprising a tilting mirror and two flanking small drawers. The case has three drawers with painted fruit decoration and wooden knob pulls. The stiles have half-turned decorations above the straight base molding, Renaissance Revival style. $995.

Pine chest of three drawers in two sections. The top part has a framed mirror flanked by two compartments, each with two open shelves and a small drawer with white porcelain pull. The chest has applied half baluster turnings to the stiles and the drawers have teal blue line decoration. The straight base molding rests on bun feet. $1095.

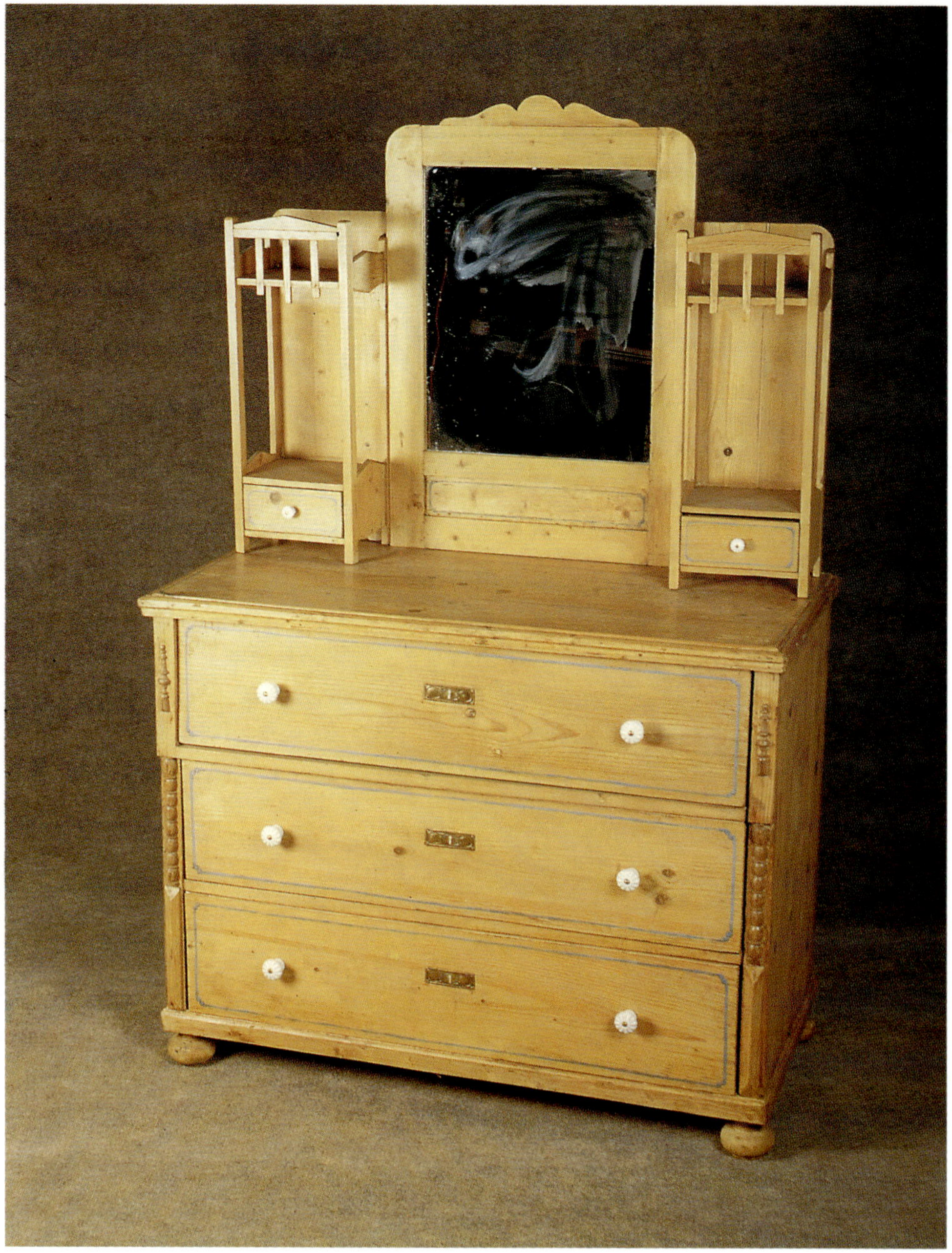

Nightstands

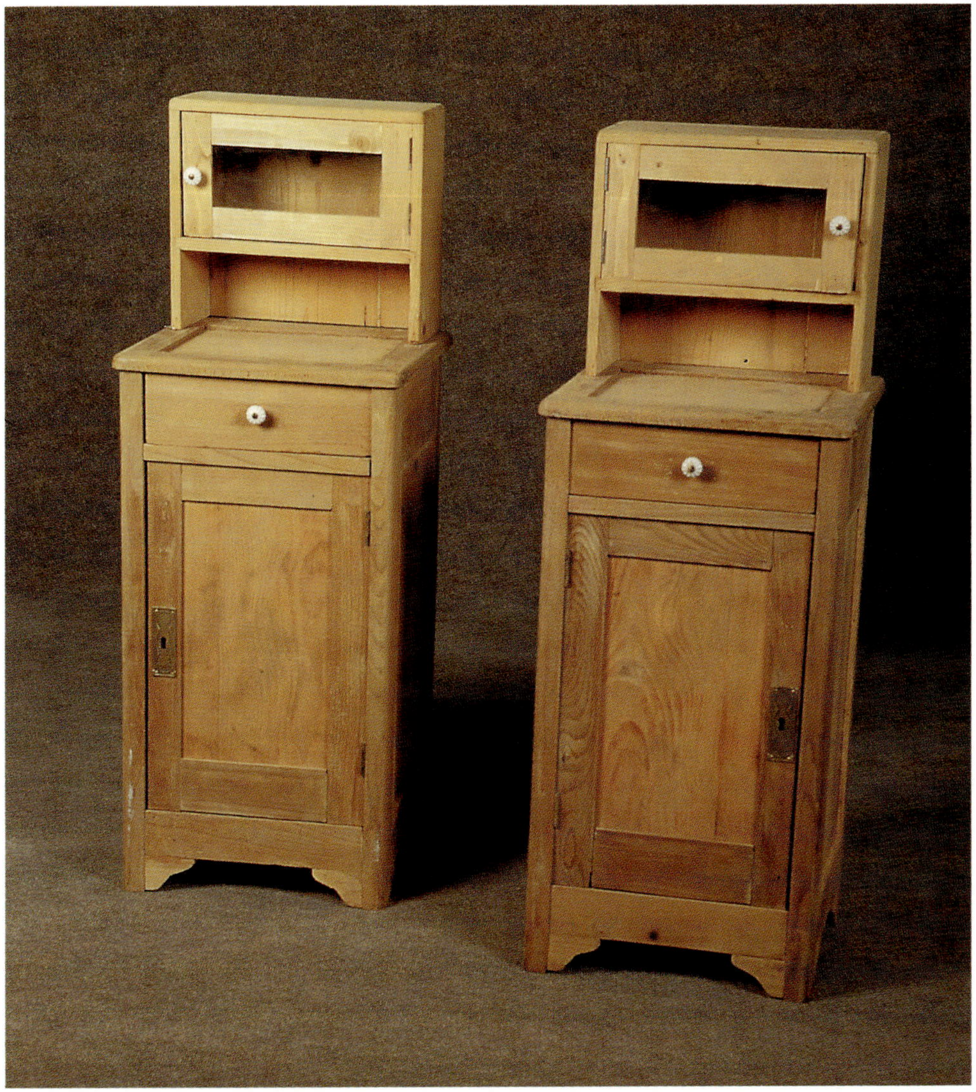

Pair of pine nightstands with raised compartments on the top each bearing a glass-enclosed shelf, the case with a single drawer with white porcelain knob, and recessed-panel door with metal escutcheon, resting on a straight base and scalloped brackets to form the feet. $295 each.

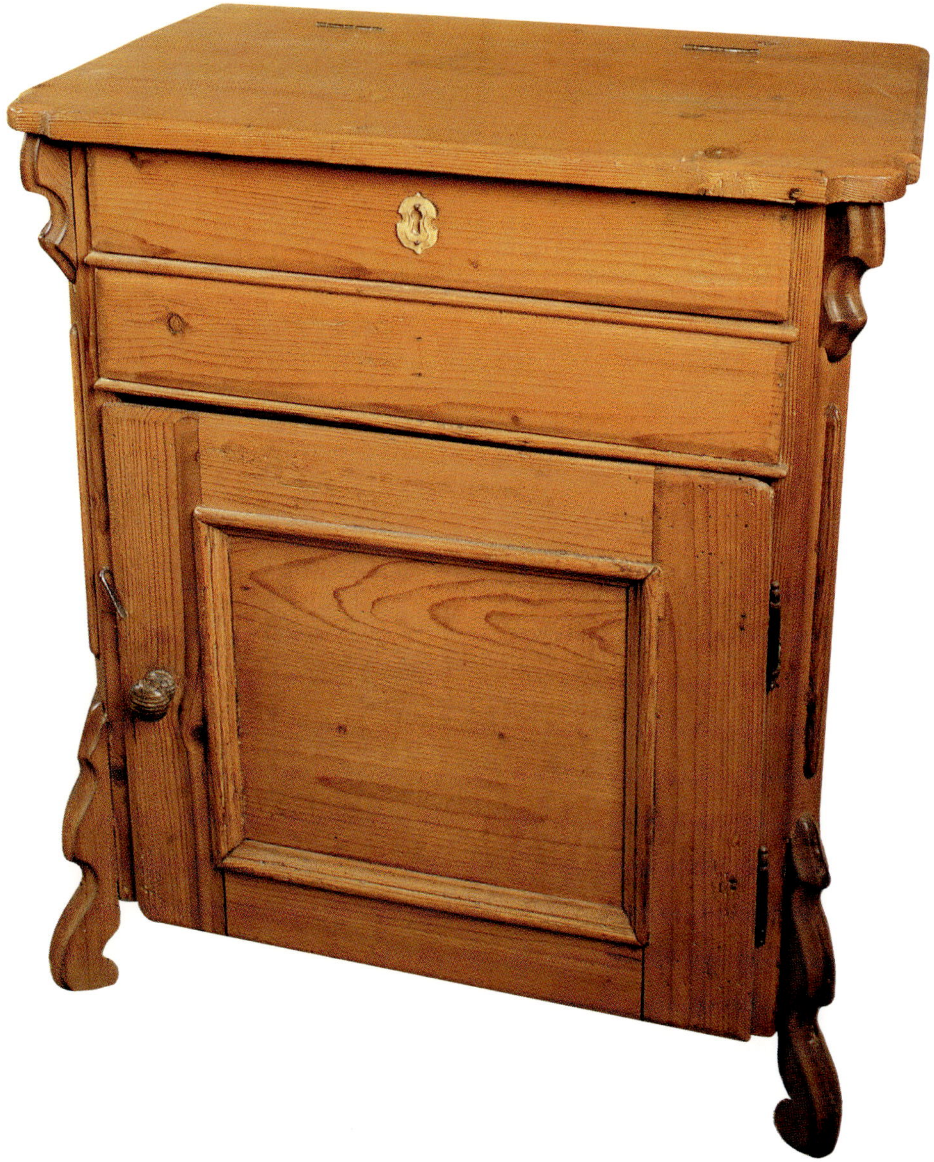

German nightstand with rectangular hinged top with shaped front corners, canted stiles with applied scrolls to the tops. The case front has a recessed-panel door with wooden knob pull and scrolled applied feet. $425.

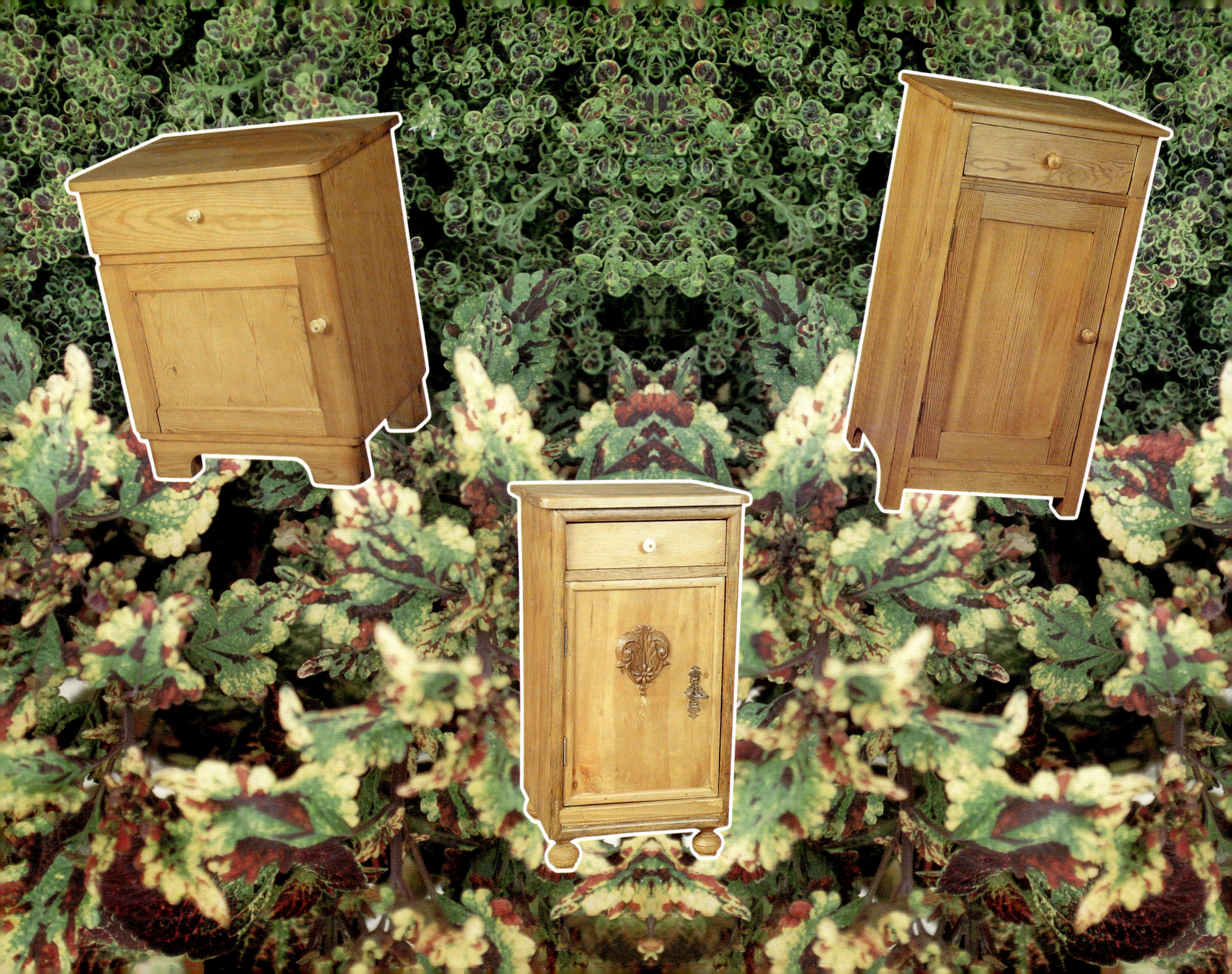

Opposite page:
Top left: Pine nightstand with drawer above a paneled door. $265.

Bottom center: Pine nightstand with drawer above a paneled door with applied relief carving. $265.

Top right: Pine nightstand with single drawer above paneled door and wooden knobs. $265.

Pine nightstand with raised splash board, single drawer and recessed-panel door; splash board and door decorated with a carved motif. $265.

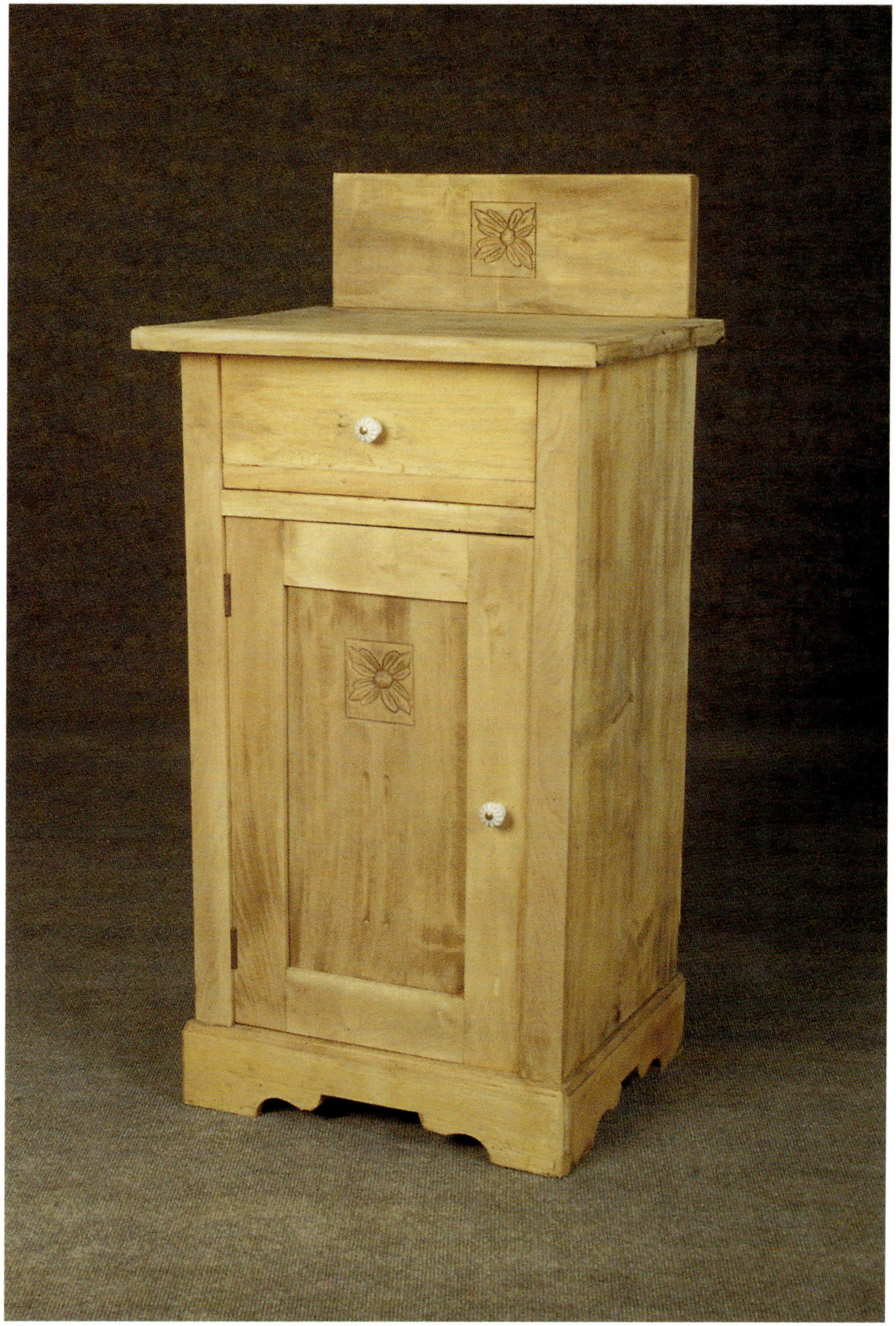

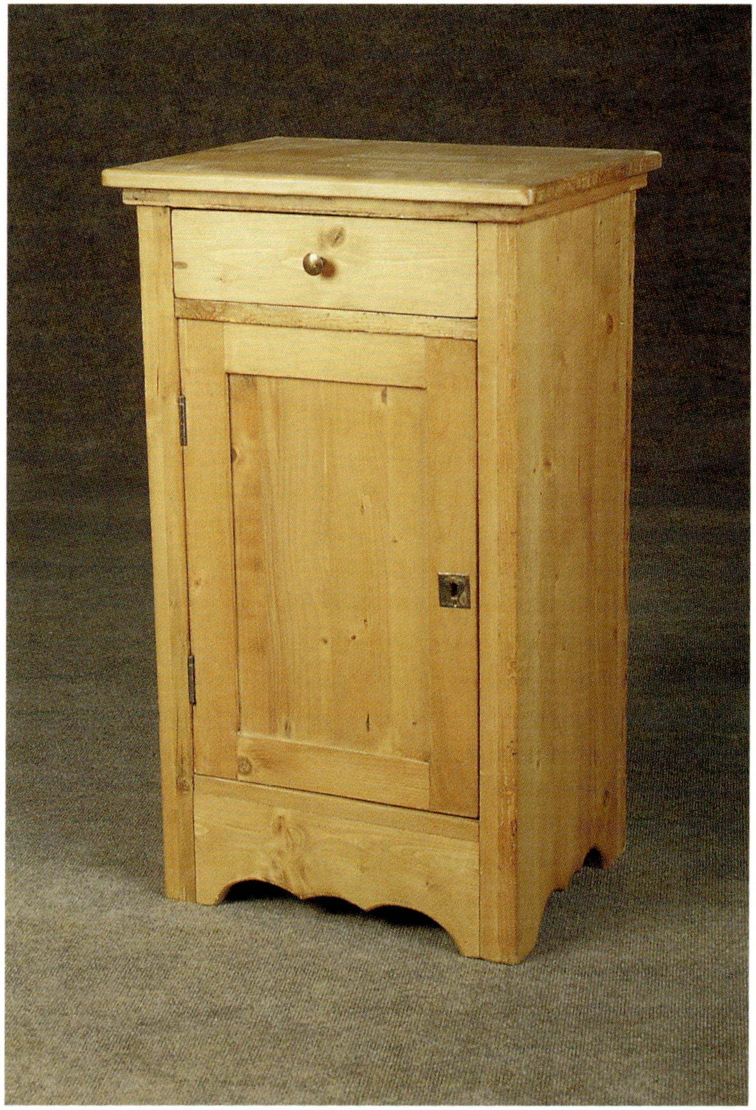

Nightstand with a rectangular top, single drawer with metal knob pull, recessed-panel door with escutcheon, and scalloped skirt. $265.

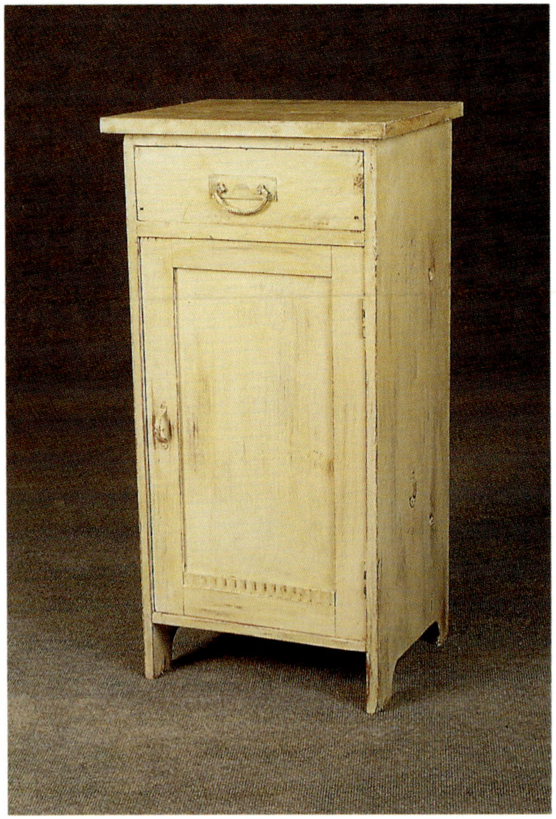

Nightstand with a single drawer with metal escutcheon pull, and rectangular recessed-panel door.

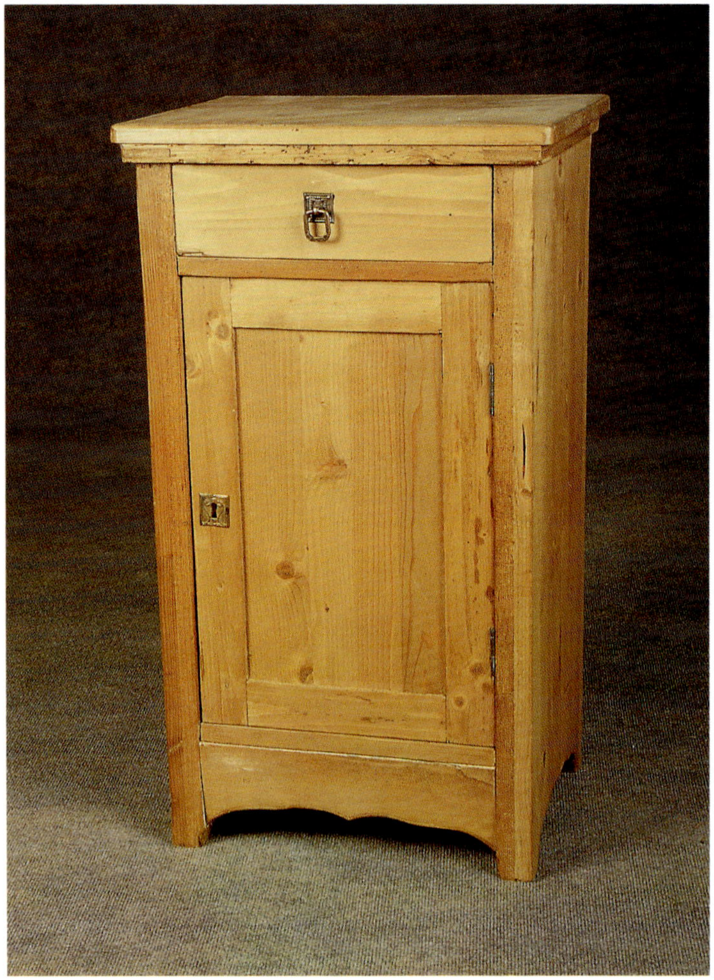

Nightstand with a rectangular top, single drawer, and recessed-panel door. $265.

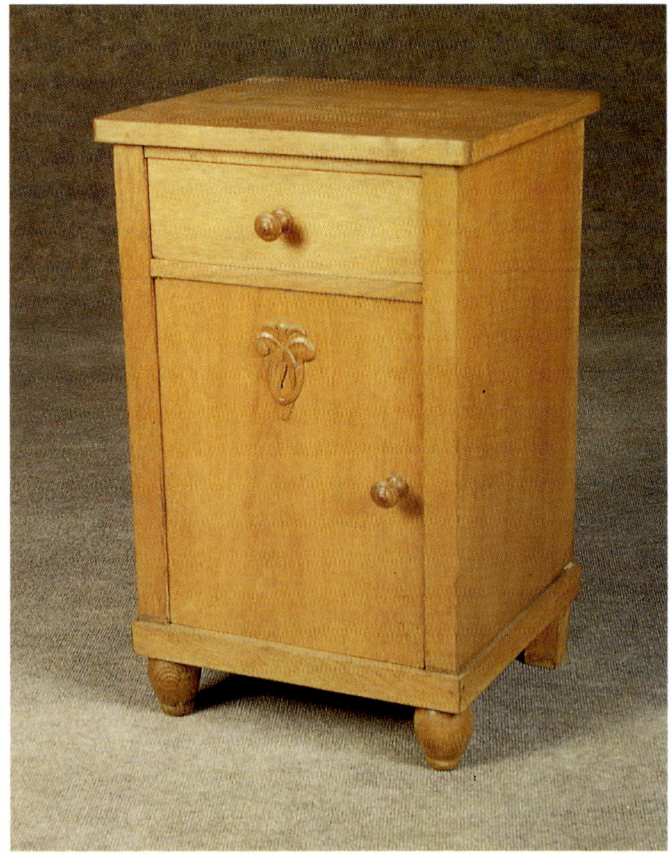

Nightstand with a plain rectangular top, single drawer, and recessed-panel door with wooden pulls and applied wooden scroll decoration, all resting on turned feet. $265.

Tables

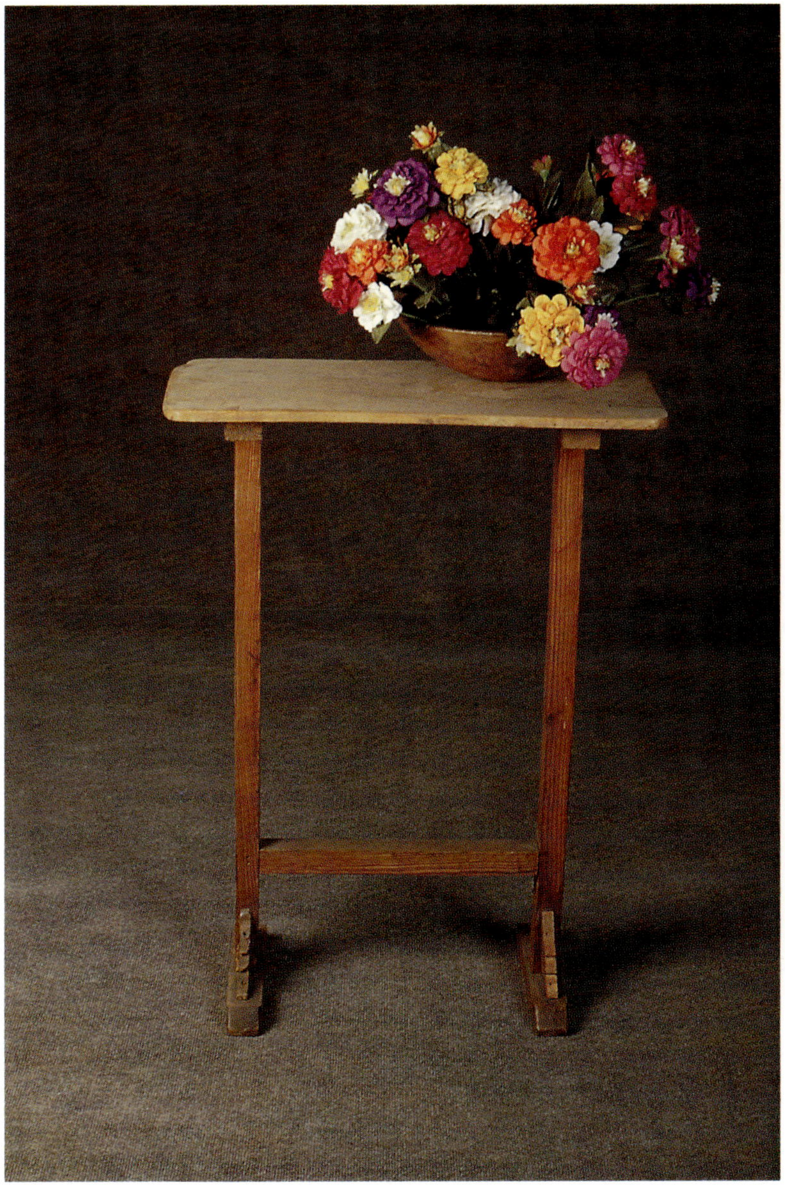

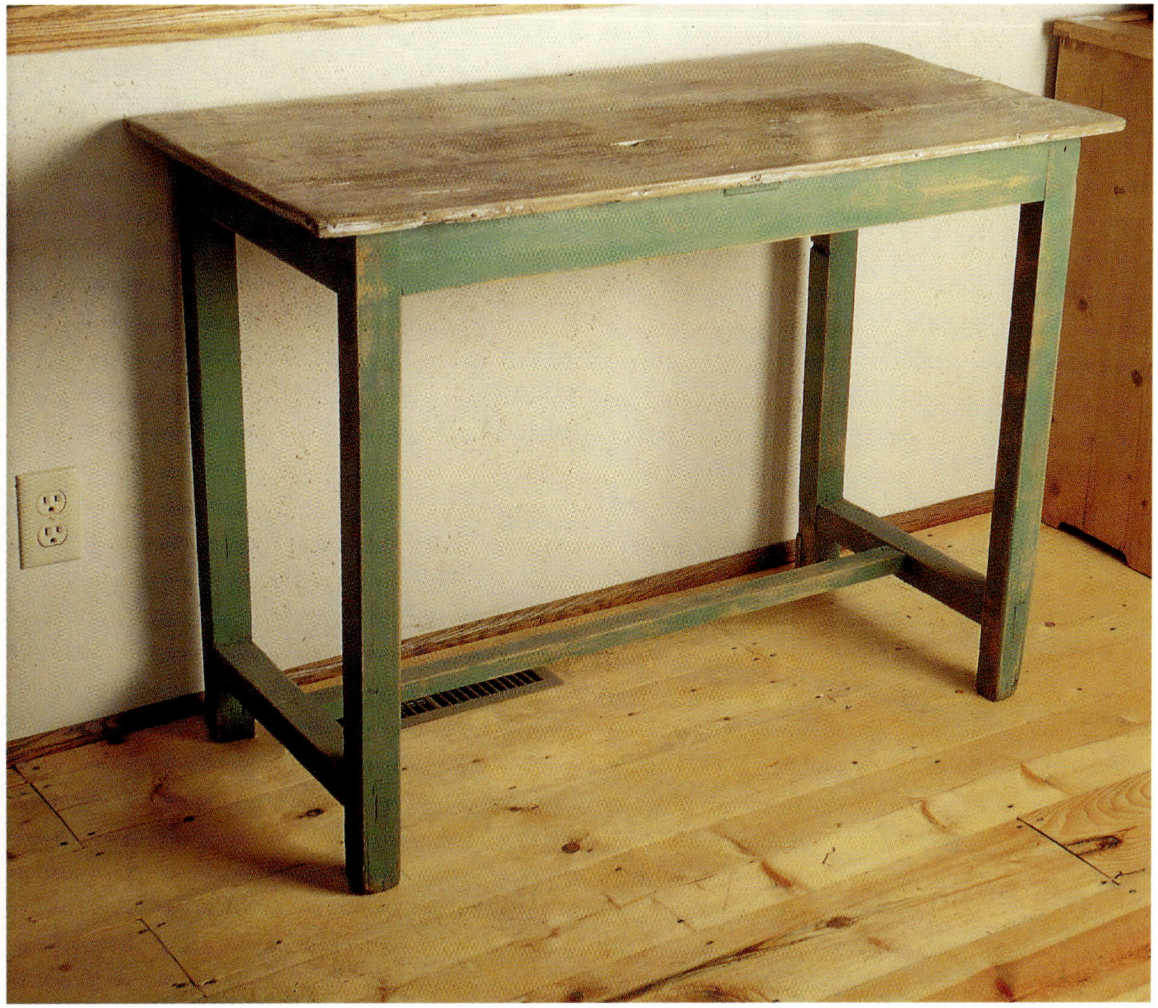

Tall table with rectangular top over straight rectangular stiles joined at the bottom by a stretcher and resting on trestle feet.

Irish painted table with white painted top and green painted skirt and four straight legs, c.1880. $495.

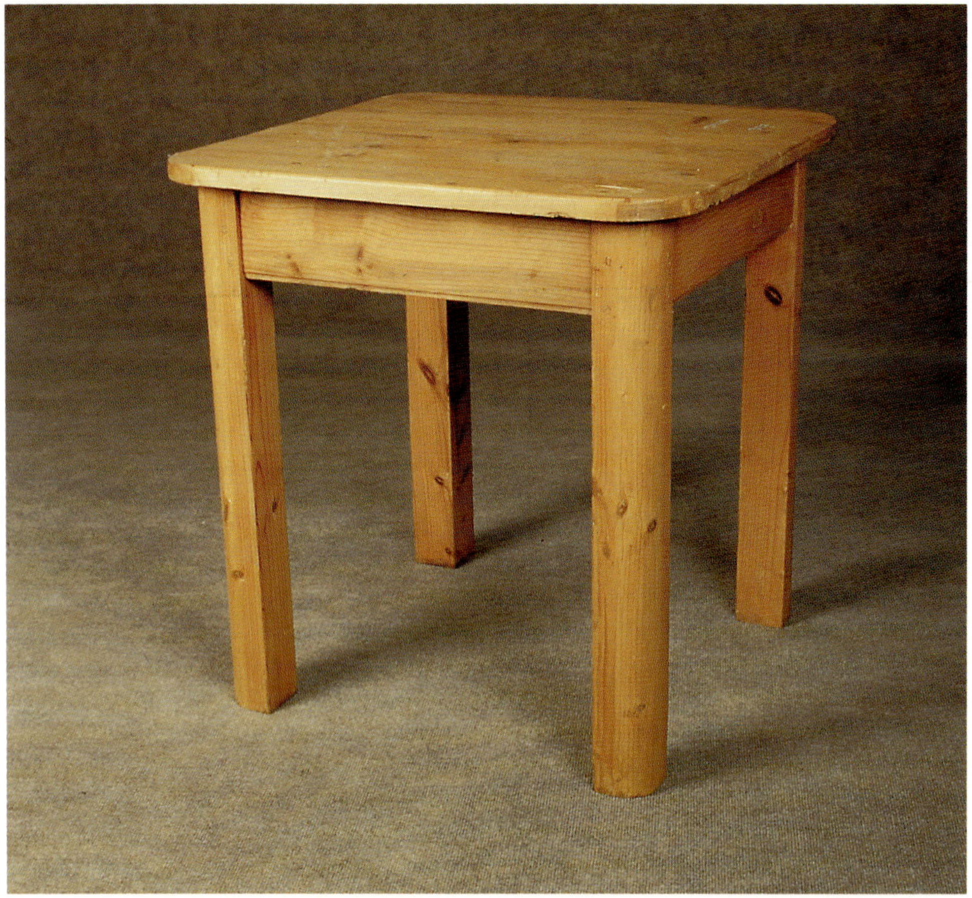

Hungarian center table with rounded corners to the square top, straight skirt with beaded edge, and straight rounded legs. $295.

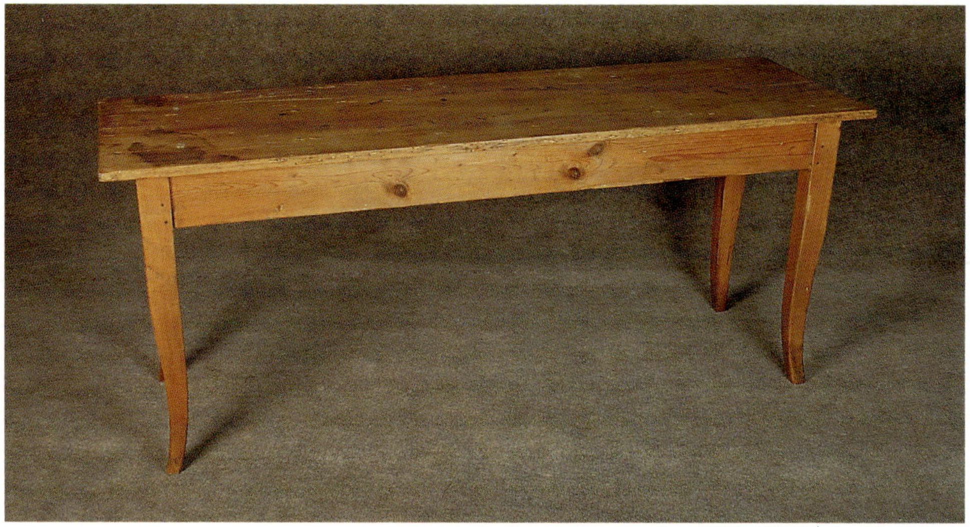

Rectangular Irish table with four serpentine square legs. $795.

Rectangular table with dough board top, single drawer and four turned legs, $495. and a yarn swift, 1880. $225.

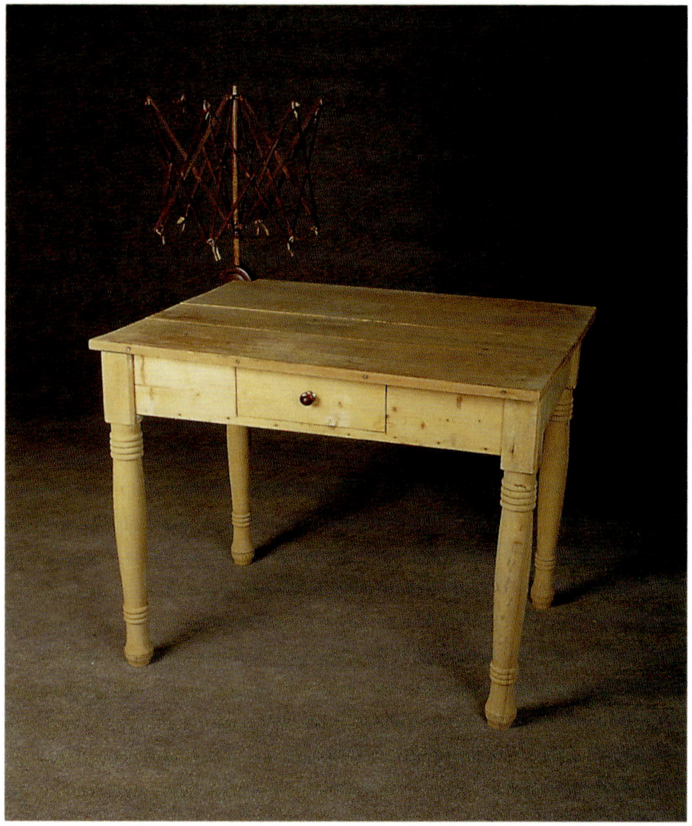

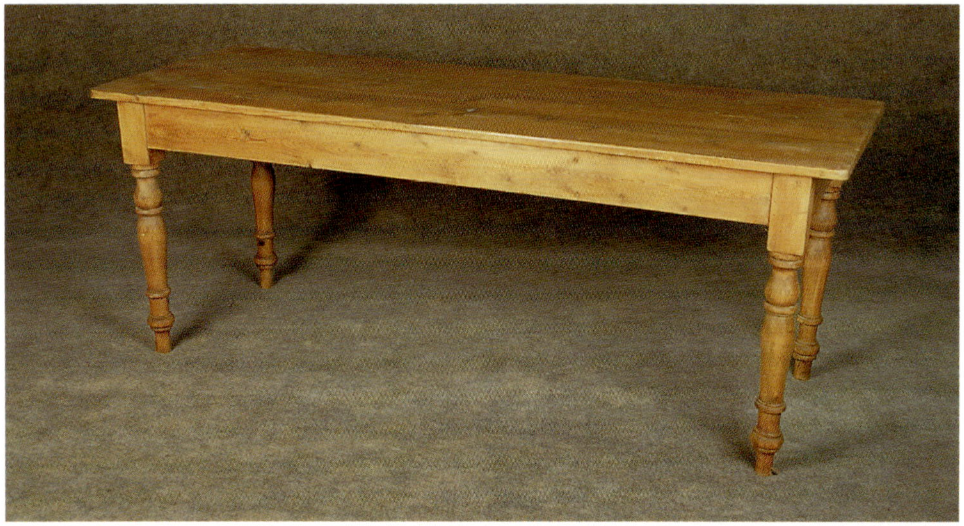

Rectangular table with straight skirt and four turned legs. $995.

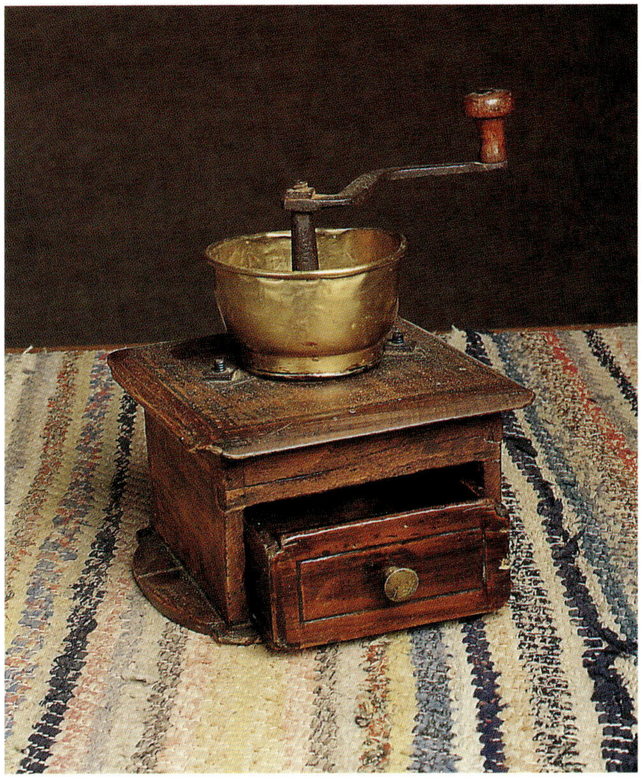

Coffee grinder

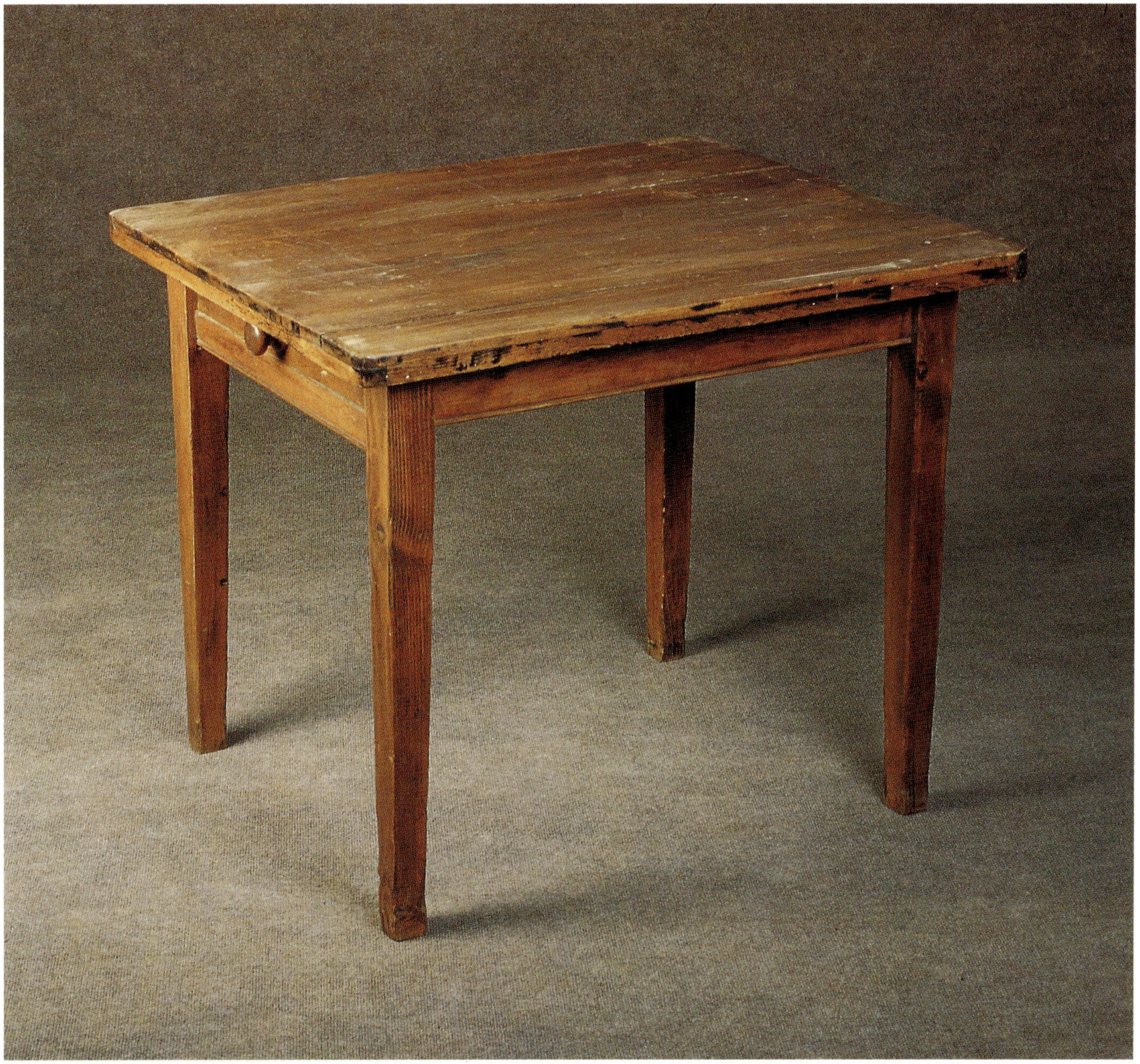

Irish table with one drawer in the straight skirt and wooden knob pull. $495.

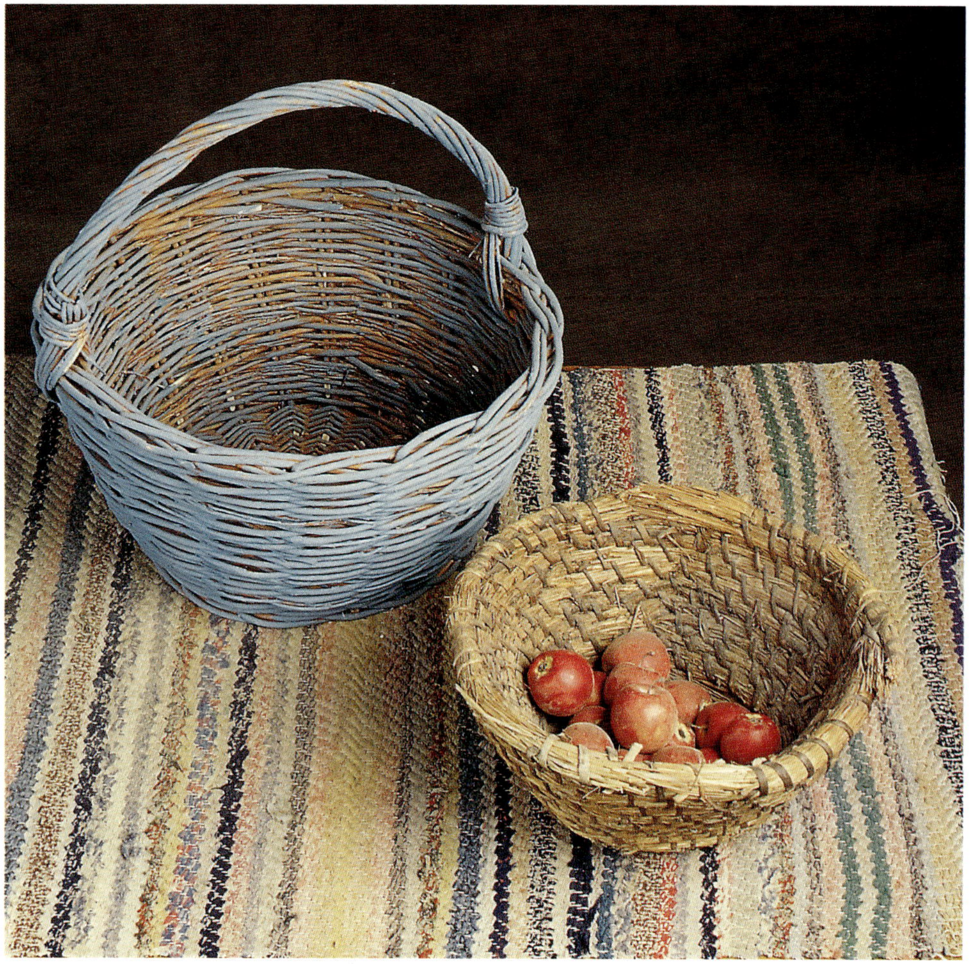

Two baskets, left woven with wicker and painted blue, right, woven with coiled, and bundled grass.

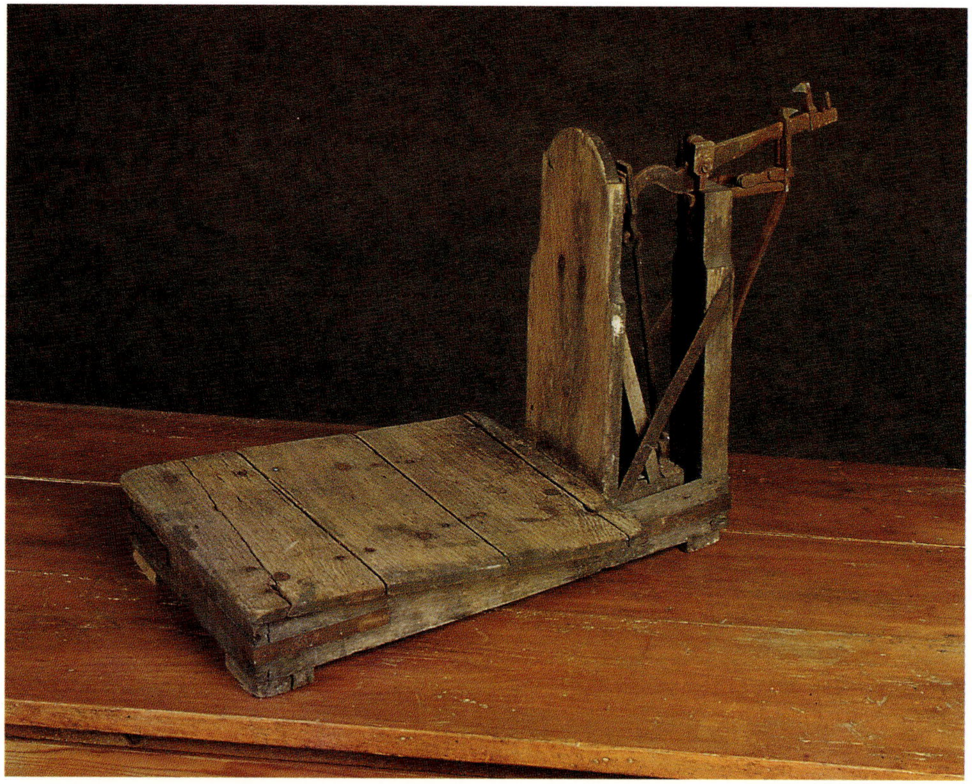

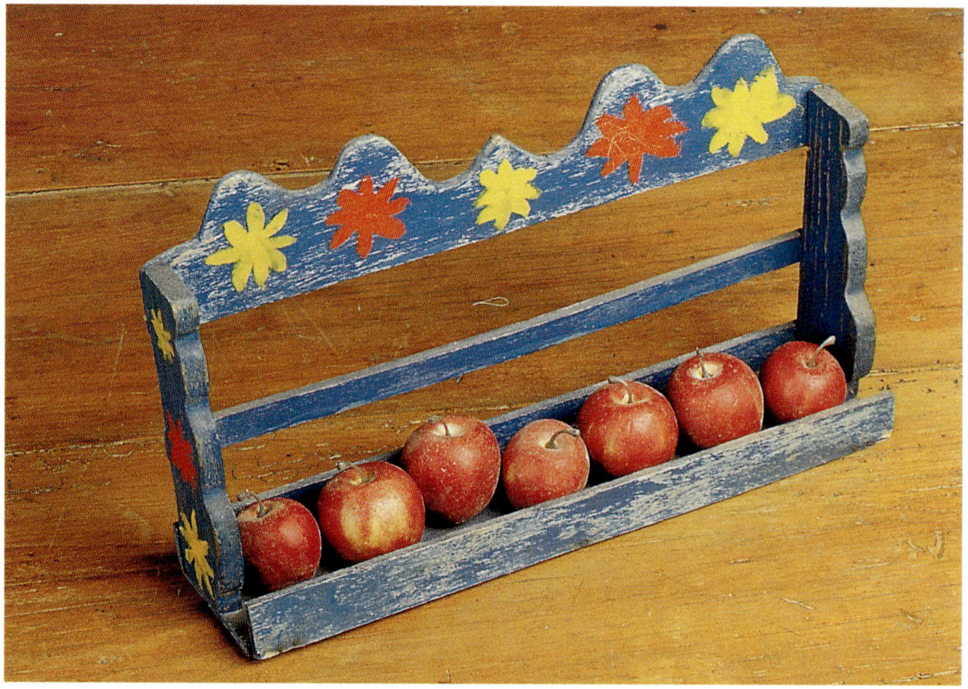

Top right: Table scale

Bottom right: Small wooden rack

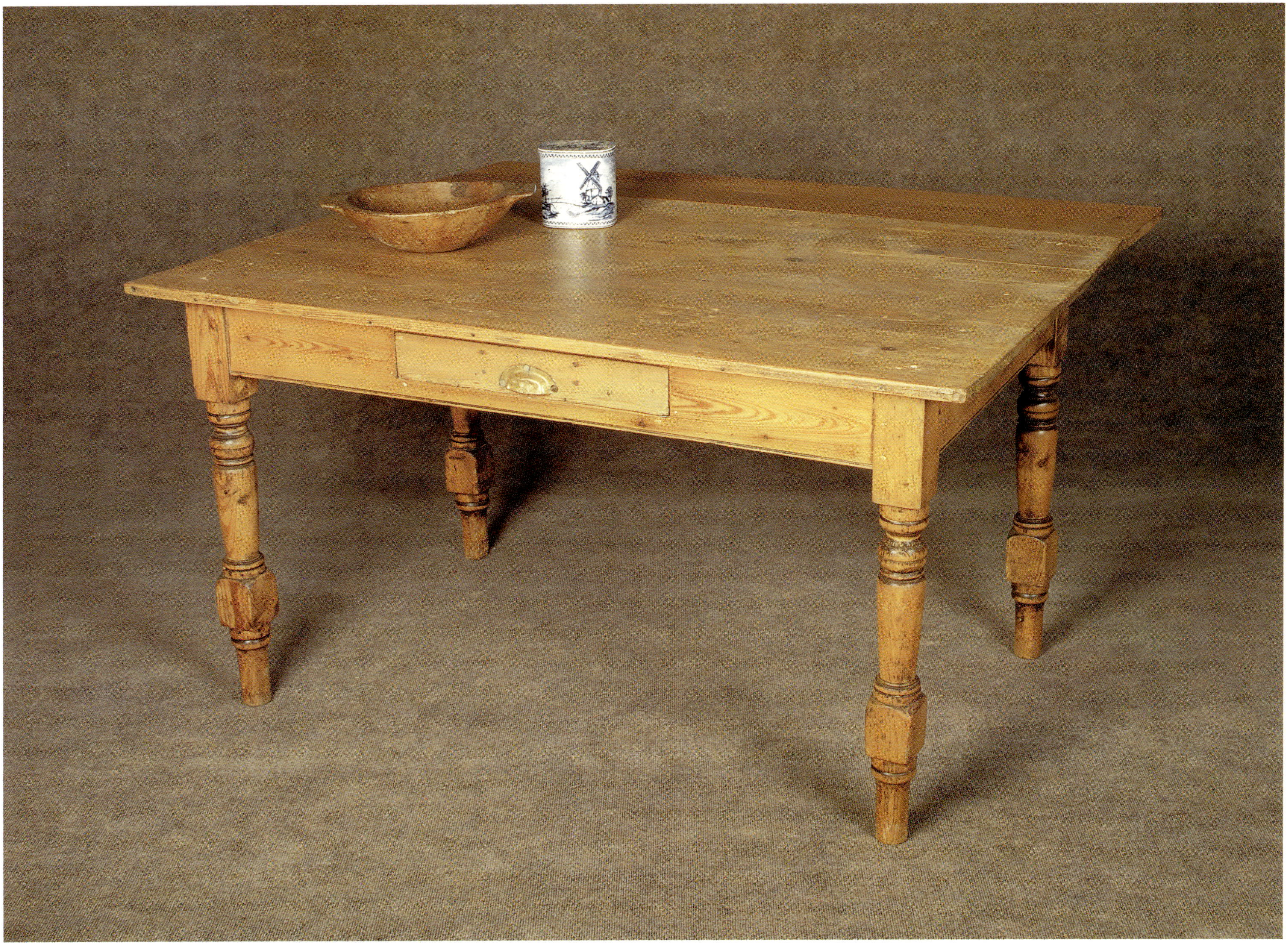

Large rectangular Irish table with single short drop leaf, single drawer, and turned legs. $1200.

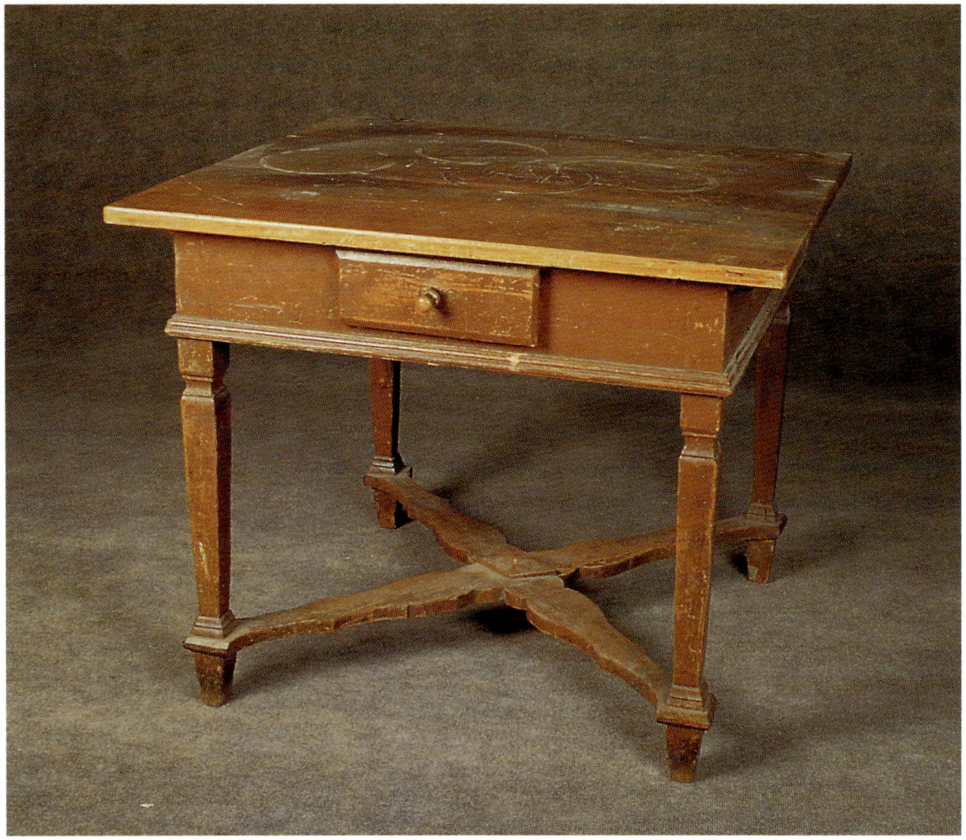

Irish pine table with rectangular top, single drawer with wooden turned pulls, and four square legs joined by a crossing flat stretcher. $695.

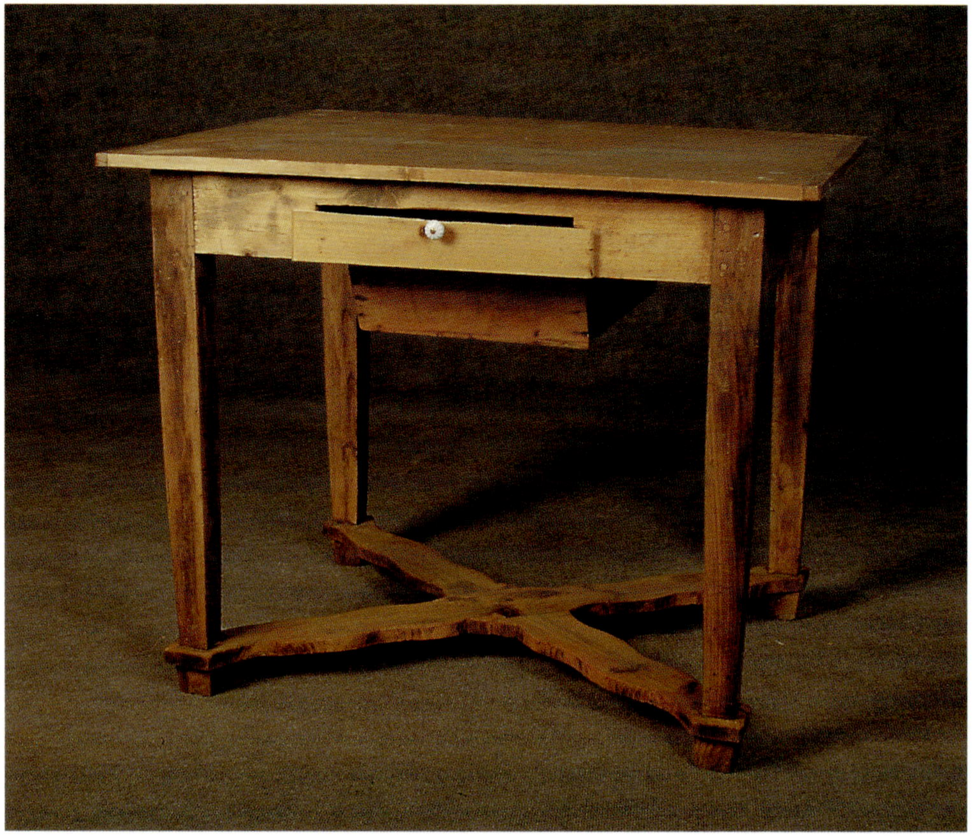

Table with rectangular top and a single dough drawer in the straight skirt, on tapering square legs joined by a crossing flat stretcher. $425.

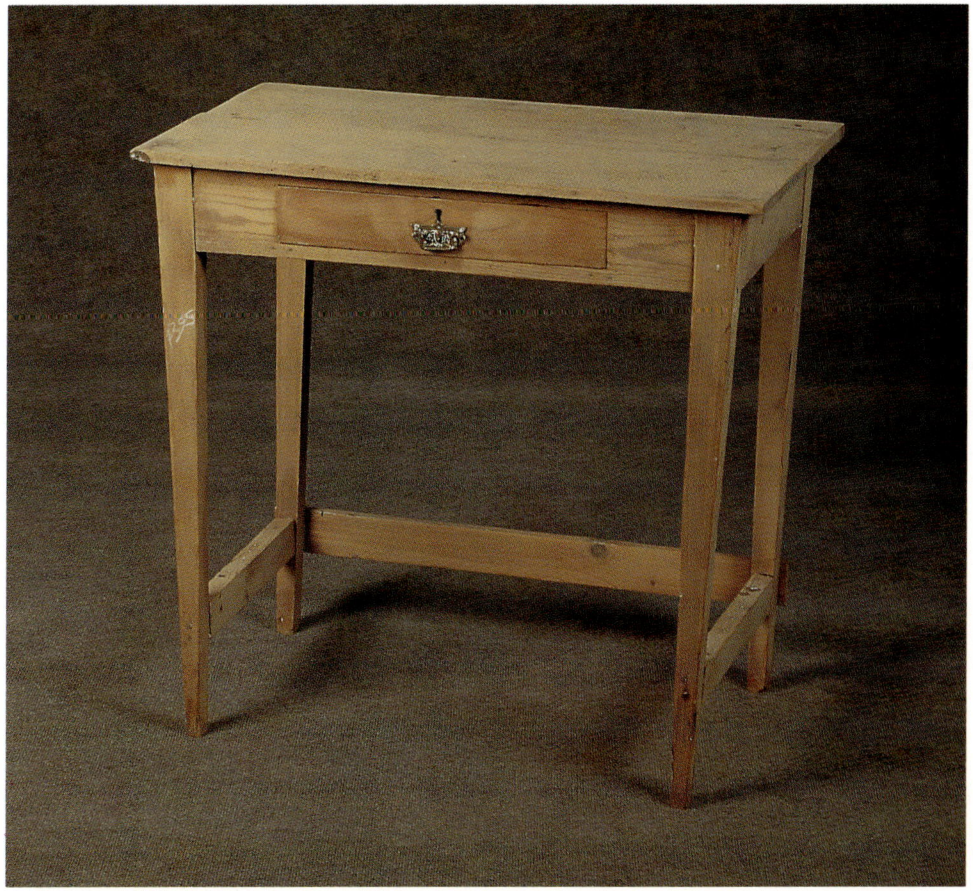

Small rectangular table with a single drawer in the straight skirt and four square tapering legs joined by side and back stretchers.

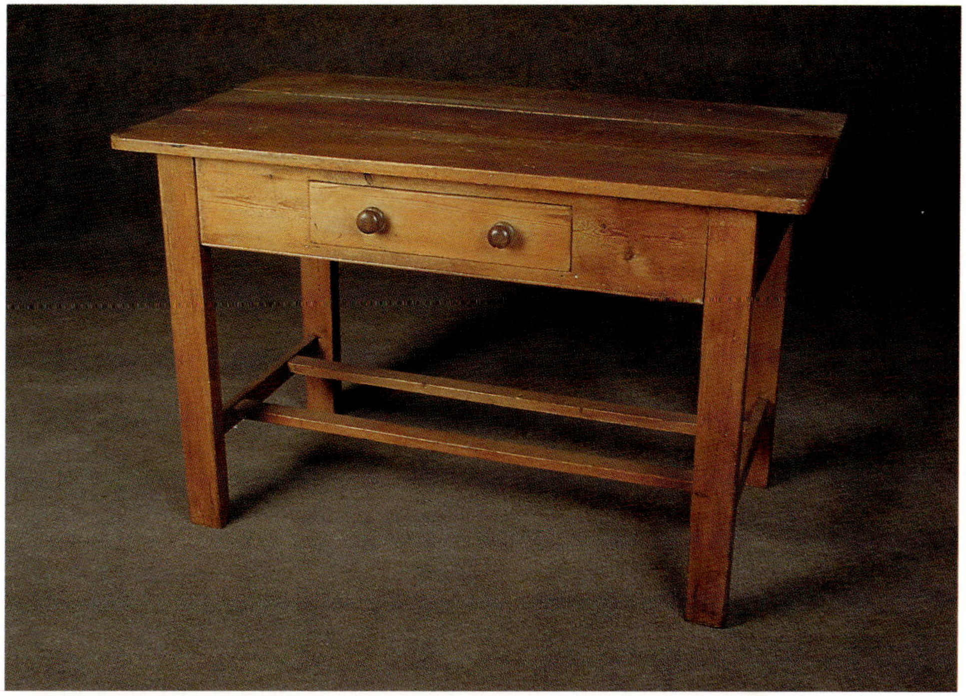

Table with grain painted surface, rectangular top, single drawer with mold trim and four square, shaped legs joined by a crossing flat stretcher. $595.

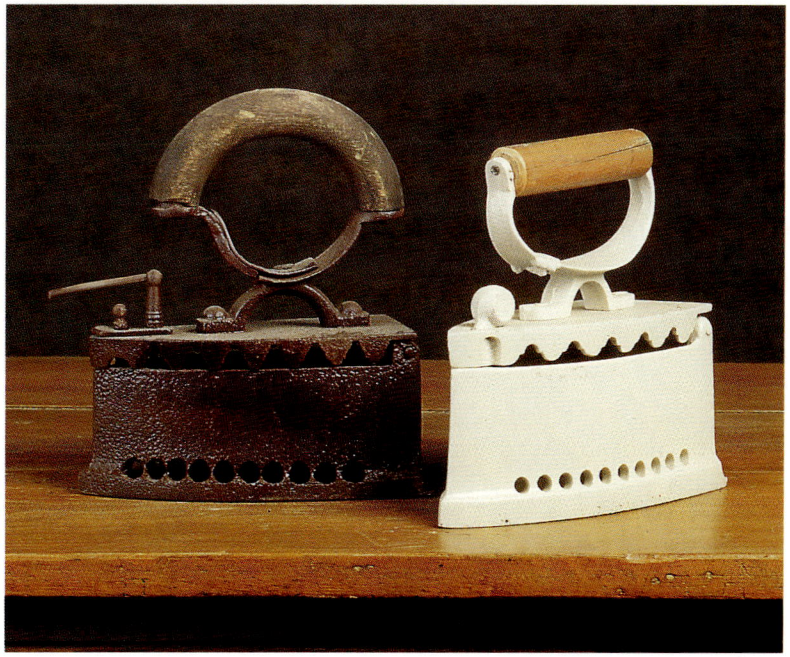

Pressing irons

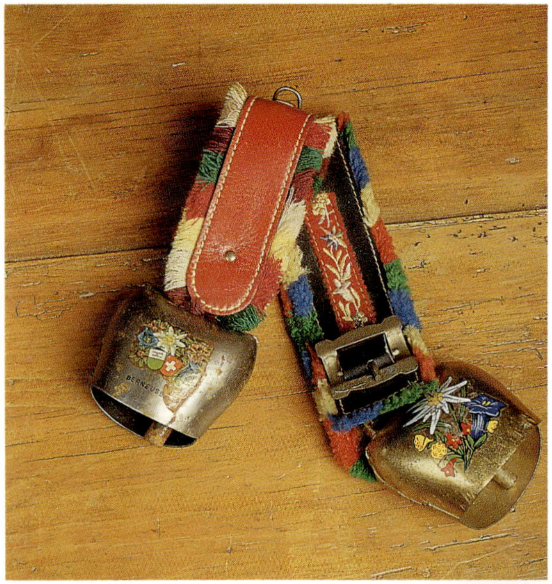

Cow bells, the beginning of the cheese-making process.

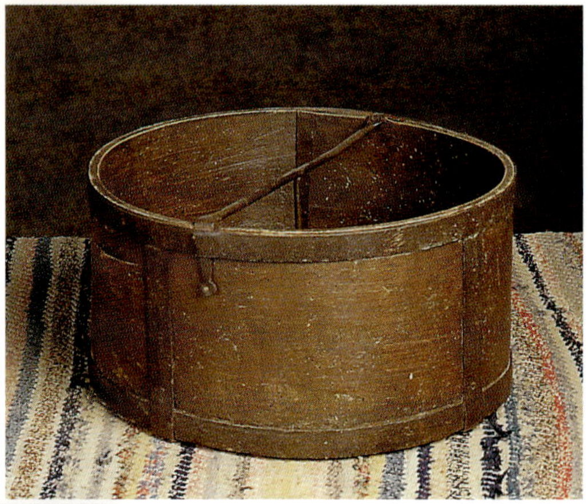

Cheese form

Cheese form

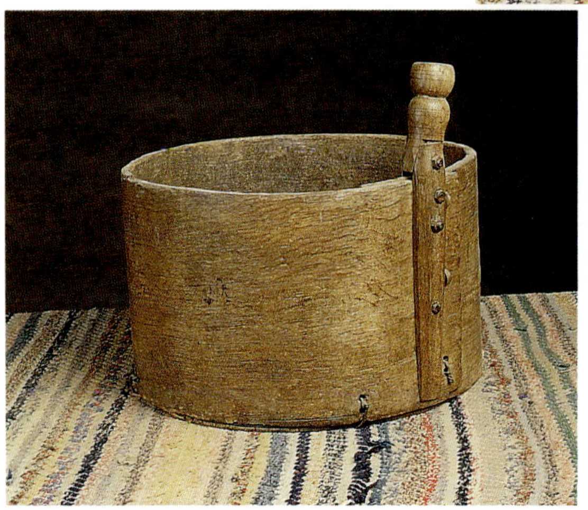

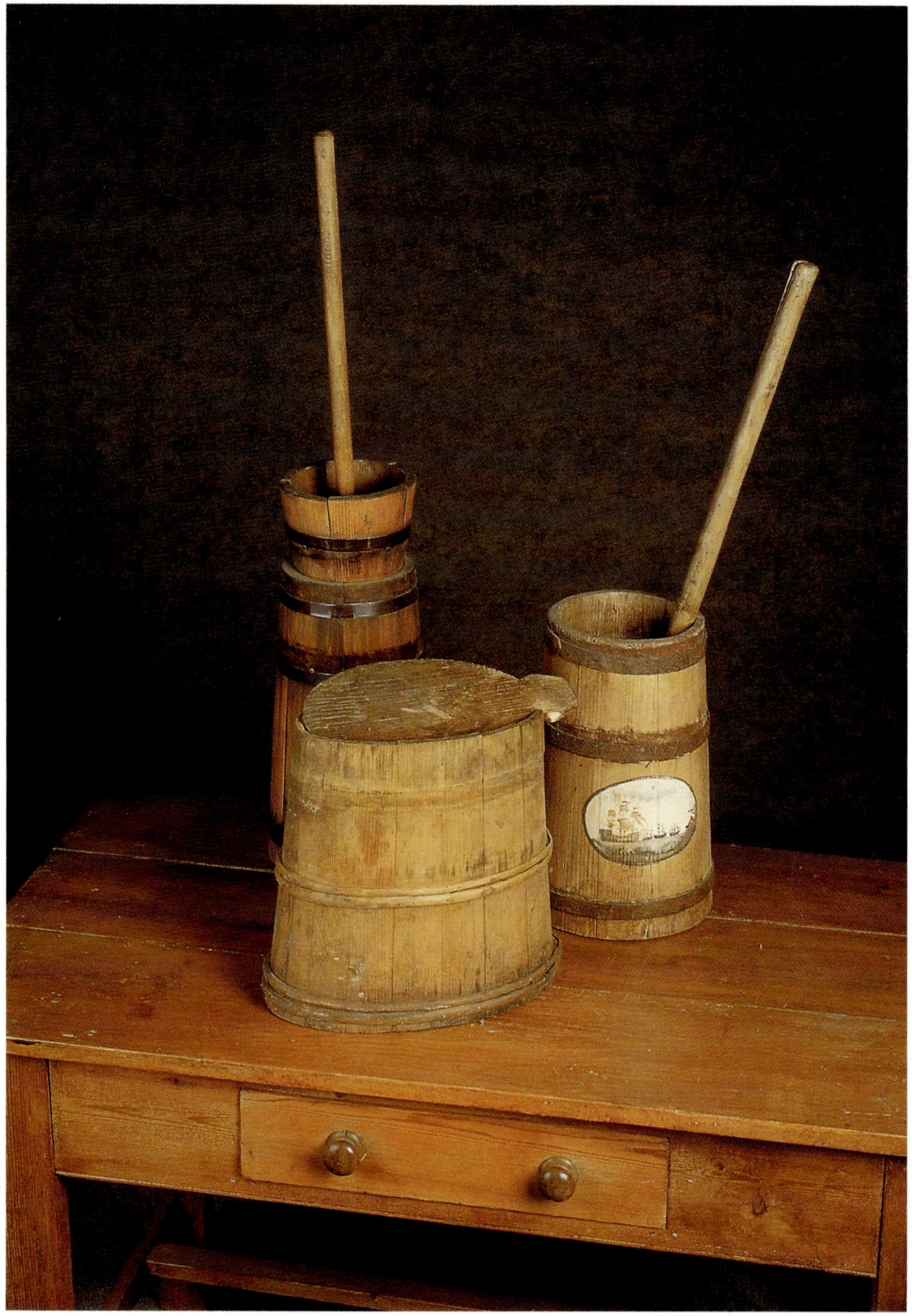

Two butter churns and a water jar

Loaf of Bread, A Jug of Wine . . .
Dough Troughs

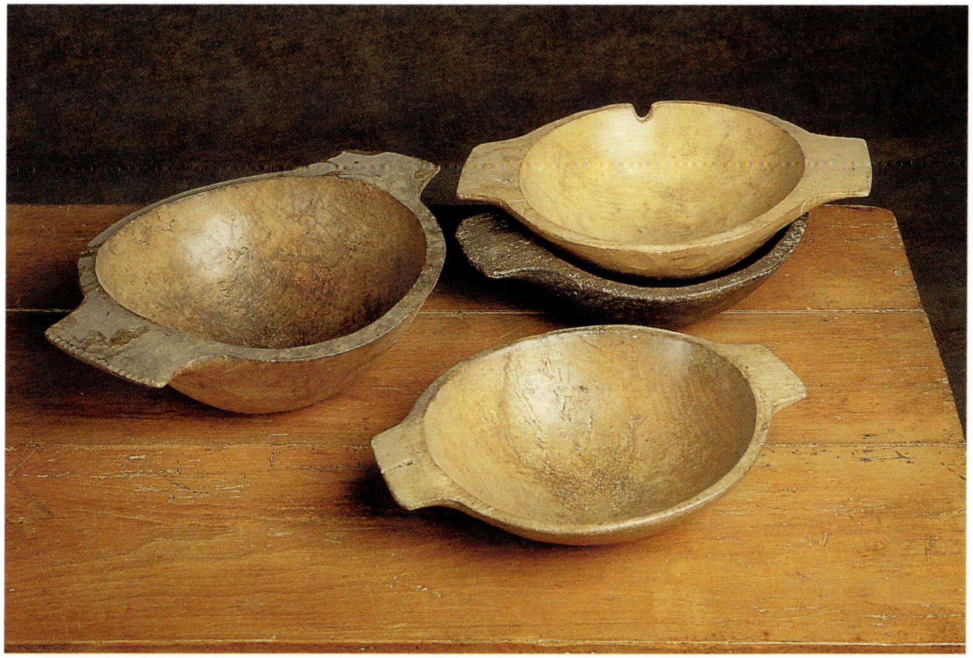

Wooden bowls

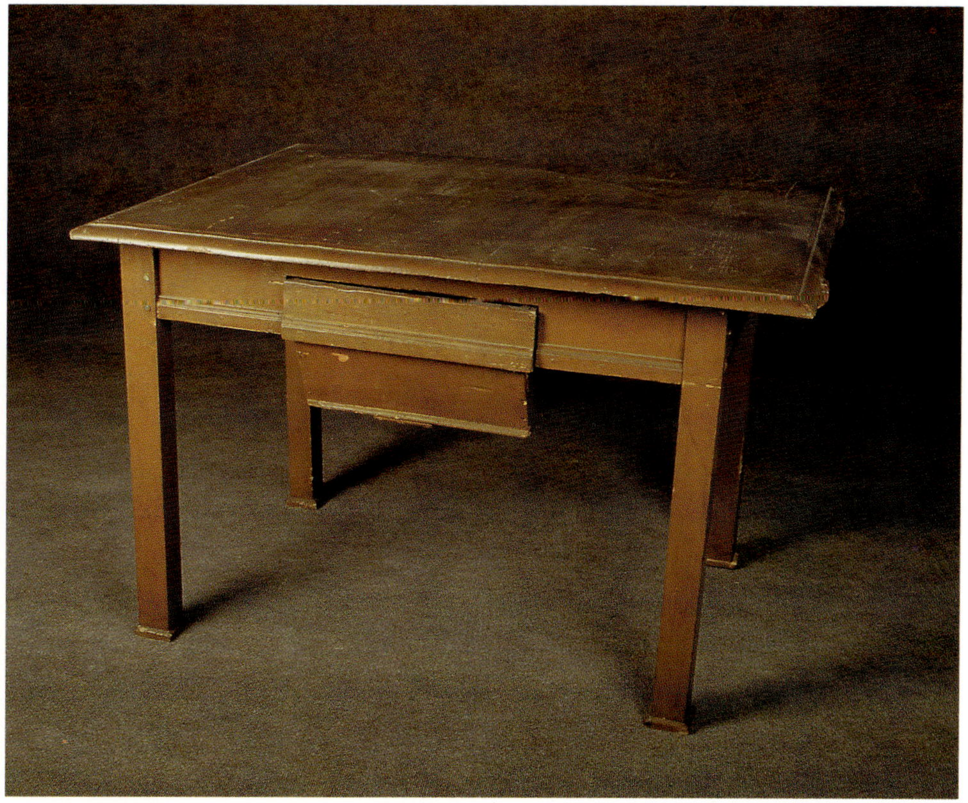

German table with painted surface, rectangular molded edge top, dough drawer in the skirt, and square legs on blocked feet. $595.

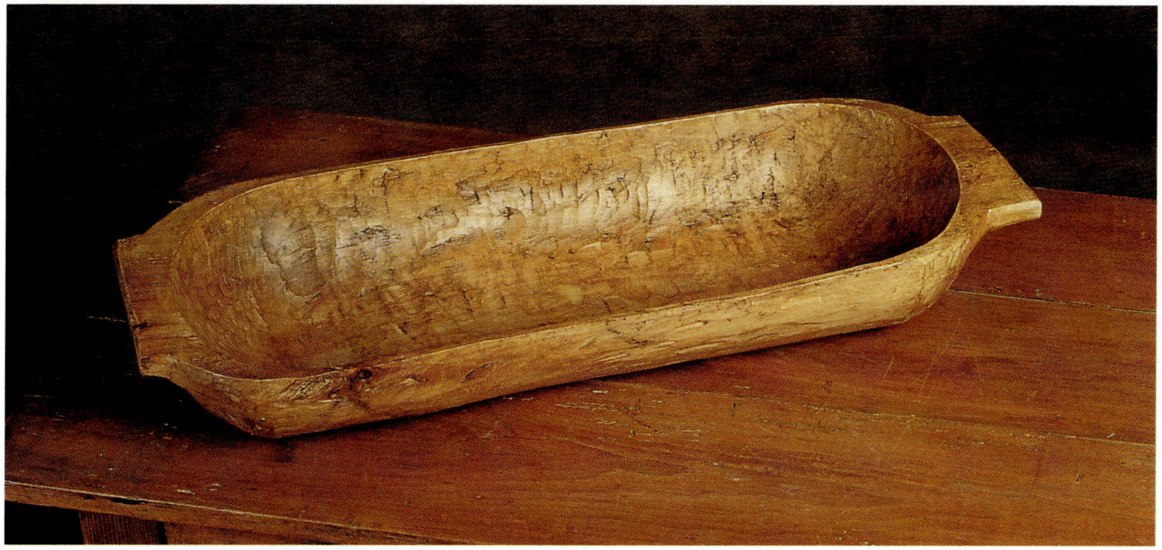

A dough bowl

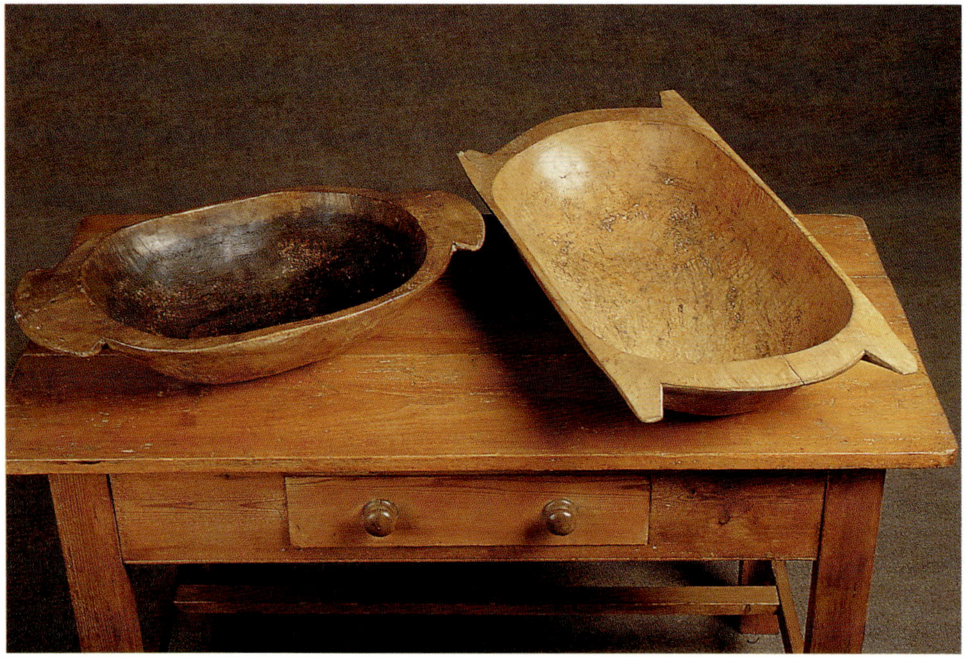

Two dough bowls

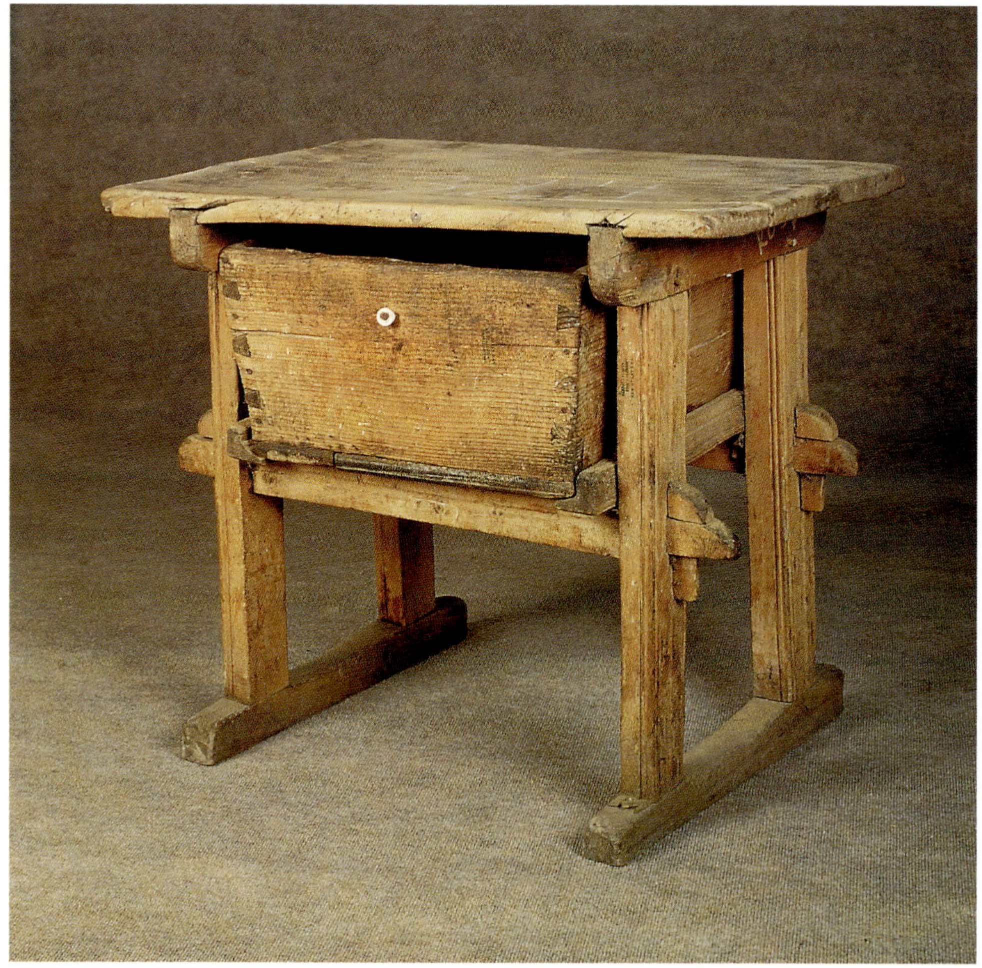

Table with rectangular top on battens above a deep dough trough with white porcelain handle and resting on four pegged legs and trestle feet, 30" wide. $795.

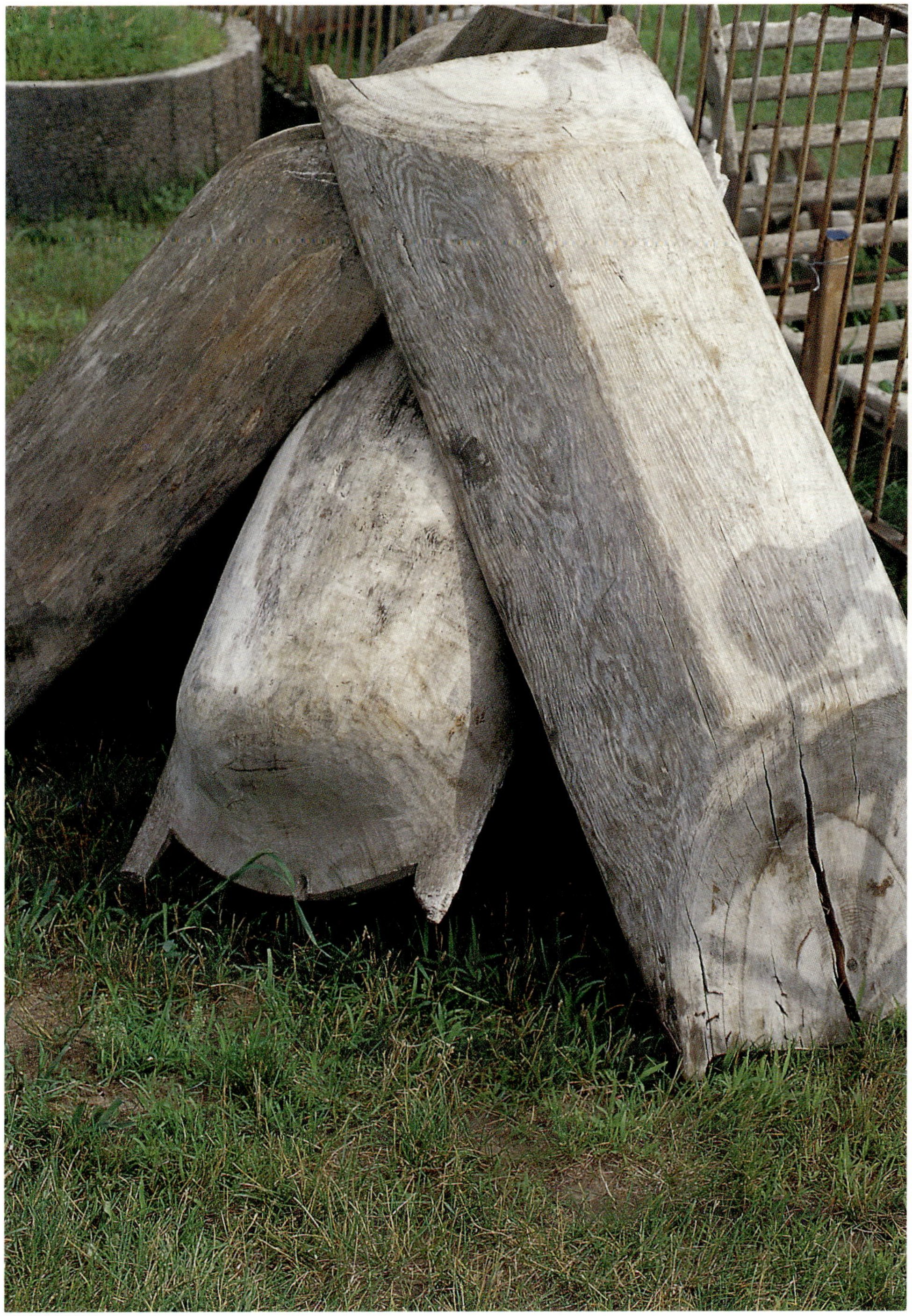

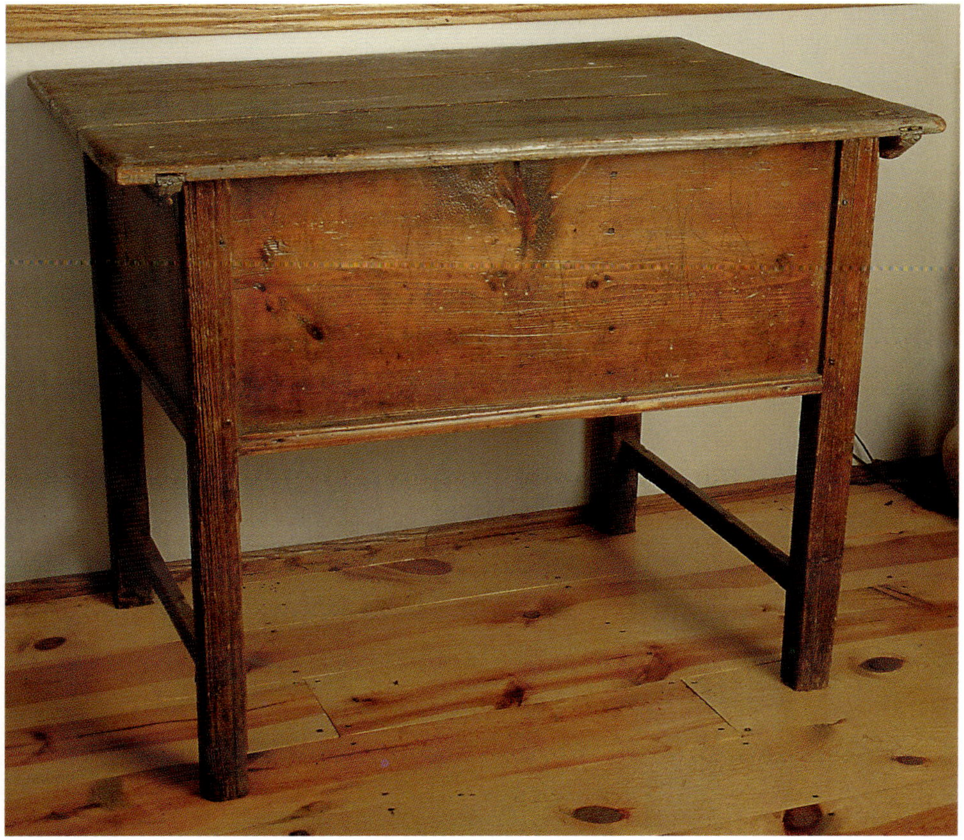

Romanian painted table with sliding rectangular top over a deep dough trough divided into two parts and resting on feet, c.1850s. $595.

Three large dough bowls ready for use

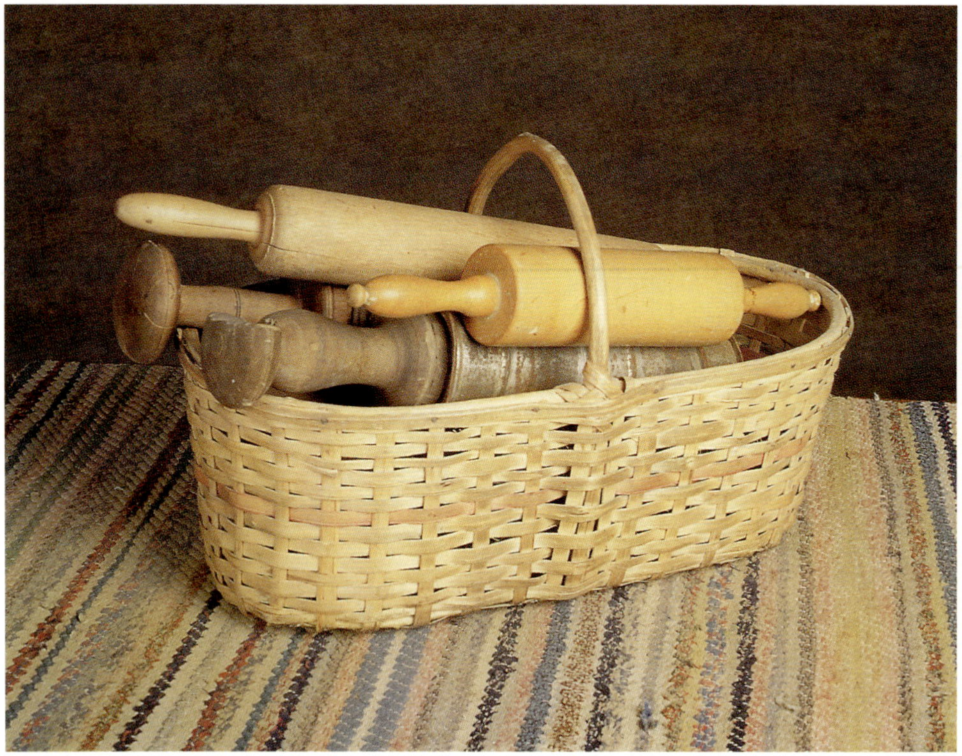
Basket with rolling pins and pastry presses

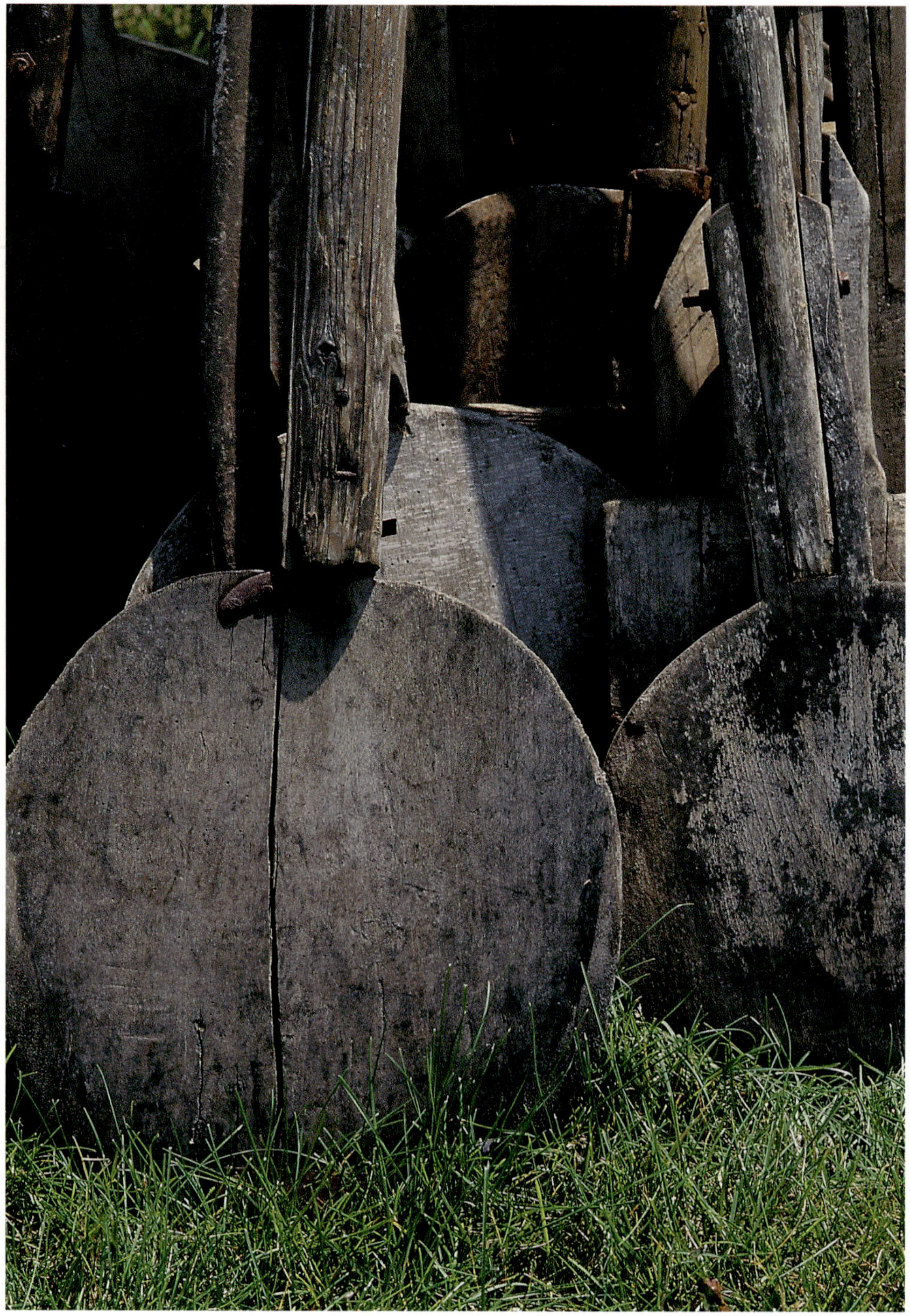
Round bread peels

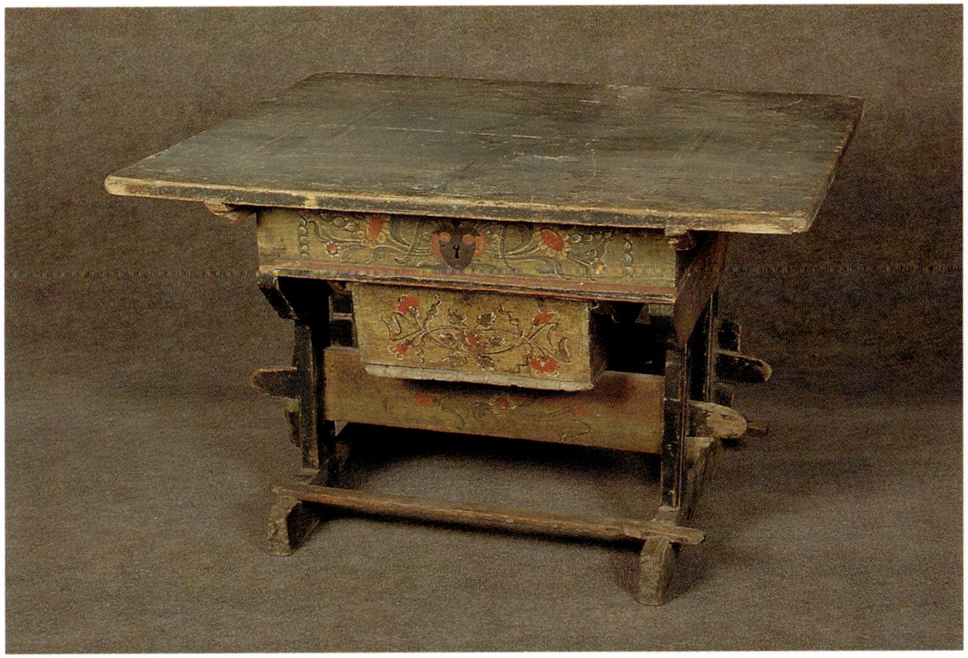

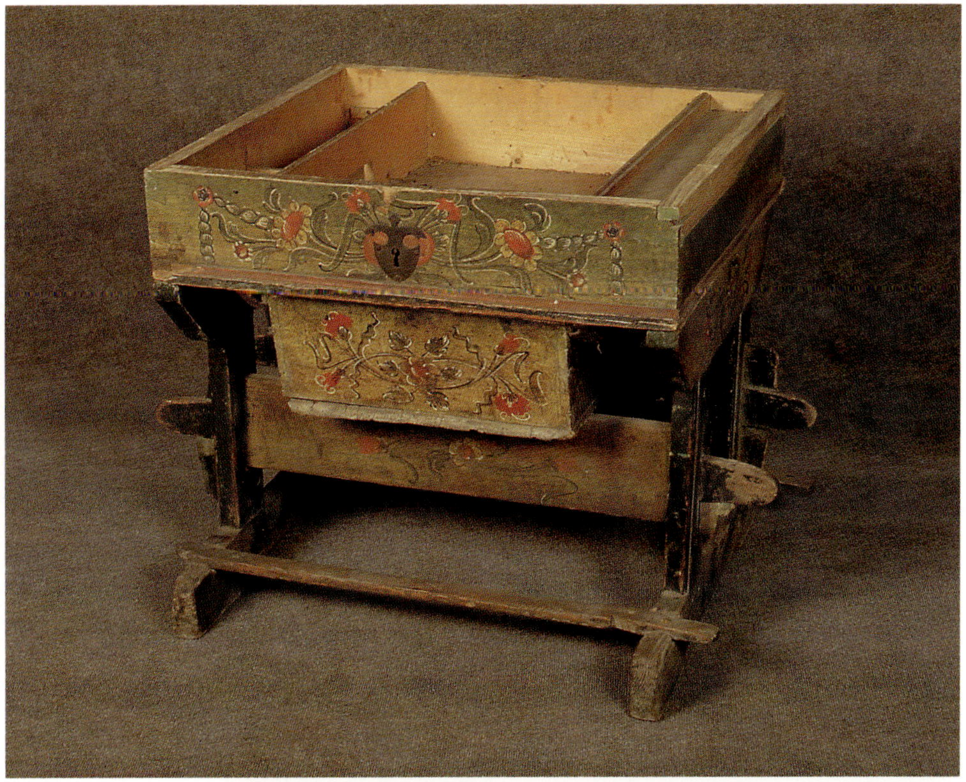

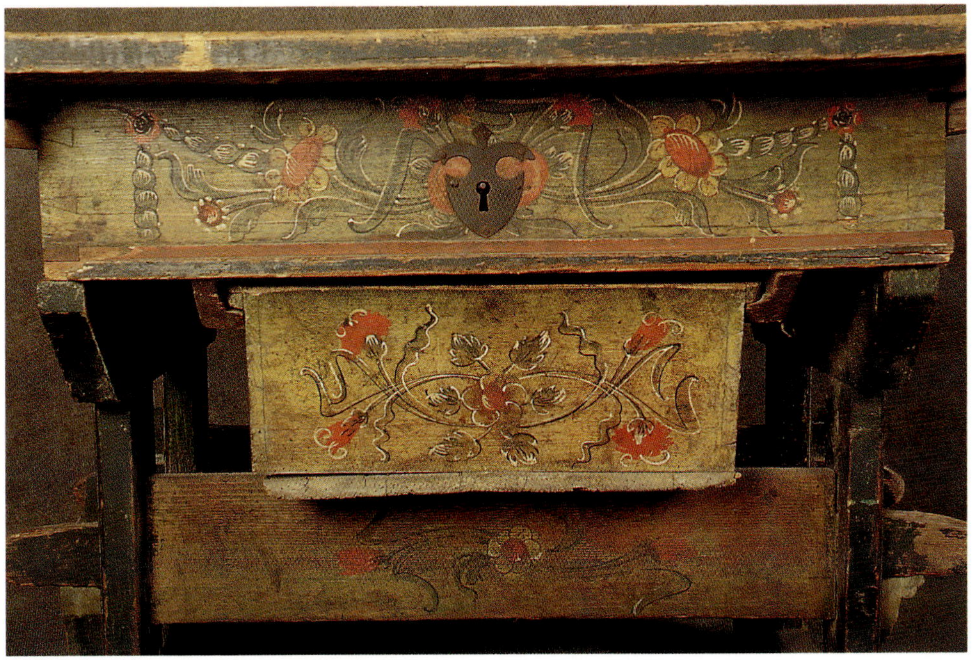

Table with its original painted decoration of floral garlands, dated 1855. The rectangular top slides on battens on the base which has a deep drawer with iron escutcheon and another, smaller, dough rising drawer, each decorated with floral ornamentation. The legs are pegged to the horizontal stretchers, also ornamented, and joined by two flat stretcher-foot rests. $7495.

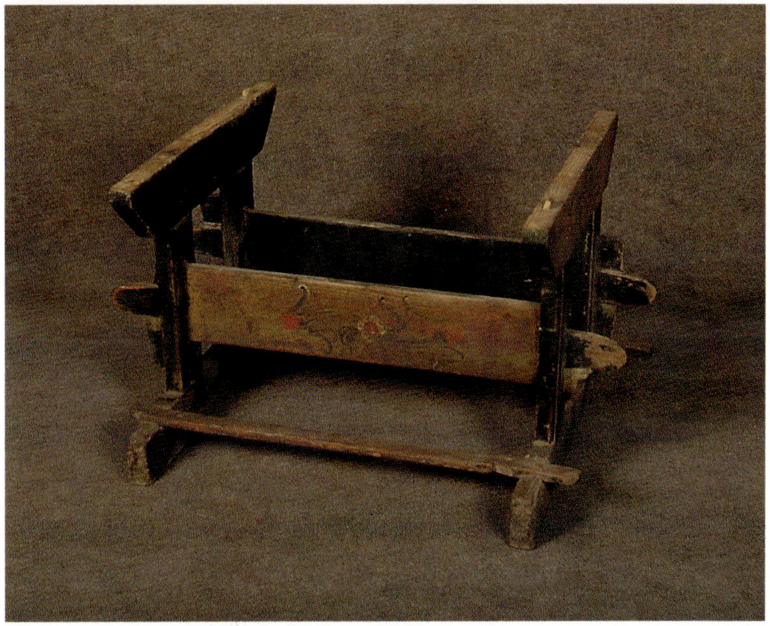

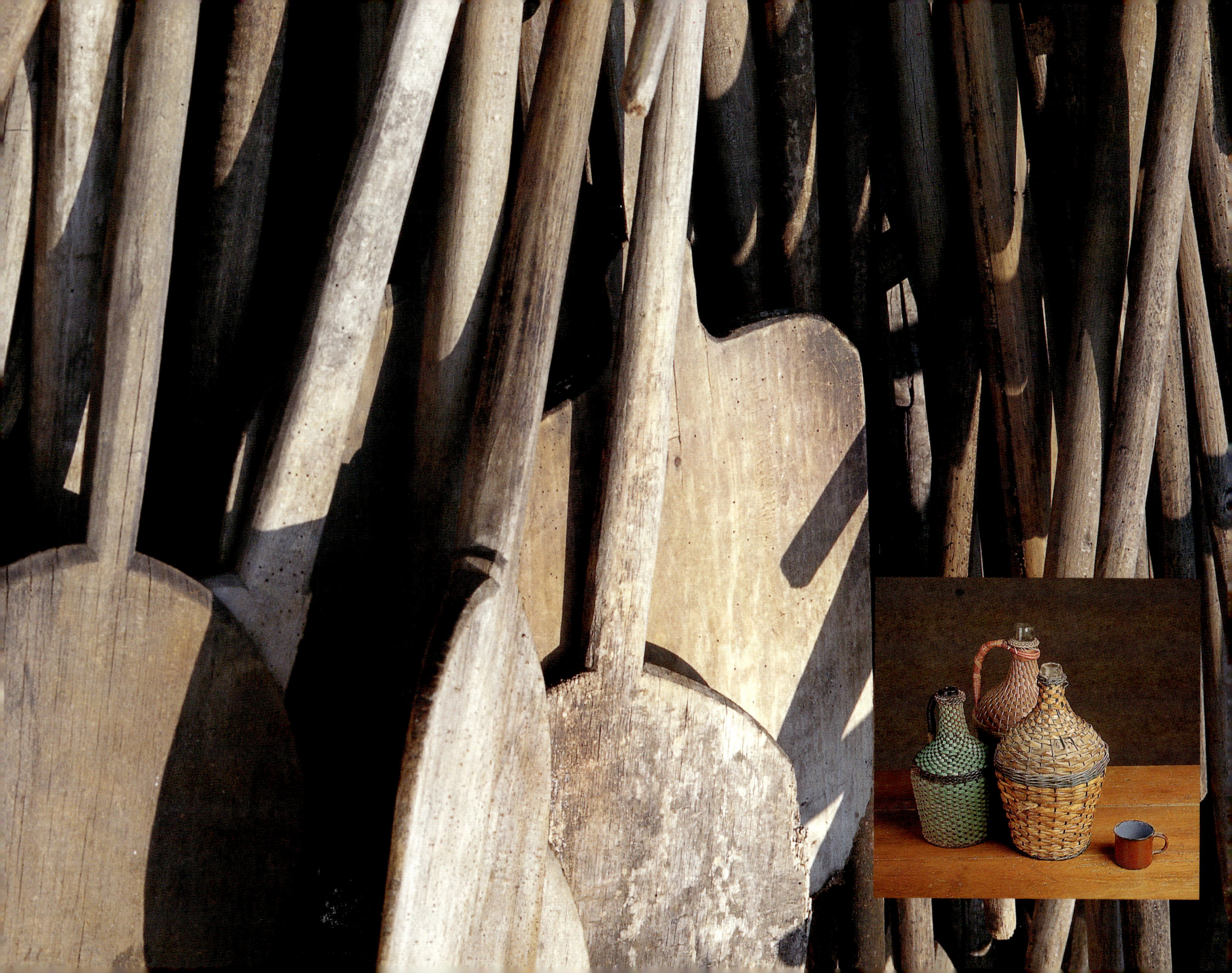

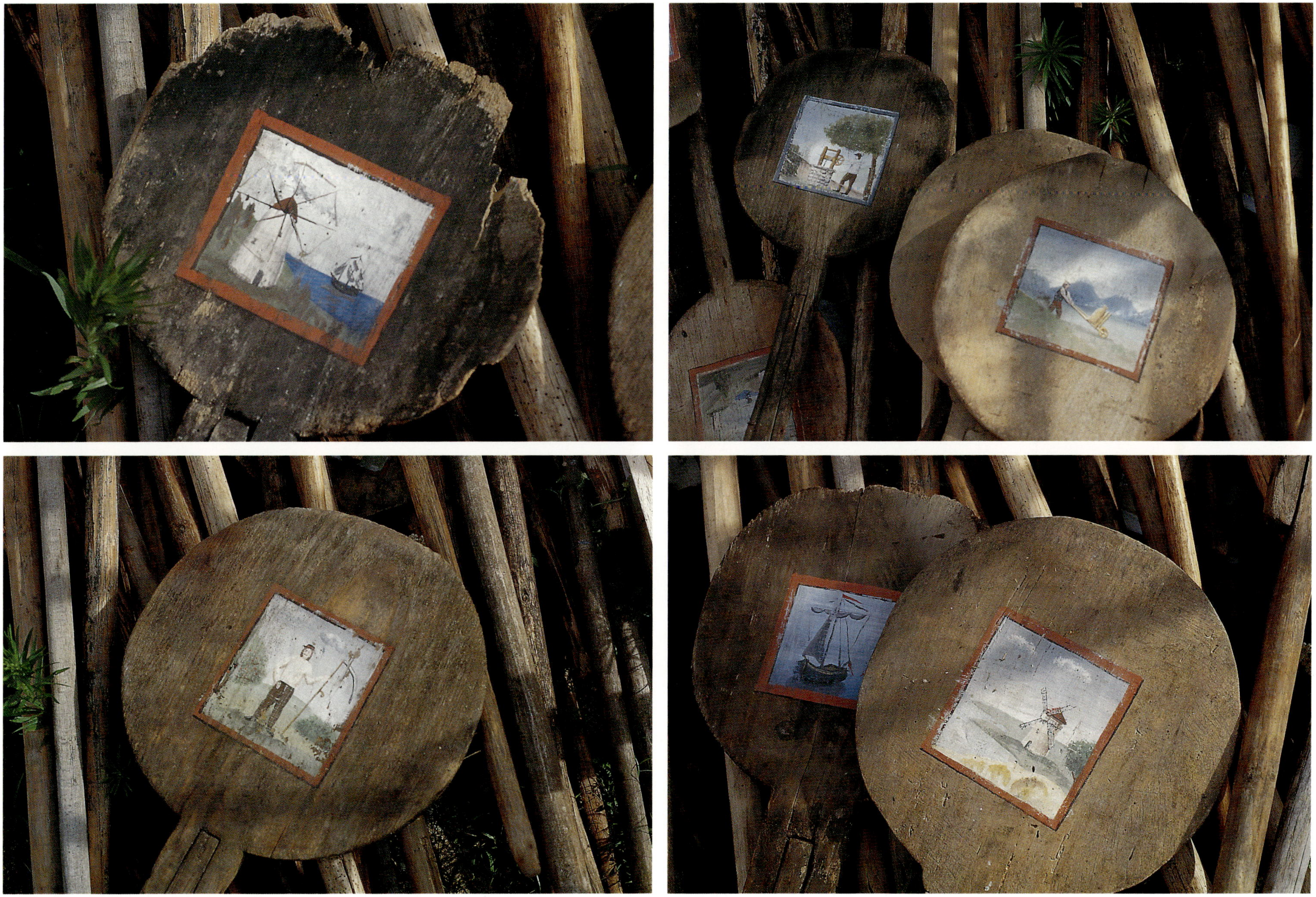

Opposite page:
Bottom right: Wine jugs

Background: Group of bread peels

Decorated peels

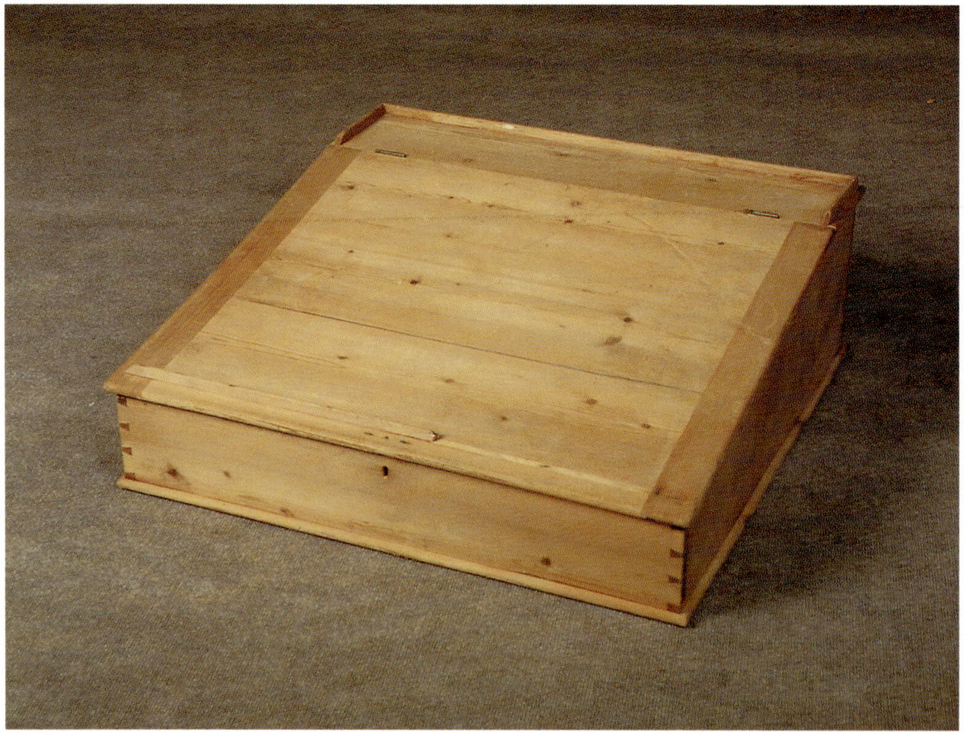

Writing desk without legs, pine, slanted lid and dove-tailed corners.

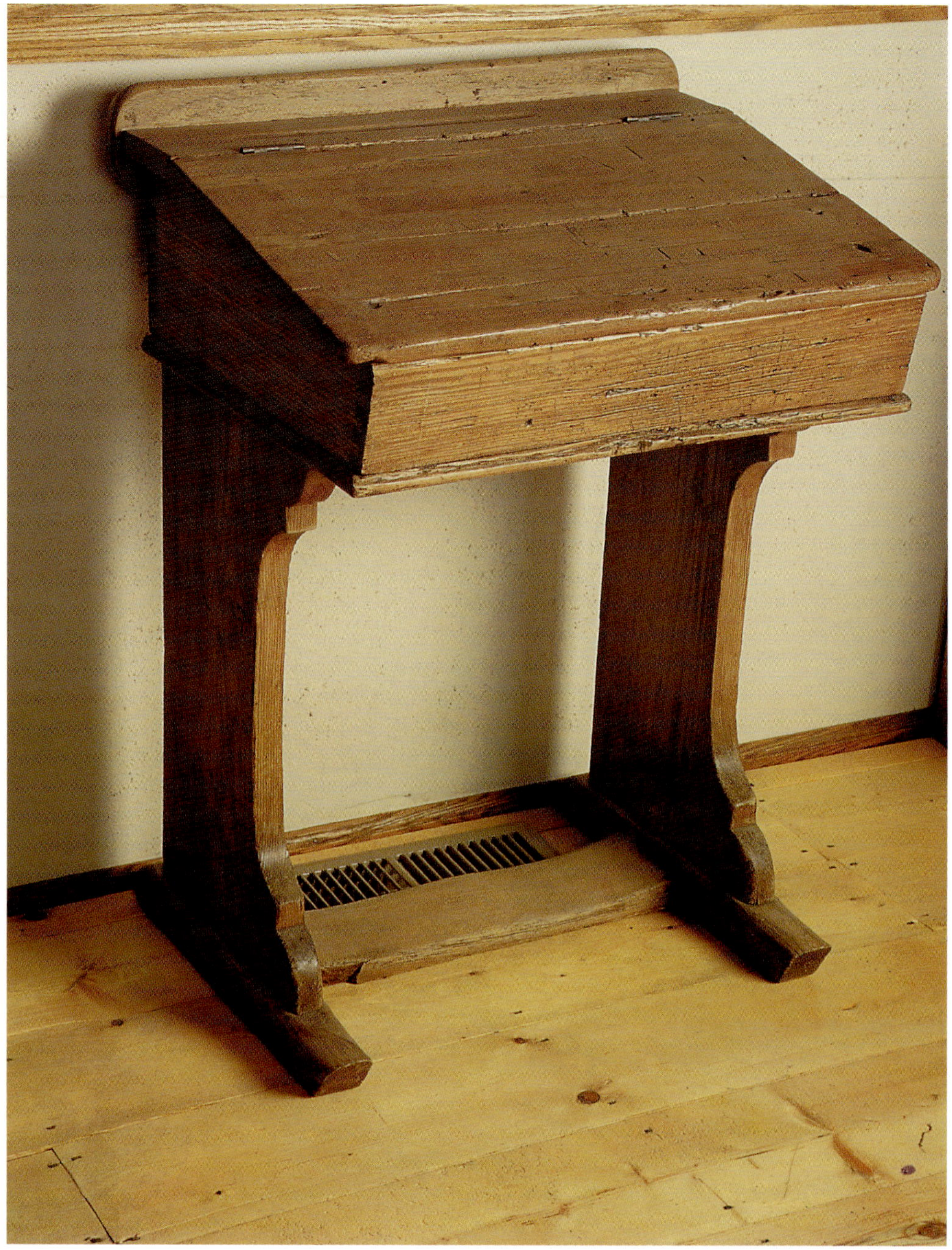

Irish child's school desk with a slant lid resting on flat stiles and trestle feet joined by a flat stretcher/footrest. $395.

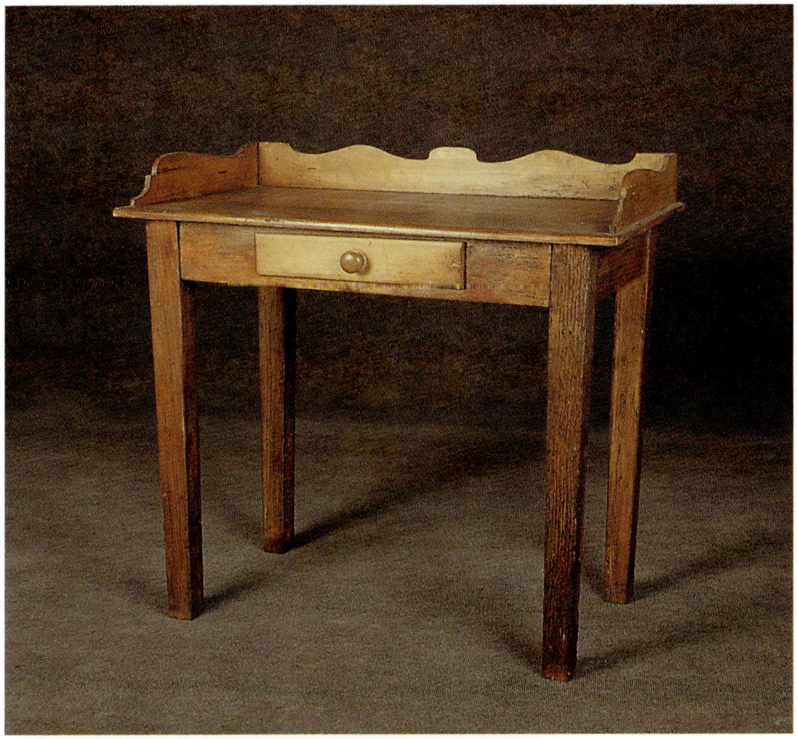

Small desk with raised back and side pieces, single drawer with wooden pull and four straight, square legs. $475.

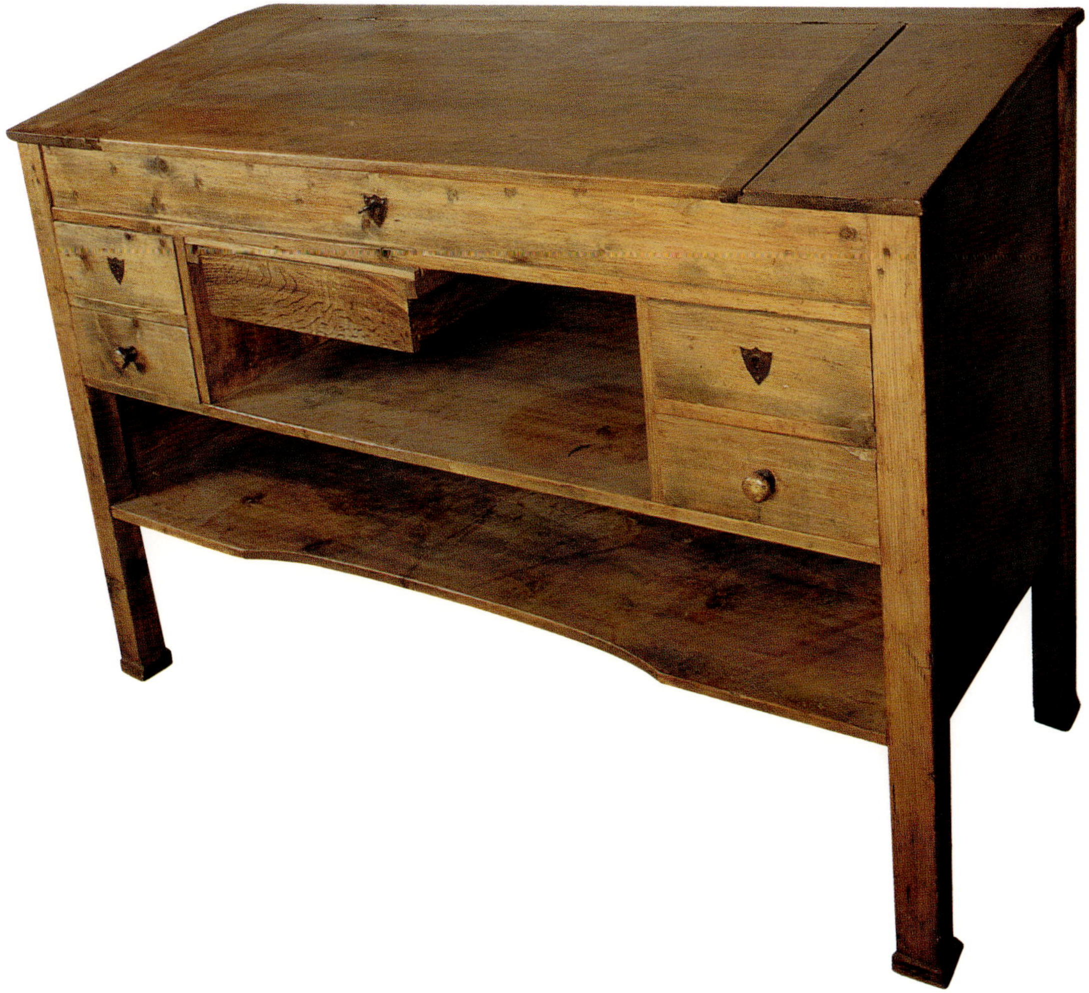

Large desk with hinged slant lid, five small drawers and two open shelves on square legs with blocked feet. $1795.

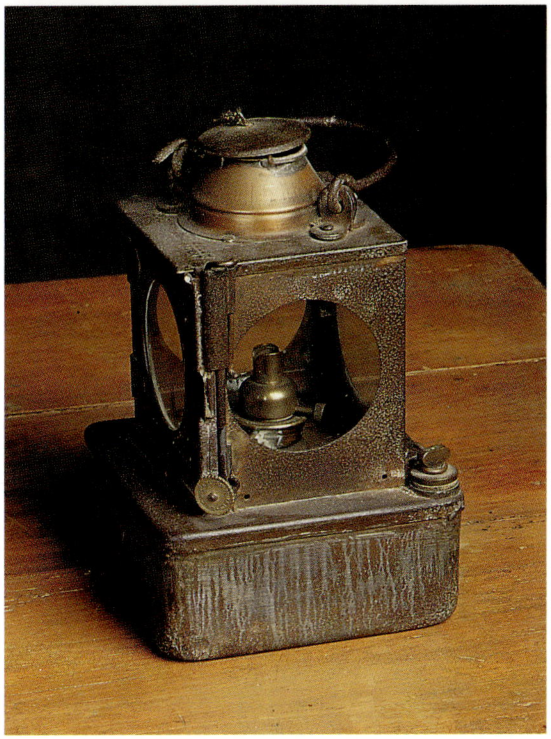

Lantern

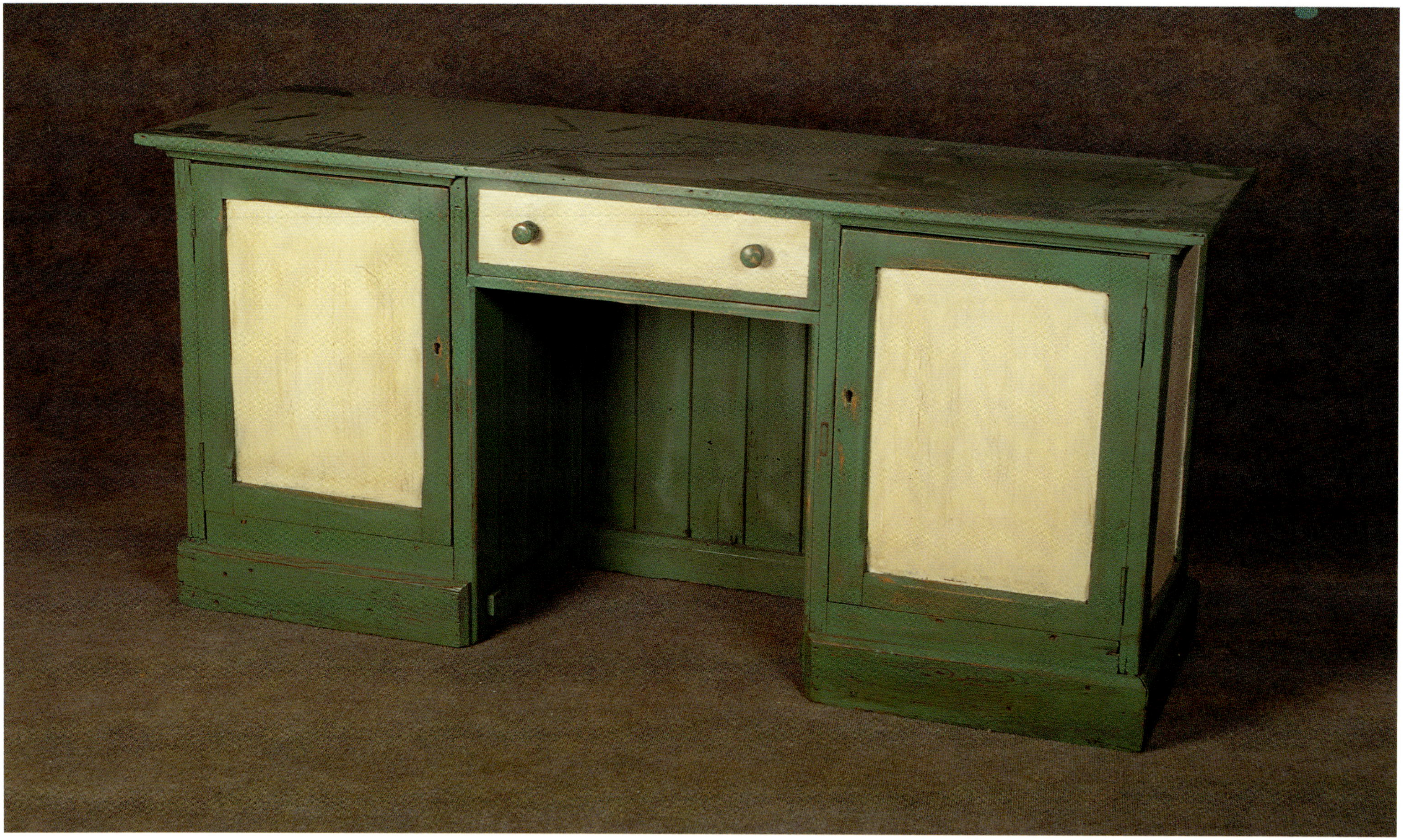

Green painted pine desk with rectangular top overhanging the two base cabinets, each with a recessed-panel door and flanking a drawer with two wooden knob pulls. The cases rest on a straight base molding. $795.

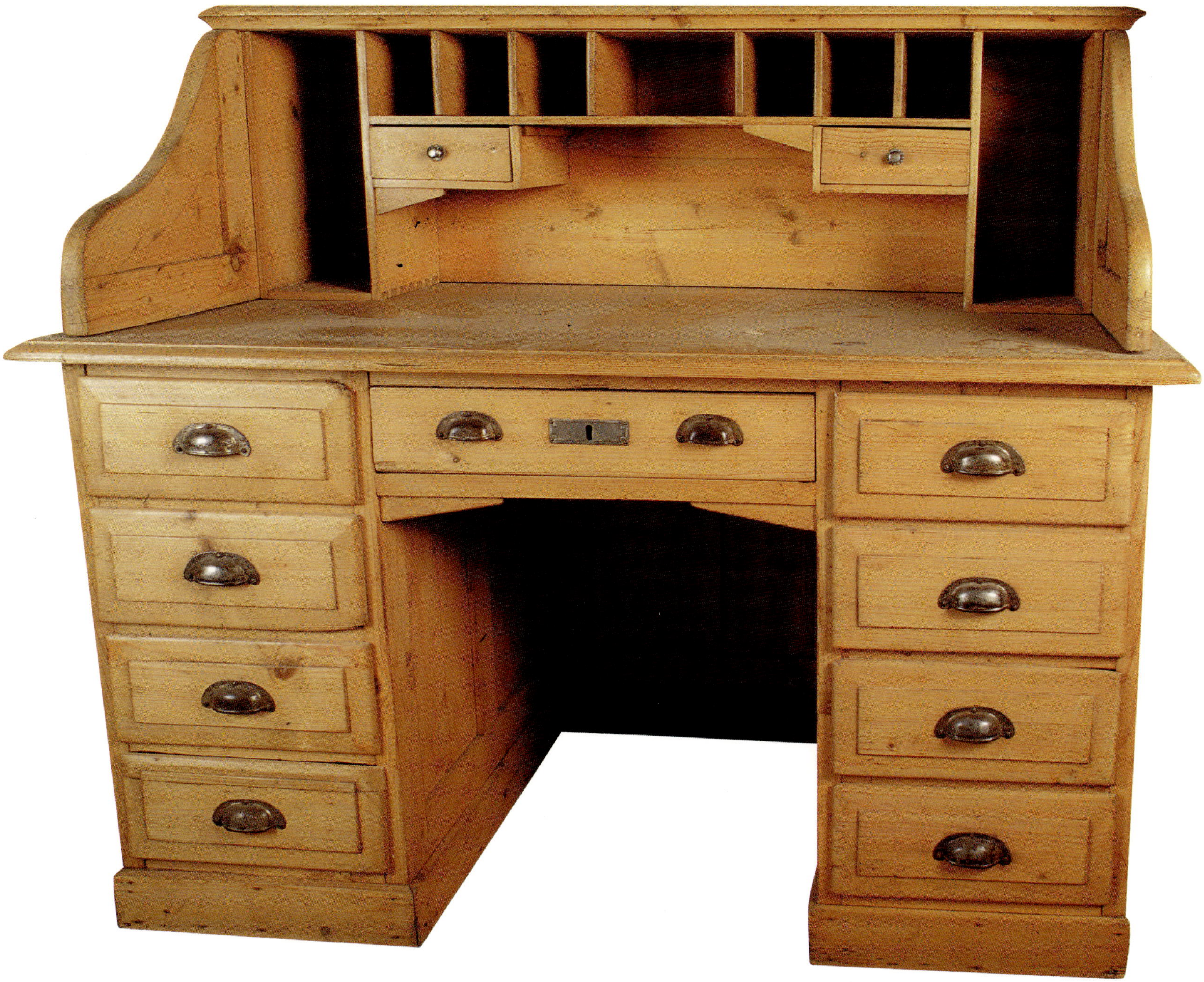

German desk with open front and raised shelves and drawers. The case has a center drawer and two stacks of four drawers each on a straight base molding. $2695.

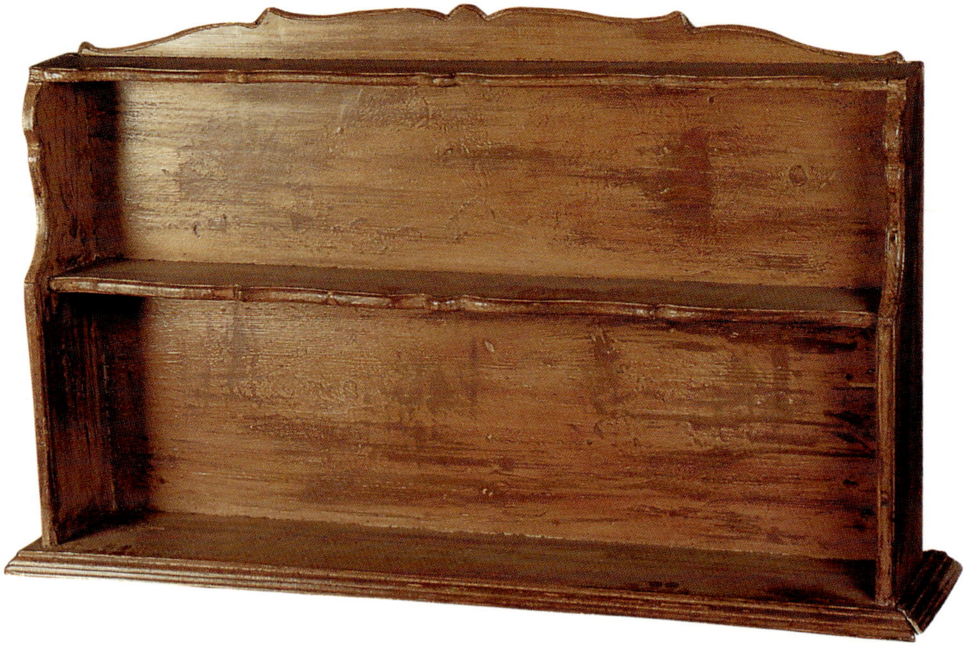

Painted two-shelf unit with scalloped top and side pieces, painted brown/red. $125.

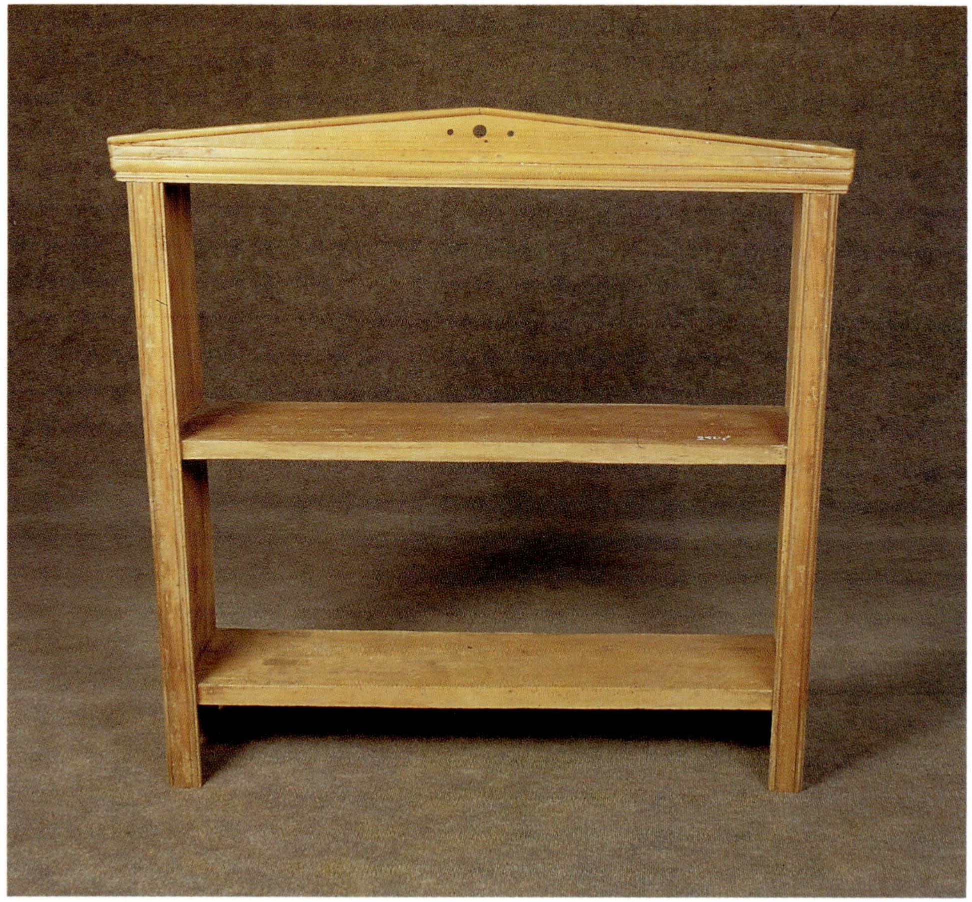

Bucket bench of pine with peaked top and two plank shelves, the ends form the feet with cut-out wedge at the floor. $295.

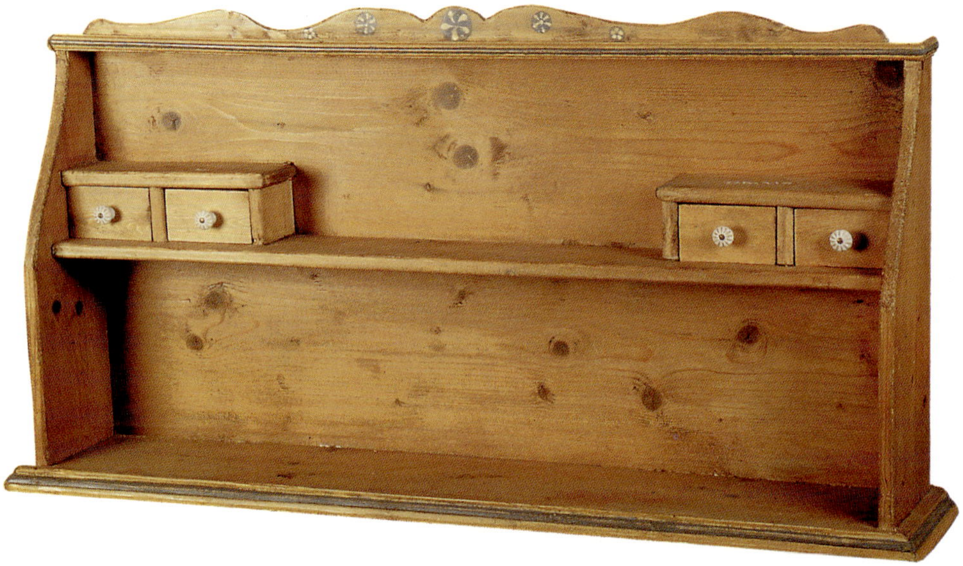

Small shelf unit of pine with a scrolled and painted top over two shelves, the top one with small drawers at the outside corners.

Living Outside

Garden Ornaments and Tools

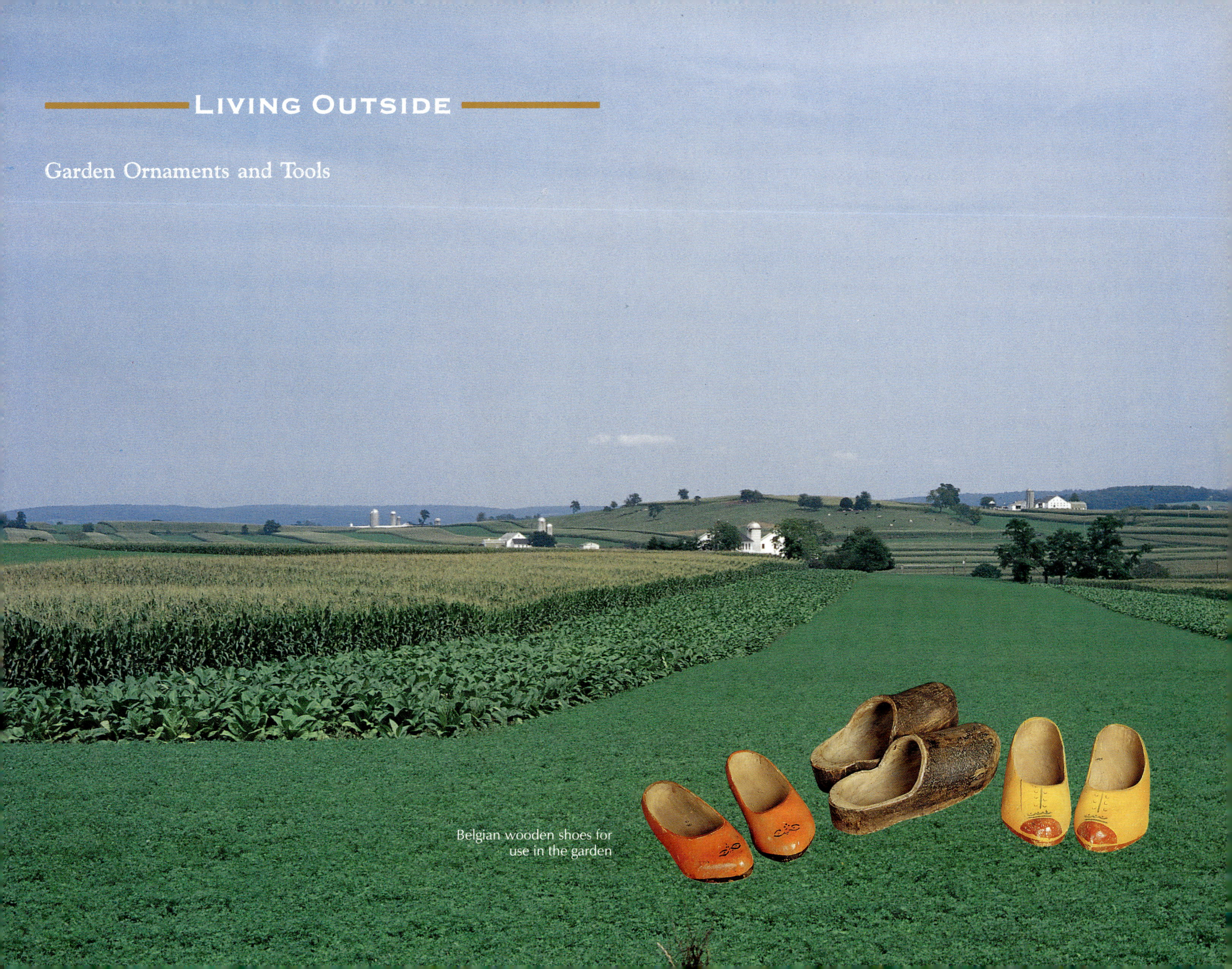

Belgian wooden shoes for use in the garden

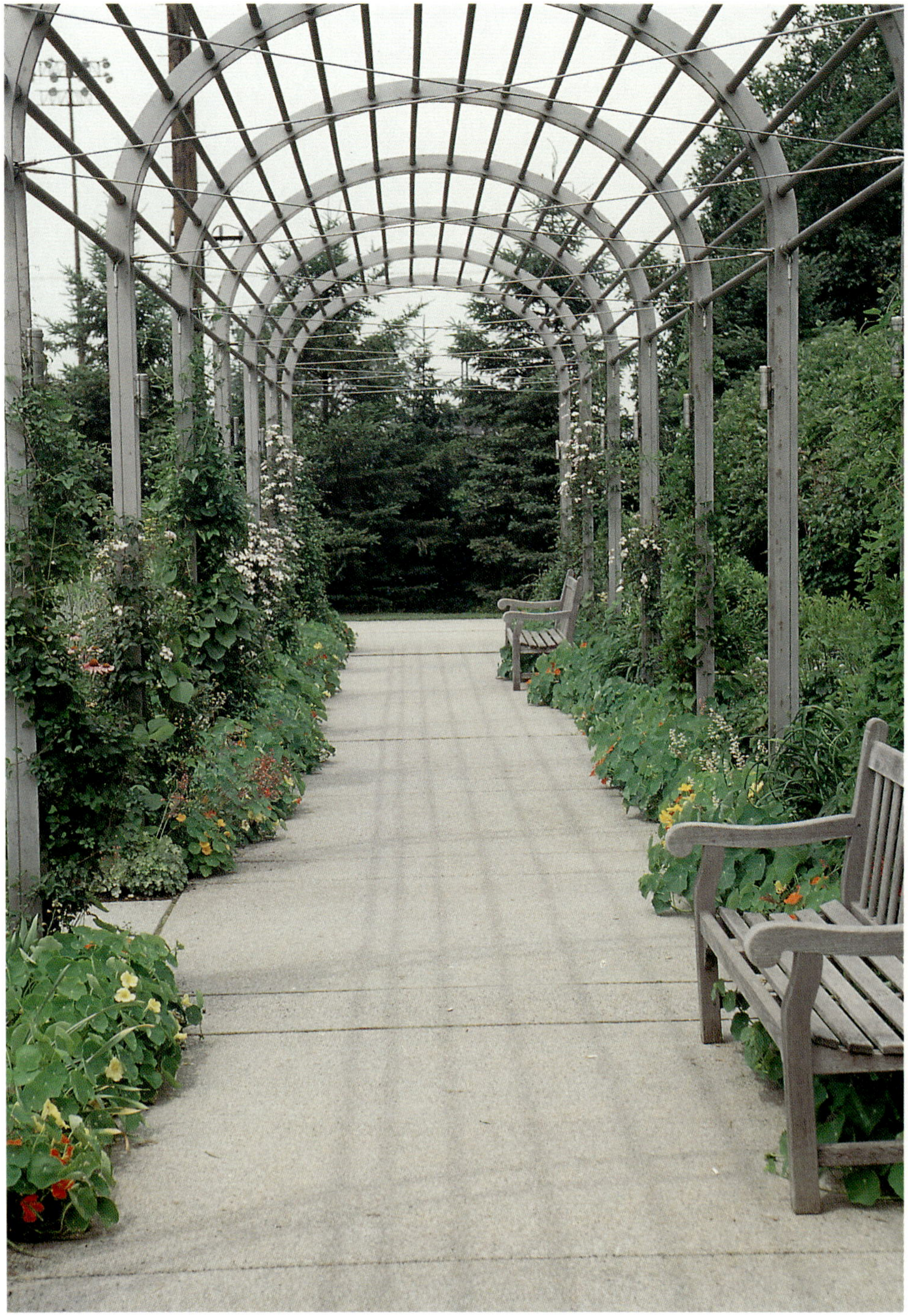

A restful garden

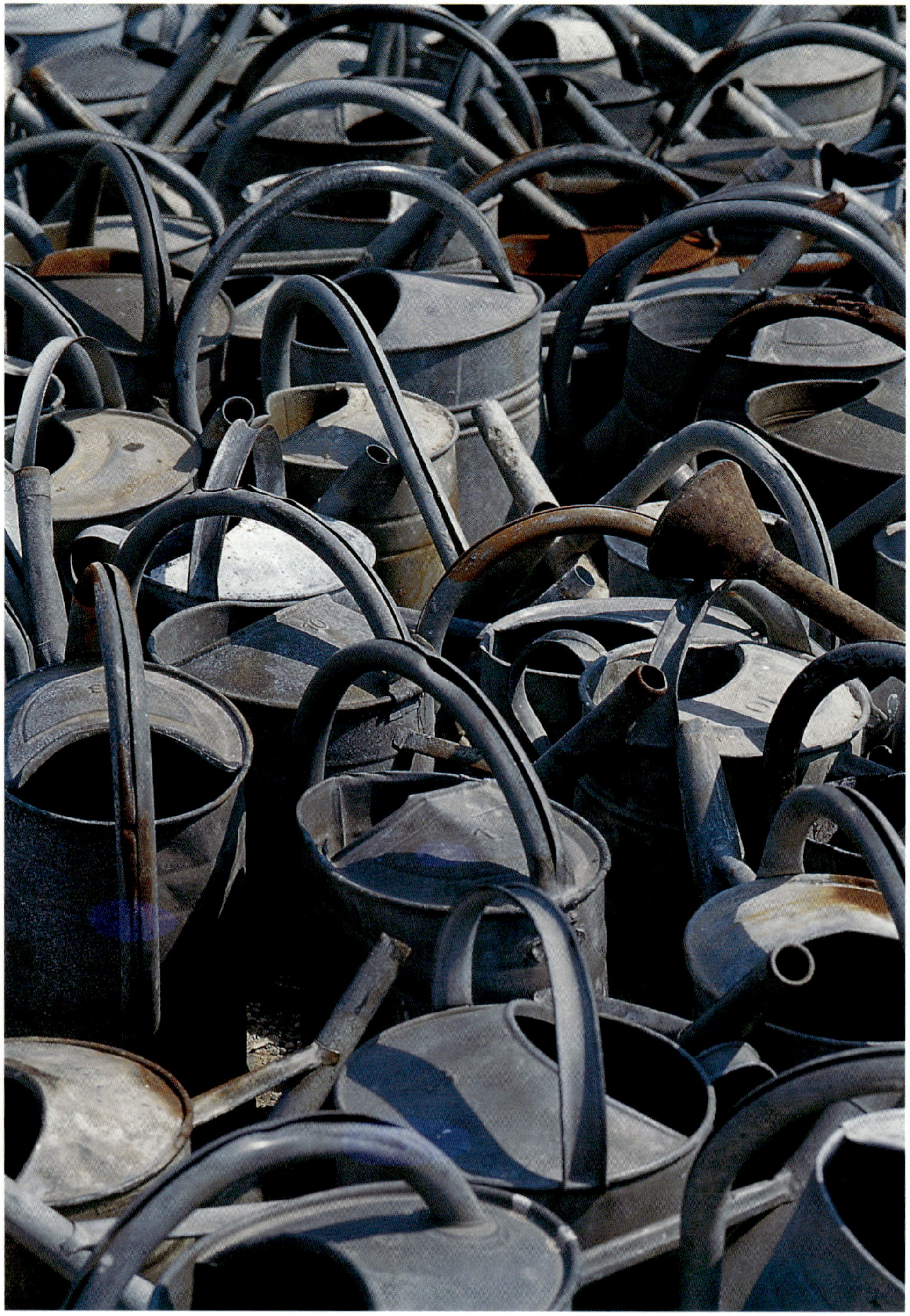

Watering cans

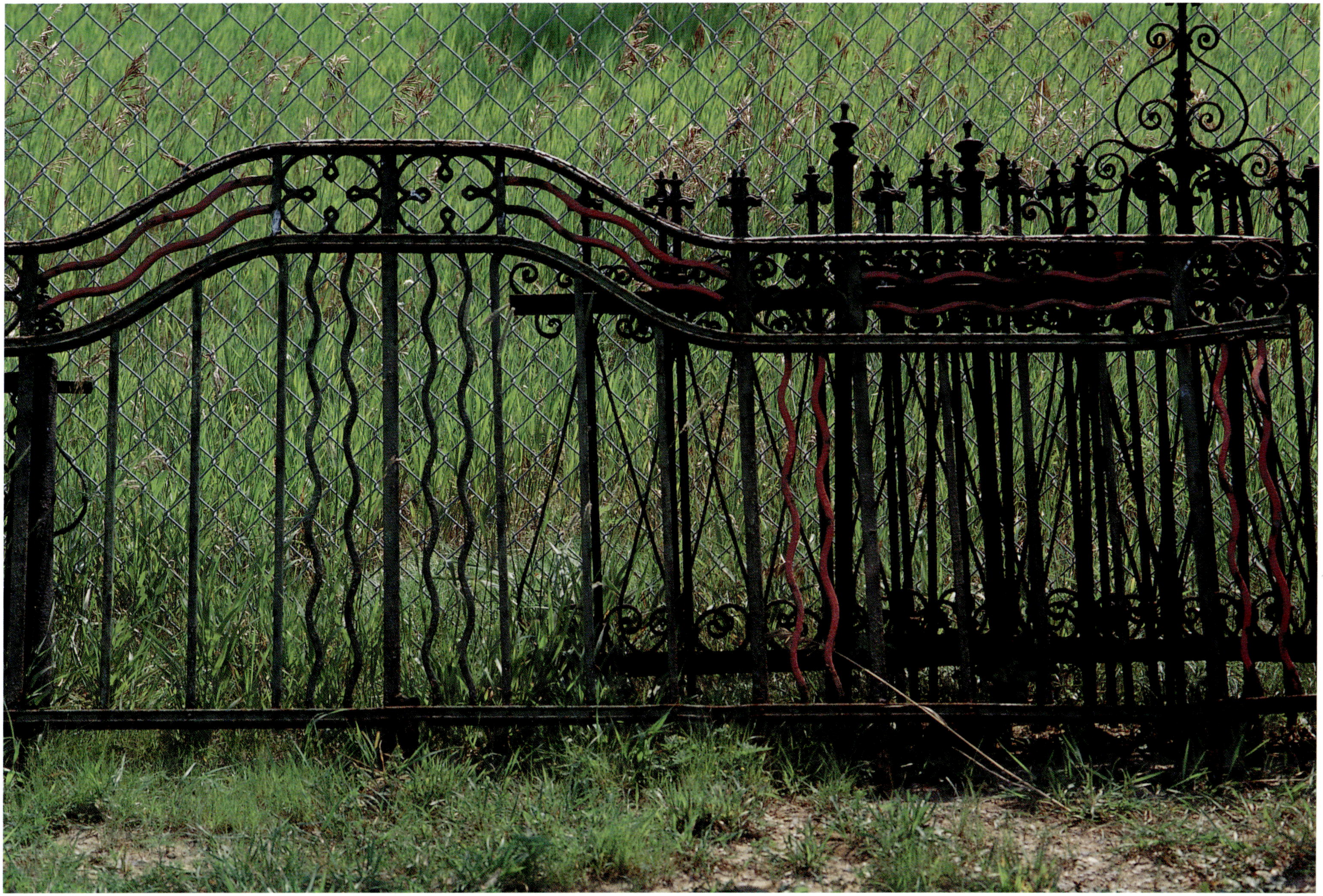

Wrought iron fencing to keep the pets in

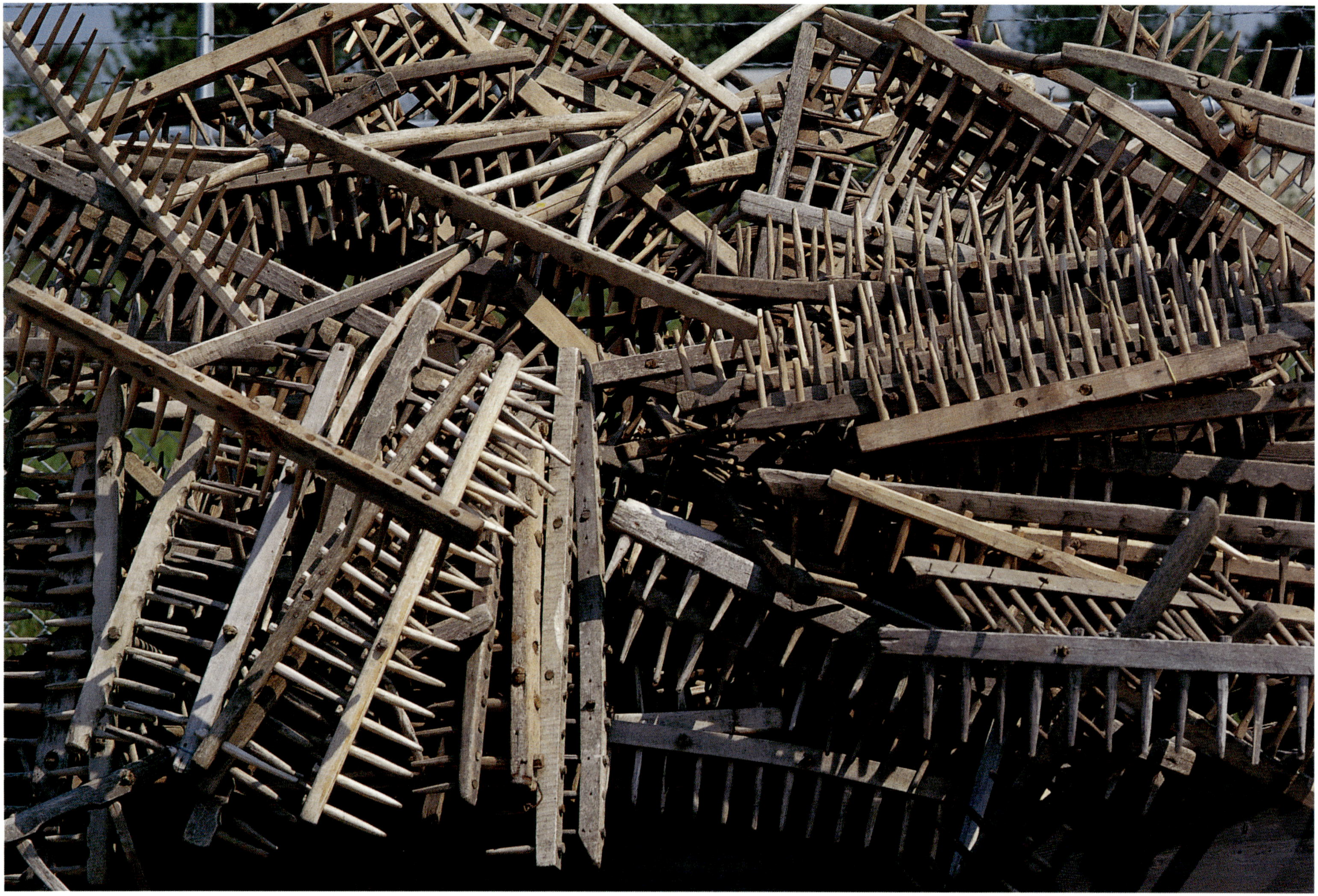

Rakes

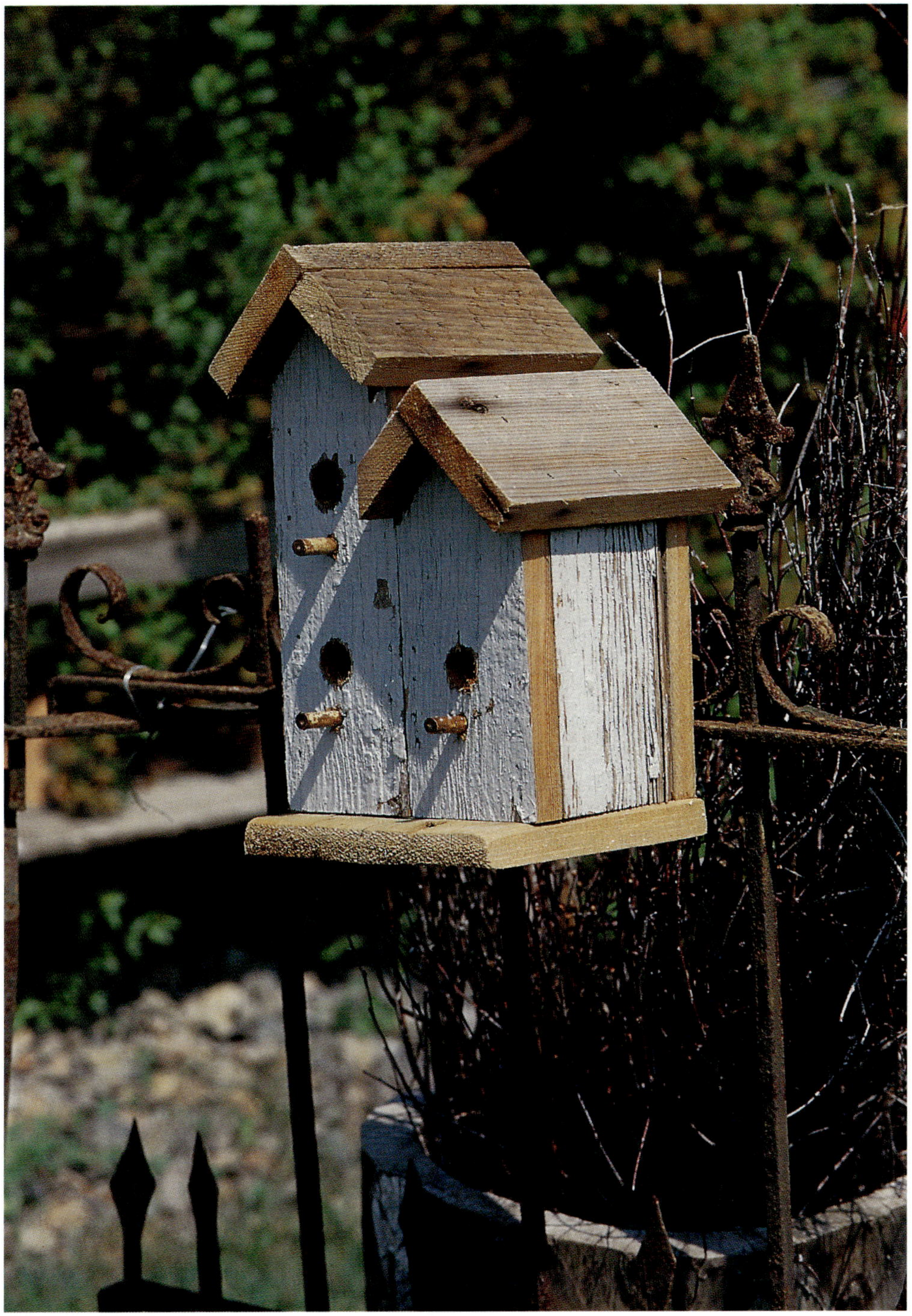
Birdhouse

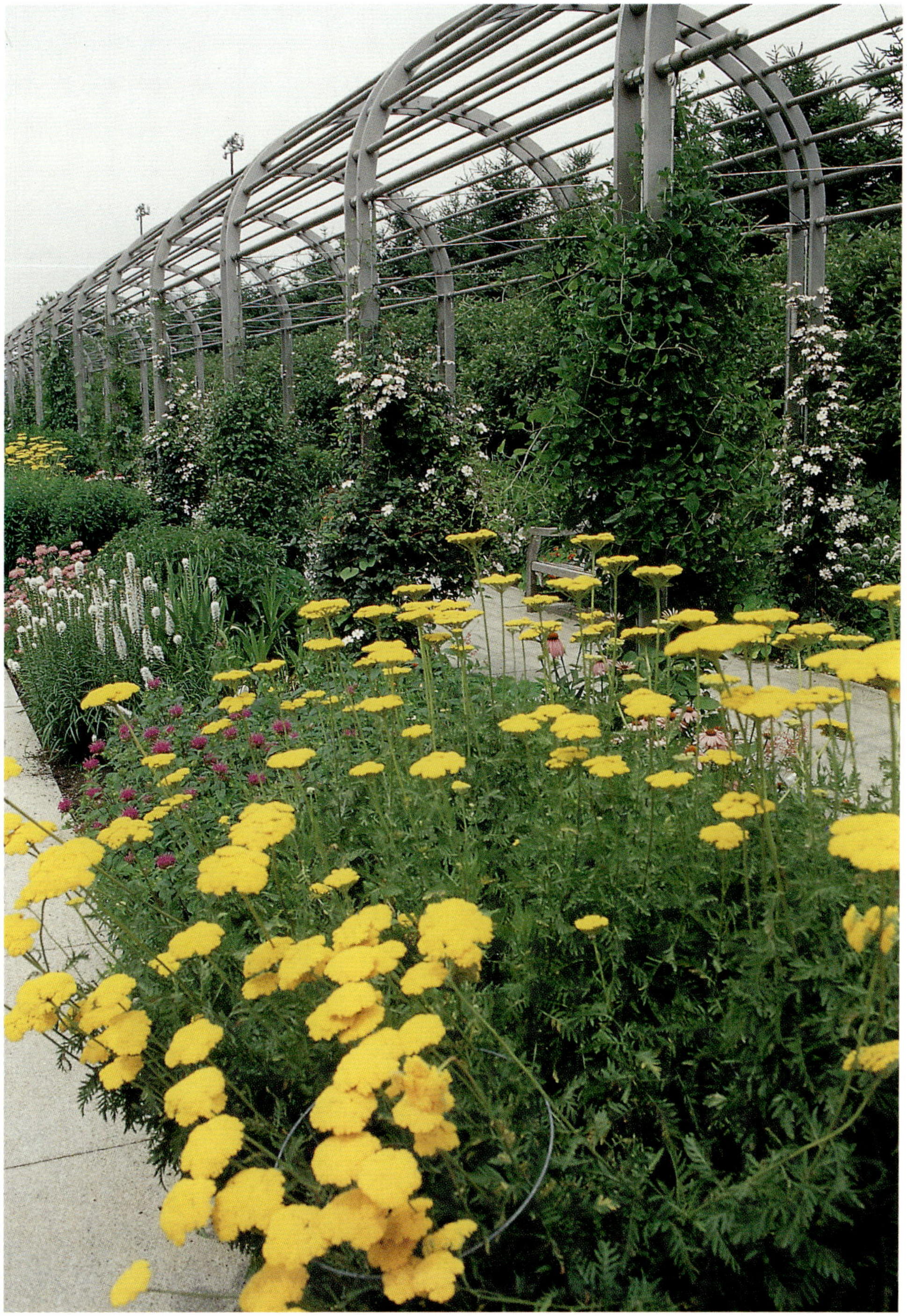

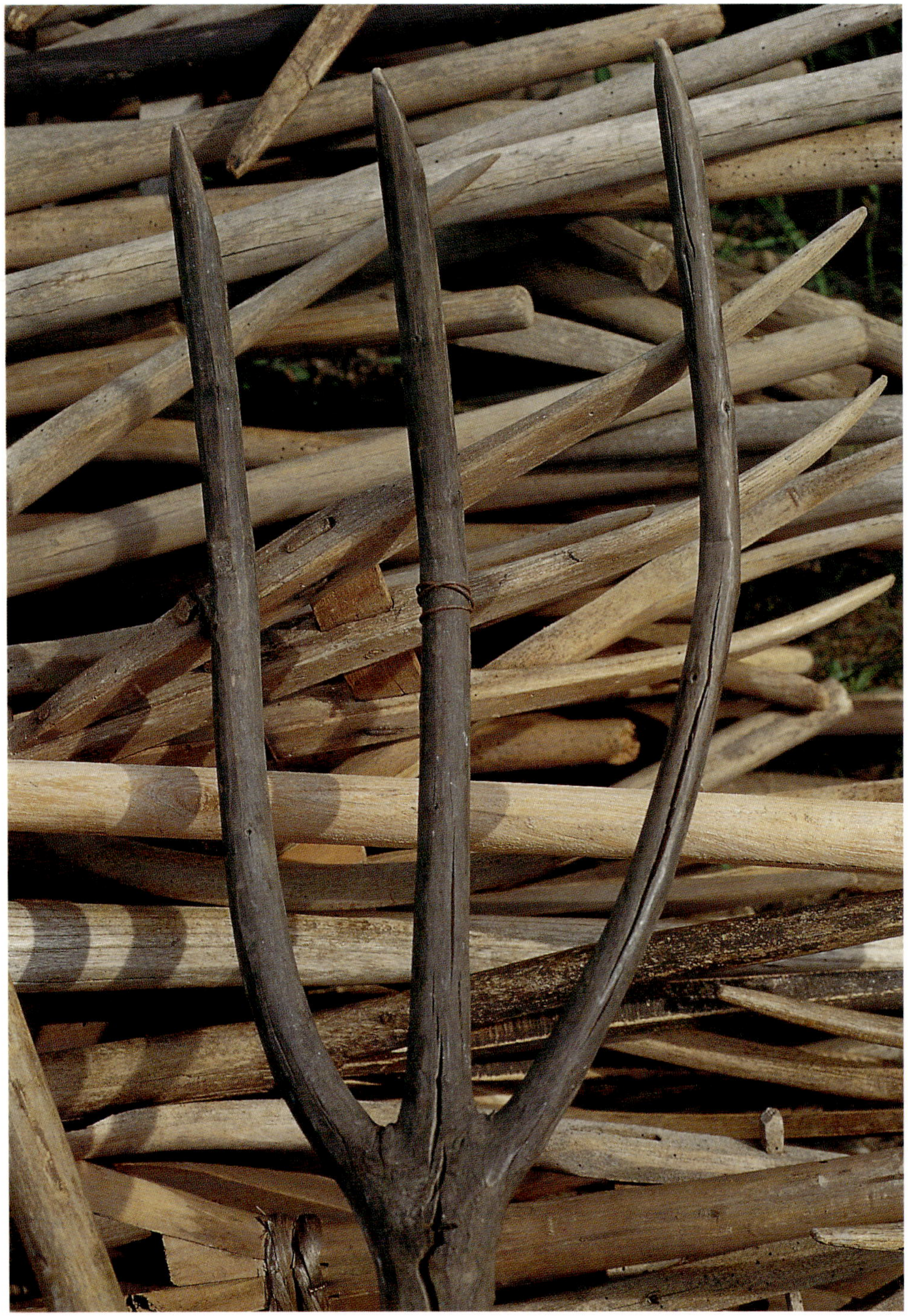

3-tine rake made from natural growth

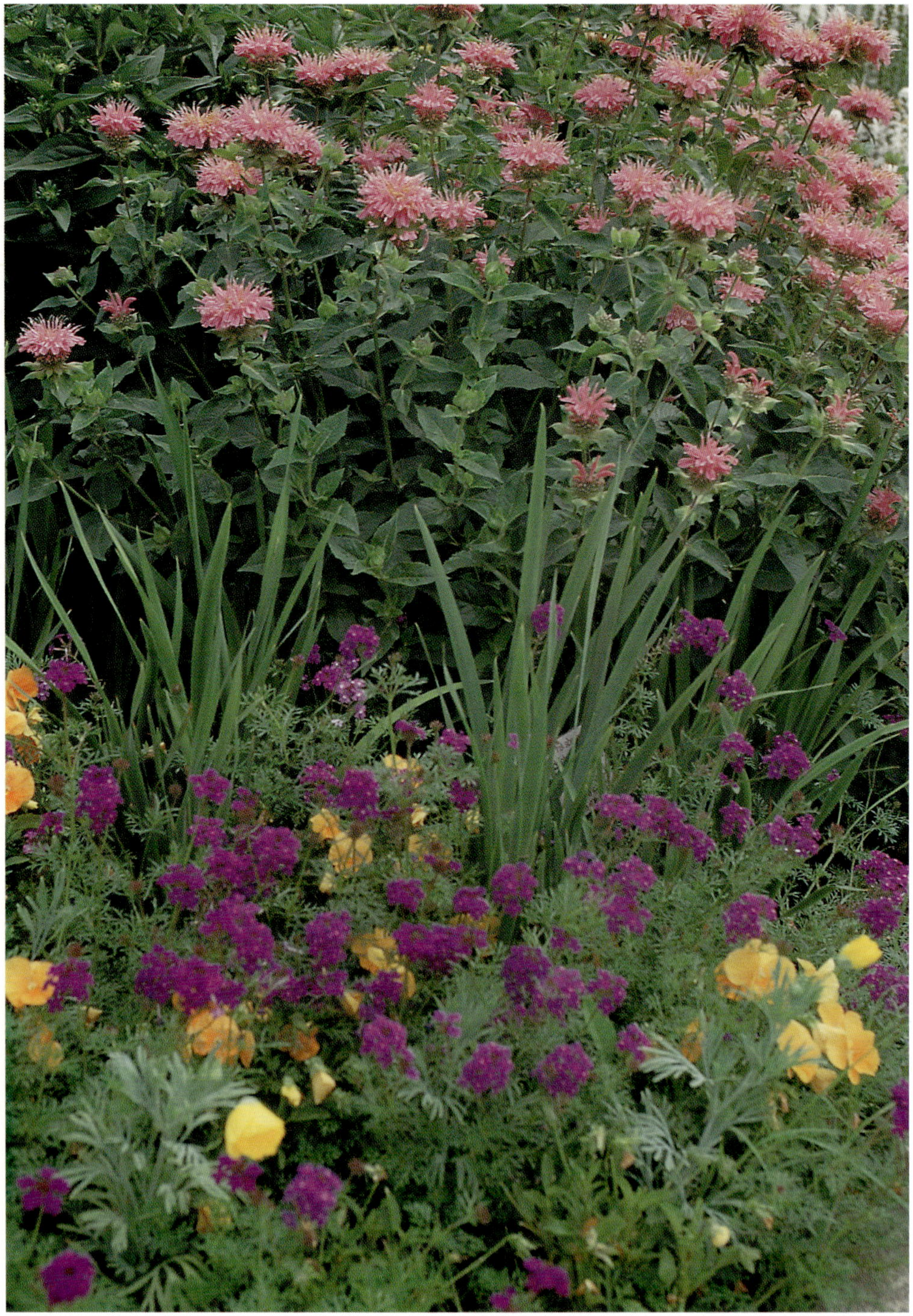

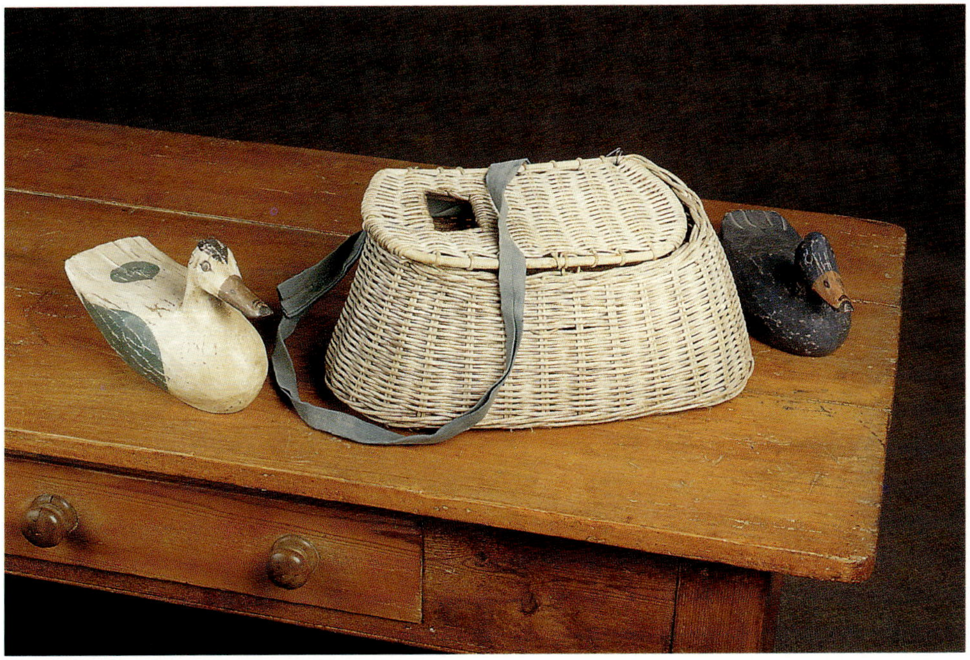

Fishing creel and two bird decoys

Three decorative clay chimney pieces

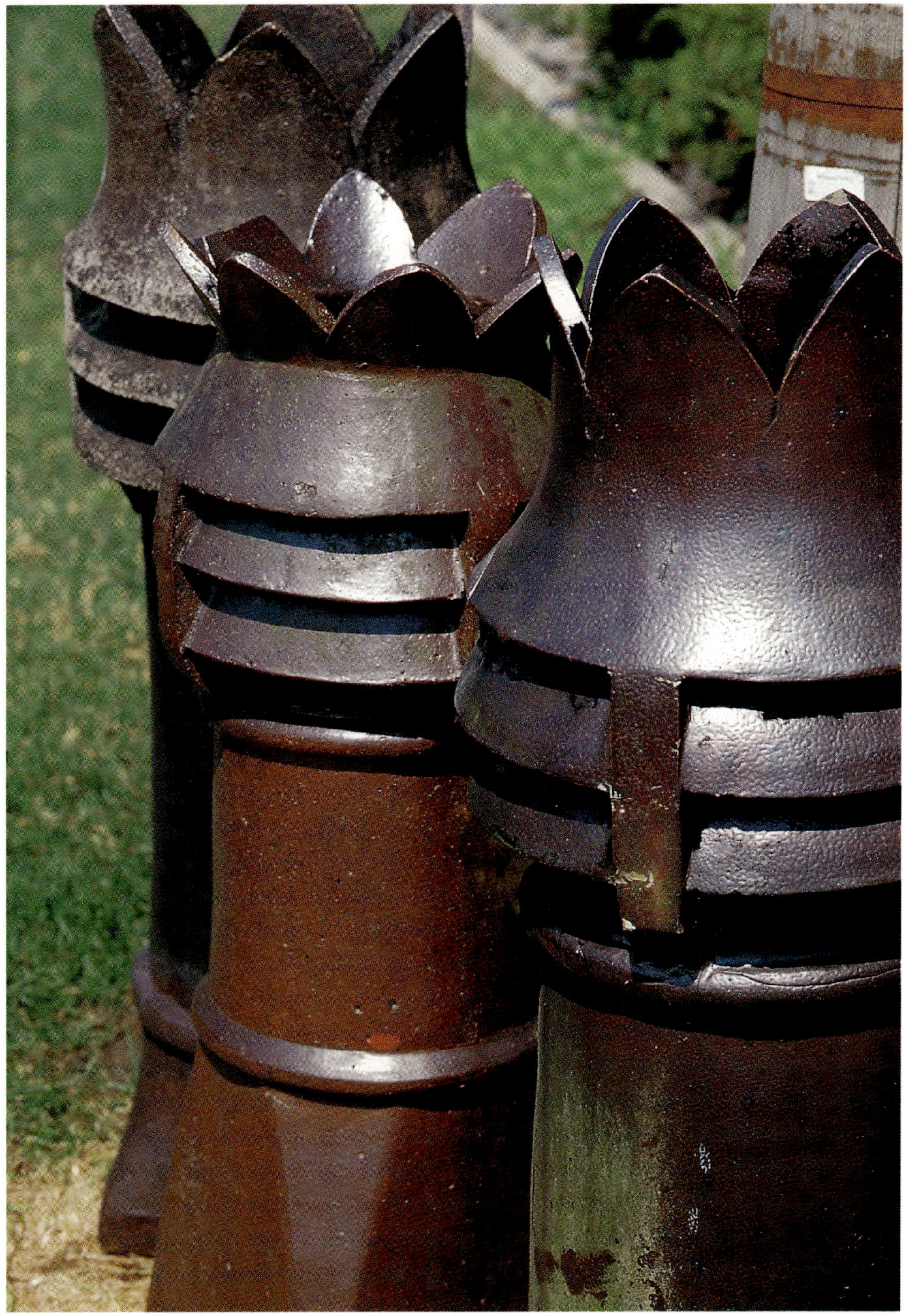

Wagons and Wheelbarrows

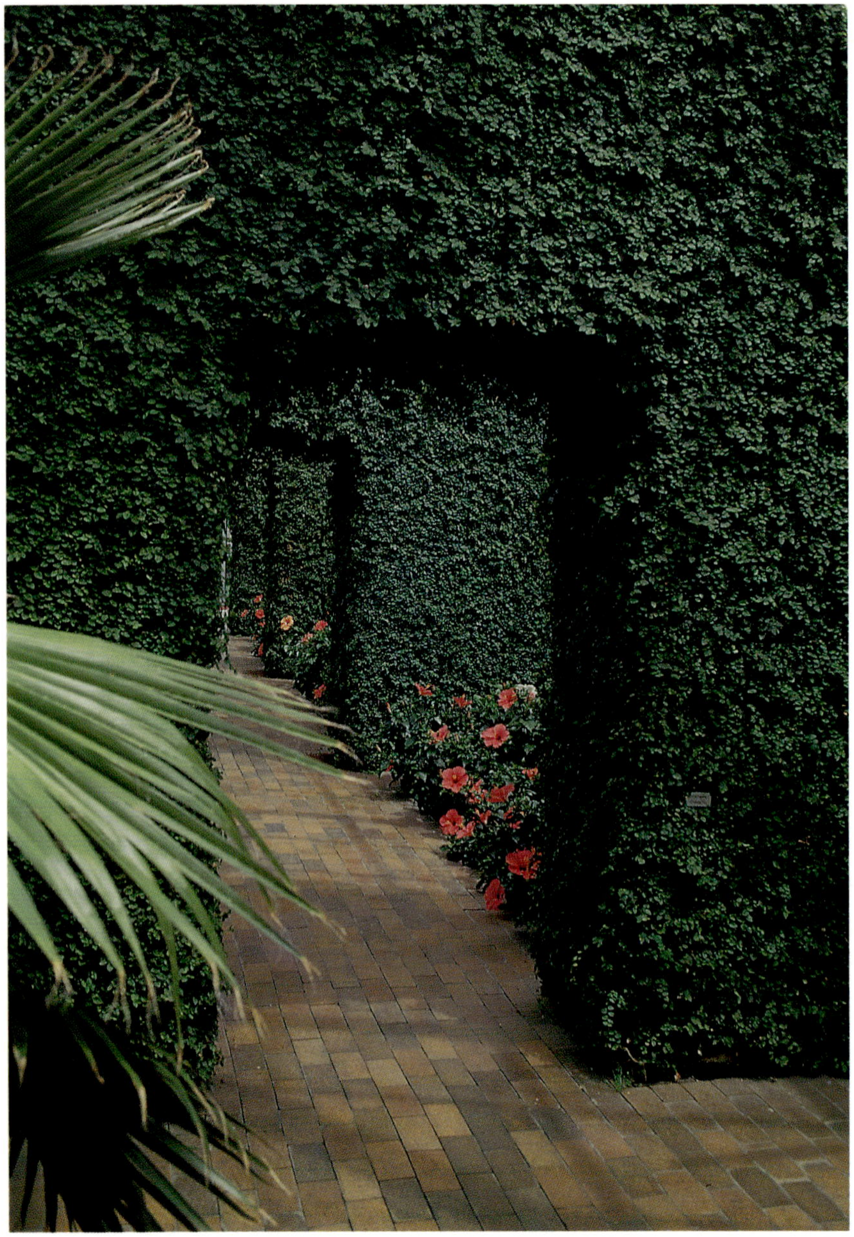

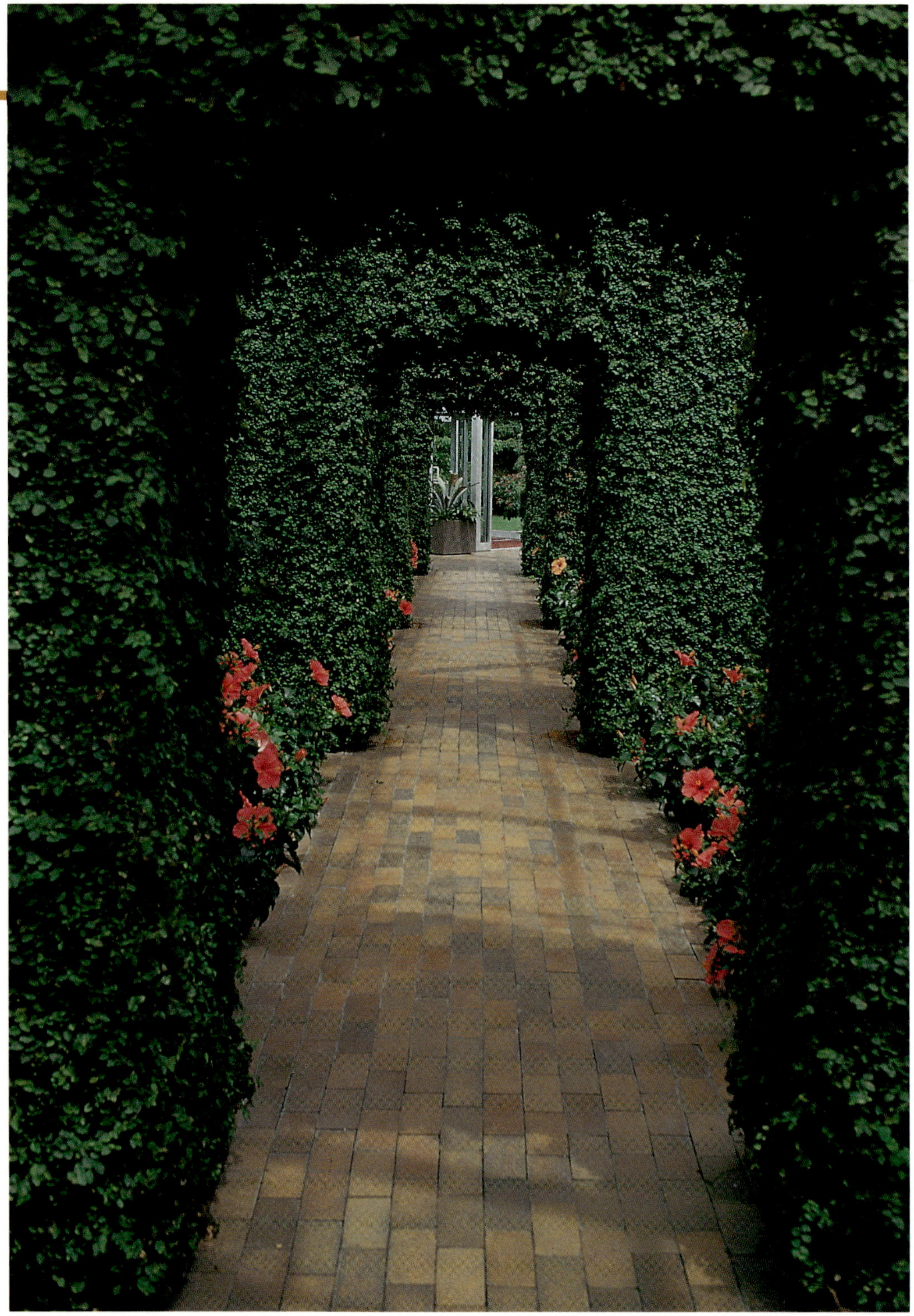

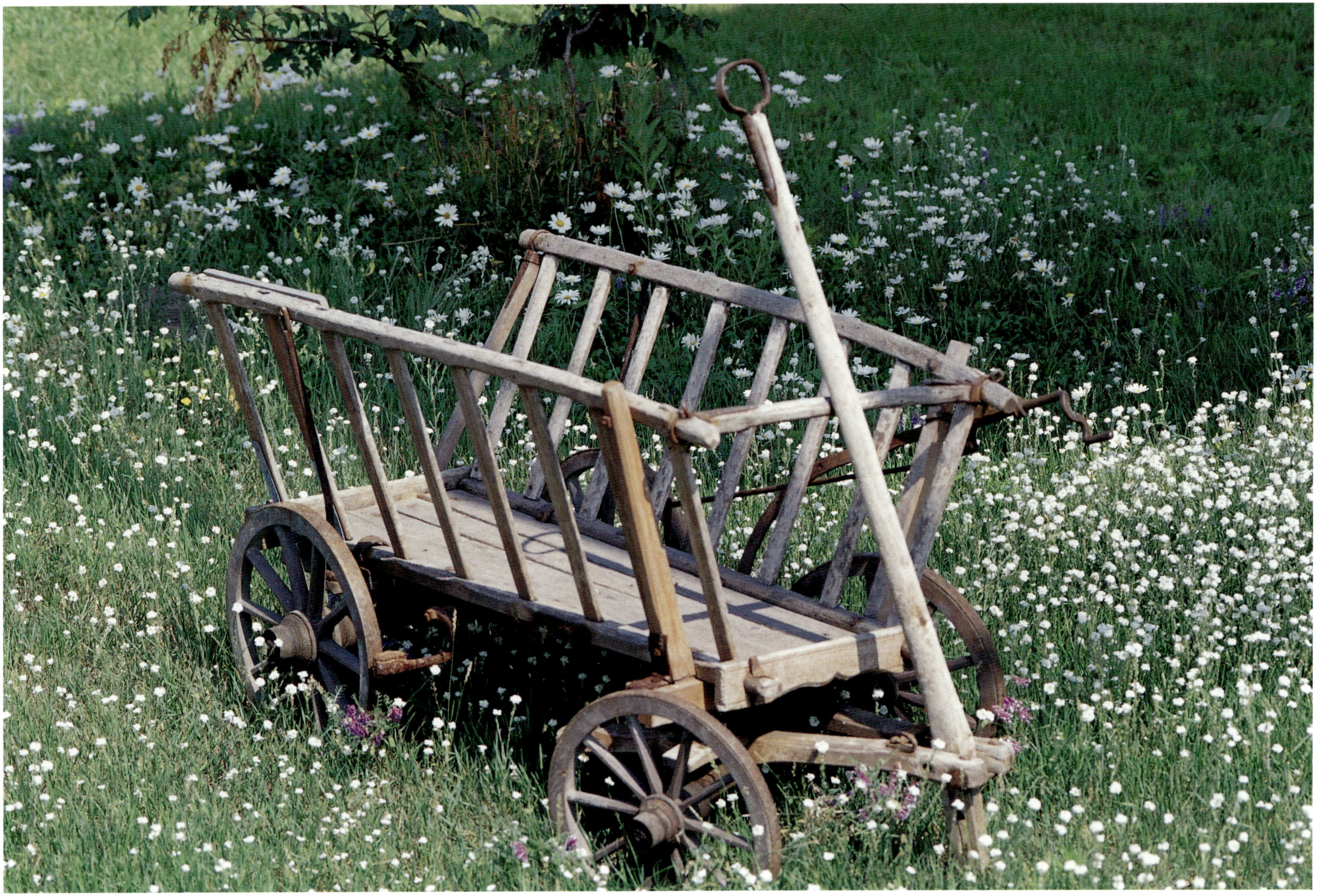

Wagon

Opposite page: Left and right: The garden takes shape

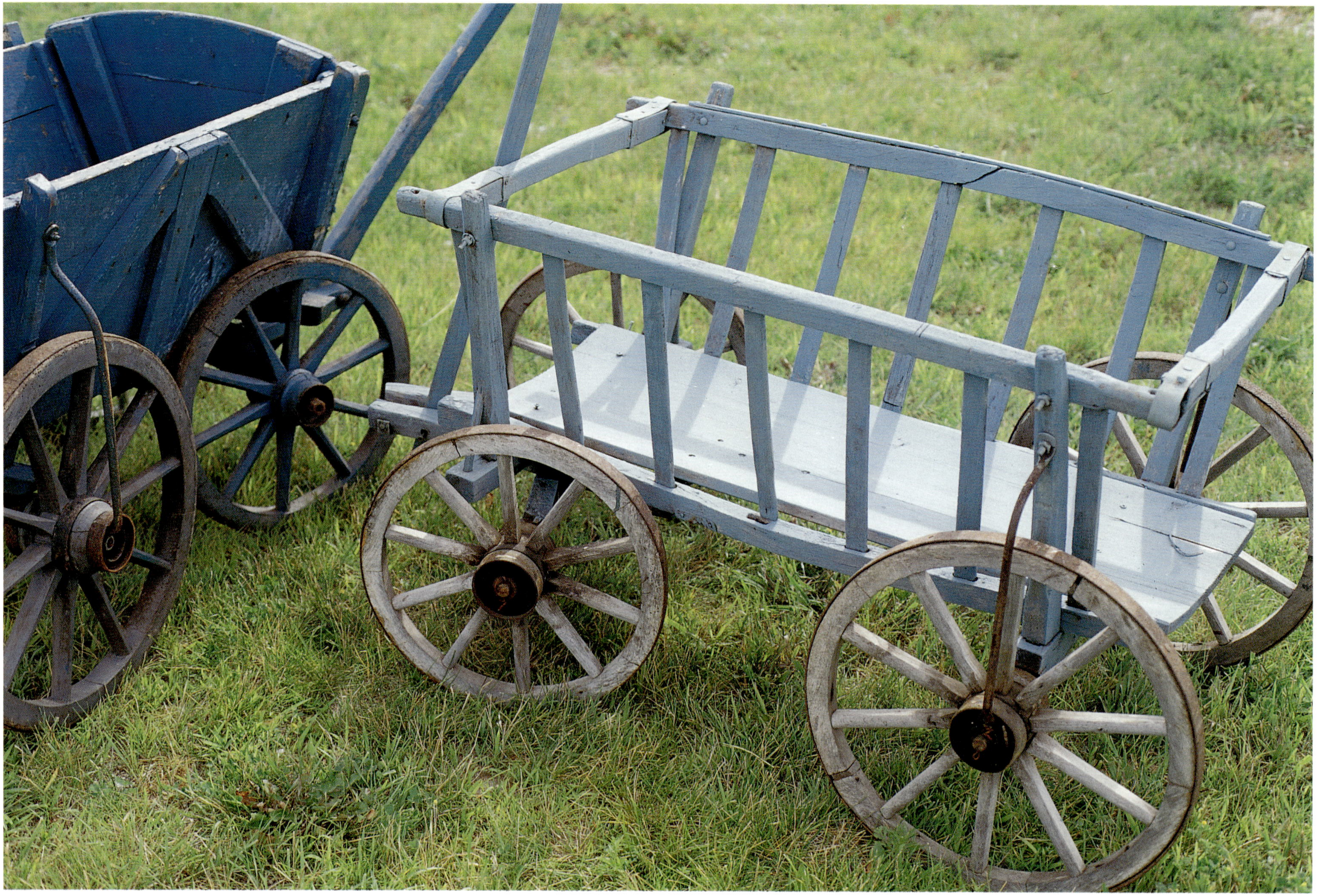

Two blue wagons

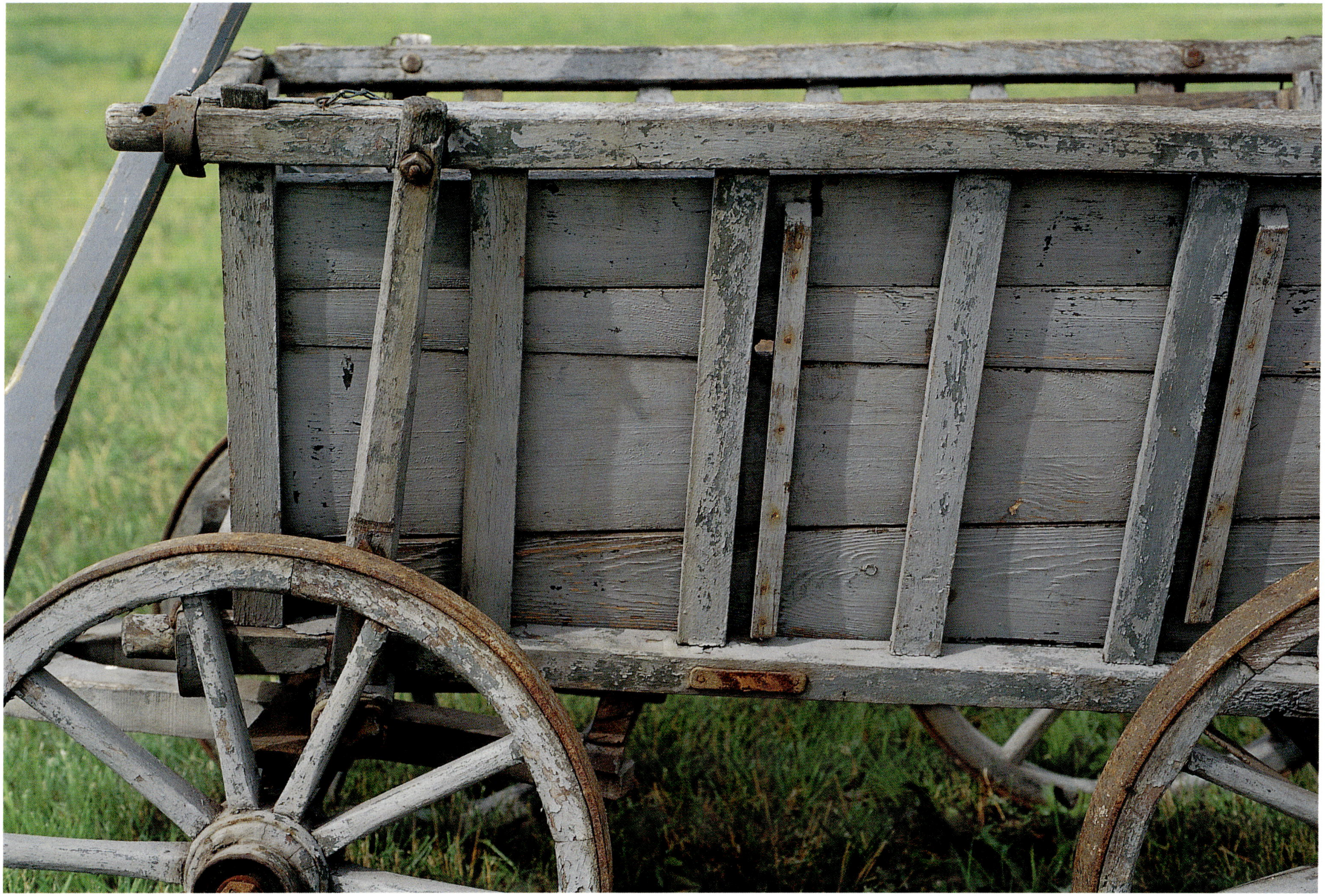

Wagon

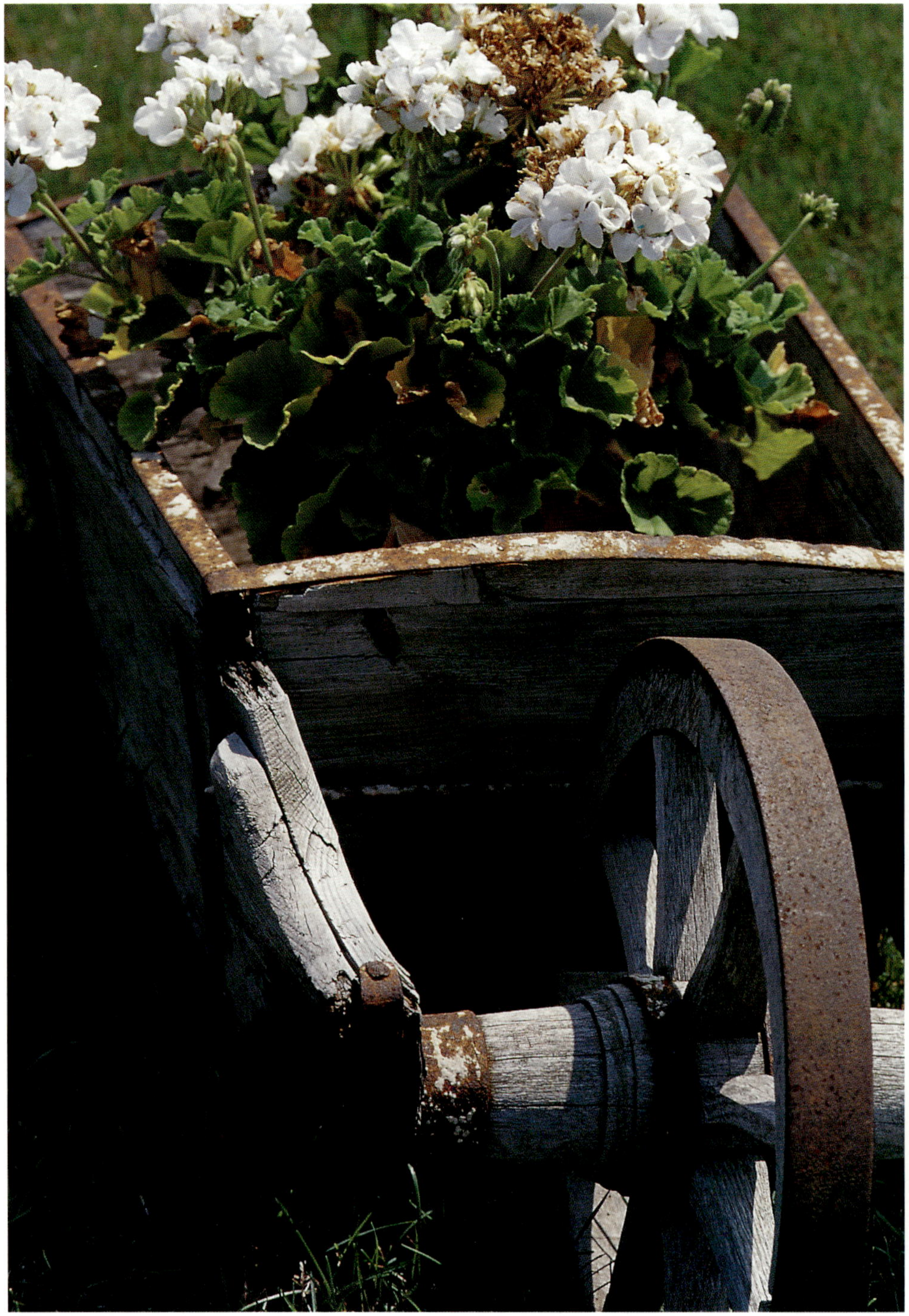

Wheelbarrow

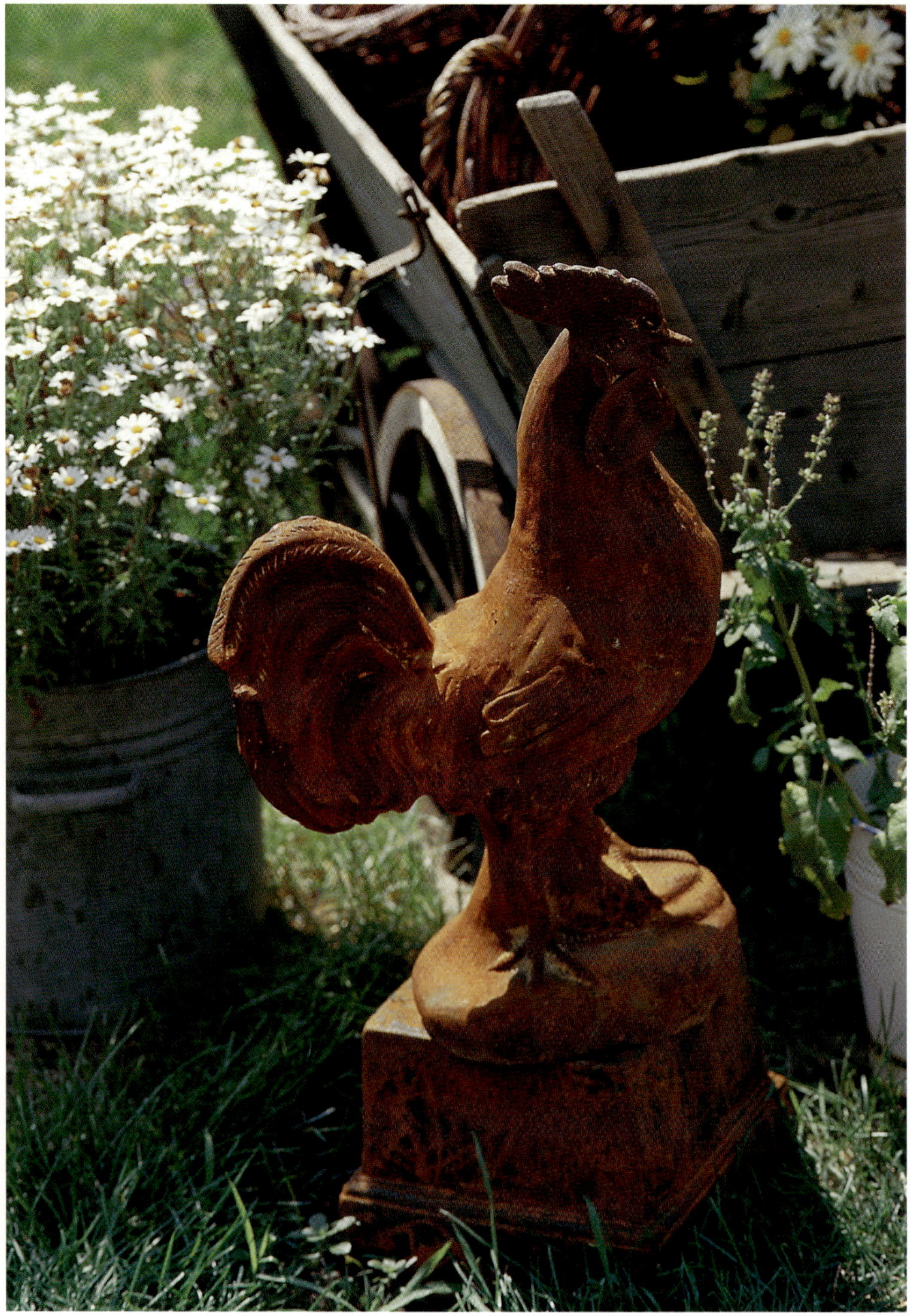

Clay rooster

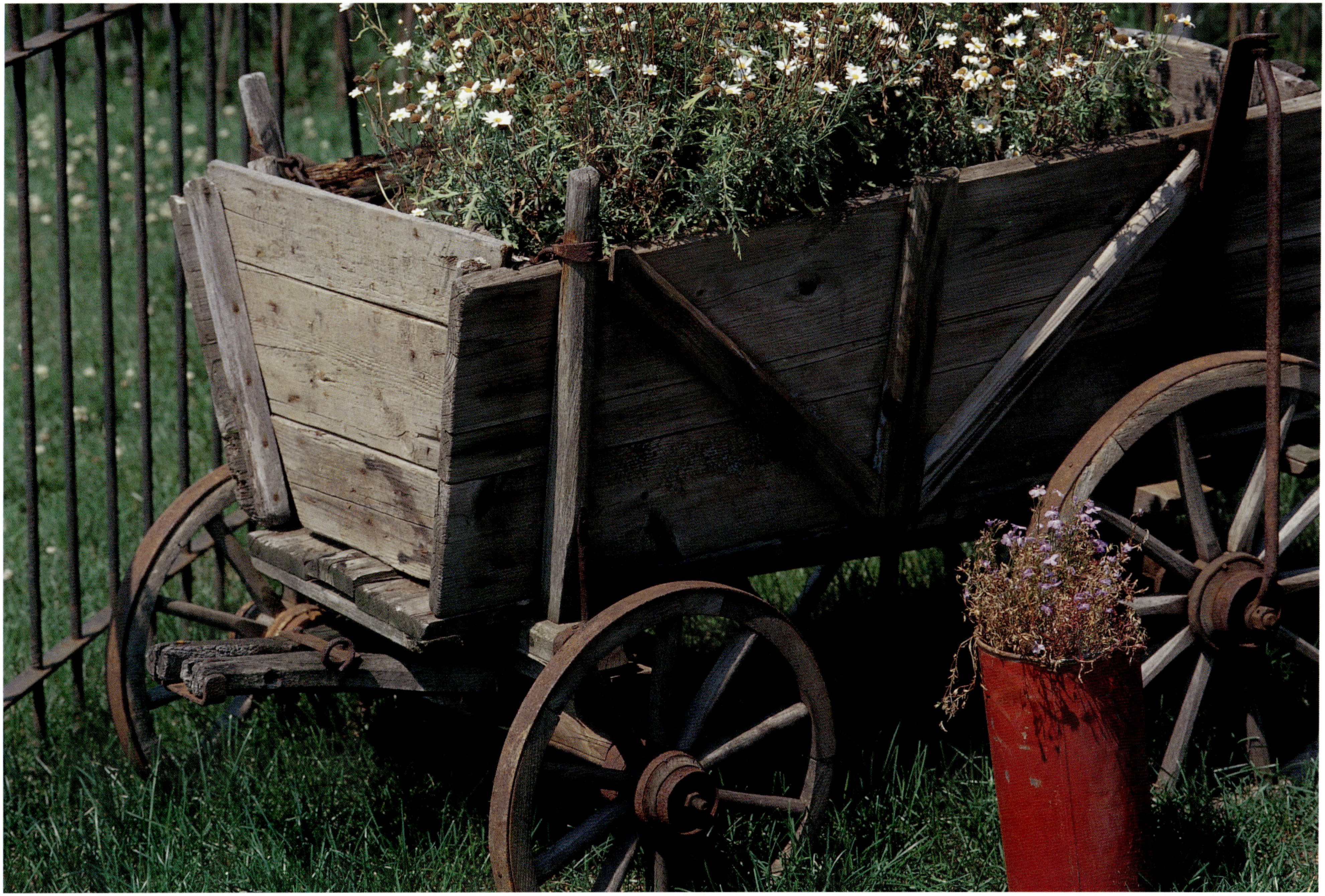

Wagon

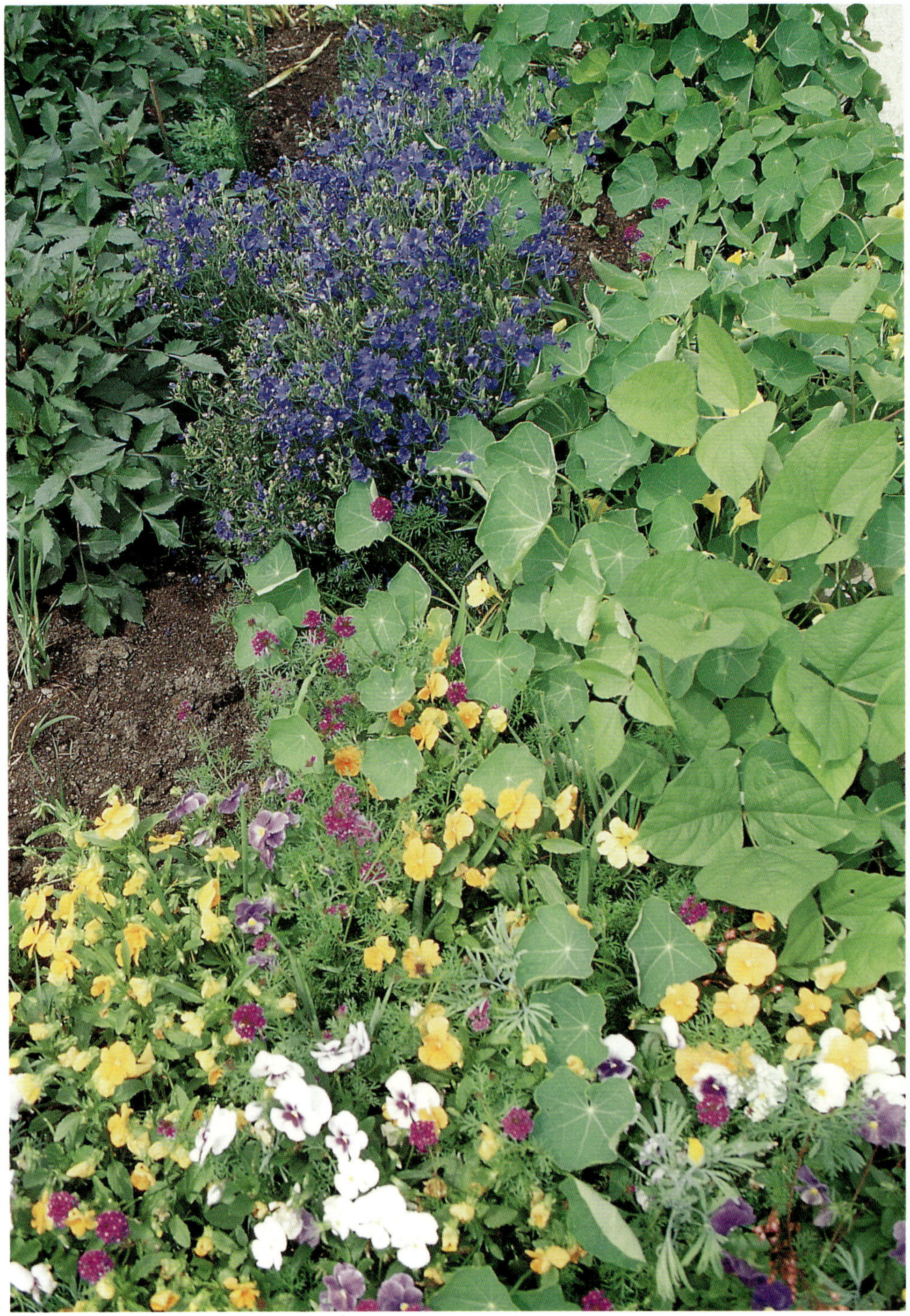

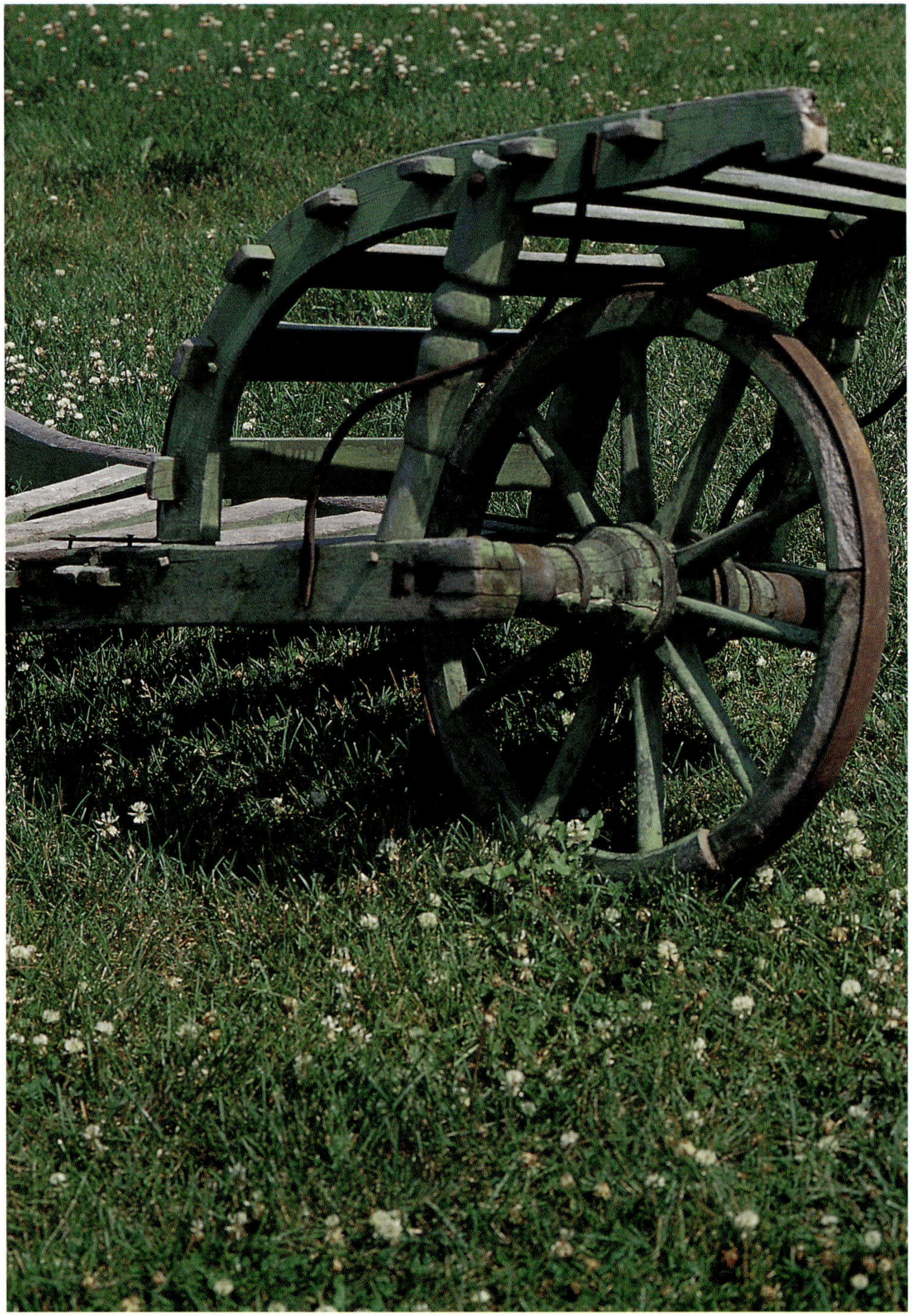

Wheelbarrow

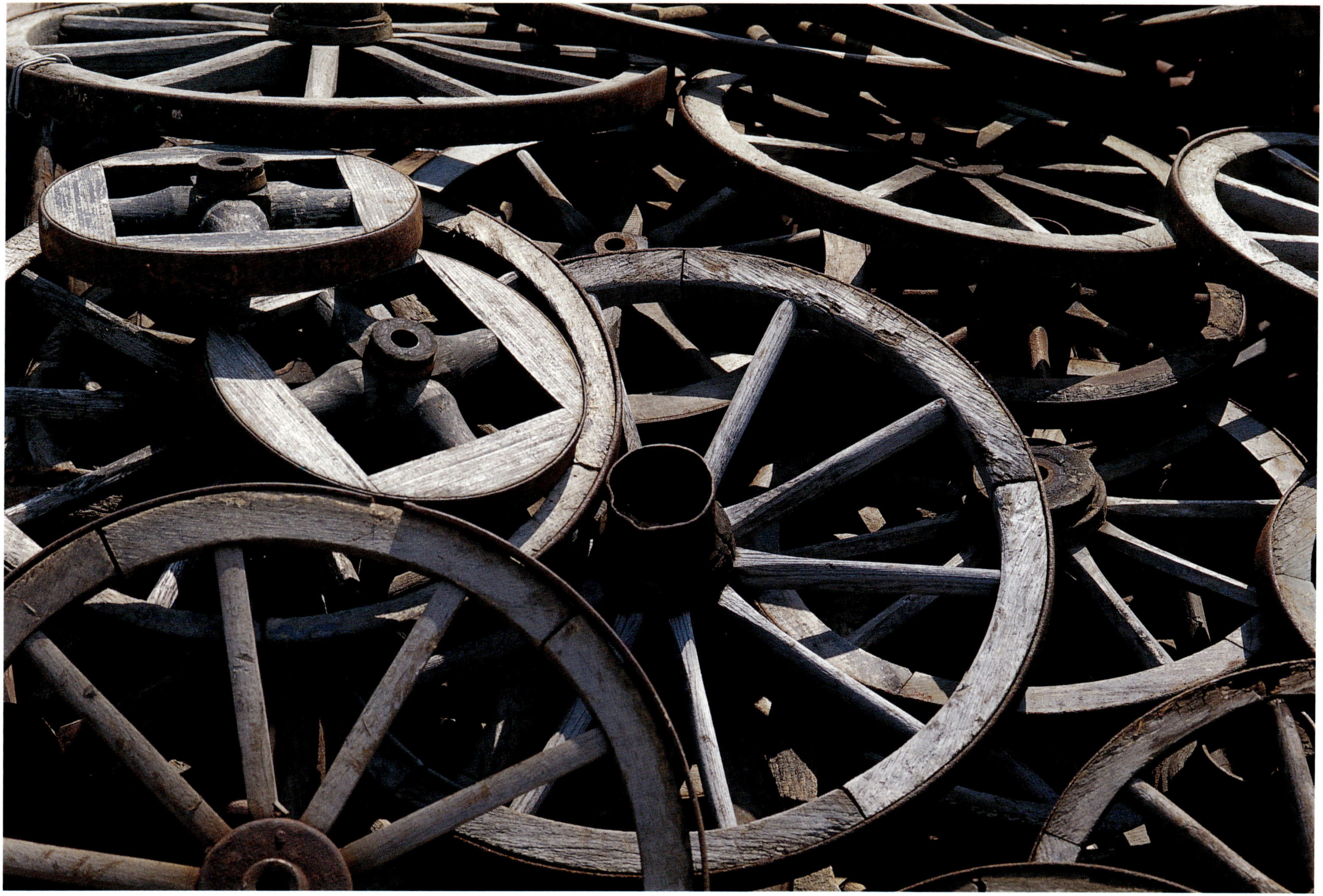

Wheels

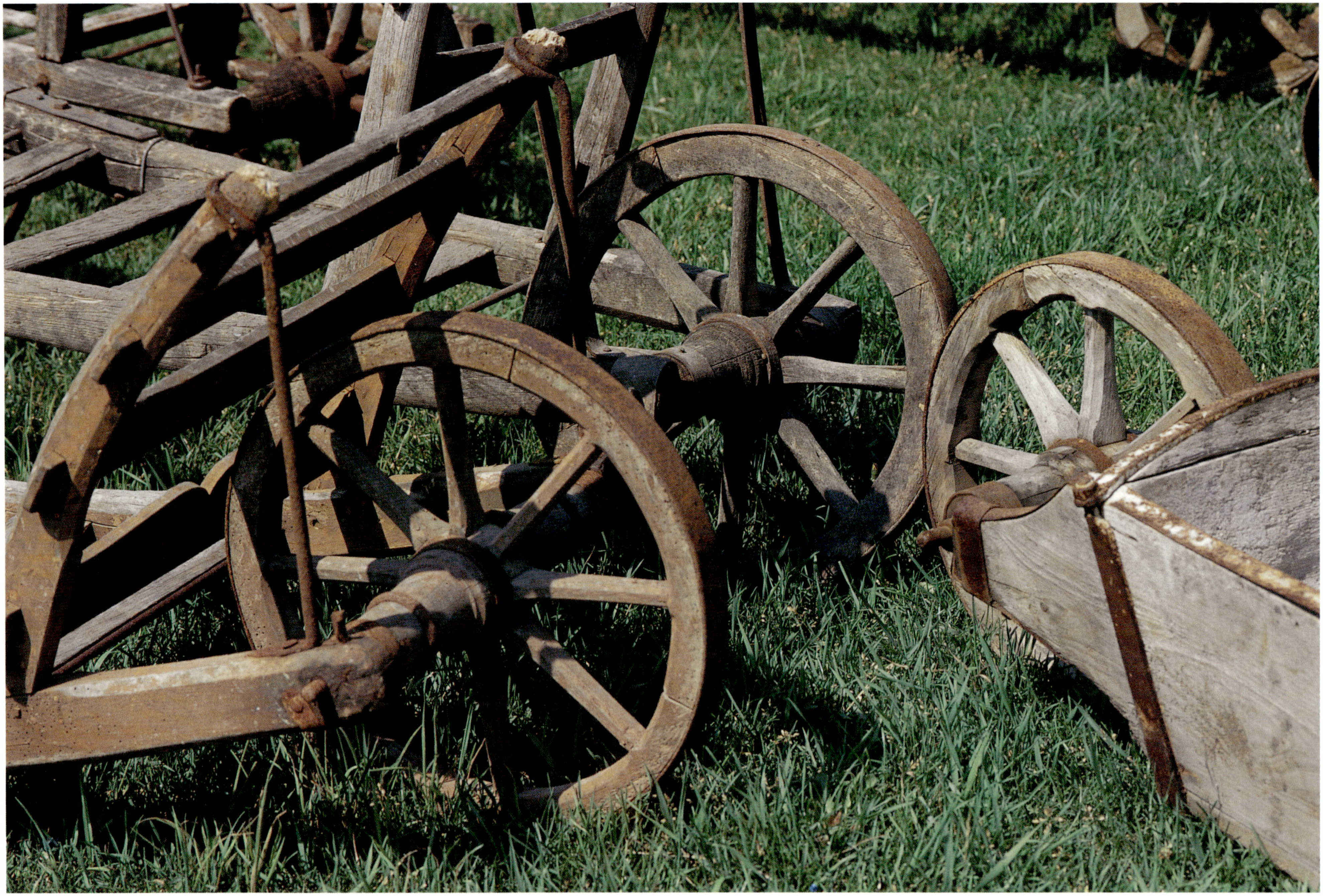

Wheelbarrows

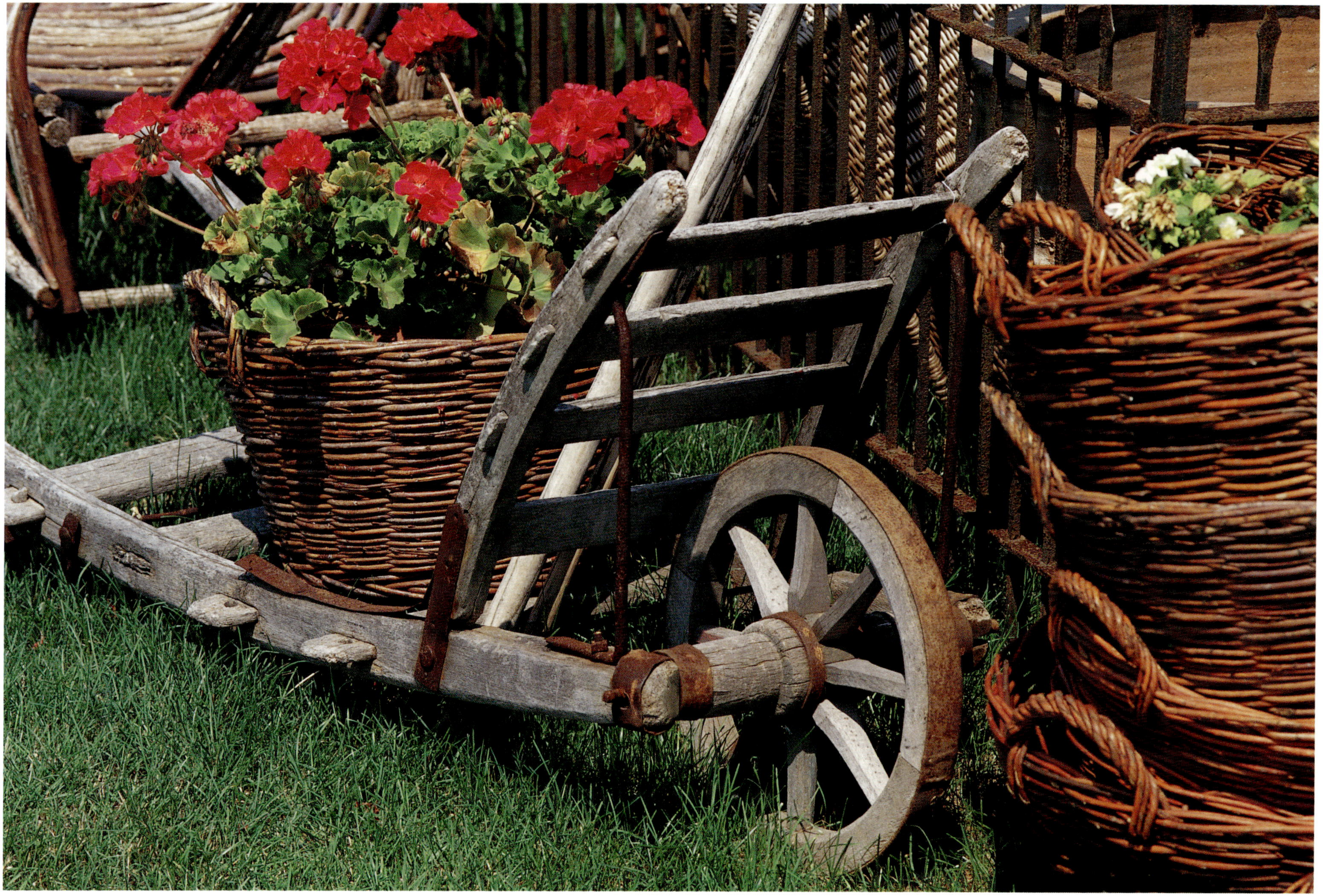

Wheelbarrow

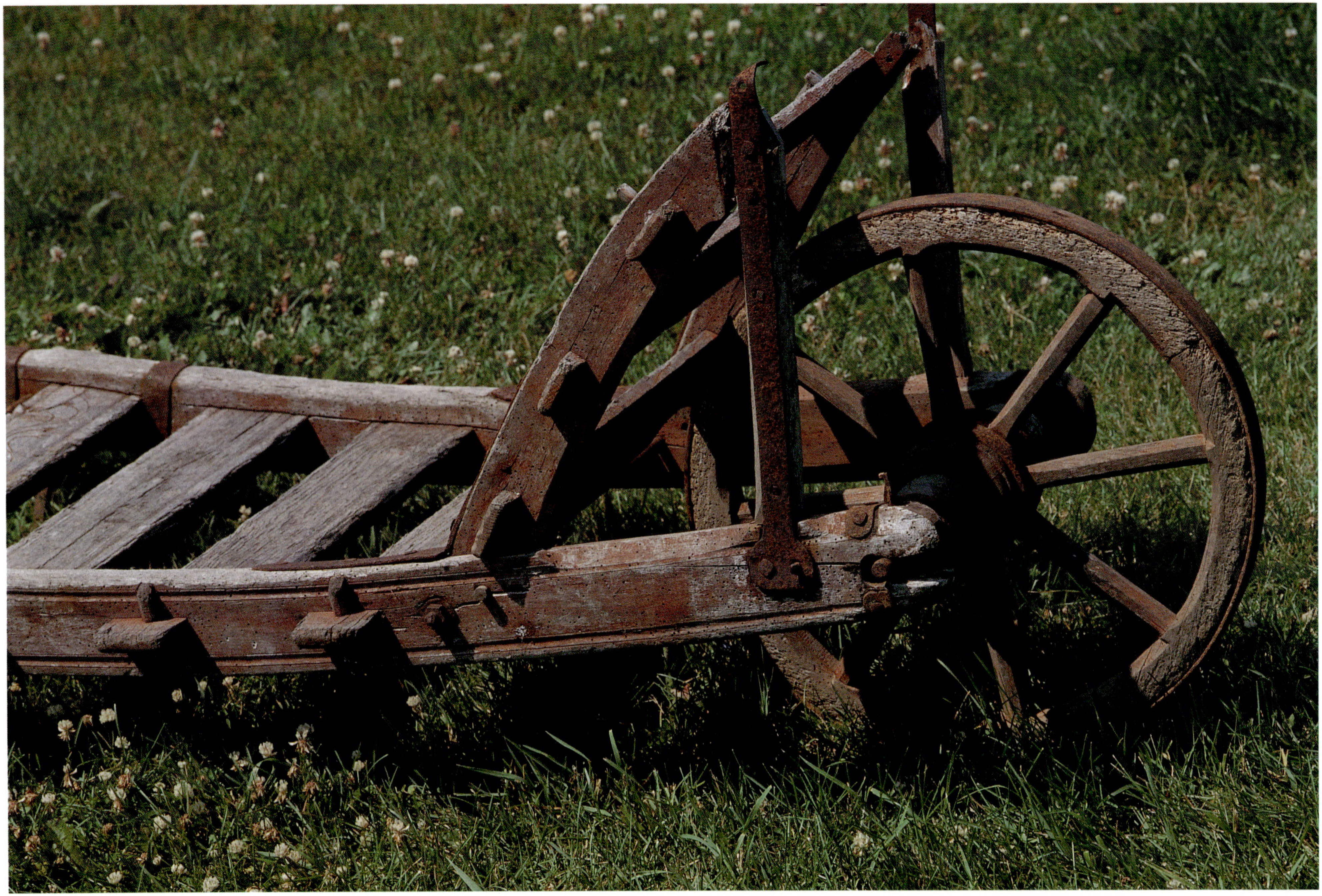

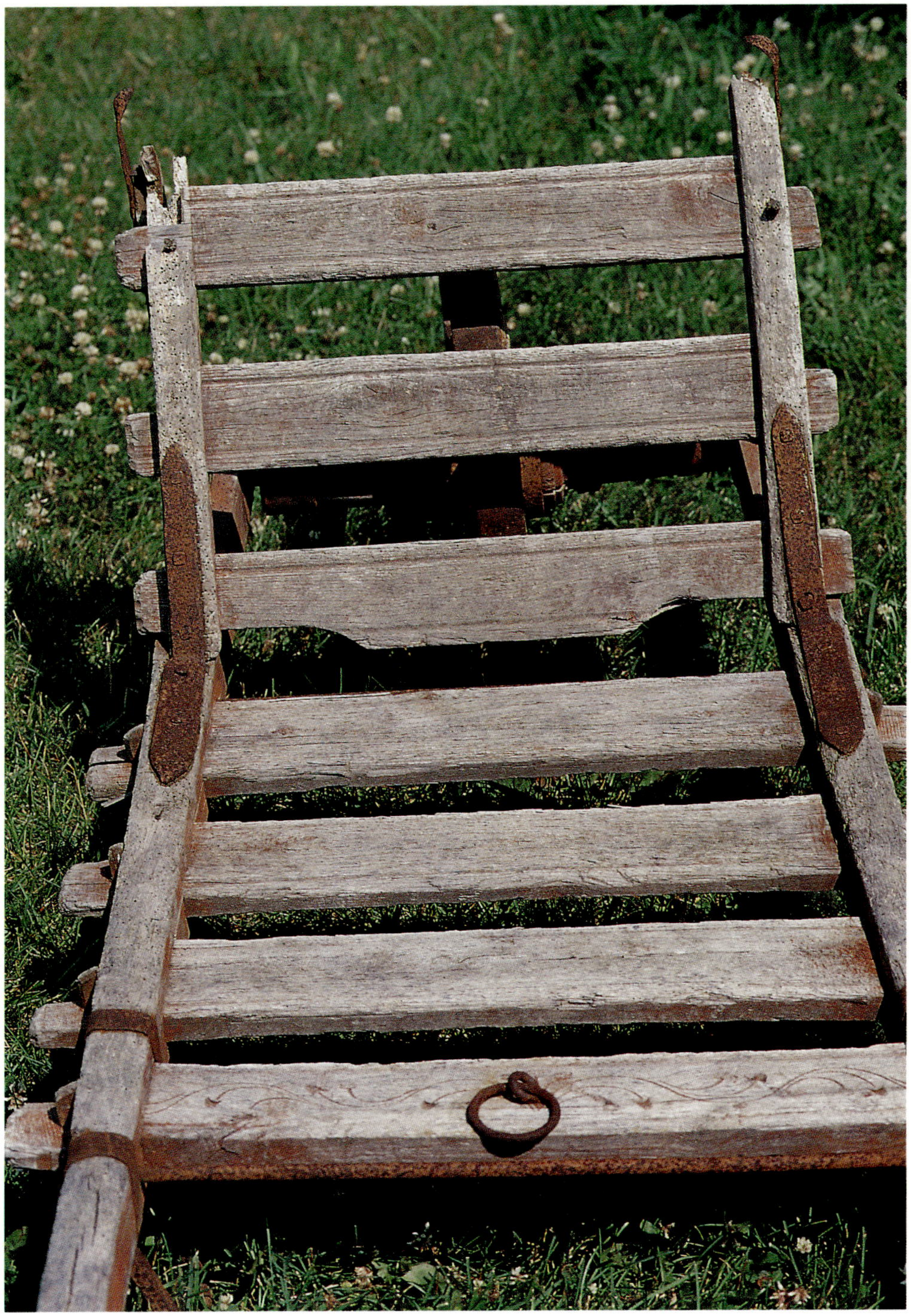

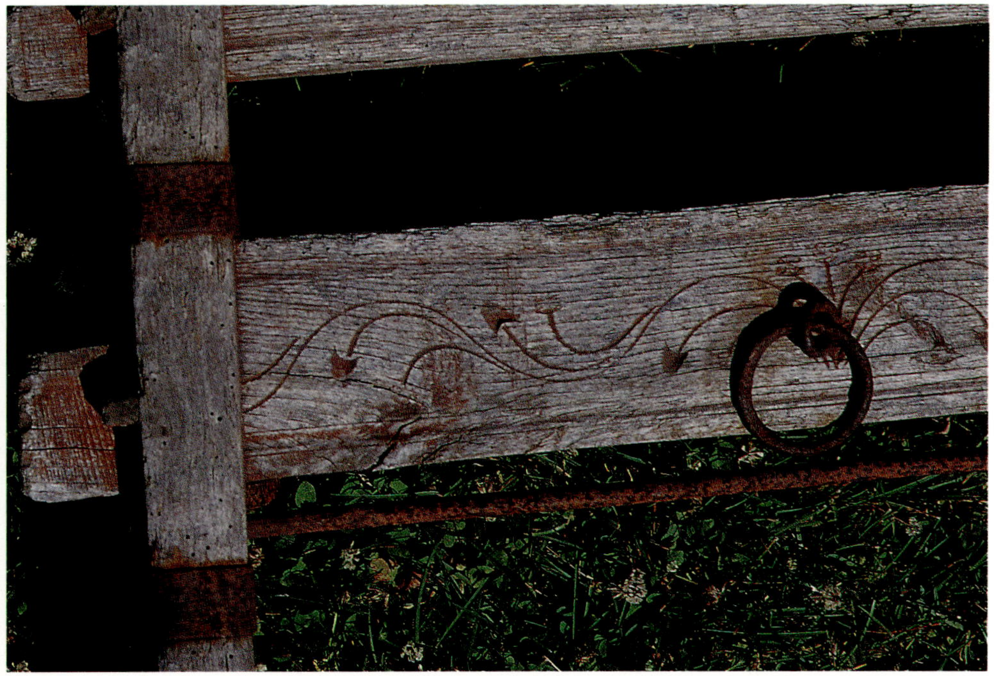

Opposite page, left and above: Slatted wheelbarrow

Sleighs, Sleds, and Ice Skates

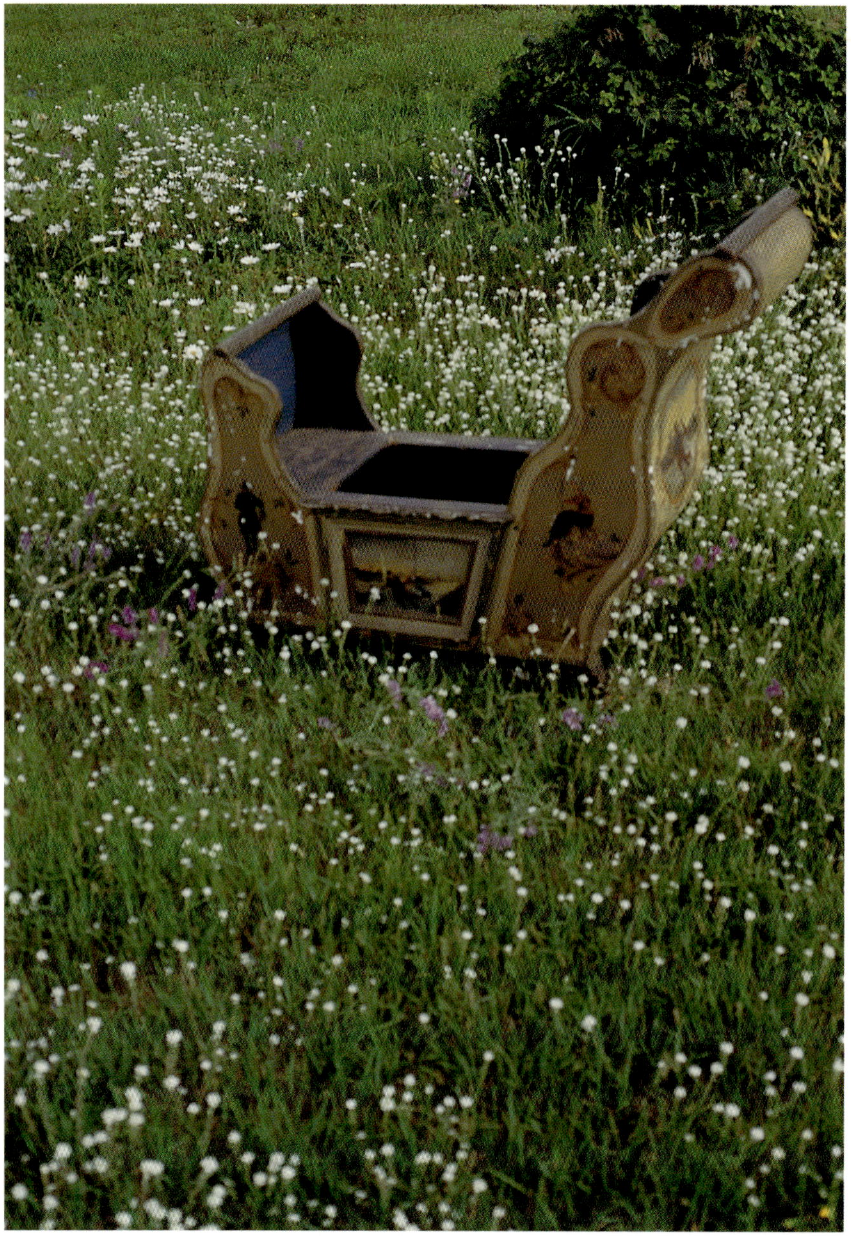

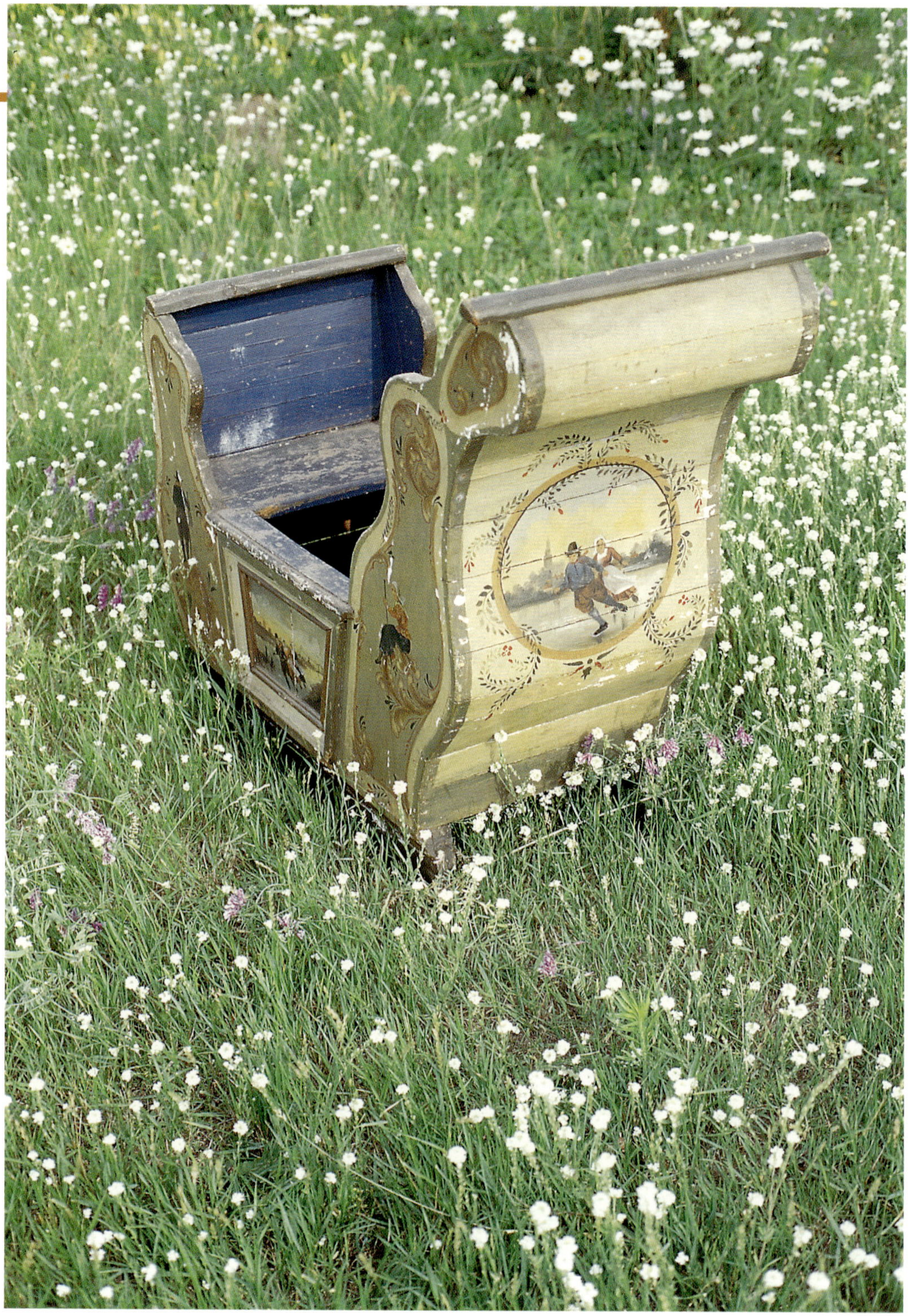

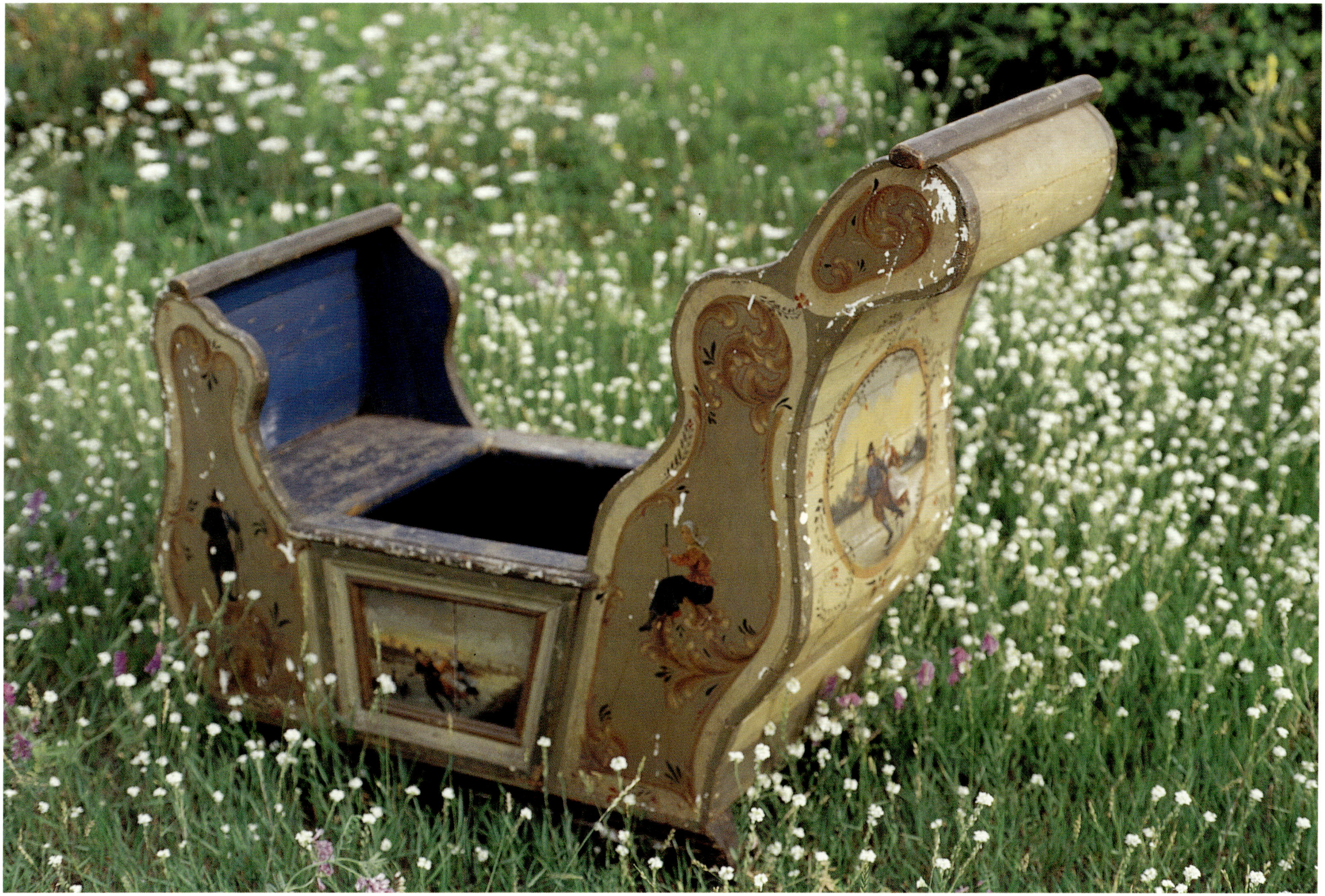

Opposite page and above: Dutch sleigh, c.1880.

Close-ups of photos on page 132 and 133: Dutch sleigh, c.1880.

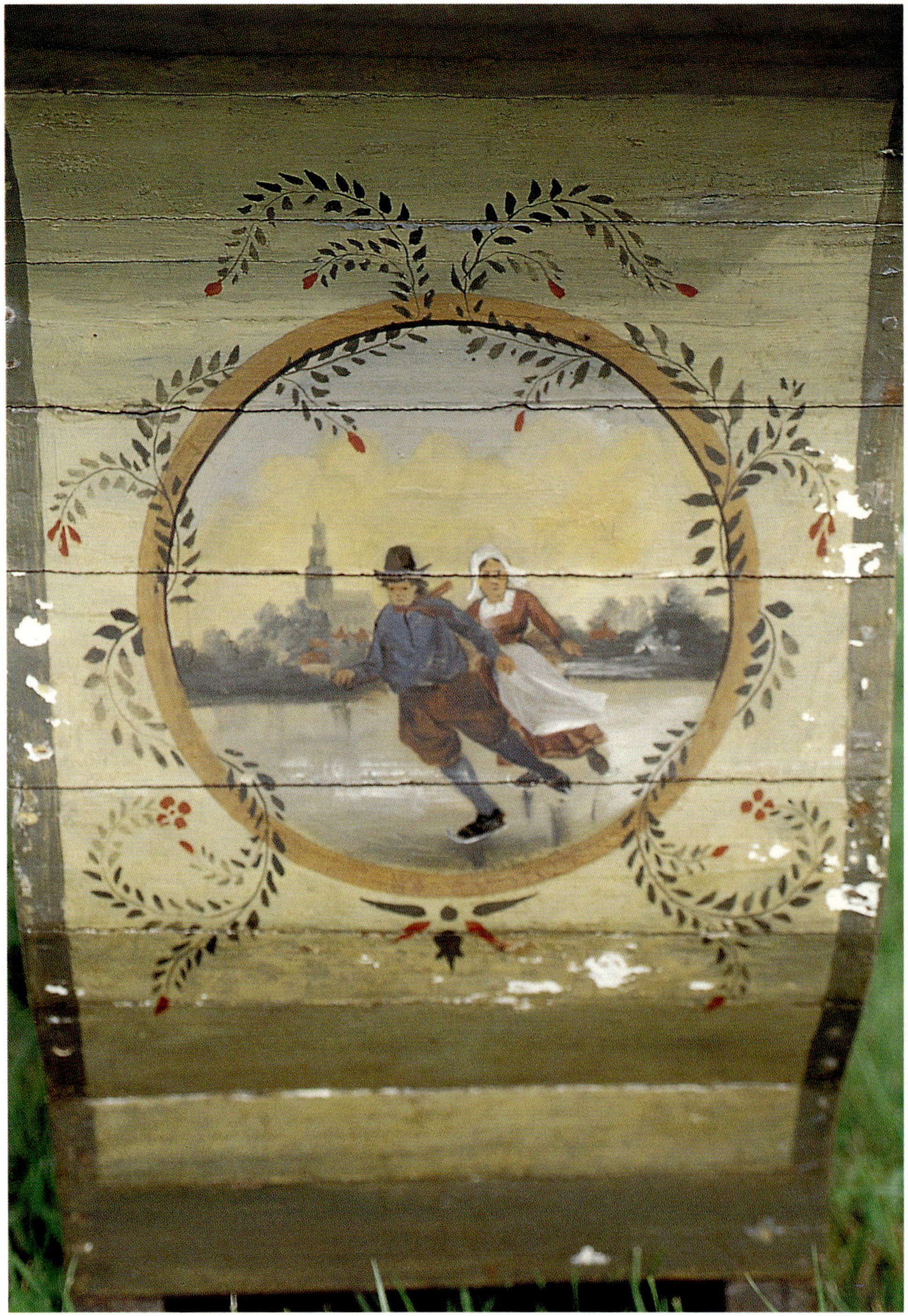

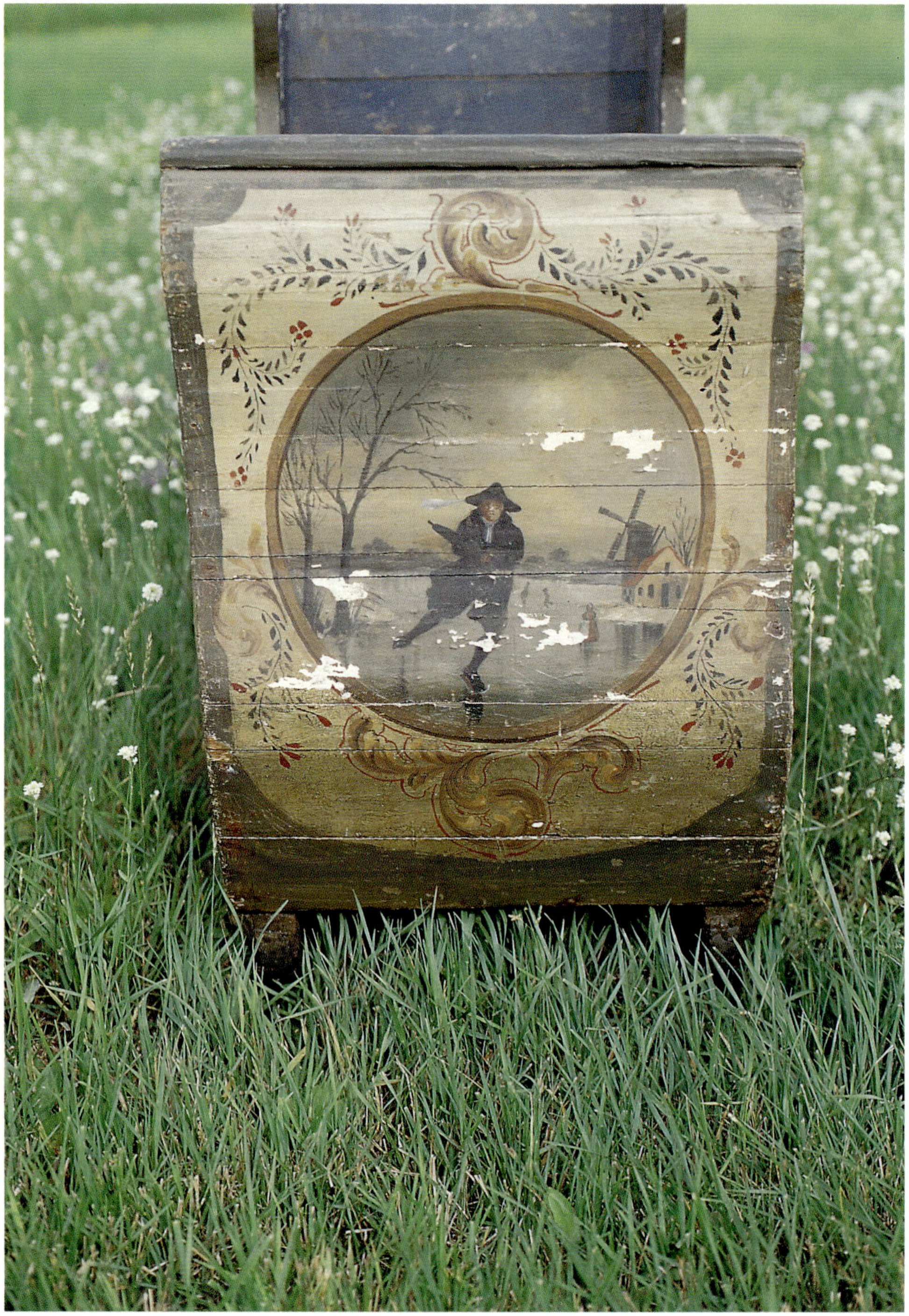

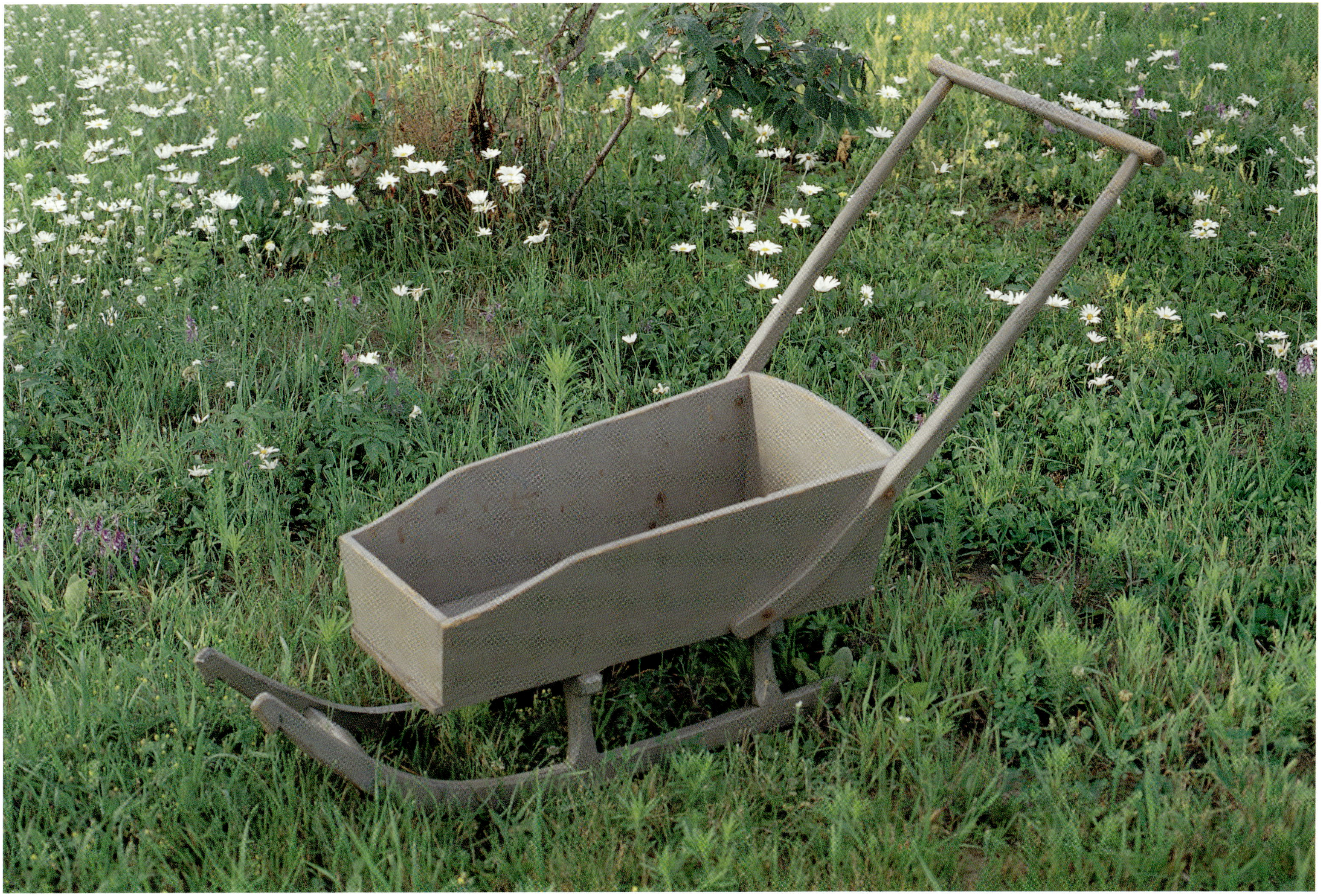

Sled barrow

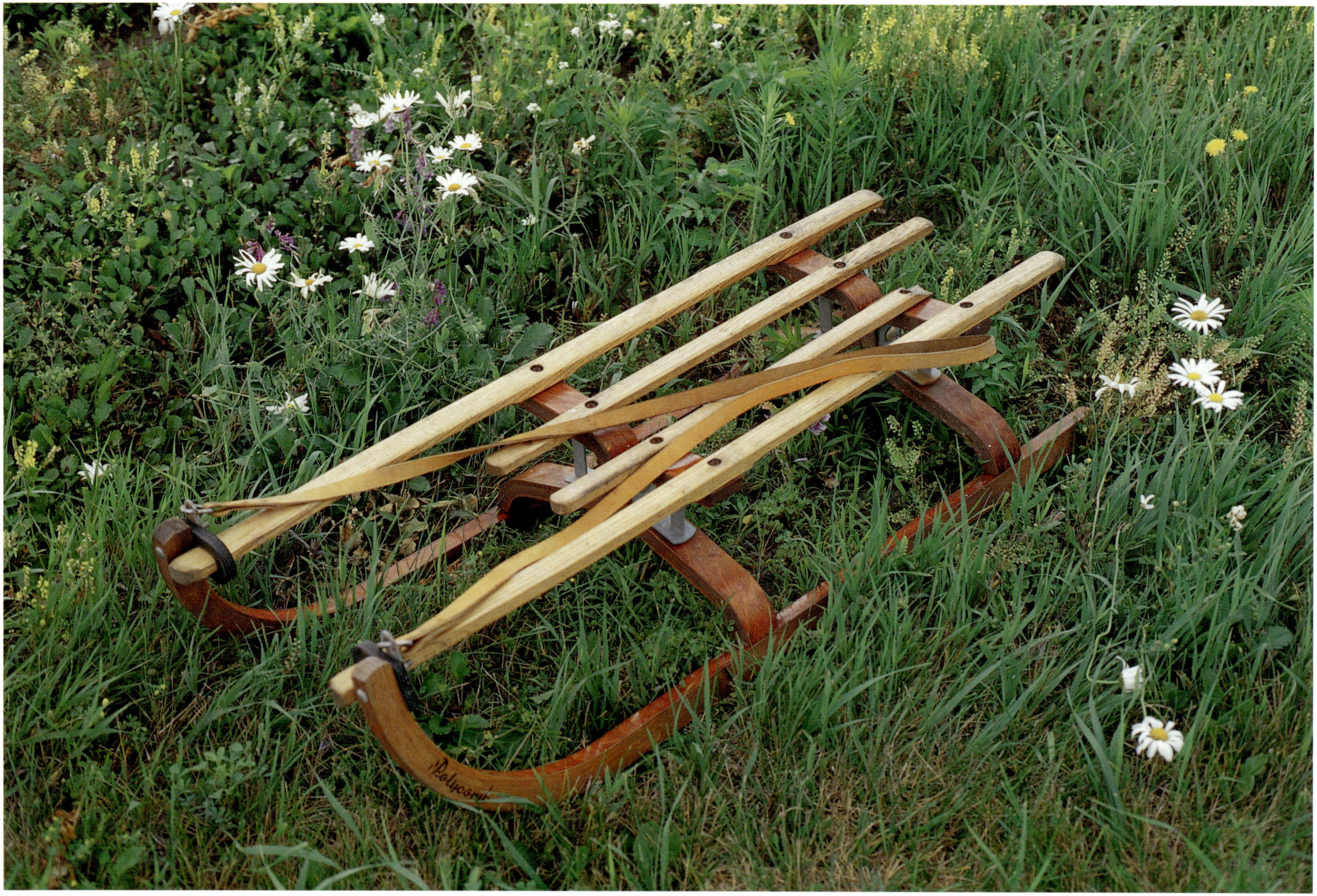

German sled. $55.

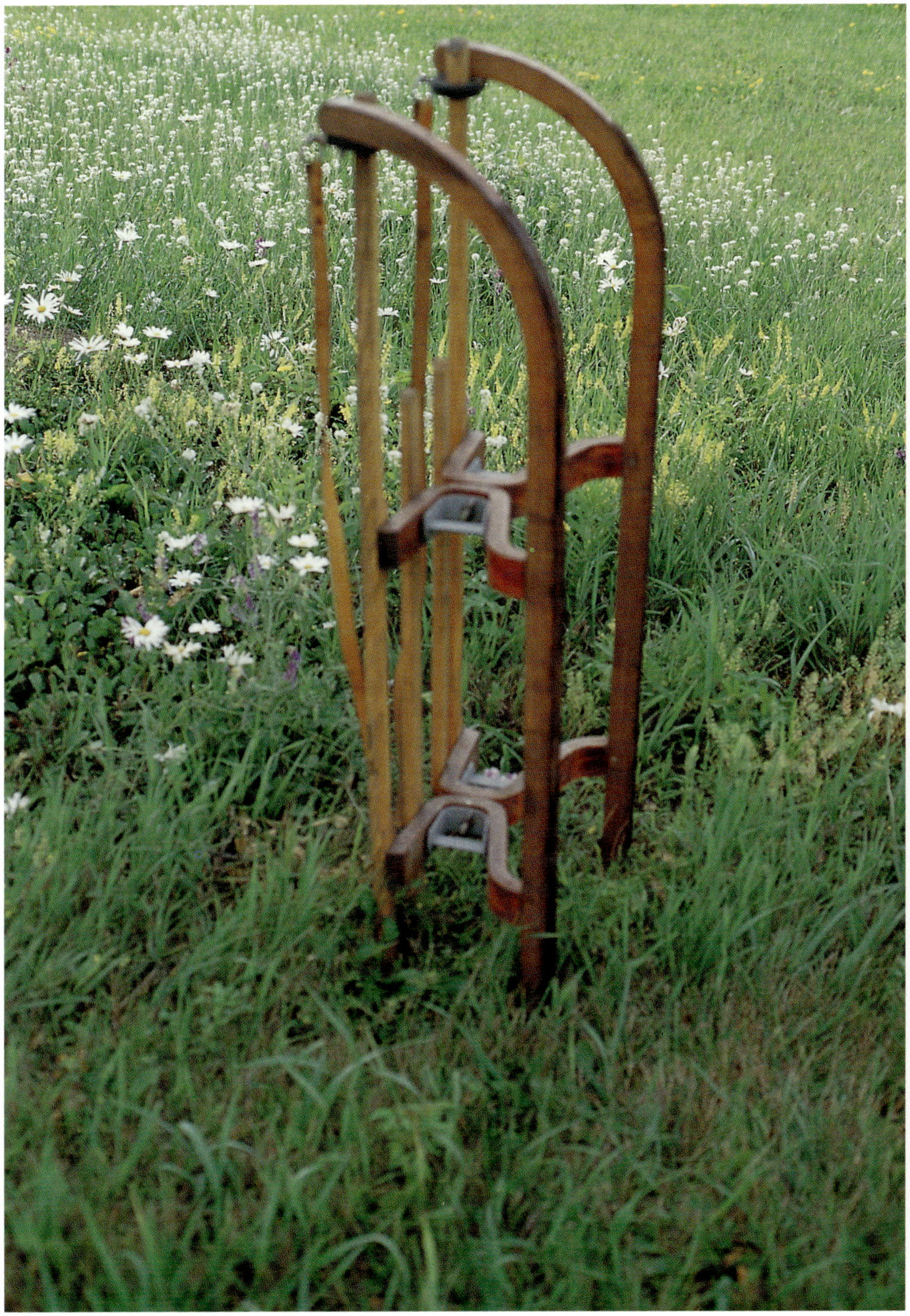

German sled. $55.

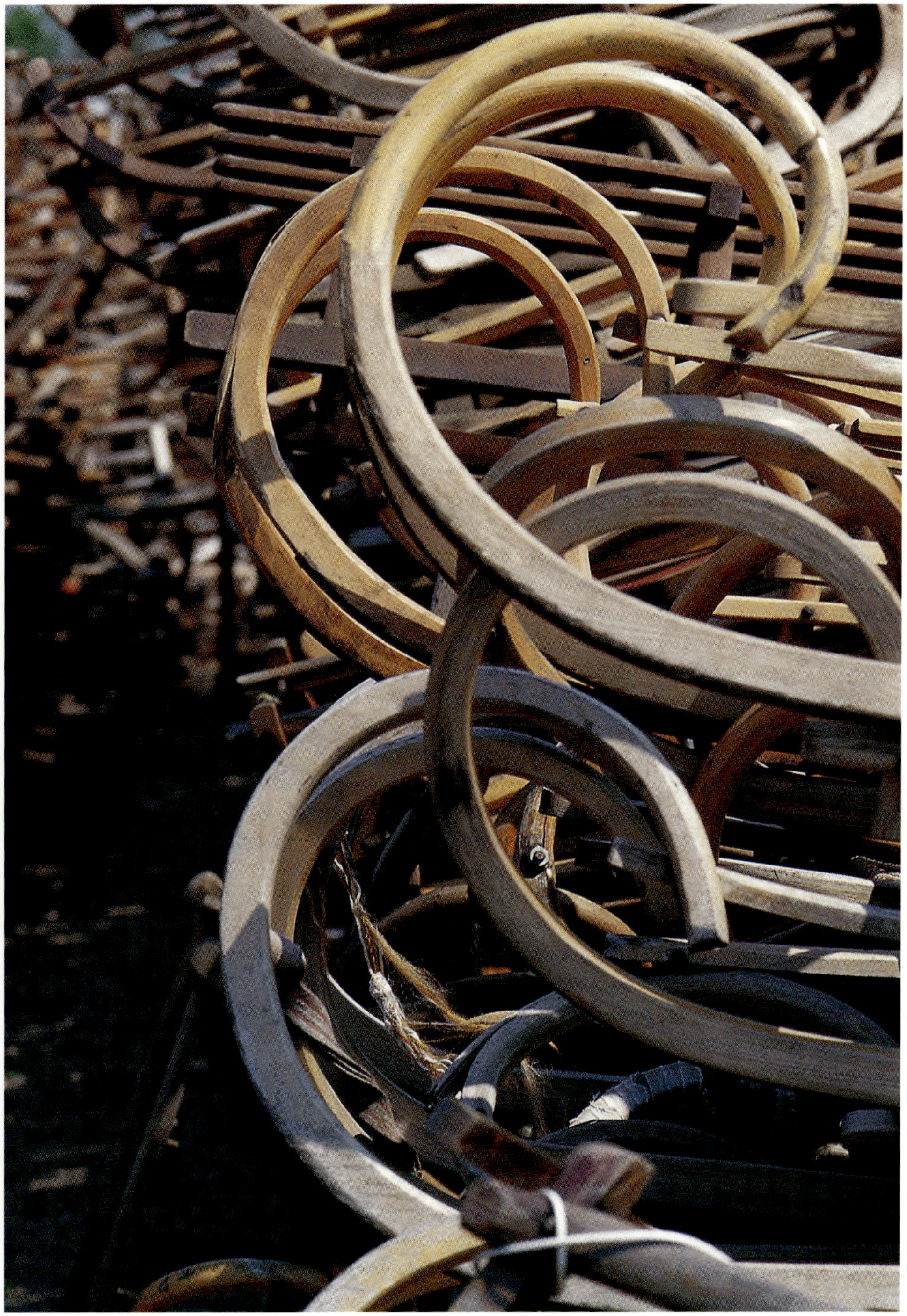

Sleds with bentwood runners

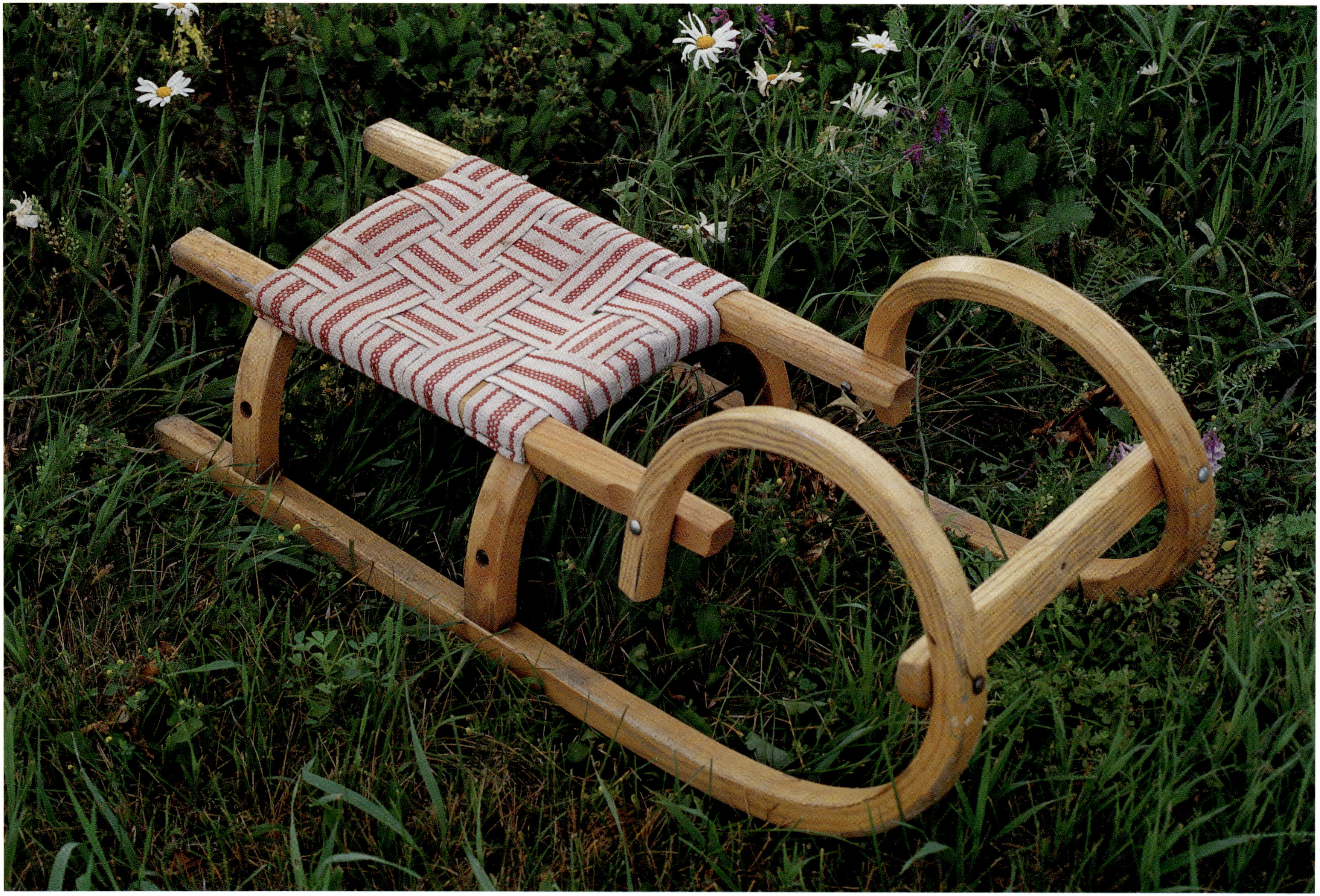

German "stag horn-style" sled with woven tape seat. $195.

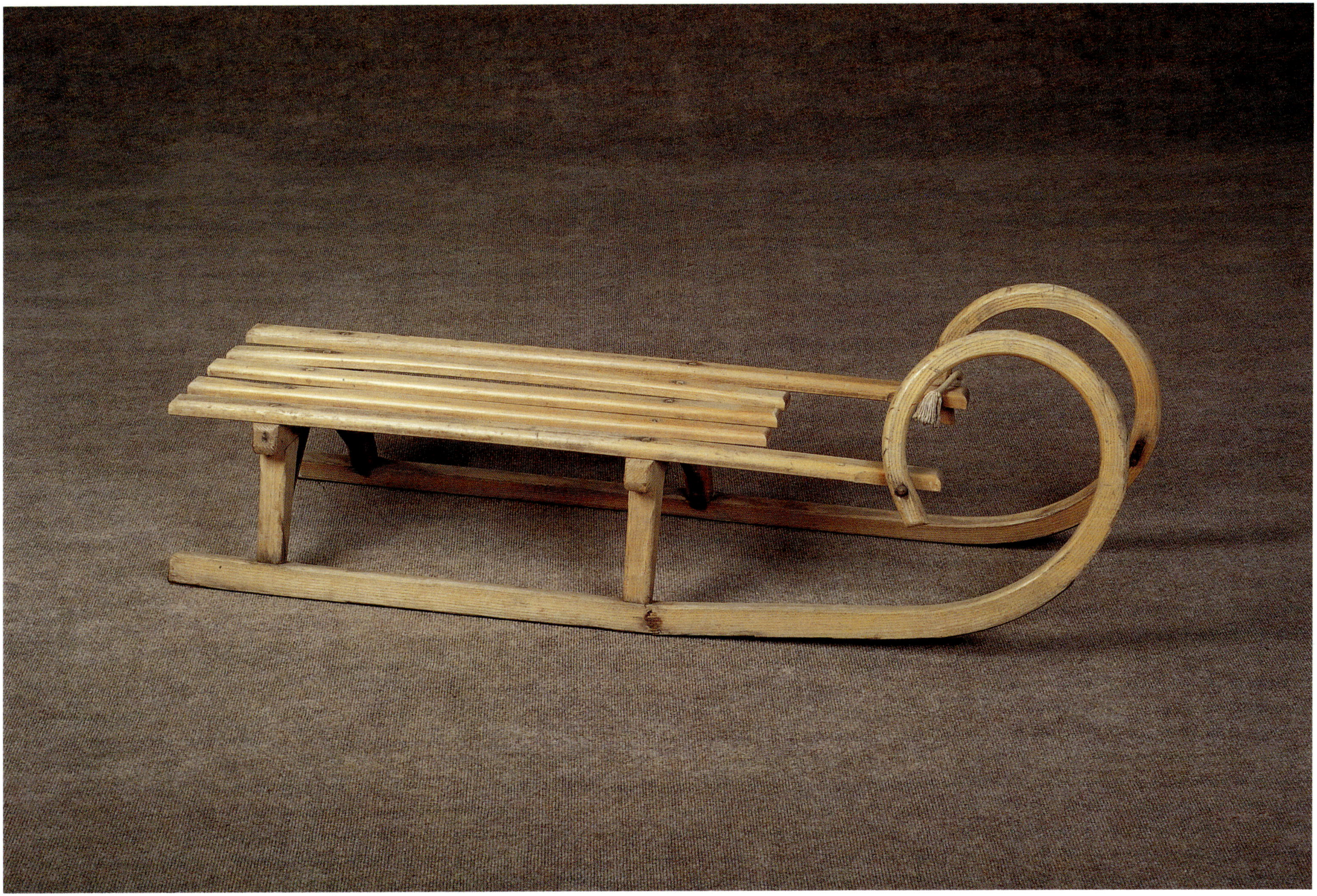

German sled with "stag horn-style" bent wood runners. $195.

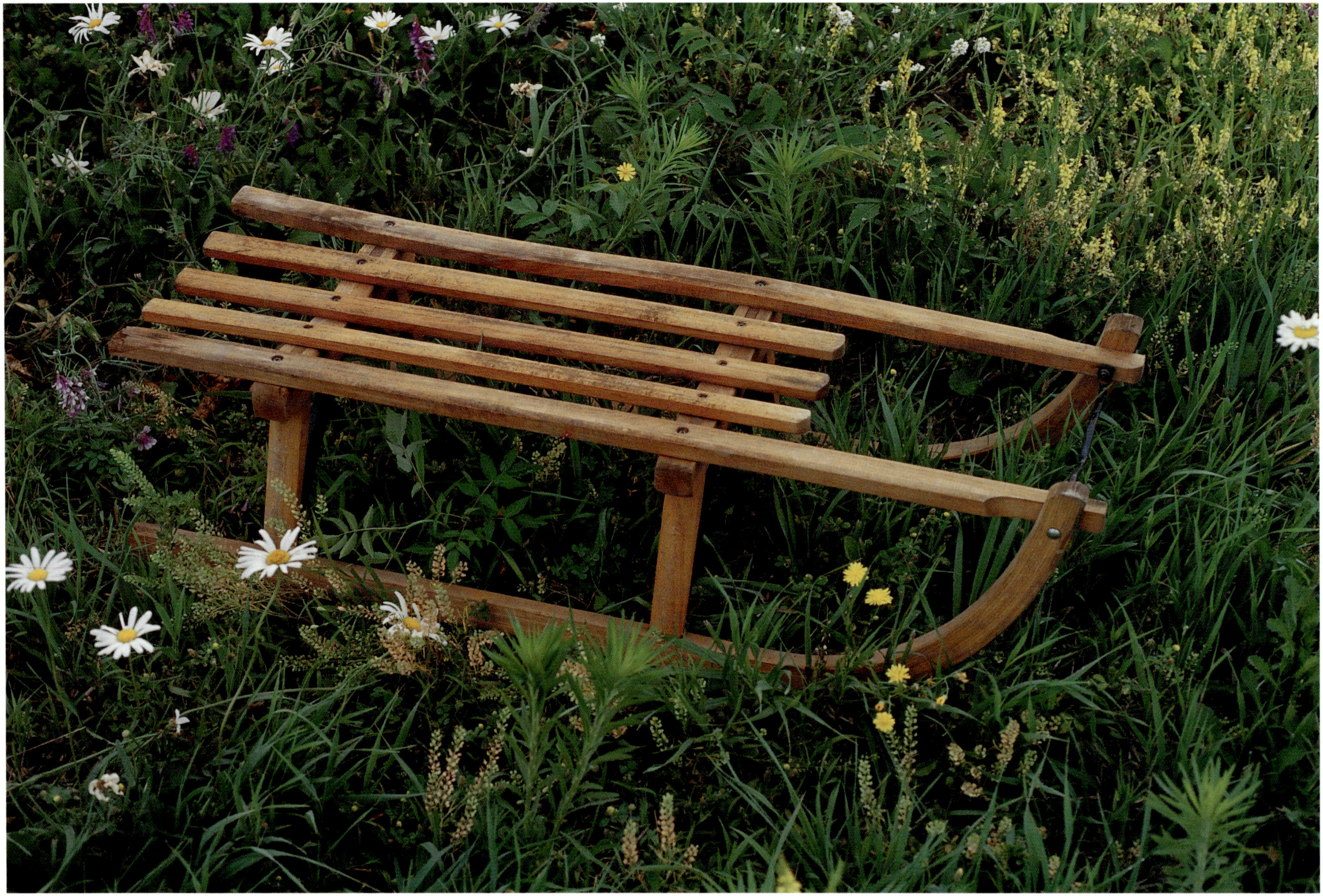

German sled. $55.

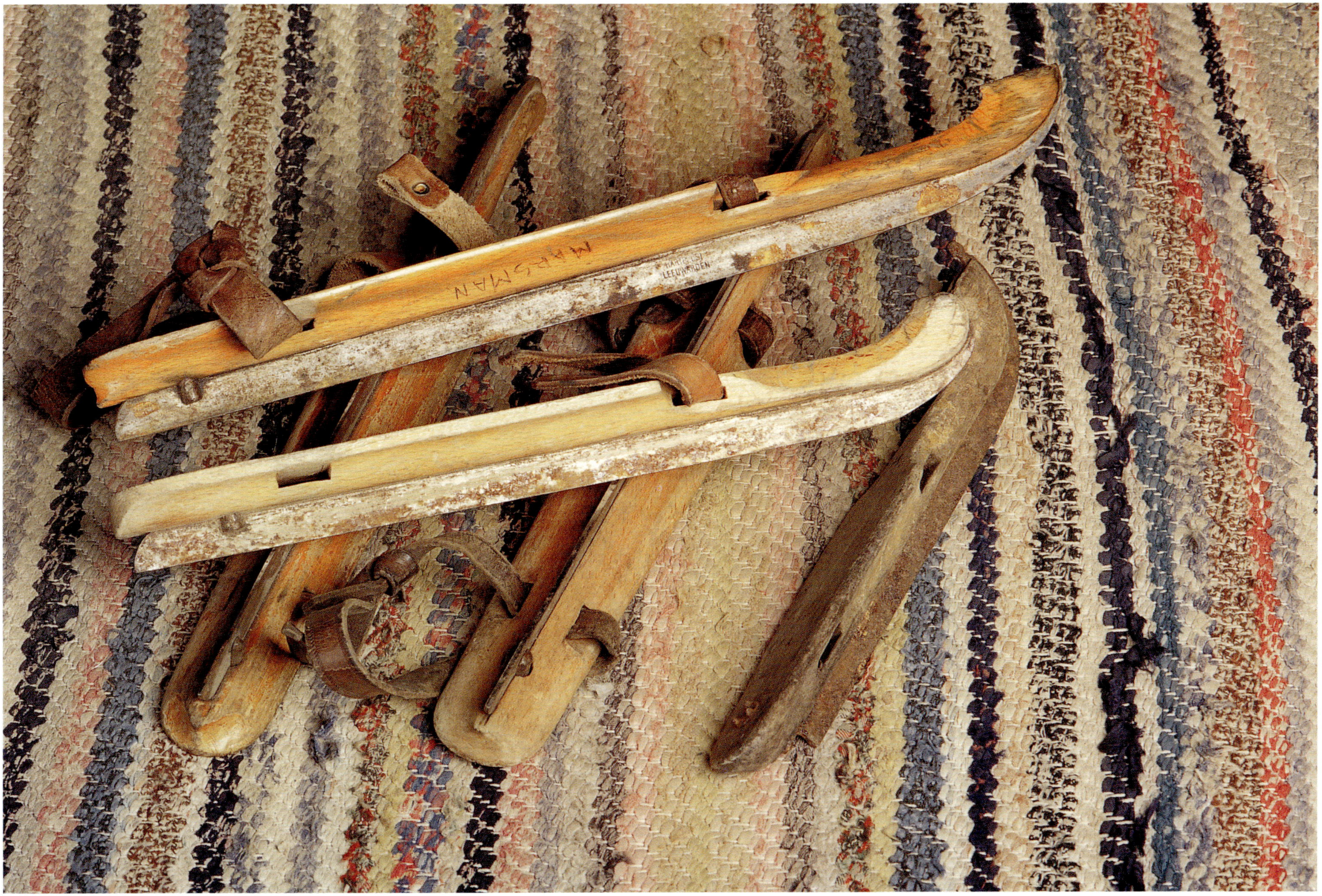

Ice skates

Closing the House

Shutters and Doors

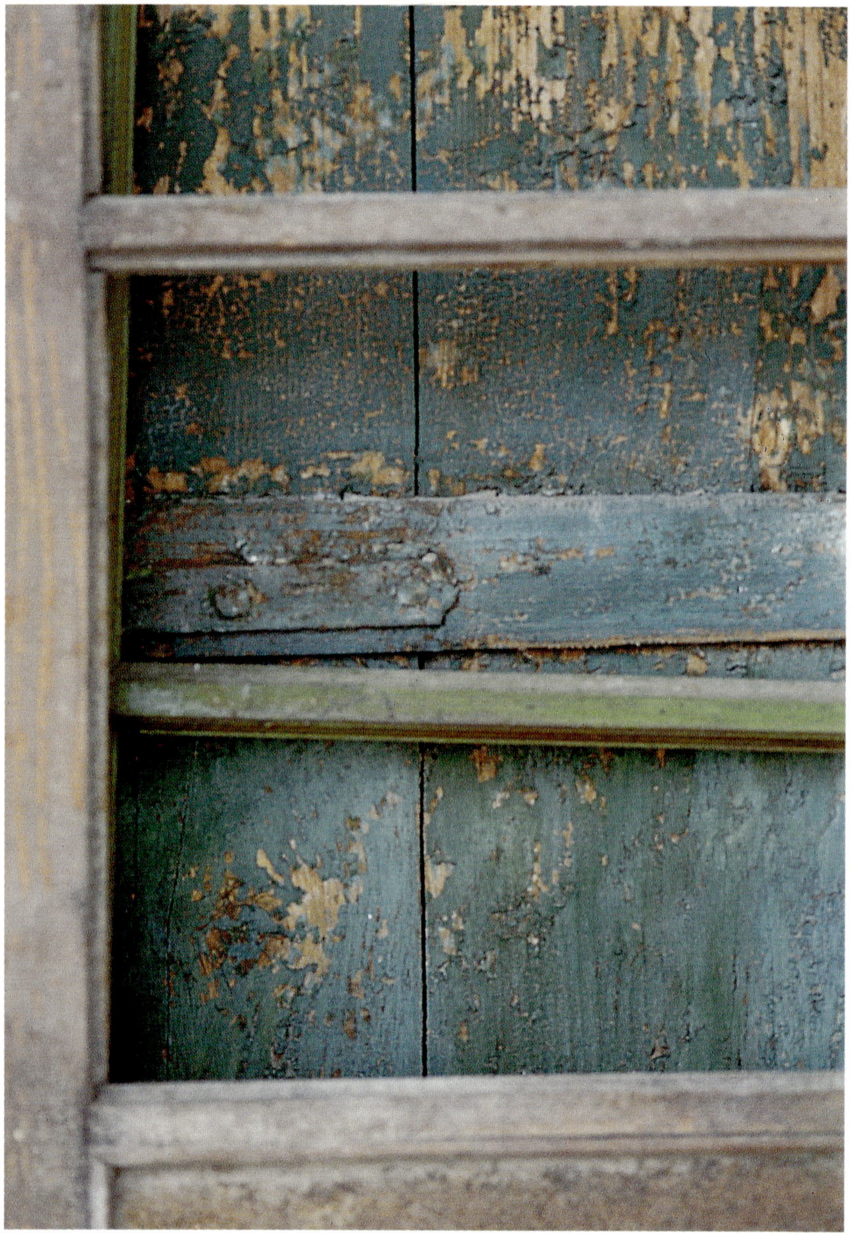

Shuttered window

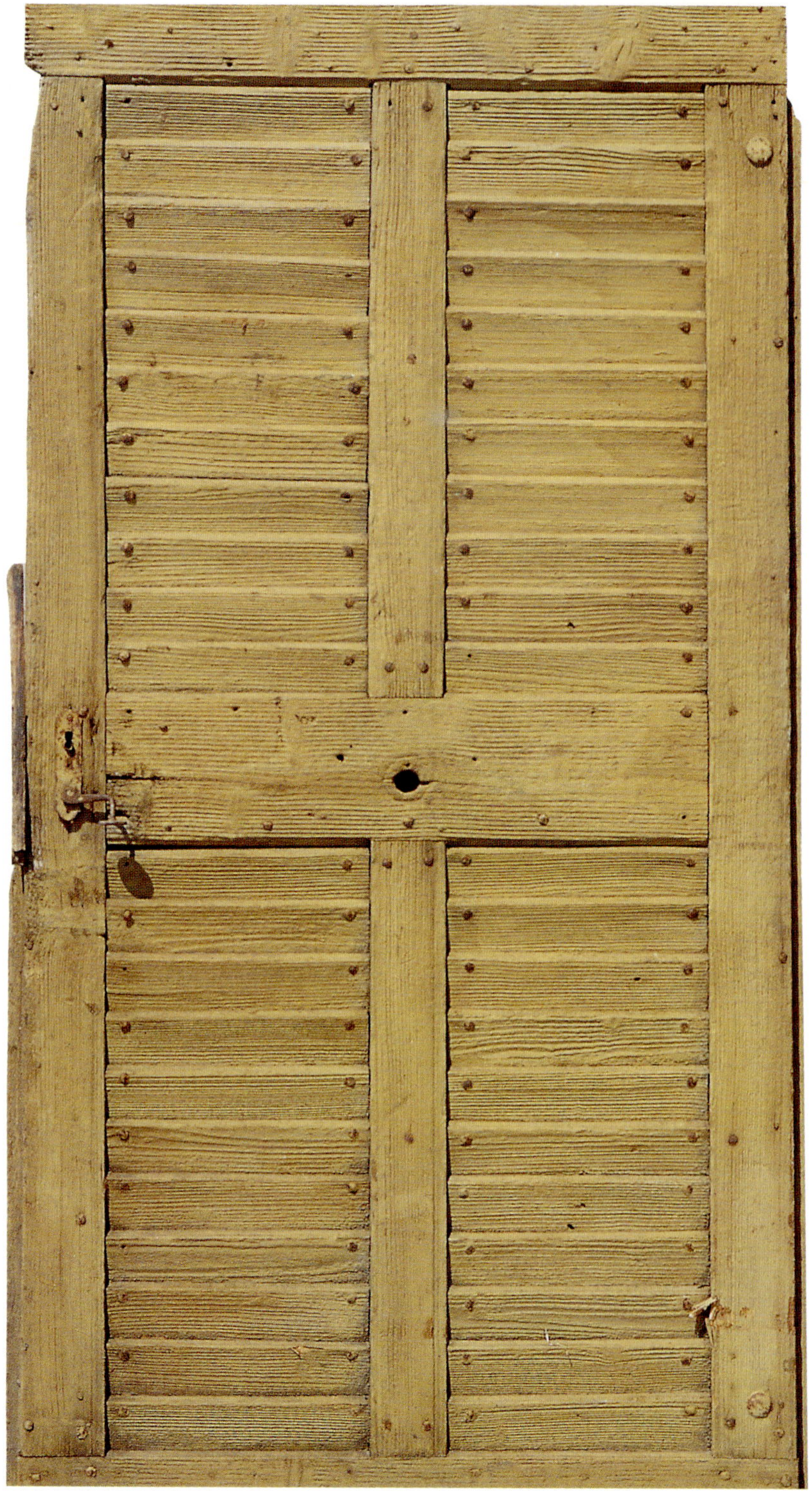

Louvered door

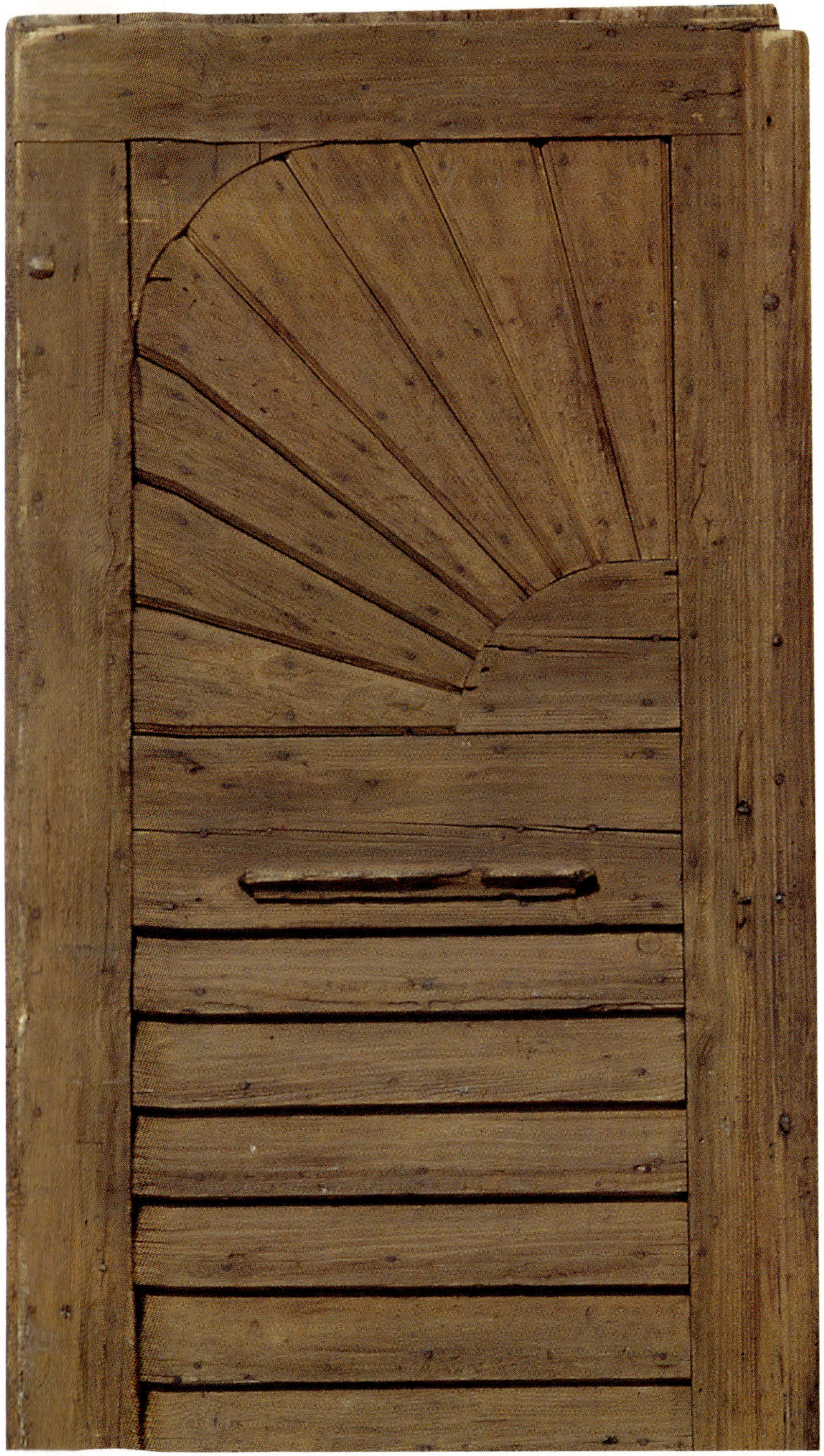
Door with louvers

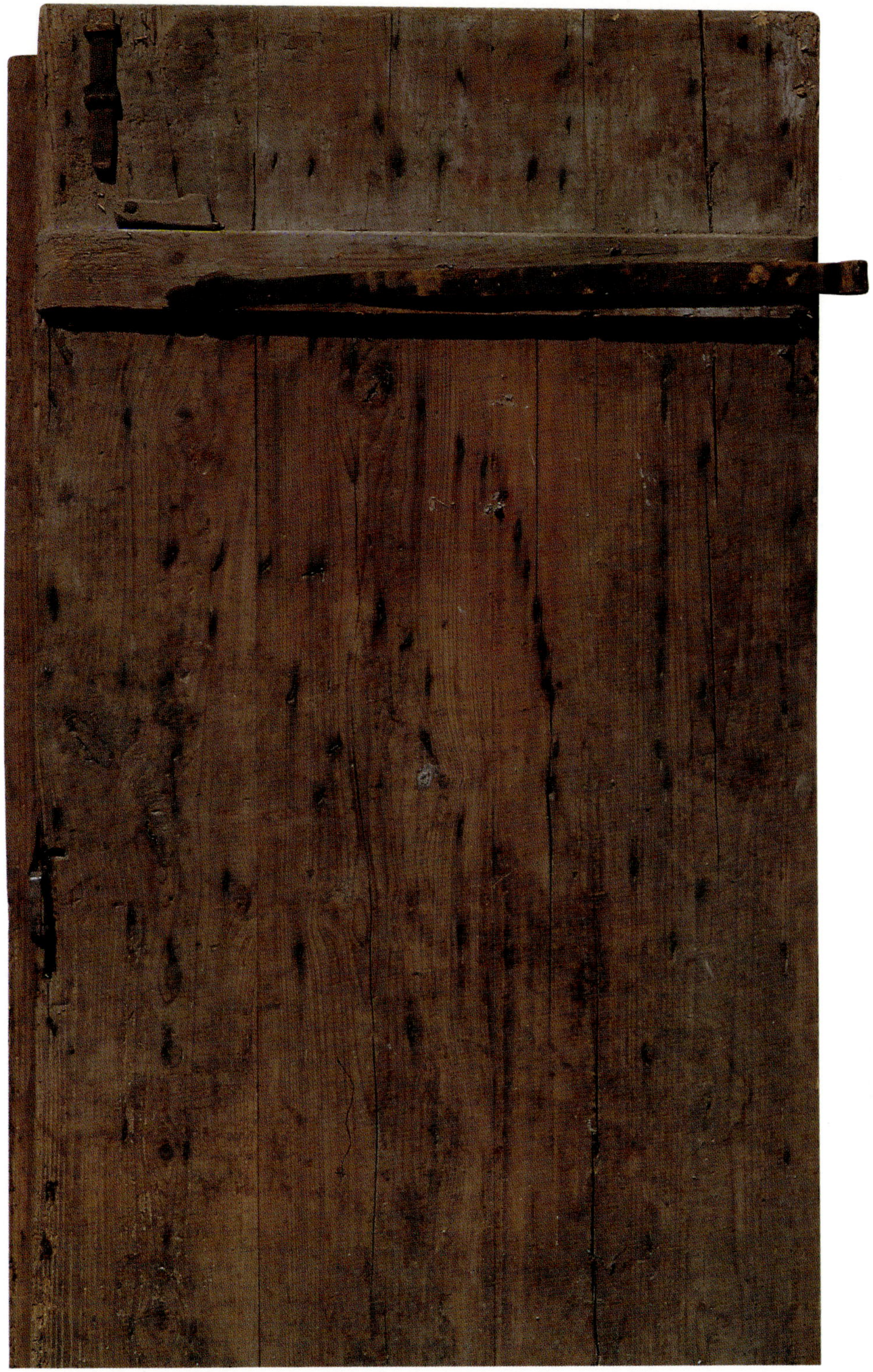
Back of louvered door

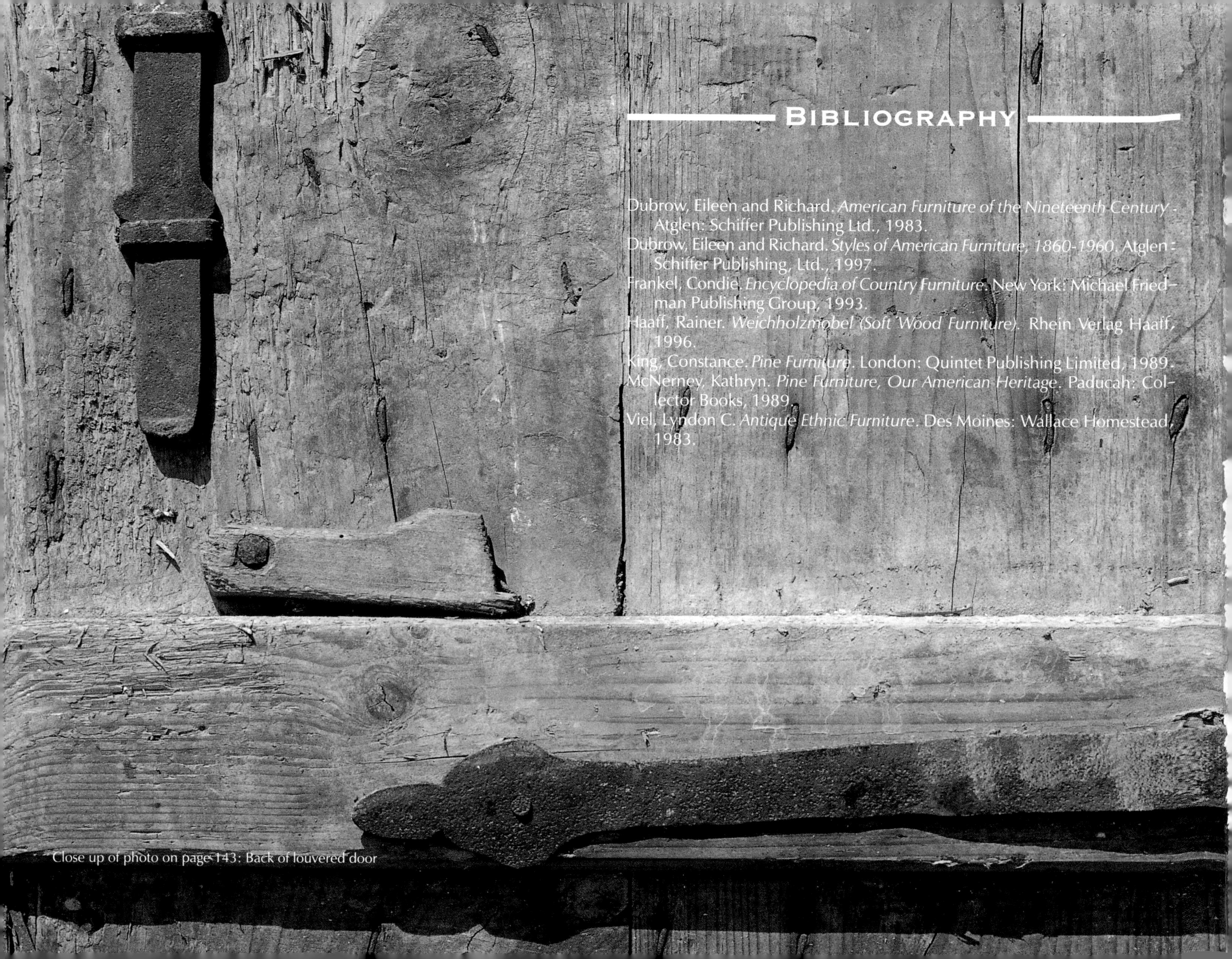

Bibliography

Dubrow, Eileen and Richard. *American Furniture of the Nineteenth Century*. Atglen: Schiffer Publishing Ltd., 1983.

Dubrow, Eileen and Richard. *Styles of American Furniture, 1860-1960*. Atglen: Schiffer Publishing, Ltd., 1997.

Frankel, Condie. *Encyclopedia of Country Furniture*. New York: Michael Friedman Publishing Group, 1993.

Haaff, Rainer. *Weichholzmobel (Soft Wood Furniture)*. Rhein Verlag Haaff, 1996.

King, Constance. *Pine Furniture*. London: Quintet Publishing Limited, 1989.

McNerney, Kathryn. *Pine Furniture, Our American Heritage*. Paducah: Collector Books, 1989.

Viel, Lyndon C. *Antique Ethnic Furniture*. Des Moines: Wallace Homestead, 1983.

Close up of photo on page 143: Back of louvered door